The Emerald Handbook on Cryptoassets

The Emerald Handbook on Cryptoassets: Investment Opportunities and Challenges

EDITED BY

H. KENT BAKER
American University, USA

HUGO BENEDETTI
Universidad de los Andes, Chile

EHSAN NIKBAKHT
Hofstra University, USA

AND

SEAN STEIN SMITH
City University of New York, USA

emerald PUBLISHING

United Kingdom – North America – Japan – India – Malaysia – China

Emerald Publishing Limited
Howard House, Wagon Lane, Bingley BD16 1WA, UK

First edition 2023

British Library Cataloguing in Publication Data
A catalogue record for this book is available from the British Library

ISBN: 978-1-80455-321-3 (Print)
ISBN: 978-1-80455-320-6 (Online)
ISBN: 978-1-80455-322-0 (Epub)

Printed and bound by CPI Group (UK) Ltd, Croydon, CR0 4YY

ISOQAR REGISTERED
Certificate Number 1985
ISO 14001

ISOQAR certified Management System, awarded to Emerald for adherence to Environmental standard ISO 14001:2004.

INVESTOR IN PEOPLE

We dedicate this book to Linda and Rory Baker; Pascale and Luciano Benedetti; Parvin, Auzin, and Daniel Nikbakht, and Ximena Romero; and Frederick Smith, Kathleen Stein Smith, Patrick Stein Smith, and Frederick Stein Smith.

Contents

List of Figures and Tables

Figures

Tables

About the Editors

H. Kent Baker, CFA, CMA, is a University Professor of Finance at the Kogod School of Business, American University. He is an award-winning author who has published 41 books and more than 200 academic articles in such journals as the *Journal of Finance* and *Journal of Financial and Quantitative Analysis*. Professor Baker has been a consultant or trainer for more than 100 organizations. He has received numerous awards for research, teaching, and service, including University Scholar/Teacher of the Year at American University and the 2019 Distinguished Scholar from the Southern Finance Association (SFA). He was also the SFA's past President. Professor Baker received a BSBA in Management from Georgetown University and an MBA, MEd, and DBA from the University of Maryland. He also has an MS in Quantitative Methods, an MA in Training and Career Development, a PhD in Educational Administration and Organizational Development, and a PhD in Counseling and Student Development from American University.

Hugo Benedetti is an Assistant Professor at ESE Business School, Universidad de Los Andes, Chile. His research focuses on entrepreneurial finance, venture capital, and FinTech, particularly blockchain technology and blockchain-enabled assets. The *Economist*, *Bloomberg*, *The Wall Street Journal*, *Nasdaq*, and several crypto-industry publications have featured his research. Professor Benedetti frequently delivers workshops on entrepreneurial finance, venture capital, and FinTech to incubators, angel investor networks, and venture capital funds. He has advised and mentored several FinTech and blockchain projects. Before joining academia, he co-founded a financial advisory boutique and held leadership roles in corporate finance, financial advisory, and venture capital at world-class firms. Professor Benedetti is a Fulbright scholar and received a PhD in Finance from Boston College.

Ehsan Nikbakht, CFA, FRM, is a Professor of Finance at Frank G. Zarb School of Business, Hofstra University. His research focuses on international finance, hedge funds, real estate, and financial blockchain. Professor Nikbakht has published in the *Journal of Corporate Finance*, *Journal of International Accounting, Auditing and Taxation*, *Journal of Financial Crime*, *Managerial Finance*, *Global Finance Journal*, and *International Journal of Business*. He is a Co-editor of *The*

Emerald Handbook of Blockchain for Business. In recognition of his research monograph, *Foreign Loans and Economic Performance*, Professor Nikbakht received a Stessin Prize for "Outstanding Scholarly Publication." He received a DBA in Finance from George Washington University.

Sean Stein Smith is Assistant Professor of Business and Economics at Lehman College, City University of New York. He serves on the Advisory Board of the Wall Street Blockchain Alliance, where he chairs the Accounting Work Group. Professor Smith has published numerous articles and several books focusing on the intersection of accounting and emerging technologies, including the *Forbes* Crypto & Blockchain vertical. He is a member of the NJCPA Board of Trustees and president of the NYSSCPA Manhattan-Bronx chapter. Professor Smith was an AICPA Outstanding CPA of Year (2022). He is on the Advisory Board of Gilded and is a Strategic Advisor to the Central Bank Digital Currency Think Tank. He served as a Visiting Research Fellow at the American Institute of Economic Research with a book due for publication in late 2022. He received a BS, MS, and MBA from Fairleigh Dickinson and a DBA from Capella University.

About the Contributors

Luis Álvaro Abarzúa is a specialist in educational policies for improving learning at the school and professional levels. He currently advises several scientific and technological-based startups. He worked at the Ministry of Education of the Government of Chile, where he supported the implementation of national educational policies. He is the Co-founder of an Ed-tech company present in six countries in the Americas. He is an enthusiastic researcher in blockchain and cryptocurrencies, delivering courses on decentralized finance and raising business ideas oriented to public education. Trained as a sociologist, he has completed postgraduate studies in Multivariate Statistical Analysis and has a Diploma in Applied Studies in Entrepreneurship and Innovation from Stanford University. He is pursuing a postgraduate degree in Innovation from Pontificia Universidad Católica de Chile.

Alevtina Dubovitskaya Ackerer is a Docent at Lucerne University of Applied Science and Arts, Switzerland. Her work as a Consultant at Swisscom and Gilded ranges from client advisory to designing and implementing blockchain-based solutions compliant with the laws and regulations. She has experience in designing protocols for privacy-preserving data aggregation and sharing. She also develops the systems using blockchain technologies, focusing on accountable and trusted interactions and reputation management in dynamic distributed systems. Her research interests are distributed data management for blockchain and cryptographic solutions for providing security and privacy. She has a PhD from the Swiss Federal Institute of Technology in Lausanne.

Damien Ackerer is a Senior Quantitative Researcher at Covario, where he works on data-driven solutions for digital asset management, such as optimal execution algorithms for cryptoassets. He is also an External Lecturer at the Swiss Federal Institute of Technology in Lausanne (EPFL), where he created a course on Machine Learning for Finance. He worked in applied research at major banks in Switzerland, UBS, and Swissquote Bank. In these institutions, he developed methodologies for risk calculation, derivatives margining, portfolio allocation, and systematic trading strategies. He has a PhD in Finance from EPFL. He focused on the pricing of financial derivatives contracts using quantitative models.

Lennart Ante co-founded the Blockchain Research Lab. As a researcher, he evaluates the use of blockchain technology across various sectors and studies the implications and characteristics of cryptocurrencies and their respective markets. He believes that blockchain technology will positively influence business models and society. Thus, he studies the technology's positive potential and assesses its barriers and risks. Besides his research activities, he is a co-founder of STOKR, which provides asset tokenization and corporate financing via blockchain technology. He studied business administration at the University of Cologne, TU Clausthal, and Universität Hamburg. He obtained a PhD in Finance at the University of Hamburg.

Antonio Brasse is the CEO of BlockQuake, a regulatory-driven digital asset and cryptocurrency trading platform. He has nearly two decades of regulatory, financial, operational, and technology audit experience within the financial services industry. He spent much of his career at AIG, Citi, and New York Life before co-founding BlockQuake. Before delving into cryptocurrency trading, his personal trading experience included stocks, options, and forex. He holds a BS in Accounting and Computer Science from the City University of New York – Brooklyn College. He also has the following certifications: Certified Information Systems Auditor, Certified Internal Auditor, Certified Financial Services Auditor, Certified Anti-Money Laundering Specialist, and Certified Public Accountant.

Christian Caceres is an Adjunct Professor of Corporate Finance and Entrepreneurship Management at Universidad Central and Universidad de las Americas. He has experience in designing, developing, and implementing business models in commercial strategies focused on innovation processes and customer experience. His research concerns the entrepreneurial ecosystem and how to build collaboration and complementation between different stakeholders. He coaches students and companies in several graduate programs at Pontificia Universidad Católica de Chile, and Impulso Chileno, a program supporting small and medium enterprises. He has also developed several ventures, including Kolife SpA and Fintelligence. He has more than 20 years of experience in the financial sector. He is a Civil Industrial Engineer with a Diploma in Computer Science. He has an MBA from Pontificia Universidad Católica de Chile and a Master's in Finance and Investments from ESE Business School, Universidad de los Andes, Chile.

Duncan Cameron is a management consultant specializing in blockchain technologies, cryptocurrencies, and tokenomics. He is currently a Manager at Capgemini Invent, the innovation, design, and transformation arm of Capgemini. His career spans a range of business and technical innovation work across digital IT strategy, IT operating model design, technical architecture, and project management. He is a former Australian Lawyer and holds an LLB with honors and a BA from Monash University.

Brett Cotler is a tax and cryptocurrency attorney at Seward & Kissel LLP. He advises investment funds, FinTech startups, and public and private companies on US federal income tax and business law matters. He also advises on business transactions, securities offerings, structured finance and securitization vehicles, and joint ventures. He received a BA and JD from Rutgers University and an LLM in Taxation from New York University.

Rocher Cyrus, CPA, CGMA, is the Managing Partner of Global International Management (GIM.cpa) and a Partner of Confirmation (part of Thomson Reuters) and Becker Professional Education. He is also a channel learning partner for the Association of International Certified Professional Accountants (AICPA). Mr. Cyrus was an early adopter of Gilded.finance, a platform unifying fiat and crypto back-office operations. He is also the Owner and Director of *Curacao Business Magazine*, which has published blockchain and technology-related articles. He has been driving innovation through technology, education, and connectivity with more than 10 years audit experience at PwC and KPMG. He holds a BS in accounting from the University of Curacao. Mr. Cyrus is enrolled in the double degree Global Masters in Blockchain Technologies program from Zigurat Innovation and Technology Business School and the University of Barcelona.

Robinpreet Dhillon is a Research Associate at Third Bridge LLC, New York. Formerly, he was an Equity Analyst at the Student Management Investment Fund, sponsored by Hofstra University. He has been on the executive board member of the Association of Latino Professionals for America chapter. He assisted organization members with professional development by leading weekly interactive meetings and giving presentations. He participated in competitive Olympic Weightlifting events. He received a BBA degree in Finance with honors from Zarb School of Business, Hofstra University.

Russell Dominic is an Australian Lawyer currently undertaking a Master of Financial Technologies at the Swinburne University of Technology. He is also a member of the Digital Law Association of Australia. Previously, he worked with an Australian FinTech company that pioneered using a capital-raising platform to accept fiat and cryptocurrency in Australia. He is now working in a PropTech company. He has first-hand knowledge of legal tech and is enthusiastic about regulation and the impact of emerging technology that could affect organizations and society. He has a Legum Baccalaureus (LLB) at the University of Tasmania. He also holds a Graduate Diploma in Legal Practice from the Leo Cussen Centre for Law.

Peter C. Earle is an Economist in the Research Faculty of the American Institute for Economic Research (AIER). Before joining AIER in 2018, he founded Intangible Economics, LLC, a cryptocurrency and gaming consultancy. He was a trader and analyst at different securities firms and hedge funds in the New York metropolitan area. His research and writing focus on financial markets, monetary policy, cryptocurrencies, and problems in economic measurement. He has written for and been cited in the *Wall Street Journal, Bloomberg, Barron's, Fortune, Forbes, Grant's Interest Rate Observer*, and other media venues. He has written and edited seven books and written hundreds of articles for various research institutes. He has a BS in Engineering from the United States Military Academy at West Point, an MBA in Finance, and an MA in Applied Economics.

Arman Eshraghi holds the Chair of Finance and Investment at Cardiff Business School, Cardiff University, United Kingdom. He is an Editor of the *International Review of Economics and Finance*, Senior Editor of *Finance Research Letters*, Director of the Cardiff Fintech Research Group, and an Advisory Board Member of Fintech Wales. His academic research spans finance, accounting, and psychology, including behavioral finance, financial technology, and corporate governance. His work appears in some leading journals in the field. Various media cite his research, including the *Financial Times*, *Washington Post*, *Harvard Business Review*, *Forbes*, and *Bloomberg*. He has also contributed to handbooks published by Cambridge University, John Wiley & Sons, Springer, and Routledge. He holds a BEng and MBA from Sharif University and a PhD in Finance from the University of Edinburgh.

Ingo Fiedler is Co-founder of the non-profit Blockchain Research Lab in Hamburg, and an Affiliate Assistant Professor at Concordia University, Montreal. He has authored nine books and over fifty articles in academic journals. He adds to the public knowledge on his main research topics – gambling and blockchain – by commenting in various media outlets and consulting with key policy stakeholders. He holds diplomas in business administration and economics and obtained his award-winning PhD from the University of Hamburg.

Samuel Hyun is the Chief Strategist of Cryptocurrency Markets at BlockQuake, with over seven years of experience trading cryptocurrencies. He has a deep understanding of CEX and DEX trading platforms and cryptocurrency markets. Before joining BlockQuake, he was an Associate in Barclay's Treasury Liquidity Risk Department and a Senior Analyst in the Internal Audit Group at AIG. He holds a BS in Mathematics and Economics from New York University.

Kristin M. Kalish is an Independent Financial Consultant. She directs an incubator program at Yale University and Georgetown University for young entrepreneurs globally. She is currently a Graduate Research Fellow at Villanova University, pursuing a Master of Science in Finance. Her prior work experience includes internships in private investment management and commodity analysis at a Chinese investment firm. She graduated summa cum laude from Hofstra University, earning a BBA with double majors in Finance and Management. She also holds a BS in Economics from Dongbei University of Finance and Economics.

Sebastián Labbé is a Research Assistant at the Institute of Concrete Structures and Building Materials at Karlsruhe Institute of Technology. His research focuses on structural dynamics, concrete technologies, and modeling impact loads due to railway traffic. *Building and Construction Materials* and *The German Federal Railway Authority* have featured his research. He is a blockchain enthusiast due to his experience with personal finance while living abroad, focusing on the technology, applications, and teaching of DeFi. He is a CHILFITEC and DAAD Alumni and received a Civil Engineering and Master of Engineering degree from Pontificia Universidad Católica de Chile and an MS at École Centrale Paris.

Paul P. Momtaz is a Professor of Financial Economics at the House of Finance at Goethe University Frankfurt. He holds a Chair of Private Equity and the Metzler Professor of International Finance at the Wharton School at the University of Pennsylvania. His research focuses on decentralized and private markets, particularly FinTech, entrepreneurship, and innovation economics. He has published in journals such as the *Journal of Corporate Finance*, *Strategic Management Journal*, *Strategic Entrepreneurship Journal*, and *Journal of Business Venturing*. He received a PhD in Economics and a *Habilitation* from the University of Hamburg, a Diploma in Applied Mathematics from the University of Paris, and an MPhil in Innovation, Strategy, and Organization from the Judge Business School at the University of Cambridge. He is also a PhD candidate in Finance at the University of California Los Angeles.

Kiran Pandian is a Graduate Student in Finance at the Frank G. Zarb School of Business at Hofstra University. He is a recipient of Dean's Scholarship and conducts blockchain research. He also mentors students in Blockchain Technology. He also holds an MS in Industrial Engineering from the University of Wisconsin, Madison.

Daniel Pfeiffer is an Equity Research Analyst at J.P. Morgan, in New York, where he covers Internet stocks. He was also an Equity Research Intern at Oppenheimer & Co. Inc. where he researched digital asset companies. He was a Team Leader for Adirondack Cup Competition and the CFA Institute Investment Research Challenge. He was the Coordinator of the Bloomberg Trading Room at the Frank G. Zarb School of Business, Hofstra University, where he received a BBA degree with a major in Finance and a minor in Accounting.

Kerem Proulx is an Independent Financial Consultant with experience working in roles involving operational risk, leveraged finance, and credit risk. He focuses on modeling tail risk using computational methods. He has a BBA in Finance from the Frank G. Zarb School of Business at Hofstra University. He received high honors for his research in applying machine learning methods to forecasting equity volatility.

Samson Qian is a Master of Finance candidate at the MIT Sloan School of Management. He was a researcher in the blockchain group at the San Diego Supercomputer Center. He engaged in data science and machine learning at the Halicioglu Data Science Institute at University of California, San Diego. As a quantitative research intern at Rebellion Research, he researched intraday patterns and assessed crypto trading strategies. He holds a BS in Data Science from the University of California, San Diego.

Gabriel Rodríguez-Garnica is an Assistant Professor of Financial Economics, Accounting, and Digital Finance at the Business Department, University Carlos III Madrid, Spain. His research focuses on entrepreneurial finance, behavioral finance, and FinTech, particularly crowdfunding and cryptoassets or blockchain-enabled assets. He was a Visiting Research Fellow at the Questrom School of Business, Boston University, where he continued his research on FinTech. He previously studied at the University of Technology Sydney, Centennial College Toronto, Middlebury Institute of International Studies at Monterey, and the University of La Rioja. He is a PhD candidate in Finance at University Carlos III Madrid, Spain.

Dimitrios Salampasis is the Director, Master of FinTech, and Lecturer, FinTech Innovation and Entrepreneurship, the Swinburne University of Technology in Melbourne, Australia. He is a Visiting Professor of FinTech at the University of Québec at Rimouski, Canada, and a Blockchain and FinTech Fellow at the Singapore University of Social Sciences. He is also a Visiting Faculty at the School of Management in Fribourg, Switzerland. His research interests concern the organizational, human, technological, and societal sides of FinTech innovation. He is a mentor and advisor for start-ups and scale-ups in Australia and abroad. He is regularly involved in speaking engagements and advisory work with international stakeholders. He has a PhD in Industrial Engineering Business and Management from the Lappeenranta University of Technology in Finland and two Executive Program Certificates from Harvard Business School Online and Columbia Business School.

Ibrahim E. Sancak is a Professor of Finance at the ZWIRN-Research Center of the Ostfalia University of Applied Sciences (Germany) with more than twenty years of hands-on experience in finance. He served as the founding director of the Market Oversight and Enforcement Division at the Capital Markets Board of Turkey. Since joining Ostfalia in February 2019, he has been actively conducting scientific research in sustainable finance and digital finance and teaching sustainable finance courses. In 2020, he took part in delivering a sustainability management guide for the "Bankenfachverband," a key financial industry association in Germany. Dr. Sancak is the lead editor of "Essential Concepts of Sustainable Finance: An A-Z Guide," a book project approved by the Routledge Editorial Board in February 2022. He holds a BSBA and MBA from Ankara University (Turkey), an MSF from the George Washington University (the U.S.), and PhD in banking from Marmara University (Turkey). Dr. Sancak also holds three certificates from the U.S. Securities and Exchange Commission (SEC) on market regulation and supervision. He is an academic member of the European Corporate Governance Institute (ECGI).

Patrick Schueffel is an Adjunct Professor at Fribourg's School of Management in Switzerland. His research focus is on banking, finance, and entrepreneurship. He also works as an advisor and founder on crypto projects spanning Europe to Asia. Before a recent three-year stint in Singapore, he worked in banking in Zurich, Switzerland, as the Chief Operating Officer of Saxo Bank. He was a member of the Senior Management at Credit Suisse's headquarters in Zurich, where he headed a global innovation team. He has published in scientific journals and practitioner outlets. He holds a PhD from the University of Reading and postgraduate degrees from Henley Business School, the Norwegian School of Economics, and the University of Mannheim.

Philip C. Sookram, CPA, is an Assistant Professor of Accounting at the Frank J. Guarini School of Business, Saint Peter's University, and Director of the Master of Science in Accountancy Graduate Program. He is an active member of the New York State Society of CPAs (NYSSCPA), serving as a Manhattan/Bronx Chapter Board Member and Chairman of the Manhattan/Bronx Chapter Next-Gen Committee. He is also involved in the New Jersey Society of CPAs (NJCPA), serving as a member of the Emerging Leaders Council. In recognition of his service, he received the Under 40 Award at the NYSSCPA in 2020. He is a recipient of the NJCPA Ovation Award in the Emerging Leader category in 2020. He has an undergraduate degree in Accounting from the University of Miami and a MAcc from Rutgers Business School — Newark and New Brunswick.

Andrew C. Spieler, CFA, CAIA, FRM, is the Robert F. Dall Distinguished Professor of Finance in the Frank G. Zarb School of Business at Hofstra University. He has published in *Real Estate Economics*, *Journal of Real Estate Finance and Economics*, *Journal of Real Estate Portfolio Management*, *Global Finance Journal*, *Journal of Applied Finance,* and other journals. He served as Chair of the Derivatives Committee at the New York Society of Securities Analysts. He also serves as Co-Director of the annual real estate conference sponsored by the Wilbur F. Breslin Center for Real Estate Studies. He received a BA in Mathematics and a BS in Economics from Binghamton University (SUNY), an MS in Finance from Indiana University, and an MBA and PhD in Finance from Binghamton University (SUNY).

John Ward is a Managing Director in Kroll's New York office and is a member of the Alternative Asset Advisory Group and the Portfolio Valuation practice. He has more than 30 years of financial and investment management experience. He evaluates operational risks for hedge funds, private equity and private credit funds, cryptocurrency funds, real estate funds, and venture capital funds. He has experience in various investment strategies and large institutional investment advisors and emerging managers. He works with endowments, foundations, public and private pensions, sovereign wealth funds, and family offices to undertake due diligence projects supporting their investment mandates. He develops best practices in investment due diligence and supports their efforts to implement institutional best practices throughout their organizations. He has a BSBA in finance and marketing from the University of Florida. He is also a Certified Due Diligence Analyst and a Board Member of the Investment Management Due Diligence Association.

David M. Waugh is the Managing Editor at the American Institute for Economic Research (AIER). He is also a Don Lavoie Fellow with the Mercatus Center at George Mason University. Before joining AIER in 2020, he worked as an Associate at S&P Global Market Intelligence. His work focuses on cryptocurrencies, financial markets, political economy, and higher education. RealClearMarkets, the Future of Freedom Foundation, the James G. Martin Center for Academic Renewal, ZeroHedge, and other outlets have featured his work. He received a BA in Economics from Hampden-Sydney College. While at Hampden-Sydney, he was a Senior Fellow with the Center for the Study of Political Economy and worked in the Economics Department as a Teaching Assistant.

Giga Zukhubaia is a graduate student in Operations Research at Fun Foundation School of Engineering and Applied Science, Columbia University. He worked as a Trading Research Analyst for the GreenEco Interments in Moscow, Russia. He also served as an Acting Chief Operating Officer for Country Cleaners Corporations through the Hofstra IdeaHub Startup Incubator, Center for Entrepreneurship. He received a BBA in Finance from Hofstra University and the Dongbei University of Finance and Economics in China.

Acknowledgments

"To write is human, to edit is divine."

Stephen King

Publishing a book is a team effort. Therefore, we have several major players to thank for their roles in this book project. For this edited book, the chapter authors created the content. We are grateful to them for devoting countless hours to writing and revising their chapters. Our role as editors was to honor their intention while helping to enhance each chapter's clarity. We wanted the book's format and style to be internally consistent so that it is more than just a collection of chapters from different authors. Michael Lee notes, "The first draft reveals the art; revision reveals the artist." We also appreciate the high degree of professionalism exhibited by Emerald Publishing's staff, especially Charlotte C. Maiorana (Vice President, Emerald Books), Kirsty Woods (Contact Development Editor), and Pavithra Mutha (Production Manager). We also thank S. Rajachitra, Lead Project Manager, KnowledgeWorks Global Ltd. We appreciate the support provided by our respective institutions: Kogod School of Business at American University; ESE Business School at Universidad de Los Andes, Chile; Frank G. Zarb School of Business at Hofstra University; and Lehman College at the City University of New York. We thank our families for their support. Finally, we dedicate this book to Linda and Rory Baker; Pascale and Luciano Benedetti; Parvin, Auzin, and Daniel Nikbakht; Ximena Romero; and Frederick Smith, Kathleen Stein Smith, Patrick Stein Smith, and Frederick Stein Smith.

Part I

The Cryptoasset Landscape

Chapter 1

Cryptoassets: An Overview

H. Kent Baker, Hugo Benedetti, Ehsan Nikbakht and Sean Stein Smith

Abstract

Bitcoin's introduction as the first cryptoasset in 2009 ushered in a new era, representing a seismic shift in the financial markets. Since then, this evolving asset class has generated much interest, excitement, and growth. This chapter begins by providing a brief background of cryptoassets. It then discusses their main types (cryptocurrencies, security tokens, and utility tokens), users (individual investors, major financial institutions, endowments, and hedge funds), and benefits and drawbacks. Next, it sets forth the book's purpose, distinguishing features, intended audience, and structure. The chapter provides a synopsis of each of the remaining 21 chapters. Although no single book can encompass all changes and iterations of these technologies as they emerge in the marketplace, this book brings together a broad collection of industry expertise and academic analysis to create a book helpful to researchers, academics, and practitioners.

Keywords: Cryptoassets; bitcoin; security tokens; utility tokens; individual investors; financial institutions

Introduction

Since bitcoin's introduction as the first cryptoasset in 2009, this evolving asset class has generated considerable interest and excitement among both academics and practitioners. A *cryptoasset* is a private digital asset that uses cryptography and serves as a medium of exchange. The most well-known cryptoassets are cryptocurrencies, such as bitcoin, that permit buying goods and services or trading them for a potential profit. However, cryptocurrencies are not like using cash and are not very "money-like." Thus, cryptoasset owners view them as investments and expect their value to rise.

The Emerald Handbook on Cryptoassets: Investment Opportunities and Challenges, 3–11

doi:10.1108/978-1-80455-320-620221001

Besides cryptocurrencies, other types of cryptoassets include security tokens, utility tokens, stablecoins, and tokenized securities. The price of cryptoassets can be unpredictable and highly volatile, making them risky investments. Some, like bitcoin, are well-known global brands trading on exchanges worldwide. Others have a much smaller market presence.

What is sure about cryptoassets is that they are here to stay. CoinMarketCap, a popular data aggregator, reports thousands of different cryptoassets, with new ones created frequently. Multiple cryptoassets exist because their creators optimize the underlying blockchains for various uses. The market capitalization of some cryptoassets exceeds $1 trillion. Those involved in cryptoassets include individual investors, major financial institutions, endowments, and hedge funds.

Cryptoassets, especially more prominent cryptocurrencies such as bitcoin, are attractive to investors because of potentially high returns. However, increased volatility accompanies high returns. Another potential benefit of including bitcoin in an investment portfolio is its low correlations with traditional assets such as stocks and bonds. Thus, including bitcoin in a portfolio offers diversification benefits. Over time, however, bitcoin's low correlations with other asset classes are likely to rise. Bitcoin is currently an early-stage investment opportunity, and its core drivers differ from those of other assets. Despite the investment opportunities offered by bitcoin and other cryptoassets, investors entering this market face substantial challenges, including low quality of information, a lack of sound or academically defensible valuation models, regulatory uncertainty, and inadequate due diligence.

About this Book

This section discusses the book's purpose, distinguishing features, and intended audience.

Purpose

This book offers curious investors and others, such as investment practitioners, academics, and students, a helpful guide to understanding cryptoassets and their role in investment portfolios.

Distinguishing Features

The following features distinguish *The Emerald Handbook on Cryptoassets: Investment Opportunities and Challenges* from others.

- This book provides a detailed examination of cryptoassets from an investment perspective. It focuses on investment opportunities and real-world challenges rather than technical or theoretical topics.
- It skillfully blends scholars' and practitioners' contributions into a single review of critical topics and issues about cryptoassets. The contributors' varied

backgrounds ensure different perspectives and a rich interplay of ideas. The book also reflects the latest trends and research.
- The book follows an internally consistent format and style while retaining the contributors' content and perspectives. Like a choir, the book's authors have separate voices. A goal of a choir and this book is to have the voices act harmoniously. This task requires skilled editing to create a smooth flow between chapters. Hence, the book is an orderly presentation of various topics organized into separate sections from different authors.
- When discussing the results of empirical studies that connect theory and practice, our objective is to make them understandable to a wide array of readers with different backgrounds.
- The end of each chapter contains four to six questions reinforcing key concepts. The end of the book includes guideline answers for each question. This feature should help faculty and students use the book in courses.

Intended Audience

The Emerald Handbook on Cryptoassets: Investment Opportunities and Challenges should appeal to its target audience of academics and practitioners because of its investor perspective. Because it covers a broad range of topics related to cryptoassets, it can serve as a guide for investors, financial practitioners, and students. The book should interest anyone seeking to become more knowledgeable about this fast-moving subject area.

This volume spans the gamut from theoretical to practical while offering the right balance of detailed and user-friendly coverage. Discussion of relevant research permeates the book. Although other books are available on cryptoassets, especially cryptocurrencies, few examine this topic from an investor's perspective. Scholarly, edited books, including academics and practitioners' contributions on the investment opportunities and challenges facing cryptoassets, are largely absent in the marketplace. This book helps to fill this gap and contributes to the growing field of cryptoassets.

Book's Structure

The remainder of this book consists of 21 chapters divided into five parts. Below is a brief synopsis of each section and chapter.

Part I. The Cryptoasset Landscape. Besides the current chapter, this part includes Chapters 2 and 3, examining the cryptoasset auditing, accounting, and investing landscapes.

Chapter 2 – The Cryptoasset Auditing and Accounting Landscape (Sean Stein Smith). This chapter examines emerging topics and trends as it connects cryptoassets to accounting, auditing, and financial reporting. It discusses the treatment of cryptoassets from a financial reporting perspective under United States and international accounting standards, frequently asked questions about auditing, attestation, and potential best practices for auditing various cryptoassets. It also discusses accounting for now and potential in the future. The chapter outlines how the rapidly changing cryptoasset landscape could lead to differentiated accounting treatment and audit best practices for practitioners seeking to attest to certain aspects of cryptoassets.

Chapter 3 – The Crypto Investing Landscape (John Ward). This chapter discusses the current landscape for digital asset investing and the operational risks facing cryptocurrency investors. It also examines the ongoing progress in the institutionalization of digital asset investment and the risks inherent when investing in cryptocurrencies and blockchain opportunities. Investors considering investing in a public or private fund that invests in digital assets must be aware of the operational risks that may directly impact their investments, including risks from portfolio concentration, illiquidity, hacking, digital asset custody, and digital asset valuations. Operational due diligence reviews of funds and fund managers are critical in assessing operational risks for digital asset investment.

Part II. Types of Cryptoassets. This part consists of Chapters 4–8, examining different types of cryptoassets: cryptocurrencies, security tokens, utility tokens, stablecoins, and tokenized securities.

Chapter 4 – Cryptocurrencies (Lennart Ante). This chapter introduces the concept of cryptocurrencies such as bitcoin, ether, or litecoin. The chapter describes the history of cryptocurrency, blockchain technology, and the quest for secure digital money, followed by a discussion of cryptocurrency as a phenomenon. Next, it discusses individual cryptocurrencies, including an overview of bitcoin and relevant subgroups, such as so-called forks or privacy coins. It also explains developments such as stablecoins or central bank digital currencies, which are potentially much more in line with bitcoin's original idea of digital cash. The chapter provides a basic understanding of cryptocurrencies, their defining characteristics, challenges, and markets.

Chapter 5 – Security Tokens (Paul P. *Momtaz*). This chapter synthesizes the economics, law, and technology of security tokens and security token offerings (STOs). Security tokens are an increasingly important instrument in decentralized finance (DeFi) markets. They are blockchain-based investment contracts that are subject to securities law. Interoperability, fractional ownership, market liquidity, and rapid settlement are the main reasons for considering security tokens a primary catalyst for digitizing finance. The chapter empirically compares STOs with initial exchange offerings (IEOs) and initial coin offerings (ICOs). STOs take longer and raise more funding. However, controlling for other factors, the amount raised in STOs and IEOs is lower than in utility token ICOs. These findings suggest an avenue for future research. Moreover, both the law and the technology of security tokens need to address critical challenges related to the competent jurisdiction in multinational activities and blockchain interoperability, scalability, and natural resource degradation.

Chapter 6 – Utility Tokens (Hugo Benedetti, Christian Caceres, and Álvaro Abarzúa). Utility tokens are digital currencies that serve as the only accepted means of payment for services and products provided through a blockchain-based platform. They finance the development of their product or service, reward and incentivize early adopters and network promoters, align economic incentives between supply, demand, and the marketplace, and enhance network effects among all participants. Their tokenomic design consists of the rules and regulations governing a token's issuance, distribution, allocation, and potential destruction. The chapter describes utility tokens, compares them with other types of cryptoassets, and discusses their value creation process and role in network economics. It also reviews standard tokenomic designs, discusses different regulatory approaches, and provides examples of current utility token applications in decentralized applications such as DeFi and virtual reality platforms (metaverses).

Chapter 7 – Stablecoins (Ingo Fiedler and Lennart Ante). This chapter introduces the concept of stablecoins such as Tether, DAI, or Ampleforth. It also provides a taxonomy of the different types of stablecoins consisting of (1) traditional asset-backed stablecoins, (2) crypto-collateralized stablecoins, and (3) algorithmic stablecoins and seigniorage shares. The chapter continues with a brief history of stablecoins, starting from BitShares as the first stablecoin implementation over Tether and market-wide stablecoin adoption to Facebook-initiated Diem. Next, the chapter explains the impact of stablecoins on cryptocurrencies and other markets and discusses trends and challenges facing stablecoins. The chapter provides a basic understanding of stablecoins, their defining characteristics, challenges, and markets.

Chapter 8 – Tokenized Assets and Securities (Hugo Benedetti and Gabriel Rodríguez-Garnica). Tokenization is a relatively new activity in digital finance. Developers can enhance the standard features and characteristics of assets and securities by tokenization, a process that creates a blockchain representation of the underlying instrument. Asset and security tokenization produces benefits. These benefits include reducing issuance and trading costs, lessening dependency on intermediaries, facilitating more liquidity in markets, and providing greater transparency around an asset's lifecycle for all parties involved. This chapter synthesizes the key characteristics, benefits, processes, tools, and techniques of tokenizing real-world assets. It also provides examples of current asset-backed token applications to help understand the rapidly growing industry and analyzes future expectations of this new technology.

Part III. Cryptoassets as Investment Opportunities. The third part contains Chapters 9–14, discussing cryptoasset products, decentralized finance, blockchain and crypto exchange-traded funds, cryptocurrency valuation, cryptoassets in a portfolio context, and cryptoasset frauds.

Chapter 9 – A Comparative Review of Cryptoasset Products (Kristin M. Kalish, Kerem Proulx, and Andrew C. Spieler). Cryptoassets are an asset class recorded digitally that does not represent a financial claim or liability for an issuer or a custodian. This chapter provides a detailed review of various cryptoassets by comparing different characteristics, products, and listing exchanges and discusses criticisms of the crypto ecosystem. It also discusses cryptoasset features, methods of tokenization, and advances in decentralized, peer-to-peer exchanges. Another topic examined is the criticisms of cryptoasset exchanges and ongoing regulatory implications due to cryptocurrency's open-source nature. The chapter evaluates various types and trends of cryptoassets, including currency, utility, platform, and transactional tokens

Chapter 10 – Decentralized Finance (Kiran Pandian, Daniel Pfeiffer, and Samson Qian). One aspect of the opportunities and challenges for cryptoassets concerns DeFi. DeFi is a growing area of cryptoassets that couples blockchain technology, digital assets, and financial services. DeFi is a publicly available system on a decentralized blockchain network, offering financial products and applications. This chapter provides an overview of the DeFi universe with massive potential in various industries in the global market. It also discusses the implications of DeFi's new wave and its applications involving ICOs and stablecoins and specific challenges like the scalability trilemma in DeFi and financial markets.

Chapter 11 – Blockchain and Crypto Exchange-traded Funds (Philip C. Sookram). This chapter examines the current state of crypto exchange-traded funds (ETFs). It focuses on issues preventing wider implementation and specific products. ETFs have become a popular investment vehicle that investors use to help achieve their long-term goals. A recurring theme is that regulators protect individual investors from exposure to cryptocurrency, which can be a highly speculative investment. Pressure from institutions and investors for a bitcoin-based ETF made progress in 2021 when Proshares, an ETF specialized investment company, debuted the first-ever bitcoin futures ETF in the United States. This event is the first-time investors could buy a fund on the New York Stock Exchange that tracks derivative futures contracts of bitcoin. This occurrence pushed this digital asset's spot price to all-time highs, serving as a breakthrough in cryptocurrency history.

Chapter 12 – Approaches to Cryptocurrency Valuation (Arman Eshraghi). Cryptocurrencies are notoriously tricky to value from a fundamental perspective. This valuation challenge is rooted in various debated issues in academia and the investments industry. For example, do cryptocurrencies and other cryptoassets have intrinsic value in the conventional sense? Can one appropriately regard cryptocurrencies as digital fiat currencies? What distinguishes cryptocurrencies such as bitcoin and ether from precious metals like gold from a financial perspective? How do cryptocurrencies compare to other cryptoassets in terms of pricing and valuation? This chapter answers these questions, discusses approaches to valuing cryptoassets, and identifies areas for future research.

Chapter 13 – Cryptoassets in a Portfolio Context (Robinpreet Dhillon and Ehsan Nikbakht). Since the inception of modern portfolio theory, traditional asset classes have been the standard investment products for portfolio construction. With the introduction of cryptoassets, including cryptocurrencies, tokenized securities, smart contracts, and blockchain-based token assets, the crypto "revolution" created a new asset class for consideration in a modern portfolio. This chapter explains cryptoassets in a portfolio, including their limitations and parameters as an asset class in a diversified portfolio. Finally, it reports an improvement in a new portfolio's reward/risk ratio using the Sharpe ratio when adding cryptoassets to simulated equity, bonds, and real estate portfolios. A caveat is that a cryptoasset's contribution to a well-diversified traditional portfolio differs from the performance of investing in a single and isolated cryptoasset.

Chapter 14 – Protection of Portfolios and Financial Consumers from Cryptoasset Frauds (Ibrahim E. Sancak). This chapter introduces the fundamentals of portfolio and financial consumer protection from frauds in the cryptoasset space. Cryptoassets pose new risks to portfolios and financial consumers, such as idiosyncratic risks stemming from their unique features and systematic risks from transitioning from centralized to DeFi. Market experience indicates that these risks threaten every portfolio and financial consumer holding cryptoassets. In the consumer protection framework, cryptoasset risks and threats are higher than traditional assets and markets. Because cryptoassets fall outside the regulatory domain in different jurisdictions, their decentralized nature, technological attributes, and the momentum of financial technology cause asymmetric technology, disarming system-based portfolios, and consumer protection mechanisms against frauds and abuses. Idiosyncratic and systematic risks of cryptoassets highlight the importance of developing more vigilant self-protection mechanisms to protect against fraud.

Part IV. Trading, Reporting, and Technical Aspects. The fourth part contains Chapters 15–19. Topics examined concern institutional considerations of blockchain and custody, provenance, and reporting of blockchain and cryptoassets. Other topics include the legal aspects of tokenized and non-tokenized assets, the underlying technology of cryptoassets, and central bank digital currencies.

Chapter 15 – General Institutional Considerations of Blockchain and Emerging Applications (Peter C. Earle and David M. Waugh). This chapter examines matters institutional investors must consider while investing or engaging in the cryptocurrency sector, whether exclusively in bitcoin or the broader universe of crypto or DeFi assets. Given the rapid change in legal and regulatory oversight and cryptocurrency and blockchain innovation, offering inviolable advice about due diligence and compliance during commercial engagement is exceedingly difficult. However, general guidelines and rules of thumb are available.

Chapter 16 – Custody, Provenance, and Reporting of Blockchain and Cryptoassets (Rocher Cyrus). Although few fully understand the evolving science of blockchain technology, many agree that such technology promises countless crypto innovative applications. However, institutions using blockchain and cryptoassets face issues. Since more institutions are beginning to explore private, public, and hybrid blockchains and their related cryptoassets, an increased need exists to understand and anticipate implementation problems. Such problems include contractual issues, privacy concerns, tax implications, jurisdictional issues, financial fraud, and data theft. Others involve intellectual property rights, money laundering, accounting and financial reporting, fork management and governance, and compliance and regulatory obligations. This chapter reviews and analyzes the problems facing institutions in using blockchain and cryptoassets as financial instruments and mediums of exchange. It focuses on these aspects concerning custody, provenance, and reporting. This chapter also discusses the compliance, disclosure, and regulatory reporting of cryptoassets.

Chapter 17 – Tokenized and Non-tokenized Assets: Legal Considerations (Brett Cotler). This chapter discusses legal considerations relating to digital assets. The legal aspects of digital assets are evolving. Although some states have enacted specific laws or regulations for digital assets, Congress and federal agencies have been slower to craft specific rules and regulations for digital assets. As a result, regulators, such as the Securities and Exchange Commission, Commodity Futures Trading Commission, and Internal Revenue Service, and market participants, must apply existing guidance to digital assets. This chapter examines using certain aspects of federal securities and tax law for digital assets. It also discusses general business law considerations for blockchain and cyber enterprises. The discussion of state law applications centers on the New York Virtual Currency License and Wyoming and Delaware crypto initiatives. This chapter does not provide a comprehensive review of all legal issues related to cryptocurrency. Each legal issue on cryptocurrency is complex and requires separate analyses.

Chapter 18 – The Underlying Technology for Cryptoassets (Alevtina Dubovitskaya Ackerer and Damien Ackerer). This chapter reviews the underlying technologies of cryptoassets, including fundamental cryptographic primitives used in distributed ledger technologies and permissionless blockchain technologies and their consensus protocols such as proof-of-work and proof-of-stake. It discusses the pros and cons of existing approaches to improve blockchain scalability and considers the requirements for security and decentralization. The chapter also examines the following techniques: layer 1 tuning, layer 1 sharding, and layer 2 solutions. It concludes with an overview of technologies to swap cryptoassets off-chain, technical requirements for cross-chain transactions, and reviews cross-chain atomic swap implementation using hashed time lock contracts.

Chapter 19 – Central Bank Digital Currencies: Opening Pandora's Box or Paving the Future of Money? (Dimitrios Salampasis, Patrick Schueffel, Russell Dominic, and Duncan Cameron). This chapter reviews developments concerning central bank digital currencies (CBDCs). It introduces, analyses, and discusses the potential implications of CBDCs on the existing cryptoassets landscape. The chapter also provides an overview of the different approaches to adopting and implementing this new form of money. It compares traditional cryptocurrencies, privately issued stablecoins, fiat currencies, and CBDCs. Although vastly divergent opinions exist on digital money's purpose, benefits, and use cases, CBDCs can provide opportunities for innovation and experimentation at a central bank and systemic level. CBDCs may pave the way for democratizing access to unbundled financial services while rethinking the overall purpose of money, monetary systems, and global business.

Part V. Other Cryptoasset Issues. The final part examines trade settlements, decentralized finance, currency exchanges, and the future of cryptoassets.

Chapter 20 – Trade Settlements (Hugo Benedetti, Ehsan Nikbakht, and Giga Zukhubaia). The current security trade settlement life cycle presents inefficiencies derived from intermediaries involved in the transaction between buyers and sellers. This chapter examines distributed ledger technology (DLT), the underlying technology of all blockchain applications, including trade settlements. It also reviews the implications of using blockchain in trade settlements for cryptoassets. Emerging blockchain technology provides investors, exchanges, regulators, and countless potential intermediaries with the most up-to-date technology with the highest efficiency, transparency, credibility, and automation enabled by smart contracts. Smart contracts allow an ecosystem to manage trade settlements starting from execution to clearing and settlement. These contracts reduce reconciliation and recordkeeping costs and streamline repetitive processes in today's trade settlement system. The chapter highlights the benefits of implementing DLT in financial markets globally in all trading aspects, including cryptoassets.

Chapter 21 – A Closer Look into Decentralized Finance (Hugo Benedetti and Sebastián Labbé). DeFi is a technological infrastructure built on a blockchain networking environment that supplies transparent, uncensorable, decentralized financial services and products. This infrastructure offers the opportunity to replicate traditional financial instruments on a decentralized platform and incorporate added features provided by blockchain technology. It also allows creating new instruments native to blockchain technology unavailable through traditional financial institutions. This chapter presents an in-depth analysis of the inner workings of stablecoins, decentralized exchanges, automated market makers, liquidity pools, decentralized lending, synthetic instruments, and asset management. It also provides specific examples for each application and presents the sector's current challenges.

Chapter 22 – Cryptocurrency Exchanges and the Future of Cryptoassets (Antonio Brasse and Samuel Hyun). This chapter differentiates between centralized and decentralized exchanges, emphasizing the importance of regulations and compliance related to the market's development and expansion for cryptoasset trading and investment. It also explains the pros and cons of using different methods to trade cryptocurrencies or virtual currencies and their tradeoffs. The chapter discusses how centralized and decentralized exchanges emerged, their history and potential future, and the possible role of future regulations and regulatory clarity around how they may operate. Additionally, it compares cryptoasset markets to other more traditional markets such as equities, real estate, and foreign exchange.

Summary and Conclusions

This chapter provides a brief synopsis of the book's contents. The book covers various issues, including a detailed description of each instrument, underlying technology, opportunities, and risks. It also discusses valuation methods, accounting and portfolio implications, regulations, legal aspects, DeFi, and the industry's future.

Where possible, the book contains non-technical language. Thus, it should be helpful to industry practitioners, students in different disciplines, and faculty in their blockchain and cryptoasset courses. Blockchain and cryptoasset applications represent a technically challenging area of financial services to examine, analyze, and forecast properly. Due to the rapid pace of change in the sector, no singular book can encompass all changes and iterations of these technologies as they emerge in the marketplace. However, it combines a broad collection of industry expertise and academic analysis to create a book helpful to researchers, academics, and practitioners.

Chapter 2

The Cryptoasset Auditing and Accounting Landscape

Sean Stein Smith

Abstract

This chapter examines some emerging topics and trends as it connects cryptoassets to accounting, auditing, and financial reporting. It discusses the treatment of cryptoassets from a financial reporting perspective under the US and international accounting standards, frequently asked questions about auditing and attestation, and potential best practices for auditing various cryptoassets. It also discusses accounting for now and potential in the future. The chapter outlines how the rapidly changing cryptoasset landscape could lead to differentiated accounting treatment and audit best practices for practitioners seeking to attest to certain aspects of cryptoassets.

Keywords: Cryptoassets; accounting; auditing; financial reporting; accounting standards; trends

Introduction

A *cryptoasset* (*crypto*) is a virtual asset cryptographically connected to an underlying blockchain that forms the foundation for how transactional data, valuation, and records are maintained and shared between network members (Alexander, 2021). Cryptoassets may take different forms and have various use cases. Still, the connection to blockchain technology is a constant across the cryptoasset ecosystem. As the highest profile cryptoasset, bitcoin maintains the most significant market capitalization compared to any other single cryptoasset in the marketplace and continues to drive the narrative around accounting treatment and

The Emerald Handbook on Cryptoassets: Investment Opportunities and Challenges, 13–24

doi:10.1108/978-1-80455-320-620221002

financial reporting. The cryptoasset ecosystem has evolved far beyond the initial idea of cryptocurrency transactions. It continues to develop and mature in ways that continuously integrate the sector into the mainstream financial conversation. As blockchain and cryptoassets evolve, researchers, practitioners, and policymakers should know how varied the sector has become since bitcoin's introduction in 2008.

A Review of the Cryptoassets Landscape

Cryptoassets mean far more than cryptocurrencies or other coins or tokens such as stablecoins or central bank digital currencies (CBDCs). Acknowledging this fact is critical in forming a foundation to contextualize the conversation around newer cryptoassets (Ossinger, 2021). Specifically, financial institutions' recent influx of investment, often in consultation with crypto-native players and actors, demonstrates the appetite for such products and the information gap in many areas (Crosman, 2021a).

Any analysis of cryptoassets should begin by discussing decentralized cryptoassets such as bitcoin and Ethereum. No issuing entity or other centralized authority organizes, manages, or controls cryptoassets in this category. Therefore, they generally experience substantial volatility. Such volatility has led to the development of other cryptoassets such as stablecoins. A *stablecoin* is a privately issued coin or token issued, governed, and managed by a centralized authority and backed, tethered, or otherwise supported by other external assets such as a commodity, fiat currency, or a combination of assets (Choi, 2021). Due to this connection to external assets and the more active management of the price levels of stablecoins, the volatility associated with these cryptoassets is much reduced compared with decentralized cryptocurrencies. Lower volatility has led to stablecoins assuming a leadership position for cryptoassets used for transactions and as a medium of exchange. Thus, stablecoins may serve as a bridge between crypto and fiat currencies and as a starting point toward CBDCs (He, 2021).

CBDCs may strike some market participants as a paradoxical development in the cryptoasset sector. However, they are a natural outgrowth and maturation of cryptos integration into the broader economic conversation (Andolfatto, 2021). Instead of being decentralized and unconnected to any sovereign nation, these cryptoassets are actively developed, managed, and governed by a central government or some equivalent financial institution like the US Federal Reserve. Introducing such direct control and engagement from a governmental agency into the cryptoassets conversation adds to the potential risk of political interference. Still, it offers several benefits. Specifically, the backstop of official government support and associated lower volatility resulting from this connection may help enable wider adoption and utilization of cryptoassets for various transactional purposes (Prasad, 2021). Additionally, the issuance and governance of these tokens by a central government or quasi-governmental agency may help resolve or push these conversations about the accounting, financial, and taxation treatment around cryptoassets to a more productive state.

The cryptoasset sector has moved far beyond even this array of cryptocurrencies to include such high-profile trends as decentralized finance (DeFi) and non-fungible tokens (NFTs). *DeFi* is the development and replication of financial products and services enabled on a blockchain platform while not requiring incumbent third-party financial institutions (Schär, 2021).

Before discussing crypto-specific accounting rules and standards, the critical point is that compliance requires clarification. Specifically, authorities enforce rules and regulations against institutions, third-party service providers, or centralized entities. DeFi makes performing these processes much more difficult because they must now be adapted to focus on individual users.

The implications of offering customary financial services without using traditional financial institutions are complex. Yet, considering compliance and regulatory implications is essential. First, any organization or entity must comply with know your customer (KYC) and anti-money laundering (AML) practices. KYC is the practice conducted by companies to verify the identity of their customers to comply with legal requirements and current laws and regulations. *AML* refers to the laws, regulations, and procedures intended to prevent criminals from disguising illegally obtained funds as legitimate income. An entity must also employ personnel with the necessary expertise to comply with these regulations. Second, any entity seeking to issue or conduct transactions denominated in cryptoassets must interoperate with other technology systems. The topic of interoperability is a technical topic but merits revisiting any conversation and analysis involving cryptoassets. For cryptoassets to become fully integrated into the broader financial ecosystem requires integrating the payment processes, technology, and settlement procedures into the current technology infrastructure at various institutions (Crosman, 2021b).

Some specific examples of DeFi operations arising after the 2020–2021 crypto bull market include lending, borrowing, and paying interest on crypto deposits in the denomination of the deposited asset. Replicating banking services without traditional financial institutions also raises several audit and attestation issues.

NFTs are digital, virtual, or cryptoassets that can be tracked, monitored, and accounted for in a traceable and transparent manner. Digital artwork has a leadership position in this sector (Chow, 2021). NFTs represent an entirely new type of cryptoasset and an opportunity for individuals and institutions to invest.

Although NFTs vary across institutions, they have several main characteristics. NFTs are *non-fungible*, meaning swapping for one another as equivalents is not possible. Subdividing NFTs like fiat currencies or crypto-like bitcoin also is not possible. The intent of NFTs is not for use as a transactional medium.

Several options are available: (1) NFTs with a non-commercial license, (2) NFTs with a commercial license, and (3) NFTs issued as a crypto or digital collectible. NFTs with a non-commercial license are the traditional or classic NFT, which is essentially a digital or crypto-enabled representation of other assets. Such assets can be traded, stored, and held by investors. Still, they have no other way to earn income and generate capital returns outside of capital appreciation.

NFTs with a commercial license option possess all the traits of a traditional NFT but can license their rights to a certain extent. Thus, besides owning the asset's digital representation, the NFT holder also can generate income and earnings linked to this virtual asset. From an accounting and auditing viewpoint, this feature suggests that two financial instruments may need to be accounted for the underlying asset and the income streams and cash flows generated from owning this asset.

NFTs treated as a collectible can create a more complicated tax situation due to the ambiguity in the tax code. Under current guidance from the Internal Revenue Service (IRS) and meeting certain income levels, the tax rates on collectible transactions can be higher than those levied on ordinary income. This situation further complicates the accounting practices and possibilities for NFTs. Suppose even a singular type of cryptoasset can have multiple iterations and potential classifications. In that case, this circumstance could discourage policymakers from creating guidance until achieving further market maturity. The accounting and tax implications around NFTs can become complicated and serve as a headwind against wide adoption. This situation also highlights the importance and urgency of establishing and maintaining consistent and comparable accounting standards connected to cryptoassets.

Current State of Crypto Accounting

Cryptoassets continue to evolve and mature, but the financial accounting standards have not kept pace with this rapid development. Under International Financial Reporting Standards (IFRS), promulgated by the International Accounting Standards Board (IASB), IAS Concept Standard Number 8 provides some flexibility. It allows organizations to perform accounting that accurately reflects economic reality via reporting assets at fair market value. US Generally Accepted Accounting Principles (GAAP) lacks such flexibility. The Financial Accounting Standards Board (FASB) has not put forward any crypto-specific accounting standards. In place of accounting standards, the consensus is to treat cryptoassets as indefinite intangible assets, such as goodwill, copyrights, and trademarks.

Several issues exist with this approach. Cryptoassets may be intangible, but they do not function like intangible assets like goodwill in terms of purpose, use case, economic reality, or impact on an organization that employs, controls, or integrates them into operations. Additionally, under US GAAP, indefinitely lived intangible assets are held at historical cost less any impairment losses incurred. *Impairment losses* are non-cash losses booked on an organization's income statement to reflect changes in the economic reality or specific changes at the organization that detrimentally affect the intangible asset's value.

Traditional assets classified in this category might operate in a manner conducive to such accounting treatment, but cryptoassets do not. This accounting treatment treats all cryptoassets alike. For example, examining the volatility commonly linked to certain cryptoassets like bitcoin illustrates why such an approach would be difficult to apply. Other indefinitely lived intangible assets do not have such volatility as an embedded component of trading activity. If other assets treated this way suffer a loss in value, this loss is almost always permanent. By contrast, cryptoassets can experience significant swings in price that can quickly reverse themselves. Such volatility can make auditing these results exceedingly difficult (Vincent & Wilkins, 2020). This fundamental difference in the trading and valuation of these assets suggests that viewing crypto and other intangible assets as equals is incorrect.

The current consensus accounting treatment fails to reflect economic realities or make logical business sense without standardized crypto-specific authoritative accounting standards. The lack of consistent accounting and reporting standards complicates any attempt to audit or attest to the values. Additionally, every organization does not have to follow GAAP or IFRS if a private organization.

The lack of crypto-specific accounting and auditing standards has implications. Publicly traded organizations cannot comply with these standards. Additionally, a growing number of private firms need not comply. For example, publicly traded firms in the United States have declined significantly over several decades, amplifying the lack of consistent and relevant accounting and reporting rules. Even private organizations without publicly traded stocks still tend to follow the authoritative accounting standards developed for public firms for comparability and consistency purposes. This lack of crypto-specific guidance means that regardless of the organization examined, accounting for cryptoasset information accurately and consistently is virtually impossible.

Current State of Crypto Auditing

The current state of crypto auditing reflects the lack of standardized accounting or auditing for crypto-specific issues. The implications of this situation for auditing and attestation engagement are two-fold. Without crypto-specific accounting guidance, the conversations between external auditors and clients center on interpreting existing rules for an emerging asset class, not on accounting codifications and standards (Sheldon, 2021). For example, if an organization's operations involve cryptoassets, auditors usually must accept and ratify management's position if it is reasonable based on business facts.

Market forces are driving the audit practitioner landscape. Specifically, the rise of *smart contracts* – executable and programmable codes connected to an underlying blockchain – raise issues that auditors and audit practices must address about how blockchain and cryptoasset operations are managed and driven (Appelbaum & Nehmer, 2020). What measures can verify that smart contracts operate as advertised, especially when business conditions change? Who has access to the underlying code and smart contract language? Who is responsible for reviewing and maintaining the smart contract language to ensure translating an agreement's intent into execution?

Although the lack of consistent auditing and attestation standards complicates the cryptoasset conversation, it is only a partial view of the landscape. Another factor complicating the crypto-financial reporting dialogue is the potential shrinking influence of public company accounting and audit standards.

Crypto-financial Reporting

Given the lack of standardized accounting or auditing standards, even with non-authoritative guidance issued by associations such as the Association for

Internationally Certified Public Accountants, the financial reporting landscape around cryptoasset represents an ambiguous area for practitioners. Businesses can report cryptoassets as inventory for specific broker-dealer firms, indefinite lived intangible assets, or some financial instruments driven mainly by the lack of liquidity in certain specific cryptoassets. However, US GAAP does not drive the reporting discussion for every organization in financial markets.

Suppose organizations seek to engage with cryptoasset transactions in any capacity but are not obligated to abide by US GAAP. In that case, these entities can account and report for cryptoassets in any manner that they choose. Accounting and auditing are disciplinary areas but do not operate in a vacuum. External market forces inform the accounting decision-making process.

Potential Reporting Options Moving Forward

The current crypto accounting and auditing landscapes are ambiguous in the United States, with the outlook equally murky in other jurisdictional areas. In 2021, neither the FASB nor IASB placed crypto accounting, auditing, and reporting issues on the agenda for resolution. Thus, the profession remains tasked with applying current accounting standards to this new sector. As cryptoassets become an increasingly integrated part of the broader economic landscape, several options merit consideration. Policymakers might not currently be addressing crypto-specific accounting standards, but this situation could change. How might this conversation develop moving forward?

Crypto Accounting Options

The argument for accounting for cryptoassets based on use case and functionality would align with the classification of other financial instruments and be more reflective of economic realities. This situation would also necessitate accounting for cryptoassets differently given their fundamental differences. For example, bitcoin might be classified as a commodity equivalent, whereas a CBDC might be more closely aligned and accounted for as a currency equivalent. If an institution is a broker-dealer, it could treat crypto holdings similarly to a financial institution that is a broker-dealer treats holdings of debt and equity financial instruments.

This conversation's complexity increases when discussing stablecoins and the so-called "utility" tokens. Stablecoins represent a crypto–fiat hybrid that involves facets of crypto and fiat currencies, complicating the accounting conversation. Specifically, how should organizations that conduct transactions with, and potentially hold, stablecoins deal with the changing values in the underlying asset stabilizing the stablecoin? Should these stablecoins be treated as the equivalent to currency, which is how some try to use them, or the equivalent to the treatment of the underlying asset?

Other complications arise when considering the DeFi sector, specifically focusing on recognizing certain crypto. Avoiding accounting minutiae issues arise when citing lending, borrowing, and other DeFi activities. The following factors represent a challenging outlook. Cryptoassets are based partly on the concept of direct ownership, which differs from how holdings in fiat funds tend to operate. Thus, the lending and borrowing of crypto create a situation where its reporting occurs on the books of two or more organizations. For example, the entity that has custody of the asset could make a case for reporting crypto on its books as an asset. The entity that borrowed the crypto could also contend that it should report it as a liability. Finally, a third party that leverages that crypto to earn block rewards or has it as a component of staking operation could also make that case.

Future Auditing Considerations for Crypto

A need also exists to improve and clarify how audits will be conducted in a business environment as blockchain and cryptoassets become more integrated into how firms manage transactions. Several specific changes that require integration follow.

How will auditors and audit firms manage the growing use of smart contracts? A *smart contract* is an application programming interface (API) allowing different blockchains and cryptoassets to interoperate (i.e., communicate). These applications are executable code embedded into an underlying blockchain allowing certain transactions to be entirely or partially automated. With such automation, a unique connection exists between privacy and cybersecurity considerations and the growing integration of cryptoassets 'and blockchain technology (Yeh, Su, Deng, Yung, & Kutylowski, 2020). Use cases for these applications allowed the implementation of blockchain options across industry sectors, including transportation, financial services, real estate transactions, healthcare, and trade financing.

From an auditing perspective, several considerations can arise from these applications. One issue involves how these smart contracts can monitor and change in response to changing business conditions. Businesses and business arrangements continuously change. Therefore, smart contracts must respond to these changes. Controls over how to implement this process must also exist. For example, modifying smart contracts requires construction that permits verification for accuracy and completeness.

The continuing implementation of blockchain-based technologies can augment straightforward auditing processes such as determining how to audit populations and select sample sizes. For example, reflecting on the continuing ambiguity around accounting and auditing standards, no consensus exists regarding what percentage would be considered a material amount. In this case, materiality is the aggregate percentage that would change the way an external user of financial statements views an organization. Given this ambiguity, private sector efforts to develop blockchain and crypto auditing and attestation standards continue to progress slowly. Audit and reporting standards remain a patchwork effort despite the multi-trillion-dollar valuation the crypto sector now commands.

Additionally, the cybersecurity policies of organizations that have implemented blockchain and cryptoassets within operations will most likely require at least a review or some other type of examination. Insurance policies, including cybersecurity policies, have not traditionally included clauses and protections linked to blockchain and cryptoasset operations. As stablecoin and other crypto transactions continue to increase in volume and include an increasing number of individuals and business owners, the need for reviewing insurance policies will most likely become part of a financial audit moving forward.

There is a need to revisit footnote disclosure and reporting practices with increasing utilization of blockchain and cryptoassets in core business operations. Specifically, the type and quantity of information publicly disclosed to the marketplace must be initially determined, revisited, and adjusted as business conditions change. Blockchains can vary significantly in programming, use cases, and cryptoasset integration. Which components of these data should be shared publicly? What actions are available to establish and increase consistent and comparable standards around this information from an audit and attestation perspective? Developing standards, even via industry best practices versus formalized accounting codification, is necessary if adopting blockchain technology continues.

A Framework for Crypto Accounting

Although significant issues remain regarding accounting for cryptoassets, several core considerations are available to construct a framework for crypto-specific accounting practices. Factors to incorporate into this framework include

- a cryptoasset's use case,
- the connection to any underlying asset or issuing entity,
- how market participants have used or integrated this asset into their financial operations,
- how liquid or actively traded the cryptoasset is in the marketplace, and
- the ability to leverage existing regulatory frameworks, such as recent updates from the Office of the Comptroller of the Currency (OCC), IRS, and Securities and Exchange Commission.

Such an approach would effectively develop cryptoasset accounting standards by considering the economic fundamentals, business use cases, and industry best practices to determine how to reflect these cryptoassets on financial statements. Although such an approach is not equivalent to the traditional FASB consultation process to develop GAAP, it would serve as an effective stopgap measure until policymakers develop authoritative standards. Additionally, this framework approach would lead to the following potential arrangements: crypto-currency, crypto-equity, cryptoasset, and crypto-commodity. The following options might represent a future state for the reporting.

- *Decentralized cryptocurrencies.* Participants could account for decentralized cryptocurrencies such as bitcoin and ether as commodities or equity securities. This differentiation would be delineated based on the development of the specific cryptoasset. Accounting for these instruments would allow (1) the changes in fair value to be reflected in real-time on the financial statements and (2) the organization to report more accurately a firm's current financial position in the marketplace.

- *Stablecoins*. Privately issued stablecoins, which resemble semi-centralized or privately issued currencies, present a situation where potentially two accounting treatments would be appropriate. Those using stablecoins backed, supported, or tethered on a one-to-one basis by the US dollar or other widely circulated fiat currency should account for them as a cash equivalent. Stablecoins supported or stabilized by some other asset must incorporate distinct accounting aspects into the reporting process. For example, an organization should report a stablecoin on its books as a currency equivalent and disclose the underlying asset. Specifically, the organization should reveal changes in the underlying asset's fair value in the footnotes or as an item in other comprehensive income. This approach allows an organization to reflect on the use case and the stablecoin's functionality while also correctly reporting the changes in value that could affect the stablecoin itself.
- *Central bank digital currencies*. CBDCs are perhaps the simplest case, with one crucial caveat. A CBDC should be accounted for and reported as a currency equivalent on the financial statements of any organization that is conducting transactions using these instruments. A CBDC intends to serve as a replacement or updated version of existing fiat currencies, the accounting treatment of these assets should mirror this functionality. Specifically, the only pertinent issue arising from widely issuing and distributing CBDCs comes from a central bank or commercial banking institution. These entities should consider the impact of newly issued digital currency on the balance sheet of different institutions. However, the transition from an existing fiat currency to a crypto–fiat hybrid or a CBDC lacks a specific connection to the GAAP financial reporting of the entity itself.

Room also exists for developing crypto-specific accounting rules and standards linked to DeFi operations and NFTs. DeFI accounting standards, unlike cryptoasset specific accounting standards, would be best served by focusing on the impact of DeFi operations on the organizations involved. Specifically, the process by which organizations can recognize certain coins or tokens engaged in these operations needs clarification. For example, what rules can organizations accurately and transparently list certain assets on the financial statements?

NFT accounting rules and standards also must address the rights and recognition of token issuers, token holders, and potential derivative instruments connected to these tokens. For example, if an NFT has a licensing component, an NFT's investor can monetize and earn income based on owning the token. This situation involves two accounting components that must be valued and reported to the external marketplace: the NFT and the income stream generated via the license option.

The crypto accounting conversation must be flexible enough to contend with different cryptoassets and create a consistent accounting environment. Since no crypto-specific authoritative accounting guidance is available, an opportunity exists for new and innovative approaches to address existing issues.

A Framework for Crypto Reporting

Underpinning any financial reporting framework is external market participants' confidence in the information itself. Such confidence is a core attribute of accounting and audit best practices. Another issue requiring attention involves how to communicates these data to the marketplace. The primary method of disclosing crypto-specific data centers around footnotes and other data not presented in the financial statement. Footnotes can report and disclose data, but that does not mean that this approach is ideal for communicating data in the future.

Conversations around establishing frameworks for accounting and auditing standards also must consider what regulatory changes may be enacted at the national level. A specific example of this situation is the report from the President's Working Group (PWG) – the PWG on Financial Markets, joined by the Federal Deposit Insurance Corporation and the OCC – issued in late 2021. This report focused exclusively on regulatory matters on stablecoins. Admittedly limited in scope by this self-imposed focus, the report may serve as a template for future regulatory and standard-setting bodies. The report contained analyses of the cryptoasset, implications of stablecoins used for payment purposes, an examination of the risks involved with stablecoin payments, and recommendations. Specific recommendations include legislative action empowering existing regulators, calling on the US Congress to create a new regulator, and mandating that stablecoin market participants operate by the same rules as incumbent organizations. Regardless of the final direction of cryptoasset regulation or the cryptoasset focused on first, these developments will inevitably inform the accounting and auditing rules created.

Valuation and accounting issues connected to cryptoassets are multifaceted. These assets' reporting standards and best practices must concurrently evolve with their accounting practices and techniques. An innovation would be to create a new asset category on the balance sheet. This approach would reflect the accounting treatment modification and bifurcation that should invariably develop going forward and be an important step toward crypto-specific accounting standards.

For example, the discussion around constructing crypto-specific footnotes raises questions of consistency, standardization, and transparency. Here are some specific questions unique to cryptoasset reporting and disclosure conversation. What type of information requires disclosure about cryptoasset holdings? Regarding stablecoins and other privately issued or semi-centralized currencies, should a disclosure or footnote relate to potential counterparty risk? Since many issuing organizations are neither banking institutions nor chartered or approved by any national banking regulator, ensuring consistent disclosure and reporting makes logical business sense.

Volatility will continue to be an aspect of cryptoassets driving debate, conversation, and analysis. Thus, a pertinent question is: What information involving this volatility requires disclosure? Assuming the eventual adoption of crypto-specific accounting standards, simply reporting volatility on the financial statements is insufficient. Instead, a hedging strategy should also be part of the financial information disclosed to combat volatility. Such information should include tactics and instruments used to hedge against crypto volatility.

A potential path forward regarding developing standardized crypto disclosure and reporting standards is likely to center around industry or sector standards instead of the all-encompassing approach traditionally governing accounting standards and standard setting. Such an approach exists in various regulatory and compliance-oriented methods from health and safety standards, regulatory reporting guidelines, and industry best practices. If framed in that context, no reason exists to expect that cryptoasset accounting and auditing standards should evolve differently.

Summary and Conclusions

The financial accounting landscape for cryptoassets continues to evolve. Yet, organizations face difficulties communicating this information transparently without crypto-specific accounting standards. Compounding this lack of comparability and consistency across the cryptoasset landscape are issues inevitably arising about the ability to audit and attest to the value of these cryptoassets. Regardless of crypto's use in a specific organization – investment choice, currency alternative, or inventory for other business operations – the process and rules guiding these assets' financial reporting and valuation need to evolve alongside the sector's growth. Although accounting and auditing standards are not the flashiest aspects of blockchain and cryptoassets, they play an integral role in the sector's evolution.

Discussion Questions

1. Explain the current accounting consensus for how organizations should account for cryptoassets.
2. Describe two differences between stablecoins and CBDCs.
3. Define an NFT and discuss how it differs from other cryptoassets.
4. List three changes needed to the audit processes as cryptoassets become more mainstream.
5. Identify two financial reporting and disclosure considerations that organizations should use related to cryptoassets.

References

Alexander, A. (2021). Decrypting cryptocurrencies. *Accounting Today*, May 17. Retrieved from https://www.accountingtoday.com/news/decrypting-crypto-opportunities-and-obstacles-for-accountants

Andolfatto, D. (2021). Some thoughts on central bank digital currency. *CATO Journal*, *41*(2), 343–351. https://doi.org/10.36009/CJ.41.2.12

Appelbaum, D., & Nehmer, R. A. (2020). Auditing cloud-based blockchain accounting systems. *Journal of Information Systems*, *34*(2), 5–21. https://doi.org/10.2308/isys-52660

Choi, G. (2021). Inner workings of collateral-based stablecoins and its implications. *IUP Journal of Bank Management*, *20*(2), 35–60.

Chow, A. (2021). NFTs and the crypto art revolution. *TIME Magazine*, March 19. Retrieved from https://www.scribd.com/article/499477194/Nf-Ts-And-The-Crypto-Art-Revolution

Crosman, P. (2021a). How decentralized finance could reshape banking. *American Banker*, January 4. Retrieved from https://www.americanbanker.com/news/how-decentralized-finance-could-reshape-banking

Crosman, P. (2021b). Playing catchup in crypto, banks ask core providers for help. *American Banker*, June 14. Retrieved from https://www.americanbanker.com/news/playing-catch-up-in-crypto-banks-ask-core-providers-for-help

He, D. (2021). Monetary effects of global stablecoins. *CATO Journal*, *41*(2), 353–365. https://doi.org/10.36009/CJ.41.2.13

Ossinger, J. (2021). BNY-backed crypto platform fireblocks seals its unicorn status. *Bloomberg.Com*, July 27. Retrieved from https://www.bloomberg.com/news/articles/2021-07-27/bny-backed-crypto-platform-fireblocks-seals-its-unicorn-status

Prasad, E. S. (2021). The case for central bank digital currencies. *CATO Journal*, *41*(2), 251–258. https://doi.org/10.36009/CJ.41.2.5

Schär, F. (2021). Decentralized finance: On blockchain- and smart contract-based financial markets. *Federal Reserve Bank of St. Louis Review*, *103*(2), 153–174. https://doi.org/10.20955/r.103.153-74

Sheldon, M. D. (2021). Auditing the blockchain oracle problem. *Journal of Information Systems*, *35*(1), 121–133. https://doi.org/10.2308/ISYS-19-049

Vincent, N. E., & Wilkins, A. M. (2020). Challenges when auditing cryptocurrencies. *Current Issues in Auditing*, *14*(1), A46–A58. https://doi.org/10.2308/ciia-52675

Yeh, K.-H., Su, C., Deng, R. H., Yung, M., & Kutylowski, M. (2020). Special issue on security and privacy of blockchain technologies. *International Journal of Information Security*, *19*(3), 243–244. https://doi.org/10.1007/s10207-020-00496-6

Chapter 3

The Crypto Investing Landscape

John Ward

Abstract

This chapter discusses the current landscape for digital asset investing and the many operational risks facing cryptocurrency investors. It also discusses the ongoing progress in the institutionalization of digital asset investment and the risks inherent when investing in cryptocurrencies and blockchain opportunities. Investors considering investing in a public or private fund that invests in digital assets must be aware of the operational risks that may directly impact their investments, including risks from portfolio concentration, illiquidity, hacking, digital asset custody, and digital asset valuations. Operational due diligence reviews of funds and fund managers are critical in assessing operational risks for digital asset investment.

Keywords: Cryptocurrency (crypto); blockchain; operational risks; illiquidity; hacking; digital assets; operational due diligence

Introduction

Since society started ascribing value to a shiny stone, seashell, tulip bulb, or piece of golden metal, people inevitably started trying to buy and sell those items to earn a profit. Despite advances over the millennia, the desire to buy and sell items hoping to profit remains. When Satoshi Nakamoto, a presumed pseudonym, issued a whitepaper on bitcoin as a digital currency in 2008, a new asset class was born – cryptocurrency (Nakamoto, 2008). For much of the first decade after the publication of the whitepaper, bitcoin traded at low prices, primarily among technical professionals and blockchain believers. Along with the expansion and institutionalization of the digital asset ecosystem came the launching of numerous global exchanges to facilitate the trading of digital assets. Soon broker-dealers

The Emerald Handbook on Cryptoassets: Investment Opportunities and Challenges, 25–41

doi:10.1108/978-1-80455-320-620221003

began to offer over-the-counter (OTC) trading services, digital asset futures and options started trading on the Chicago Mercantile Exchange (CME), and various counterparties and service providers entered the market.

This chapter discusses the current landscape for digital asset investing and the many risks facing cryptocurrency investors. It also examines the ongoing progress in the institutionalization of digital asset investment and inherent risks when investing in cryptocurrencies and blockchain opportunities.

The Regulatory Climate for Digital Asset Investing

Several landmark regulations enacted by the US Congress guide much of the modern securities industry. For example, the Securities Act of 1933 (the '33 Act) (United States Congress, 1933) was the first US federal legislation regarding the offer and sales of securities. The Securities Act of 1934 (the '34 Act) (United States Congress, 1934) regulated securities in the secondary market. It also authorized the formation of the Securities and Exchange Commission (SEC) and the Investment Company Act of 1940 (the '40 Act) (United States Congress, 1940), codifying many rules associated with the mutual fund industry. These rules form the bedrock for US fund managers and fund investors and determine the types of investments and investors allowed in various fund vehicles.

The '33 Act includes an important group of rules within Regulation D (Reg D) that discuss how an organization can offer securities privately and without requiring formal securities registration with the SEC. Congress updated Reg D in 1982 to facilitate capital raising efforts by small companies, including hedge funds, private equity funds, and other similar investment schemes. Most importantly, Rule 506(b) of Reg D (United States Securities and Exchange Commission, 1982) prohibits the general solicitation of investors and includes a restriction on public advertising.

The SEC's Investment Company Act of 1940 (the '40 Act) codified many of the rules associated with the mutual fund industry (United States Securities and Exchange Commission, 1940). The '40 Act, including the more recent edits and enhancements, regulates the creation of investment companies and how they market their shares to the public. A critical component of the '40 Act was Section 3(c)(1) and Section 3(c)(7), which are exemptions to the filing requirements for "private investment companies." Private investment companies organized as exempt under Section 3(c)(1) have no more than 100 investors, while funds organized under the Section 3(c)(7) exemption do not have this limitation. However, all investors must be *qualified purchasers* who have a minimum income level or an overall level of wealth.

In the United States, private and public fund managers investing in digital assets must adhere to the same rules and regulations that are in place for non-digital asset fund managers. They must follow the same regulations as non-digital asset fund managers for registration, advertising, fraud, and market manipulation.

Globally, however, the regulatory environment for digital assets is inconsistent and fluid:

- China announced on September 24, 2021, a ban on all digital asset transactions. Before the announcement, China was a major hub for digital asset mining (Reuters Staff, 2021).

- On September 7, 2021, El Salvador became the first country to accept bitcoin as legal tender (Hernandez, 2021).
- On September 2, 2021, Australia, Malaysia, Singapore, and South Africa announced they would undertake a trial for cross-border payment transactions using various central bank digital currencies (CBDCs) (Alun, 2021).

Unlike China, most nations are not taking an all or none approach to digital assets. Instead, they are trying to adapt existing regulatory frameworks to address the evolving digital currency markets. However, the inconsistency in adapting regulatory frameworks has confused investors and fund managers.

According to the Alternative Investment Management Association (AIMA, 2021), about 43 percent of all crypto hedge fund managers are in the United States, 19 percent in the United Kingdom, and 11 percent in Hong Kong. Yet, the United States has not enacted a clear regulatory framework for digital assets. Instead, the SEC takes an incremental approach and leverages the existing regulatory frameworks already in place.

In the United Kingdom, the primary securities regulator is the Financial Conduct Authority (FCA). The FCA issued Consultation Paper CP19/3 (Financial Conduct Authority, 2019) to provide some much-needed clarity on various digital asset regulatory matters. The FCA has segregated digital assets into three broad categories – each with different regulatory requirements:

- *Exchange tokens* are digital assets not issued or backed by any central authority and intended and designed for use as a means of exchange "outside the perimeter" of the FCA.
- *Security tokens* are digital assets contracted for fractions of an existing asset like real estate, corporate stock, artwork, collectibles, or other assets, meeting the FCA's definition of a Specified Investment. Therefore, all security tokens are "within the perimeter" of the FCA and are fully regulated entities.
- *Utility tokens* are digital assets allowing the holder to access a service or a current or prospective product. They fall into two general categories. Utility tokens that act like fiat cash are e-money in certain circumstances and would be "within the perimeter" of the FCA. Other utility tokens where the exact fiat value is unknown would not function as a type of e-money and be "outside the perimeter" of the FCA. Two real-world, non-blockchain examples of "utility tokens" that most people would recognize are gift cards with a specific cash value and reward points/reward miles granted by an organization but have no specific cash value.

Many fund managers operating their businesses out of one country register their funds in different countries and may have global staff. Because crypto trades continuously and crypto exchanges are worldwide, funds often have staff in Asia, the United States, and Europe. Due to the complex nature of global securities regulations and tax policies, investors considering a private fund investment should speak with legal counsel, tax professionals, or due diligence professionals to ensure that the fund manager operates the fund by all global regulatory and taxation frameworks.

Private Funds

Digital asset investing requires technical knowledge of a fast-emerging technology asset class combined with unique asset management characteristics. Most investors who lack a deep understanding of the fast-moving digital asset space but want to add digital assets to their portfolios should rely on a third-party fund manager to invest their assets.

Investors may consider using a sophisticated hedge fund or venture capital (VC) fund to manage their digital asset investments. Funds considered *liquid*, allowing investors to invest or redeem monthly, quarterly, or semi-annually, are organized as a hedge fund. Funds with longer investment horizons that limit investors' ability to redeem for several years often have private equity or VC organizational structures.

Liquid Private Funds

Liquid private funds, typically organized as hedge funds include a management fee paid to the fund manager and calculated as a percentage of the assets under management (AUM). Additionally, most hedge funds have a performance fee paid to the fund manager, typically at year-end, where the fund manager receives part of any profits earned for their investors. Hedge fund investors also incur all costs for operating the fund, including an annual fund audit, the services of a fund administrator, custodian, insurance, and fund research costs.

Liquid private fund investors usually receive a private placement memorandum (PPM) or an offering memorandum (OM). The fund's PPM or OM should thoroughly discuss the manager's investment style and experience, important service providers to the fund, including the fund auditor, fund administrator, asset custodians, lawyers, and consultants. The fund should fully disclose all fees and expenses and fund subscription and redemption terms. There should be a discussion on valuing the portfolio's assets. Investors should closely read the fund's PPM or OM in its entirety and consult with competent professionals to discuss if the investment is appropriate given their risk tolerance.

Liquid hedge fund managers often follow one of several common investment styles:

- *Long/short*. Many label managers buy and sell digital assets and digital asset derivatives based on various inputs gathered from research, market statistics, charts, or news events as long/short managers. Long/short managers can differ in deploying capital, using leverage, and accessing long and short positions. Their portfolios can also have different holding periods and liquidity.
- *Arbitrage*. Managers who seek price discrepancies across markets or trading exchanges and then buy and sell instruments to capture the profits generally follow an arbitrage strategy. When digital asset markets had less trading, large differences in the price of bitcoin or ether occurred on different global exchanges. Today, with many more market participants and much heavier trading volumes, significant price discrepancies are less common.

- *Quantitative*. Many view fund managers who rely on computers to quickly identify investment opportunities and affect trading activities as quantitative ("quant") traders. Some managers use computer programs to identify price discrepancies across markets to seek profits. In contrast, others use trend following, mean reversion, or technical trading programs. Quant managers may also have different holding periods, depending on their strategy. Some fund managers trade only once per day, while others make thousands of trades per hour.
- *Multi-strategy*. Some fund managers use more than one investment strategy when managing their fund portfolios. By combining the best attributes of different strategies, a fund manager may feel better equipped to guide investor assets during periods of market volatility. The chief investment officer of a multi-strategy fund is responsible for allocating the fund's capital across the different strategies available within the firm. Therefore, a manager's internal asset allocation skills determine fund profits and losses.

Illiquid Private Funds

Longer-term investors may seek out illiquid private funds that make investments over many years. Illiquid digital asset fund managers often look for investment opportunities in early-stage digital asset technology, a standard agreement for future tokens (SAFTs), or blockchain technology to invest in private companies with profitable products or services. Illiquid fund managers use a structure like a private equity or VC fund structure. Common attributes of an illiquid private fund scheme follow.

- A fund uses a close-ended structure to lock up an investor's capital with no opportunity for redemptions for several years.
- Fund investors commit to a maximum level of investment into an illiquid fund before its launch.
- A manager looks for private, early-stage investment opportunities consistent with a fund's investment mandate.
- After a fund purchases a private investment, a manager sends out a demand notice asking each investor to send some committed capital to the fund to pay for the investment.
- Most private funds allow managers at least three to five years to identify investment opportunities to purchase for the fund's investors. The *investment period* is the first several years after a fund launch.
- Private fund managers collaborate closely with the purchased firms to help them grow in value. Many private funds have a 5 to 10-year period for a fund manager to help support and grow the early-stage business after acquisition and then sell the investments or help them go public. This period is *the harvesting period.*
- Illiquid private fund managers receive a management fee generally based on the amount of committed capital during the investment period and then the amount of invested capital during the harvesting period. Private fund managers may also receive part of an investment's profits, typically called the *carry*, after selling an investment or becoming a publicly traded company or digital asset.

Illiquid private fund investors typically receive a limited partnership agreement (LPA). A fund's LPA should thoroughly discuss the manager's investment style, experience, and any critical service providers to the fund, including the fund auditor, fund administrator, asset custodians, lawyers, and consultants. Standard disclosures include all fees and expenses, fund subscription and cash call terms, and the procedure for valuing the portfolio's assets. As with a PPM or OM, investors should closely read the fund's LPA in its entirety and consult with competent professionals before investing.

Public Funds

As noted earlier, public funds are widely available to all investors. Firms offering public funds go through formal filings with the appropriate securities regulators. The managers must follow all appropriate investment restrictions and guidelines. Public funds have fewer restrictions on the fund manager's ability to market the fund to investors to raise fund assets. Like publicly traded trusts or exchange-traded funds (ETFs), the market typically prices public funds as exchange-traded securities. Investors can choose to buy or sell their investments whenever the market or exchange is open for business. Public funds organized as a mutual fund usually have daily liquidity. Additionally, investors buy or sell a mutual fund at the closing price at the end of the business day. Managers of public mutual funds broadly make public the daily price for the fund soon after the trading markets close.

Global securities regulators have been slow to approve selling digital asset-focused mutual funds and ETFs to the public due to their concerns about protecting public investors who lack sophistication. The slow bureaucratic nature of many securities regulators makes them hesitant to approve new investment products in a marketplace that is evolving at a breakneck pace. Many digital asset industry watchers expect a rush of assets into the public fund marketplace once a major global securities regulator approves a public investment fund or ETF that directly invests in digital assets.

As of December 2021, the SEC had yet to approve a mutual fund or an ETF that directly invests in digital assets. ProShares, an investment management firm, launched the ProShares Bitcoin Strategy ETF in late 2021. It lists on the New York Stock Exchange (NYSE) under the ticker BITO. The ETF tracks bitcoin prices through futures contracts traded at the CME (Dossett, 2021). Other mutual funds and ETFs that provide digital asset exposure do so by investing in bitcoin futures that trade on the CME and not actual digital coins or tokens. Some mutual funds or ETFs invest in the publicly traded equities of firms involved in blockchain technologies, public digital asset payment companies, public digital asset mining companies, or public digital asset exchanges. Further, certain public companies, like Tesla, have made statements about owning or holding digital assets on the firm's balance sheet. A mutual fund or an ETF may hold all these public companies.

In recent years, several firms have come to market using publicly traded closed-end trusts. The trusts directly buy digital assets like bitcoin or ether and then issue a fixed number of shares to the public. The value of the shares reflects the value of the digital assets held in the trust's portfolio and all trust fees and expenses. A fund manager or fund advisor manages the trusts and receives a fee for rebalancing the fund's portfolio. Most closed-end trust structures currently trade at a discount to the fund portfolio's *net asset value* (NAV), reflecting overall market sentiment around the complex fund structures and concerns about costs and fees that could vary over time.

Digital Asset Investment Risks

Investors interested in investing in a public or private digital asset fund should understand the risks inherent to the crypto asset class, especially those for which they receive no compensation. Besides the many regulatory and taxation-related risks affecting a potential digital asset investment, other risks include operational risks unique to the digital asset class requiring proper vetting by investors before investment.

Operational risks are the risks investors face, excluding the risks present in the investment portfolio. Such risks may materially affect the value of their invested assets. Institutional investors regularly undertake operational due diligence (ODD) assessments of private funds before investment to identify operational risks.

An institutional ODD typically includes a fund's structure, fees, expenses, and liquidity terms. The review covers the fund manager's systems, technology, controls, cyber security, trading and settlement operations, reporting, leverage, counterparties, and service providers. ODD professionals are acutely interested in cash controls, asset custody and safety, compliance, regulatory filings, conflicts of interest, audited financial statements, and the background and experience of the manager's senior staff members. A typical ODD review includes speaking or meeting with a fund manager's chief operating officer, chief financial officer, chief compliance officer, chief technology officer, and portfolio managers. Other key members of a firm's operations include the controller, business development officer, and operations manager. This review involves analyzing numerous documents and contacting fund counterparties, service providers, board directors, and consultants to identify the services supplied to the fund. An institutional review of a fund manager often takes about four to six weeks.

Common operational risks affecting fund investors include having the fund's assets stolen, systems and technology failures, regulatory risks, fraud, accounting errors, and portfolio valuation errors. However, the media do not report most operational failures. Thus, many investors are unaware of the enormous sums lost to fraud, theft, and malfeasance every year.

To further clarify the impact of possible operational risks on an investment opportunity consider the following three scenarios: (1) Investor A invested $500,000 in stocks or bonds held at a bank or brokerage firm, (2) Investor B invested $500,000 to buy a building, and (3) Investor C invested $500,000 in various digital assets.

- Investor A's investment returns vary based on the value of portfolio holdings. The investor can easily buy or sell his investments, and the banks or brokers move the money and securities as needed. His assets are usually safe from the failure of the bank or brokerage firm. Experiencing someone stealing their investments from the bank or brokerage firm is highly unlikely. Investor A can focus on investment returns as he has a generally low level of operational risk.

- Investor B's returns vary based on the building's value and any tenants' rent. Real estate investors face several external operational risks like fires, floods, or storm damage that could affect their investment returns. Other risks include tenants who stop paying rent, tax increases, and varying costs for electricity or other services. Investor B can buy insurance to mitigate some of the most significant external risks. Investor B can also ask for security deposits and other assurances against more minor losses. An astute real estate investor considers all cash flows from rents and leases, all expenses from building operations, taxes, and insurance, and makes an investment decision based on the expected net returns. Investor B has a moderate level of operational risk. Although insurance and other arrangements can mitigate some risk, Investor B faces greater investment complexity.
- Investor C's returns involve the value of the digital asset investments. Unlike Investors A and B, Investor C should consider several operational risks, including how she wants to hold her digital assets (in a hot wallet, a cold wallet, or at a custodian or on an exchange). She is likely to incur the costs of moving assets into and out of fiat currencies and into digital currencies. Investor C should also consider data security for her digital private keys or seed phrases and be concerned about a cyber security event such as hacking an exchange. A *seed phrase* is a series of words generated by someone's cryptocurrency wallet, giving that person access to the crypto associated with that wallet. Investor C cannot buy insurance to mitigate these and other risks. Additionally, the digital asset investment returns do not reflect all her technical and operational risks. Investor C has higher-level operational risks associated with the investment program that she cannot easily offset by insurance or other mitigation strategies.

When evaluating an investment opportunity, rational investors should consider their portfolio and operational risks. In the previous examples, if all three investors had the same annual returns, Investor A achieved the returns at a much lower level of risk than Investor C. Investors should understand all investment risks and ensure proper compensation for taking such risks. Many investors focus only on a portfolio's returns when determining investment success or failure and ignore the full impact of operational risks on their investments.

Investors who invest in a digital asset private or public fund should investigate all risk areas likely to have a material impact on their investment returns and do not receive compensation. By reducing or eliminating those extraneous operational risks, investors can more confidently focus on the returns generated by the portfolio investments. The following sections discuss the most prominent digital asset investment operational risk areas and suggest some methods for risk mitigation.

Digital Asset Custody

The most critical risk element with digital assets and the biggest hindrance to global institutional investors fully adopting the asset class is digital asset custody. Investors may accept the risks associated with digital asset investment strategies but are unwilling to risk their assets being lost or stolen due to custody-related risks.

Institutional investors in hedge funds that trade traditional securities have become accustomed to the safety and security offered by large banks, global custodians, and prime brokerages. Although, the collapse of Lehman Brothers highlighted unexpected problems that could occur with large banks, the assets of the bank's clients were not at risk, and Lehman's clients generally received the assets. Trillions of dollars of stocks, bonds, derivatives, currencies, and commodities move among various custodians safely and effectively every day. Institutional investors also demand a similar asset safety and security level within the digital asset class.

Certain digital asset hedge funds have increased exposure to custody-related risks due to their investment style. For example, managers who employ a high frequency or quantitative investment strategy are at a much higher risk of loss since they must maintain their digital assets on an exchange for trading them as quickly as needed. Hackers have successfully stolen assets from digital asset exchanges. Any investment strategy that requires maintaining a fund's assets on an exchange is at a higher risk of loss from theft.

News stories about cyber hackers stealing digital assets from various exchanges are familiar. The following news items exemplify events occurring during 2021:

- The BitMart hack in early December 2021 resulted in the exchange quickly suspending all customer withdrawals to undertake an investigation. The estimated losses are $200 million (Tidy, 2021).
- Hackers stole more the $130 million from Cream Finance, a De-Fi protocol, in October 2021. Other hacks occurred in August 2021, resulting in losses of 1,300 Ethereum valued at over $4 million, and February 2021 when Cream Finance lost $37.5 million (Chipolina, 2021).
- In August 2021, Poly Network, a DeFi exchange, experienced the largest hacking loss of about $611 million (Brennan, 2021).
- A hack of Liquid, a Japanese crypto exchange, occurred in August 2021, resulting in a loss of $97 million in digital cryptocurrencies from the exchange's hot wallets (Browne, 2021).
- Hackers stole $285 million in digital assets from client accounts of KuCoin, a Seychelles-based crypto exchange. The exchange recovered much of the stolen crypto in early 2021, and KuCoin's insurance paid $45.55 million to make exchange clients whole (Roy, 2021).

According to Groves (2022), at least 46 cryptocurrency exchanges have suffered significant hacks since 2012. Hackers compromised a record number of 19 crypto exchanges in 2019 alone. Cumulatively, hackers have stolen nearly $2.66 billion in assets from crypto exchanges since 2012.

Investors must keep in mind that digital assets are essentially bearer assets. To most unsophisticated investors, every stolen bitcoin looks exactly like any other legally owned bitcoin. Hackers and digital thieves have become adept at hiding digital assets by (1) using crypto "mixers," (2) using exchanges in jurisdictions that do not have strong know your customers or clients (KYC) and anti-money laundering (AML) policies, (3) moving stolen assets quickly to cold wallets, and (4) quickly trading stolen assets into privacy-protecting digital currencies like Zcash, Monero, Verge, and DASH.

Numerous companies have entered the market to offer custody solutions to public and private funds. Custody providers have different approaches and limitations to their services. Perhaps most importantly to fund managers, custodians typically limit asset custody to bitcoin, ether, and perhaps a few other highly liquid cryptocurrencies. Finding an institutional custodian for many cryptocurrency investors is difficult. Many custodians require several time-consuming processes to validate owner authenticity. Moving assets into and out of custody may take 15 minutes to several hours. Because of the complexity of transferring assets into and out of custody, many fund managers who trade their portfolios with even moderate frequency have chosen to leave digital assets in hot wallets on exchanges. A *hot wallet* is a form of digital storage that someone can access on a computer or phone and is connected to the internet.

As noted earlier, hackers have stolen billions of dollars in crypto from exchanges. The reality is that fund managers are putting client assets at material risk of theft, especially managers who maintain their fund's assets on higher risk global digital asset exchanges organized in jurisdictions with weak AML requirements.

Investors considering a public or private fund investing in digital assets need to inquire about how a fund holds its assets in custody. Further, they should consider the hacking risks associated with a manager using exchange hot wallets. Investors also need to determine if they receive adequate compensation for the custody-related risks they assume.

Portfolio Development

Several risks are intrinsic to cryptocurrencies. Among them are the difficulties in creating a broadly diversified and appropriately liquid portfolio, finding investment management talent that is sufficiently knowledgeable about digital assets, and identifying scalable fund managers. A convention of portfolio management is creating a well-diversified portfolio. However, institutional digital asset fund managers have difficulty investing in a broad list of digital assets while maintaining sufficient portfolio liquidity. Table 3.1 provides digital asset market capitalizations on Coinmarketcap.com in late November 2021.

Bitcoin and ether would rank among the top 25 most valuable companies globally. The tenth most valuable digital asset, Avalanche, has a market cap of $30.86 billion and the twentieth most valuable digital asset, Algorand, has a market cap of $10.7 billion. To create a portfolio of digital assets not completely dominated by bitcoin, portfolio managers must have exposure to smaller digital assets with

Table 3.1. A Comparison of Digital Asset and Public Company Market Capitalizations: November 30, 2021.

Asset	Symbol	Market Cap	Similar Equity Market Cap	Global Equity Market Cap Ranking
Bitcoin	BTC	$1.059 trillion	Between Tesla ($1.188T) and Facebook ($960.60B)	6 and 7
Ethereum	ETH	$481.21 billion	JP Morgan Chase ($490.00B)	12
Binance Coin	BNB	$92.82 billion	Lam Research ($92.80B)	178
Tether	USDT	$73.126 billion	Hikvision (China) ($73.93B)	231
Solana	SOL	$65.280 billion	Petrobras (Brazil) ($65.05B)	2,809

Note: This table shows how quickly the market capitalization of the most prominent digital assets drops off compared to global equities.
Source: Coinmarketcap.com.

materially lower market capitalizations, lower daily trading volumes, less liquidity, and higher price volatility.

To further illustrate the challenge in creating a broadly diversified portfolio of digital assets, consider the following. Bitwise created a fund that tracks the top 10 digital assets based on a market value called the Bitwise 10 Crypto Index Fund. Table 3.2 shows that the fund had the following exposures in late November 2021. Bitcoin and ether represent almost 90 percent of the fund's exposure, whereas digital assets 6 through 10 collectively comprise only 3.02 percent of the index. Creating a well-diversified digital asset portfolio that is liquid yet not entirely dominated by bitcoin and ether, the two highest valued digital assets, is difficult.

According to the AIMA (2021), the earliest digital asset-focused hedge funds began operating in 2013 and 2014. Many of those funds did not survive the crypto winter of 2018 when the value of bitcoin dropped from about $18,000 to about $3,000. AIMA further notes between 150 and 200 active crypto hedge funds globally, with 81 percent launched since 2017 and 18 percent since 2020. The digital asset management fund space is a vibrant, growing asset class with a short performance history.

However, identifying digital asset managers with extensive crypto experience and stable investment returns is hard. At year-end 2020, the average liquid crypto hedge fund had about $43 million in AUM. Less than 10 percent of digital asset hedge funds had over $250 million in fund assets, and the 10 largest crypto hedge funds controlled 63 percent of total AUM. A concentration of assets exists within

Table 3.2. Market Capitalization Weighting of the Bitwise 10 Crypto Index Fund: November 30, 2021.

Name	Portfolio Weight (percent)
Bitcoin	60.77
Ethereum (ether)	28.20
Solana	3.82
Cardano	3.37
Litecoin	0.84
ChainLink	0.74
Algorand	0.60
Bitcoin Cash	0.60
Polygon	0.60
Uniswap	0.48

Note: This table shows that bitcoin and ether dominate all digital tokens in market capitalization.
Source: Bitwise.

a small number of digital asset hedge funds. Stated differently, institutional investors wanting to represent less than 10 percent of a fund's assets will have difficulty allocating outside of a small group of funds and fund managers. Institutions preferring to diversify their exposure among several managers within an asset class may not properly diversify their digital asset investments due to the lack of investable funds. Given the high concentration of digital asset market capitalization within a small number of digital assets, mainly bitcoin and ether, even if investors diversify among several fund managers, they are likely to correlate to the same few digital assets.

Lastly, the design of several tokens is to avoid transparency on the public blockchain. Using privacy coins enables actively shields against criminal activity, including hacking, theft, pornography, ransomware, drug dealing, and other unauthorized activities on the dark web. Institutional investors should be concerned about a fund manager's use of privacy coins or investments in privacy coins within the fund's portfolio. Any fund manager choosing to invest in privacy coins may be opening institutional investors to serious headline risk if any privacy coins within a fund can, at some future point, be tied to illegal activity. *Headline risk* is the possibility that a news story adversely affects an investment's price.

Fund Counterparties and Service Providers

Many industry participants manage their firms at the forefront of technology and innovation. Most digital asset funds managed long-only portfolios only three or four years ago. Accessing short exposure to crypto for hedging purposes or alpha was challenging. Today, decentralized finance (DeFi) is among the fastest-growing sectors of digital assets, and non-fungible tokens (NFTs) are regularly in the news. Traditional custodians, auditors, administrators, and counterparties may also consider adapting their services to the digital asset class.

Institutional investors interested in digital asset fund investments must invest considerable time learning the strengths and weaknesses of service providers focusing on digital assets and not well-known in traditional asset investments. The largest and most familiar traditional hedge fund administrators are not actively involved in digital asset fund administration. Most top-tier auditors are not actively auditing public or private digital asset funds, and those conducting fund audits are only doing so in limited jurisdictions.

Equally, most fund counterparties common to digital asset funds are uncommon in traditional assets. The largest traditional asset custodians, including The Bank of New York Mellon, State Street, JP Morgan Chase, and Northern Trust, are not materially involved in crypto custody. The largest global securities exchanges – The NYSE, Nasdaq, Shanghai Stock Exchange, Hong Kong Stock Exchange, London Stock Exchange, and the Japan Stock Exchange – are all uninvolved in trading digital assets.

Regulators have banned some of the largest exchanges focusing on digital assets from operating in various countries. According to CoinMarketCap.com, Binance is the most prominent digital asset exchange based on trading volume. Several countries, including the United Kingdom, the United States, China, Japan, the European Union, Thailand, and Malaysia, have banned Binance from operating or investigated it (Geron, 2021). Institutional investors should be concerned about investing in any fund conducting business with any digital asset exchange under active investigation. The ownership of many of these exchanges, financial health, and cyber security safeguards may be unknown. Client data may be sold, trading activity may be shared with state actors, and some exchanges may be involved, directly or indirectly, with illegal activities due to the lax AML rules present in their home country.

Institutional investors in digital assets need to know which counterparties, exchanges, brokers, and banks a fund manager uses. Any public or private digital asset fund that uses a counterparty operating out of a high-privacy country and is unwilling to publicly disclose its ownership, financial health, data security, and cybersecurity protocols should be a major concern. Investors should also be concerned about managers reluctant to disclose counterparty relationships or exchanges and brokers.

Digital Asset Valuation

A fund's portfolio value is critical for determining liquid funds' investment management and performance fees. Liquid public and private digital asset funds typically charge an investment management fee based on a fund's AUM and the performance fees earned as a percentage of any profits created, both realized and unrealized. Fund managers calculate performance fees by comparing a fund's value at year-end to its value at the beginning of the year. If the fund increases in value, net of all subscriptions and redemptions, the manager earns a performance fee payable by the fund's investors.

Besides properly determining fees, public and private liquid funds allow investors to subscribe and redeem at specific intervals, as noted in the fund's offering documents. Subscriptions into and redemptions out of the fund typically occur at month-end using a fund's NAV. To calculate a fund's NAV, a manager or fund administrator must first determine the fund's portfolio value. Any errors in determining a fund's portfolio value cause investors to pay an incorrect price when investing, and existing fund investors receive an incorrect amount when redeeming fund shares.

Digital Assets Traded on an Exchange

Investors trade many cryptocurrencies on numerous global exchanges. The Binance exchange lists over 400 coins, KuCoin lists values on over 600 coins, and Gate.io lists more than 1,275 coins on its exchange (CoinMarketCap, 2022). Institutional investors familiar with listed equities, but not cryptocurrencies, may incorrectly assume that the pricing of an exchange-list coin uses the closing price on the primary exchange. However, determining a coin's price is more complicated.

- Digital asset exchanges trade continuously with no exchange closing time. With no official closing time for a crypto exchange, what time should a manager use as a cutoff for determining coin values?
- Most digital assets trade on multiple exchanges, so there is no primary exchange. How should a fund manager determine which exchange to use to determine a coin's value with no primary exchange?
- Digital asset exchanges express coin prices in different currencies. What is the correct currency conversion price for calculating a coin's value?
- Fund managers may only trade on a few exchanges. Should investors use a volume-weighted average price (VWAP) from one of the aggregator pricing services like CoinMarketCap.com or Bloomberg, which access all global exchanges when determining coin prices?

Although industry conventions address some of these concerns, no absolute regulatory requirements are available for exchange-traded digital asset valuations. Most, but not all, fund managers value their fund portfolios at midnight Greenwich Mean Time. Most, but not all, fund managers use a readily available pricing service like coinmarketcap.com, which calculates a VWAP for the most common digital assets. Whatever pricing convention a manager uses and discloses in offering documents, the process must be consistent every month and repeated when valuing a portfolio.

A more troublesome issue is that certain digital assets list on only a few exchanges and trade only in shallow volumes and or irregularly. Any fund manager who uses coin values based on stale trading history, limited trade volumes, or trades from a single exchange runs the risk of improperly valuing a fund's portfolio. According to Financial Accounting Standards Board (2011), best practices for valuing illiquid coin investments would be to treat the coin as an ASC 820 Level 2 security, meaning that limited price transparency exists. However, determining an illiquid coin's value requires data other than market prices. A fund administrator or fund manager would collect market bids and ask for quotes from reliable exchanges where the coin is listed. The manager would then determine if the bids and offers are actionable and at or near the market. Lastly, the manager would combine the various bids and offers using an average or a mean value to estimate a coin's value. Whatever pricing convention the manager uses and discloses in the offering documents, the process must be consistent every month and repeated when valuing a portfolio.

Illiquid Investments

Illiquid digital asset funds and many liquid digital asset funds may include some illiquid investments within their fund portfolios. Managers may invest in SAFTs, pre-ICOs, or private investments within a liquid fund portfolio. According to Financial Accounting Standards Board (2011), illiquid investments are typically ASC 820 Level 3 securities. Such securities require various value estimating processes, including similar observable market values (comparables), recent funding rounds, project milestones, and other standard valuation processes. Managers who invest in illiquid investments must value these hard-to-value investments whenever calculating a fund's NAV and used for subscriptions, redemptions, or determining advisor or performance fees. Further, for highly technical valuations, a best practice is to retain the services of a third-party valuation provider to ensure the proper valuation of illiquid investments.

Institutional investors considering investing in a public or private digital asset fund first must determine if the fund makes investments in less liquid Level 2 coins, or illiquid Level 3 investments. Next, investors must decide if they have the requisite knowledge and experience to evaluate a manager's complex asset investment valuation policies. Any fund that invests in Level 2 or Level 3 securities must have an explicit, detailed valuation policy that it rigorously follows whenever calculating its NAV. Any fund valuation policy that allows a fund manager or fund administrator to value Level 2 or Level 3 investments at cost without reassessing the value on an ongoing basis has material operational risks.

Summary and Conclusions

Digital assets investing represents both tremendous opportunities and considerable risks. Investors must have the requisite knowledge to evaluate a public or private fund manager before investment. This chapter explores the most common operational risks associated with public and private digital asset fund investing. This discussion is not comprehensive and may not include other material operational concerns that may negatively impact a fund's investment outcome. A fund manager's background and experience, the experience of a fund's operations staff, the competence of compliance officers and technology officers, and the quality of the firm's systems and technology are all critical areas of operational risk. Investors should ask numerous questions before they invest. If they do not feel sufficiently knowledgeable about the various potential risks, they should seek a due diligence professional to help guide their fund manager analysis.

Discussion Questions

1. Discuss the main US rules and regulations applying to fund managers investing in digital assets and how they differ from traditional fund managers.
2. Identify three main categories of digital assets determined by the FCA and those under its regulation.
3. Explain the operational risks unique to digital asset funds: asset custody, portfolio management, counterparties, and service providers.
4. Explain three challenges in determining the NAVs of a fund's investment in digital assets trading on crypto exchanges.

References

Alternative Investment Management Association. (2021). The 3rd annual global crypto hedge fund report 2021. Retrieved from https://www.aima.org/educate/aima-research/third-annual-global-crypto-hedge-fund-report-2021.html

Alun, J. (2021). Australia, Malaysia, Singapore, and South Africa launch central bank digital currency scheme. *Reuters*, September 2. Retrieved from https://www.reuters.com/business/finance/australia-singapore-south-africa-test-cross-border-cbank-digital-payments-2021-09-02/

Brennan, M. (2021). Poly network hacked for $611 million which is biggest Defi hack ever. *The Crypto Basic*, August 10. Retrieved from https://thecryptobasic.com/2021/08/10/poly-network-hacked-for-611-million-which-is-biggesst-defi-hack-ever/

Browne, R. (2021). More than $90 million in cryptocurrency stolen after a top Japanese exchange is hacked. *CNBC*, August 19. Retrieved from https://www.cnbc.com/2021/08/19/liquid-cryptocurrency-exchange-hack.html

Chipolina, S. (2021). Cream finance suffers third hack, loses over $130 million. *Decrypt*, October 27. Retrieved from https://decrypt.co/84590/cream-finance-suffers-third-hack-losing-over-130-million

CoinMarketCap. (2022, December). Top cryptocurrency spot exchanges. Retrieved from https://coinmarketcap.com/rankings/exchanges/

Dossett, J. (2021). First Bitcoin-linked ETF starts trading on the New York Stock Exchange. *CNET*, November 15. Retrieved from https://www.cnet.com/personal-finance/crypto/the-first-bitcoin-linked-etf-starts-trading-on-the-new-york-stock-exchange/

Financial Accounting Standards Board. (2011). Fair value measurement (topic 820). Accounting Standards Update No. 2000-4. May. Retrieved from https://asc.fasb.org/imageRoot/00/7534500.pdf

Financial Conduct Authority. (2019, July). Guidance on cryptoassets feedback and final guidance to cp19/3, policy statement ps19/22. Retrieved from https://www.fca.org.uk/publication/policy/ps19-22.pdf

Geron, T. (2021). Here's everything going wrong at Binance, the world's biggest crypto exchange. *Protocol*, September 22. Retrieved from https://www.protocol.com/fintech/binance-regulation-crypto

Groves, K. (2022). The complete list of crypto exchange hacks. *HedgewithCrypto*, February 3. Retrieved from https://www.hedgewithcrypto.com/cryptocurrency-exchange-hacks/

Hernandez, J. (2021). El Salvador just became the first country to accept bitcoin as legal tender. *NPR*, September 17. Retrieved from https://www.npr.org/2021/09/07/1034838909/bitcoin-el-salvador-legal-tender-official-currency-cryptocurrency

Nakamoto, S. (2008). *Bitcoin: A peer-to-peer electronic cash system*. Retrieved from https://bitcoin.org/bitcoin.pdf

Reuters Staff. (2021). China's top regulatory ban crypto trading and mining, sending bitcoin tumbling. *Reuters*, September 24. Retrieved from https://news.trust.org/item/20210924141810-3ymbi

Roy, A. (2021). KuCoin hack: Exchange recovers 100% of stolen funds. *AMBcrypto*, February 3. Retrieved from https://ambcrypto.com/kucoin-hack-exchange-recovers-100-of-stolen-funds/

Tidy, J. (2021). BitMart: Crypto-exchange loses $150m to hackers. *BBC*, December 6. Retrieved from https://www.bbc.com/news/technology-59549606

United States Congress. (1933). The Securities Act of 1933. Retrieved from https://www.govinfo.gov/content/pkg/COMPS-1884/pdf/COMPS-1884.pdf)

United States Congress. (1934). The Securities Exchange Act of 1934. Retrieved from https://www.sec.gov.about/laws/sea34-12g.pdf

United States Congress. (1940). The Investment Company Act of 1940. Retrieved from https://www.govinfo.gov/content/pkg/COMPS-1879/pdf/COMPS-1879.pdf

United States Securities and Exchange Commission. (1940). Laws and rules. Retrieved from https://www.sec.gov/investment/laws-and-rules

United States Securities and Exchange Commission. (1982). Rule 506 of Regulation D. Retrieved from https://www.investor.gov/introduction-investing/investing-basics/glossary/rule-506-regulation-d

Part II

Types of Cryptoassets

Chapter 4

Cryptocurrencies

Lennart Ante

Abstract

This chapter introduces the concept of cryptocurrencies such as bitcoin, ether, or litecoin. The chapter describes the history of cryptocurrency, blockchain technology, and the quest for secure digital money, followed by a discussion of cryptocurrency as a phenomenon. Next, it discusses individual cryptocurrencies, including an overview of bitcoin and relevant subgroups, such as so-called forks or privacy coins. It also explains developments such as stablecoins or central bank digital currencies, which are potentially much more in line with bitcoin's original idea of digital cash. Overall, the chapter provides a basic understanding of cryptocurrencies, their defining characteristics, challenges, and markets.

Keywords: Cryptocurrency; bitcoin; ether; litecoin; stablecoins; central bank digital currencies; privacy coins; digital cash

Introduction

The internet represents a technology for securely exchanging information (Cameron, 2005). Digital applications and services such as email provide a basis for social, political, and economic value creation (Amit & Zott, 2001; Verhoef et al., 2021). However, the internet's basic structure does not provide a value or identity layer (Cameron, 2005). Consequently, copied information is always the basis of conventional applications. The senders of emails keep the original in their mailbox and send a digital copy to one or more recipients. Senders cannot monitor what recipients do with this information. For example, they cannot control or see whether recipients forward the email to others. Suppose someone sends a unique value like a currency via an e-mail-like system. No one could verify how much of

The Emerald Handbook on Cryptoassets: Investment Opportunities and Challenges, 45–60

doi:10.1108/978-1-80455-320-620221004

that currency exists and whether a given digital "coin" is a copy or an original. This situation for a digital currency is known as the double-spending problem (Osipkov, Vasserman, Hopper, & Yongdae, 2007). *Double-spending* is the risk that someone could use (spend) a cryptocurrency more than once. It creates accounting and security challenges and makes a system unsuitable for transferring unique values or information worth protecting.

The traditional solution to the double-spending problem is to secure value transfers through trusted intermediaries who centrally manage and update digital ledgers. For example, banks centrally manage the digital account balances of their customers. When initiating a wire transfer between two individuals, at least one bank is involved as a securing intermediary, covering, and preventing the risk of double-spending. An intermediary expects a fee for the service of maintaining and updating the ledger. Therefore, involving intermediaries entails transaction costs, which according to transaction cost theory (Williamson, 1979), can result in additional coordination costs, such as monitoring or controlling. Furthermore, trust problems (moral hazard) can arise as intermediaries may be tempted to exploit asymmetric information (adverse selection) (Akerlof, 1970; Jensen & Meckling, 1976; Rothschild & Stiglitz, 1976), and their ledgers constitute centralized single points of failure (Mendling et al., 2018). For example, manipulating or deleting a bank's ledger affects customer account documentation and security.

The bitcoin whitepaper (Nakamoto, 2008), the first reference to blockchain technology, introduced a novel solution to the double-spending problem. In January 2009, the launch of the bitcoin network put blockchain technology into practice. Bitcoin is a decentralized network whose users can conduct secured peer-to-peer (P2P) transactions through transparency, redundancy, cryptography, and mining. Bitcoin or blockchain technology is not entirely new but a clever combination of various pre-existing technologies, some dating back decades. They include, for example, time-stamping (Bayer, Haber, & Stornetta, 1993; Haber & Stornetta, 1990), Merkle trees (Merkle, 1980), Byzantine fault tolerance (BFT; Castro & Liskov, 1999; Lamport, Shostak, & Pease, 1982), and proof-of-work (PoW; Dwork & Naor, 1992). Other researchers had previously proposed ideas or concepts similar to bitcoin, such as hashcash (Back, 2002) or bit gold (Szabo, 2005).

The concept of blockchain technology builds on a shared ledger, which is updated at regular intervals by network participants and represents the network's entire state and history (Nakamoto, 2008). A major component of the network's security is redundancy – all network participants store a complete record of the distribution of value in the network and update the records regularly. So-called miners, who expect economic rewards (e.g., newly issued cryptocurrency and transaction fees), collect and verify the state changes (i.e., transactions). After solving a cryptographic puzzle, they bundle transactions in digital blocks and attach them to previously verified blocks. This cryptographic puzzle differs across blockchains. The basis of the Bitcoin network is PoW, where a proving entity provides proof of its work (computational effort) to other entities (verifiers). By trial and error, miners must find a specific combination of numbers and letters called the hash. If a miner guesses this combination correctly, it is shared on the network by publishing a new block containing previously unconfirmed transactions. Having published a block, the miner receives a "block reward" (i.e., newly issued bitcoins) and the fees of the newly confirmed transactions. Other miners can easily verify and confirm the solution. Once someone confirms a block, the process starts anew (Dwork & Naor, 1992; Nakamoto, 2008). This process results in a chain of blocks — the blockchain. Unlike "traditional" centralized solutions, all information about values stored on the blockchain is public knowledge, and anyone can monitor it. For example, anyone can look up the Bitcoin blockchain using online block explorers such as www.blockchain.com or by downloading the blockchain (e.g., by setting up a blockchain node or using third-party services such as Google BigQuery). If one miner misbehaves, all other miners can simply reject the provided information and refuse to update their ledgers accordingly. With bitcoin, for example, anyone can see how many bitcoins exist, who owns them, and when someone transfers them. Updating the distributed ledgers occurs every 10 minutes, on average, thus validating new transactions. Logging all historical behavior occurs transparently once assigning an address to an entity.

The derivation of the term cryptocurrency comes from the underlying methodology of cryptography. Cryptography, redundancy, and economic incentive systems ensure the security of cryptocurrencies such as bitcoin or litecoin (Nakamoto, 2008). These digital "currencies" represent the underlying units of distributed or decentralized networks (e.g., blockchains). Primary uses of such currencies include transmitting value or paying for services. Although cryptocurrency suggests that the phenomena are currencies, cryptocurrencies may be financial assets or investments. The rationale is that cryptocurrencies are usually subject to high price fluctuations, limiting their suitability as a means of payment (Baur & Dimpfl, 2021).

The first and most known virtual currency is bitcoin (Nakamoto, 2008), introduced in 2008 and launched in 2009. Any internet user can download the bitcoin software and access the decentralized network. Many view bitcoin as a software-based payment system, a store of value, and a monetary unit that operates and is managed decentrally in a network. Transactions are processed based on a transaction database jointly managed and stored by users. To join this network, users only need to install the software or use the appropriate third-party providers that offer access to users. Thus, the network is not subject to any restrictions other than the need for internet access. Users can divide bitcoins into smaller units to make even the smallest (micro) transactions possible. The cryptocurrency's main properties include transaction security, decentralization, scarcity (i.e., a maximum of 21 million bitcoin), and irreversibility of transactions.

Besides bitcoin, thousands of other cryptocurrencies exist. One example is the currency litecoin, created in 2011 as a copy of the bitcoin codebase. The reasons for litecoin's creation included criticism of bitcoin's mining process. Litecoin contains properties such as a shorter block time, more maximum coins, and the use of a different hashing algorithm as a cryptographic basis. Due to its similarity to bitcoin, some describe litecoin as digital silver to bitcoin's digital gold. The fact that cryptocurrencies are published decentrally as open-source software means that market participants can copy this code and create cryptocurrencies with little effort. Additionally, disputes in processing transactions or updating the code base in blockchain networks can lead to forks. This situation means that networks can split up so that one part of the network uses one codebase and the other uses another codebase. An example is the bitcoin fork "bitcoin cash."

Privacy coins are a special type of cryptocurrency that represents privacy and anonymity as defining characteristics. They strive to enable anonymous blockchain transactions to provide users with the highest possible privacy. This purpose uses privacy-enhancing techniques such as zero-knowledge proofs, so-called mixing or ring signatures.

The chapter proceeds as follows. The following section introduces the concept of cryptocurrency, including a definition of the phenomenon. The next section describes bitcoin, the largest and most significant cryptocurrency. The subsequent section presents major alternative cryptocurrencies, including forks and privacy coins. The final section contains a summary and conclusions.

Cryptocurrencies

Cryptocurrencies are digital or virtual "currencies" secured by cryptography. Using cryptography ensures that no counterfeiting or double-spending is possible. Most cryptocurrencies are applications of blockchain technology, meaning that a distributed or decentralized ledger represents the underlying data and settlement infrastructure. A key feature of cryptocurrencies is that a decentralized computer protocol rather than a centralized entity usually issues them. This situation reduces how centralized or state institutions can directly or indirectly interfere with or manipulate them. The term cryptocurrency lacks a uniform and generally accepted definition. Consequently, many use the term various blockchain-based currencies, assets, or tokens, which may only partially or not correspond to the actual concept of digital currency.

The phenomenon of cryptocurrencies is associated with various potentials, advantages, disadvantages, and risks. One advantageous feature is that the transfer of value can occur directly without intermediaries' involvement (e.g., banks or payment processors). Public and private key encryption and economic and technical incentive systems (e.g., PoW) replace their security role. Users can conduct any transaction directly via the internet and permit comparatively low transaction costs depending on the cryptocurrency. Furthermore, the network's transparency ensures how much cryptocurrency exists and, depending on the privacy-related characteristics of the network, its location, and transfer.

The degree of transparency or pseudo-anonymity is also a possible disadvantage or risk of cryptocurrency. The high level of privacy or complete anonymity is only comparable with cash transactions, making cryptocurrencies attractive for individuals and entities looking to protect their privacy. Cryptocurrencies offer one of the most suitable methods to send values privately on the internet, which criminals can use for tax evasion or money laundering. However, traditional cryptocurrencies such as bitcoin, ether, or litecoin are only suitable for criminal behavior to a minimal extent due to their transparent architecture. All transactions are publicly visible, providing law enforcement with a database to identify criminal actors through forensic analysis. This situation is not the case for privacy-centric cryptocurrencies, such as monero or zcash, that guarantee maximum anonymity. Most cryptocurrency transactions are non-reversible. Once a transaction takes place, no way is available to refund or charge back its value.

The phenomenon of cryptocurrencies has shown continuous growth since Satoshi Nakamoto's bitcoin whitepaper in 2008, evident in bitcoin's price development and the number of people owning cryptoassets. For example, 9 percent of the German population owns cryptocurrency (Steinmetz, von Meduna, Ante, & Fiedler, 2021). Cryptocurrencies continue to develop into a relevant investment asset for individual and professional investors. Compared to traditional financial markets, these cryptocurrency markets are still less regulated. Other characteristics range from high returns to total losses and fraud (e.g., Benedetti & Nikbakht, 2021; Momtaz, 2021; Le Pennec, Fiedler, & Ante, 2021). This development continues with no end in sight. Accordingly, individuals or companies should understand these markets, individual cryptoassets, and technical characteristics.

Besides understanding existing cryptocurrency markets, they should assess the potential of future cryptocurrencies or digital currencies. Although bitcoin represents a decentralized cryptocurrency, central bank digital currencies (CBDCs) with central banks as issuers may significantly shape the future of digital commerce and society. For example, in July 2021, the European Central Bank launched a 24-month phase to study a digital euro. This development involves a design based on user preferences and technical advice from traders and intermediaries (European Central Bank, 2021). A national or supranational regulated digital currency could potentially make online payments essentially free of charge. Although, this situation could sustainably strengthen the economy, it could also lead to the disintermediation of traditional payment processors. Therefore, this development requires detailed planning to assess its social consequences.

Bitcoin

Bitcoin currently represents the oldest and most significant use case of blockchain technology. As of 2021, the market capitalization of all bitcoins rose above \$1 trillion (Coingecko, 2021). Transfer of over \$6.3 trillion occurred via the Bitcoin blockchain throughout 2020. This value would amount to \$29 trillion for 2021 if the settled amount remains at the same price level as the first two months (Glassnode, 2020). This amount would represent about 250 percent of the annually settled value of the VISA network (VISA, 2020). However, one should view this popular comparison between bitcoin and VISA critically. VISA is a payment service on top of various layers of a traditional financial system, while bitcoin is a settlement (base) layer. Accordingly, bitcoin is more comparable to the American Fedwire or European TARGET2 systems. For example, when comparing Fedwire's daily settlement value of about \$3.3 trillion per day (The Federal Reserve, 2021) to bitcoin, the cryptocurrency still occupies a niche market as a financial settlement layer.

But what exactly is bitcoin? The title of the bitcoin whitepaper reads "Bitcoin: A Peer-to-Peer Electronic Cash System" (Nakamoto, 2008), suggesting that bitcoin represents digital cash. But this answer is too simple. Although potentially conceived as digital cash, this cryptocurrency and its uses have evolved.

The literature offers details on how to classify or define bitcoin. Publications assess whether it represents a medium of exchange, asset, or store of value (Baur & Dimpfl, 2021; Baur, Hong, & Lee, 2018), to what extent bitcoin corresponds to a "classic" currency or money (Hazlett & Luther, 2020; Yermack, 2015), to what extent it is an entirely new asset or investment class (Corbet, Lucey, Urquhart, & Yarovaya, 2019; Hayes, 2017) or if bitcoin exhibits safe-haven property, similar to gold or commodities (Bouri, Gupta, Tiwari, & Roubaud, 2017; Bouri, Molnár, Azzi, Roubaud, & Hagfors, 2017; Dyhrberg, 2016; Shahzad et al., 2019; Urquhart & Zhang, 2019). In summary, bitcoin is a financial asset because the cryptocurrency's actual utility is currently more like an investment/store of value and not a medium of exchange. For example, Baur and Dimpfl (2021) show that bitcoin's volatility is much too high– almost 10 times higher than fiat currencies such as the US dollar or the Euro – to be useful as a medium of exchange. Researchers need to conduct additional studies to develop bitcoin and cryptocurrency ecosystems further.

Regardless of what bitcoin is, this cryptocurrency is becoming increasingly relevant. Its price development reflects support for this view. Bitcoin reached an all-time high price of $68,521 on November 5, 2021, supporting its relevance. Investments in publicly traded companies also illustrate the growing significance as a digital investment object. For example, NASDAQ-listed MicroStrategy, Inc. bought over $2 billion worth of bitcoin, which doubled its value as of March 2021. Another example is the $1.5 billion investment by Tesla, Inc., which rose to an estimated value of over $2.5 billion within a few months due to bitcoin's price increase. Overall, projections indicate that by December 2021, about 7.1 percent of all existing bitcoins are located in treasuries of countries and publicly traded, private or exchange-traded funds (ETFs) like firms (Bitcointreasuries, 2021). An up-to-date overview of public investments in bitcoin is available on bitcointreasuries.org.

Against the backdrop of the increasing relevance of bitcoin as a decentralized settlement layer and "digital gold" is a challenge for the scientific community to gain a detailed understanding of this phenomenon. Suppose bitcoin and other cryptocurrencies become a new asset class. In that case, understanding how this asset class differs from others, its characteristics, and resulting implications becomes increasingly important. Bitcoin's underlying blockchain technology with its features such as transparency, pseudo-anonymity, or the decentralized consensus procedure and energy consumption represents a fundamental difference between established systems and assets. Bitcoin mining follows a Poisson point process, meaning that although the average time between blocks (i.e., transaction verification) is known, the exact timing is a random distribution. Miners are as likely to mine a new block after one minute as after 30 minutes. Depending on the average time over a window of about two weeks, the complexity of the mining process is adjusted to target the desired average of 10 minutes (Nakamoto, 2008). The network is a pseudonymous system that uses public and private key cryptography. The public key represents a public address on the blockchain that anyone can look up and monitor. It usually consists of letters and numbers (e.g., 1HLoD9E4SDFFPDiYfNYnkBLQ85Y51J3Zb1). The private key resembles a password that grants access to the value stored on an address and signing transactions (i.e., making transfers). Accordingly, market participants in the blockchain network can see how much value an address contains, but in principle, they cannot use the public key to ascertain the entity behind it.

Bitcoin runs on energy. Solving the network's PoW consensus mechanism requires repeatedly trying out number and letter combinations. Hence, a higher computational capacity increases the probability of solving the problem. If the expected block reward's value is higher than the energy costs, miners have an incentive to use more energy for successfully mining a block. As the bitcoin price increases, mining profitability and the network's energy consumption also increases. Figure 4.1 shows the projected annualized energy consumption of the bitcoin network based on the Cambridge Bitcoin Electricity Consumption Index (CBECI) (Rauchs, Blandin, & Dek, 2021).

As of December 2021, the estimated annual energy consumption of the bitcoin blockchain is 116 TWh, which would be about 0.52 percent of the world's energy consumption (IEA, 2020). According to Blandin et al. (2020), about 39 percent of the energy used for bitcoin mining comes from renewables. Bitcoin has an average carbon intensity of 480–500 gCO_2eq per kWh (Stoll, Klaaßen, & Gallersdörfer, 2019). Bitcoin's high energy consumption is undoubtedly one of its key challenges, which is why other cryptocurrencies rely on less energy-intensive approaches to reach consensus, such as BFT-based mechanisms or proof-of-stake (Castro & Liskov, 1999; Lamport et al., 1982; Steinmetz et al., 2021).

The bitcoin network is fully transparent. Tracking all activities occurs in real-time, including the amount of bitcoin stored in any address and when and where

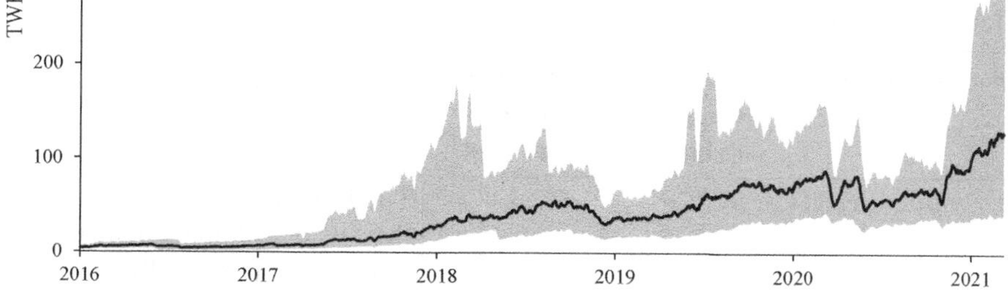

Figure 4.1. Estimated Annualized Energy Consumption of the Bitcoin Blockchain. *Notes*: This figure shows the estimated annualized energy consumption in terawatt-hours (TWh) of the Bitcoin blockchain according to the CBECI. The gray area indicates upper and lower bounds.

its transfer occurs. These characteristics represent a clear difference compared to fiat currencies or stocks, where markets may be partially transparent (Boehmer, Saar, & Yu, 2005). Still, the underlying settlement layers remain non-transparent to the public. Accordingly, the question arises whether and, if so, which implications result from a transparent settlement layer.

Public blockchains such as bitcoin are usually pseudonymous, meaning they are fully transparent but use public addresses as identifiers consisting of alphanumerical strings. Accordingly, acting anonymously but transparently as an entity or person is possible in the bitcoin network. Criminals have used this possibility to trade illicit goods, ransom, or extortion on the internet. Such behavior is also due to the lack of alternatives for anonymously transacting value, or cash, digitally on the internet (Turner & Irwin, 2018). However, the actual level of anonymity in the bitcoin network is limited because a unique connection or link between the real and digital worlds transparently reveals a user's complete transaction history. Thus, not causing such a connection is extremely difficult (Reid & Harrigan, 2013). The successful conviction and closure of criminally active cryptocurrency exchanges (e.g., due to money laundering), darknet marketplaces, or extortionists illustrates this situation (Koshy, Koshy, & McDaniel, 2014; Reid & Harrigan, 2013).

Alternative Cryptocurrencies

Besides bitcoin, thousands of other cryptocurrencies and blockchain-based tokens are available, each with different characteristics. However, users often generically use the term cryptocurrency for all blockchain-based assets (i.e., cryptoassets). The following chapters discuss specific forms of cryptoassets in more detail to better differentiate the term cryptocurrency. Table 4.1 provides an overview of the major cryptocurrencies described in this chapter, sorted by market capitalization in August 2021. A more detailed summary is available on various websites such as coingecko.com. For example, bitcoin makes up about 39 percent and ether 20 percent of the overall market valuation of $2.17 trillion. The 10 selected cryptocurrencies represented over 70 percent of the total market valuation in December 2021.

Table 4.1. Overview and Description of Selected Cryptocurrencies.

#	Coin (Ticker)	Market Capitalization ($ billion)	Market Share (percent)	Description
1	Bitcoin (BTC)	915.20	42.1	The Bitcoin blockchain is the first distributed payment settlement network. Bitcoin (BTC) is the native asset of the network and represents the first digital currency without a centralized administrator of a central bank

#	Coin (Ticker)	Market Capitalization ($ billion)	Market Share (percent)	Description
2	Ethereum (ETH)	376.96	17.3	Ethereum is a distributed blockchain computing platform for smart contracts and decentralized applications. The primary uses of the native token ether (ETH) are to pay transaction fees and to serve as collateral. The network plans to shift from PoW to PoS
3	Cardano (ADA)	92.44	4.25	Cardano is a smart contract blockchain platform that uses proof-of-stake consensus to secure the network. The native token ADA entitles stakers a claim on newly issued ADA. Its primary use is to pay transaction fees
6	XRP (XRP)	53.42	2.46	XRP is the native token of the XRP Ledger, an open-source cryptographic ledger powered by a P2P network of nodes. It aims at making transferring money between financial institutions more efficient. XRP is a bridge for financial institutions exchanging value between multiple fiat currencies
7	Dogecoin (DOGE)	37.05	1.70	Dogecoin (DOGE) is a blockchain and digital currency popularized by adopting the Shiba Inu internet meme. It is based on the Bitcoin protocol and is one of the largest cryptocurrencies
8	Solana (SOL)	26.93	1.24	Solana is a blockchain protocol and platform for smart contracts and decentralized applications. It is optimized for scalability, one of the significant challenges of other blockchains, such as Ethereum

(*Continued*)

Table 4.1. (*Continued*)

#	Coin (Ticker)	Market Capitalization ($ billion)	Market Share (percent)	Description
13	Bitcoin Cash (BCH)	12.81	0.59	Bitcoin Cash (BCH) is a hard fork of bitcoin that advocates interpreting bitcoin as a "peer-to-peer electronic cash system." It aims at cheap peer-to-peer transactions as the network's core value proposition and uses increased block sizes to improve scalability
15	Litecoin (LTC)	11.92	0.55	Litecoin is a fork of bitcoin with four times faster block times and a four times larger supply. Some describe litecoin as digital silver and bitcoin as digital gold
21	Ethereum Classic (ETC)	8.32	0.38	Ethereum Classic (ETC) is a hard fork of Ethereum with the same overall goals. The network split occurred due to a community disagreement handling a hack in 2017
32	Monero (XMR)	5.37	0.25	Monero (XMR) is a privacy-preserving blockchain network for anonymous value transfer on the web. By default, the network offers privacy using ring signatures, stealth addresses, and confidential transactions
	Overall market (9,129 coins)	2,173.76	100.0	

Notes: This table describes 10 cryptocurrencies. The symbol # indicates the global rank of the cryptocurrency based on market capitalization in August 2021.

The second largest cryptocurrency, blockchain network, and distributed blockchain computing platform are *Ethereum* (Buterin, 2013; Wood, 2014). It enables so-called *smart contracts* – decentrally anchored computer code that enables process automation (Ante, 2021). Creating blockchain tokens involve smart contracts, representing any value held and transferred independently on the blockchain. Examples of such tokens are access authorizations for decentralized protocols, shares in ventures or real estate, energy units or fiat currency, and so-called stablecoins. Accordingly, unlike bitcoin, ether, the native currency of the Ethereum blockchain, is stored and transferred on the Ethereum blockchain. Many different assets are subject to the same degree of pseudo-anonymity and transparency. Cardano, Binance Smart Chain, Solana, and Ethereum Classic are blockchain networks whose primary goal is also applying smart contracts. They differ from Ethereum by other basic features, such as the consensus mechanism for validating transactions.

The underlying protocols are usually freely accessible (i.e., open source) in decentralized networks. Thus, they can be copied, changed, and rebuilt. Accordingly, prominent cryptocurrencies, such as litecoin or dogecoin, have emerged as copies of the Bitcoin protocol. Slightly different characteristics, such as the time interval of transaction processing or level of monetary expansion, distinguish these protocols from bitcoin.

Another defining characteristic of blockchain networks is that they can split up into so-called *hard forks* where one part of the validators confirms a block, and another part of the validators confirms another block. Effectively, the network forms two forks, which exist autonomously from each other in the future. The two cryptocurrencies – bitcoin cash (as a hard fork of bitcoin) and Ethereum classic (as a hard fork of Ethereum) – are examples of such forks. For pre-fork cryptocurrency owners, a hard fork means that they own both cryptocurrencies post-fork. They can decide to hold both, sell one of the cryptoassets, or both.

For the first time, a digital infrastructure makes the complete lifecycle of various digital values, assets, and markets transparent and publicly traceable. Privacy coins start here and pursue the goal of maintaining transparency and decentralization at the network level while guaranteeing individual privacy and anonymity of actors and transactions. Monero (XMR) is one of the most significant privacy coins and uses features such as RingCT, stealth addresses, and ring signatures to promote the comprehensive anonymity of the blockchain network. To verify or prove that a transaction has occurred, users need to know a specific transaction ID, a private uniquely generated transaction key, and the recipient's public blockchain address. Only when market participants know these three pieces of information can they uncover blockchain network data.

Another major privacy coin is Zcash (ZEC), which allows network participants to choose whether to hide transactions via privacy and non-traceability mechanisms called shielded transactions and zk-SNARKS or to execute them transparently. Privacy coins represent a central part of the crypto ecosystem and are most comparable to the classic anonymity of analog cash transactions. This fact also makes them suitable for criminal processes on the internet, which is a major criticism of these networks.

Examining these digital assets can help understand future blockchain markets and have potential implications for traditional markets. For example, examining the issuance of digital *blockchain dollars* (i.e., stablecoins such as Tether or USD Coin) or the lifecycle of privacy coins in the context of the resulting impact on other markets can provide relevant insights for discussing the level of transparency of new monetary issuances by central banks or the development of CBDCs. Practitioners planning or working on blockchain-based products and markets should evaluate the effects of different degrees of market transparency. For example, a regulated CBDC (e.g., a blockchain-based Euro issued by the European Central Bank) is unlikely to be designed as a fully transparent, pseudonymous system such as Bitcoin. This situation is due, for example, to concerns about individuals' digital privacy or the protection of sensible company payment data. However, a central bank issuing a digital currency or national regulators may require full market transparency. Accordingly, such a system is likely to provide different levels of transparency for different groups of users.

The thousands of cryptocurrencies differ based on underlying technical characteristics and fundamental use cases. For example, the two largest and most significant cryptocurrencies, bitcoin (digital cash or gold) and Ethereum (a computing network), pursue distinctly different goals. However, bitcoin, with a market share of 39 percent, and ethereum, with over 20 percent, account for significant portions of the overall market. Prices of cryptocurrencies are generally highly correlated, as shown in Table 4.2.

Table 4.2 shows Pearson correlation coefficients between the prices of selected cryptocurrencies over one year. The numbers quantify the estimated strength of the linear relationship between two variables. In this situation, the prices of the respective cryptocurrency pairs. Correlations range between +1 (perfectively positive) and −1 (perfectly negative). A 0 indicates no linear correlation. All cryptocurrencies have positive correlation coefficients, meaning that their prices move together. This table illustrates that cryptocurrency markets are still immature or highly interrelated.

Table 4.2. One-year Pearson Correlations Between Prices of Major Cryptocurrencies.

	BTC	**ETH**	**LTC**	**XRP**	**ADA**	**BCH**	**ETC**
Bitcoin (BTC)							
Ether (ETH)	0.66						
Litecoin (LTC)	0.72	0.78					
XRP (XRP)	0.52	0.52	0.58				
Cardano (ADA)	0.38	0.60	0.48	0.59			
Bitcoin Cash (BCH)	0.55	0.74	0.90	0.49	0.42		
Ethereum Classic (ETC)	0.37	0.68	0.68	0.37	0.47	0.75	
Dogecoin (DOGE)	0.27	0.50	0.54	0.33	0.40	0.64	0.80

Notes: This table shows Pearson correlations between eight major cryptocurrencies. The metrics indicate the degree of linear correlation between each cryptocurrency pair. The data from August 2020 to August 2021 are detrended using the first differences.

The underlying base layer transparency of blockchain technology distinguishes it from traditional financial infrastructures and markets. It allows market participants to process additional information. Against this background, activity on the blockchain (e.g., a transaction) represents public information regarding the semi-strong form of the efficient market hypothesis (Fama, 1970, 1991). *Semi-strong form efficiency* refers to a market where share prices fully and fairly reflect all publicly available information, including all past information. Consequently, a market based on blockchain technology should be more efficient than a "non-blockchain" copy of that market.

Summary and Conclusions

This chapter explained that the internet emerged without a suitable basis for transferring values. Additionally, bitcoin, cryptocurrencies, and blockchain technology stem from searching for a solution to the double-spending problem. After describing the concept of cryptocurrency, the chapter describes bitcoin as a prevalent and significant example, followed by a discussion of alternative crypto-currencies and their major subgroups. In summary, the chapter provides a basic understanding of the complex topic of cryptocurrencies, which can form a basis for more in-depth studies.

Cryptocurrencies have evolved into a significant market with broad adoption. This growth and development indicate that the phenomenon is here to stay. However, understanding cryptocurrencies can be a substantial challenge for players in the financial sector and beyond. The innovative and disruptive use of cryptocurrency has only begun.

Discussion Questions

1. Explain the double-spending problem.
2. Define bitcoin and discuss if it represents cash, currency, a financial asset, a medium of exchange, a commodity, or something else.
3. Explain how so-called privacy coins differ from bitcoin.
4. Discuss whether cryptocurrency prices are correlated and why this situation might occur.

References

Akerlof, G. A. (1970). The market for 'lemons': Quality uncertainty and the market mechanism. *Quarterly Journal of Economics*, *84*(3), 488–500.

Amit, R., & Zott, C. (2001). Value creation in E-business. *Strategic Management Journal*, *22*(6–7), 493–520.

Ante, L. (2021). Smart contracts on the blockchain – A bibliometric analysis and review. *Telematics and Informatics*, *57*(March), 101519.

Back, A. (2002). Hashcash – A denial of service counter-measure. Retrieved from www.hashcash.org/hashcash.pdf

Baur, D. G., & Dimpfl, T. (2021). The volatility of bitcoin and its role as a medium of exchange and a store of value. *Empirical Economics*, *61*(5), 2663–2683. https://doi.org/10.1007/s00181-020-01990-5

Baur, D. G., Hong, K. H., & Lee, A. D. (2018). Bitcoin: Medium of exchange or speculative assets? *Journal of International Financial Markets, Institutions and Money*, *54*(C), 177–189.

Bayer, D., Haber, S., & Stornetta, S. W. (1993). Improving the efficiency and reliability of digital time-stamping. In R. M. Capocelli, A. De Santis, & U. Vaccaro (Eds.), *Sequences II* (pp. 329–334). New York, NY: Springer.

Benedetti, H., & Nikbakht, E. (2021). Returns and network growth of digital tokens after cross-listings. *Journal of Corporate Finance*, *66*(C), 101853.

Bitcointreasuries. (2021, March). *Bitcointreasuries.org*. Retrieved from https://bitcointreasuries.org/

Blandin, A., Pieters, G., Wu, Y., Eisermann, T., Dek, A., Taylor, S., & Njoki, D. (2020). Cambridge centre for alternative finance 3rd global cryptoasset benchmarking study. Retrieved from http://www.jbs.cam.ac.uk/wp-content/uploads/2021/01/2021-ccaf-3rd-global-cryptoasset-benchmarking-study.pdf

Boehmer, E., Saar, G., & Yu, L. (2005). Lifting the veil: An analysis of pre-trade transparency at the NYSE. *Journal of Finance*, *60*(2), 783–815.

Bouri, E., Gupta, R., Tiwari, A. K., & Roubaud, D. (2017). Does bitcoin hedge global uncertainty? Evidence from wavelet-based quantile-in-quantile regressions. *Finance Research Letters*, *23*(C), 87–95.

Bouri, E., Molnár, P., Azzi, G., Roubaud, D., & Hagfors, L. I. (2017). On the hedge and safe haven properties of bitcoin: Is it really more than a diversifier? *Finance Research Letters*, *20*(C), 192–198.

Buterin, V. (2013, March). Ethereum white paper – A next generation smart contract and decentralized application platform. Retrieved from http://blockchainlab.com/pdf/Ethereum_white_paper-a_next_generation_smart_contract_and_decentralized_application_platform-vitalik-buterin.pdf

Cameron, K. (2005, May). The laws of identity. *Identityblog.com*. Retrieved from http://www.ict-21.ch/ICT.SATW.CH/IMG/Kim_Cameron_Law_of_Identity.pdf

Castro, M., & Liskov, B. (1999). Practical Byzantine fault tolerance. In M. Seltzer & P. Leach (Eds.), *Proceedings of the third symposium on operating systems design and implementation*, New Orleans, LA, February 1 (pp. 173–186). Retrieved from https://www.usenix.org/legacy/publications/library/proceedings/osdi99/full_papers/castro/castro_html/castro.html

Coingecko. (2021, November 24). Bitcoin market capitalization. Retrieved from https://www.coingecko.com/en/coins/bitcoin

Corbet, S., Lucey, B., Urquhart, A., & Yarovaya, L. (2019). Cryptocurrencies as a financial asset: A systematic analysis. *International Review of Financial Analysis*, *62*(C), 182–199.

Dwork, C., & Naor, M. (1992). Pricing via processing or combatting junk mail. In E. F. Brickell (Ed.), *CRYPTO '92: Proceedings of the 12th annual international cryptology conference on advances in cryptology*, Santa Barbara, CA: Springer, Berlin, August 12–20 (pp. 139–147).

Dyhrberg, A. H. (2016). Hedging capabilities of bitcoin. Is it the virtual gold? *Finance Research Letters*, *16*(C), 139–144.

European Central Bank. (2021, July 14). Eurosystem launches digital euro project. Retrieved from https://www.ecb.europa.eu/press/pr/date/2021/html/ecb.pr210714~d99198ea23.en.html

Fama, E. F. (1970). Efficient capital markets: A review of theory and empirical work. *Journal of Finance*, *25*(2), 383–417.

Fama, E. F. (1991). Efficient capital markets: II. *Journal of Finance*, *46*(5), 1575–1617.

Glassnode. (2020, August). Glassnode. Retrieved from https://glassnode.com

Haber, S., & Stornetta, S. W. (1990). How to time-stamp a digital document. In A. J. Menezes & S. A. Vanstone (Eds.), *Advances in cryptology-CRYPTO'90. CRYPTO*

1990. Lecture Notes in Computer Science (Vol. 537, pp. 437–455). Berlin: Springer. https://doi.org/10.1007/3-540-38424-3_32

Hayes, A. S. (2017). Cryptocurrency value formation: An empirical study leading to a cost of production model for valuing bitcoin. *Telematics and Informatics*, *34*(7), 1308–1321.

Hazlett, P. K., & Luther, W. J. (2020). Is bitcoin money? And what that means. *Quarterly Review of Economics and Finance*, *77*(2), 144–149.

IEA. (2020, August). Electricity information: Overview. Retrieved from https://www.iea.org/reports/electricity-information-overview

Jensen, M. C., & Meckling, W. H. (1976). Theory of the firm: Managerial behaviour, agency costs and ownership structure. *Journal of Financial Economics*, *3*(4), 305–360.

Koshy, P., Koshy, D., & McDaniel, P. (2014). An analysis of anonymity in bitcoin using P2P network. In R. Safavi-Naini & N. Christin (Eds.), *Financial cryptography and data security – 18th international conference, FC 2014, Revised selected papers* (pp. 469–485). Berlin: Springer Verlag.

Lamport, L., Shostak, R., & Pease, M. (1982). The Byzantine generals problem. *ACM Transactions on Programming Languages and Systems (TOPLAS)*, *4*(3), 382–401. Retrieved from https://www.microsoft.com/en-us/research/publication/byzantine-generals-problem/

Le Pennec, G., Fiedler, I., & Ante, L. (2021). Wash trading at cryptocurrency exchanges. *Finance Research Letters*, *47*, 101982.

Mendling, J., Weber, I., Van Der Aalst, W., Vom Brocke, J., Cabanillas, C., Daniel, F., … Zhu, L. (2018). Blockchains for business process management – Challenges and opportunities. *ACM Transactions on Management Information Systems*, *9*(1), 1–16.

Merkle, R. C. (1980). Protocols for public key cryptosystems. In G. I. Davida & R. Turn (Eds.), Proceedings – IEEE *symposium on security and privacy*, April 14 (pp. 122–134). Oakland, USA: IEEE, New York.

Momtaz, P. P. (2021). The pricing and performance of cryptocurrency. *European Journal of Finance*, *27*(4–5), 367–380.

Nakamoto, S. (2008, June). Bitcoin: A peer-to-peer electronic cash system. Retrieved from https://bitcoin.org/bitcoin.pdf

Osipkov, I., Vasserman, E. Y., Hopper, N., & Yongdae, K. (2007). Combating double-spending using cooperative P2P systems. In *The 27th international conference on distributed computing systems (ICDCS '07)*, June 25, Toronto, Canada (p. 41).

Rauchs, M., Blandin, A., & Dek, A. (2021). Cambridge bitcoin electricity consumption index (CBECI). Retrieved from https://ccaf.io/cbeci/

Reid, F., & Harrigan, M. (2013). An analysis of anonymity in the bitcoin system. In Y. Altshuler, Y. Elovici, A. Cremers, N. Aharony, & A. Pentland (Eds.), *Security and privacy in social networks* (pp. 197–223). New York, NY: Springer.

Rothschild, M., & Stiglitz, J. (1976). Equilibrium in competitive insurance markets: An essay on the economics of imperfect information. *Quarterly Journal of Economics*, *90*(4), 629–649.

Shahzad, S. Hussain, J., Bouri, E., Roubaud, D., Kristoufek, L., & Lucey, B. (2019). Is bitcoin a better safe-haven investment than gold and commodities? *International Review of Financial Analysis*, *63*(May), 322–330.

Steinmetz, F., von Meduna, M., Ante, L., & Fiedler, I. (2021). Ownership, uses and perceptions of cryptocurrency: Results from a population survey. Technological Forecasting and Social Change, *173*(C), 121073.

Stoll, C., Klaaßen, L., & Gallersdörfer, U. (2019). The carbon footprint of bitcoin. *Joule*, *3*(7), 1647–1661.

Szabo, N. (2005, December 29). Bit gold. Retrieved from https://nakamotoinstitute.org/bit-gold/

The Federal Reserve. (2021, March). Fedwire® funds service – Annual statistics. Retrieved from https://www.frbservices.org/resources/financial-services/wires/volume-value-stats/annual-stats.html

Turner, A., & Irwin, A. S. M. (2018). Bitcoin transactions: A digital discovery of illicit activity on the blockchain. *Journal of Financial Crime*, *25*(1), 109–130.

Urquhart, A., & Zhang, H. (2019). Is bitcoin a hedge or safe haven for currencies? An intraday analysis. *International Review of Financial Analysis*, *63*(May), 49–57.

Verhoef, P. C., Broekhuizen, T., Bart, Y., Bhattacharya, A., Dong, J. Q., Fabian, N., & Haenlein, M. (2021). Digital transformation: A multidisciplinary reflection and research agenda. *Journal of Business Research*, *122*(C), 889–901.

VISA. (2020, February). VISA 2019 corporate responsibility and sustainability report. Retrieved from https://usa.visa.com/dam/VCOM/download/corporate-responsibility/visa-2019-corporate-responsibility-report.pdf

Williamson, O. E. (1979). Transaction-cost economics: The governance of contractual relations. *Journal of Law & Economics*, *22*(2), 233–261.

Wood, G. (2014, May). Ethereum: A secure decentralised generalised transaction ledger. Retrieved from https://ethereum.github.io/yellowpaper/paper.pdf

Yermack, D. (2015). Chapter 2 Is bitcoin a real currency? An economic appraisal. In D. Lee & K. Chuen (Eds.), *Handbook of digital currency* (pp. 31–43). Cambridge, MA: Academic Press.

Chapter 5

Security Tokens

Paul P. Momtaz

Abstract

This chapter synthesizes the economics, law, and technology of security tokens and security token offerings (STOs). Security tokens are an increasingly important instrument in decentralized finance (DeFi) markets. They are blockchain-based investment contracts that are subject to securities law. Interoperability, fractional ownership, market liquidity, and rapid settlement are the main reasons security tokens are a primary catalyst for digitizing finance. The chapter empirically compares STOs with initial exchange offerings (IEOs) and initial coin offerings (ICOs). STOs take longer and raise more funding. However, controlling for other factors, the amount raised in STOs and IEOs is lower than in utility-token ICOs. These findings suggest an avenue for future research. Moreover, both the law and the technology of security tokens need to address critical challenges related to the competent jurisdiction in multinational activities and blockchain interoperability, scalability, and natural resource degradation.

Keywords: Security tokens; security token offerings; decentralized finance; blockchain; initial exchange offerings; initial coin offerings

Introduction

Blockchain technology and smart contracts are transforming financial markets. Startups raising venture capital via utility token offerings were the main driving force for the initial blockchain adoption phase (Adhami, Giudici, & Martinazzi, 2018; Benedetti & Kostovetsky, 2021; Fisch, 2019; Howell, Niessner, & Yermack, 2020; Momtaz, 2020b). However, the lack of regulation deterred institutional investors and slowed adoption by firms. With the development of token-specific

The Emerald Handbook on Cryptoassets: Investment Opportunities and Challenges, 61–78

doi:10.1108/978-1-80455-320-620221005

case law, security tokens may facilitate blockchain adoption. *Security tokens* are blockchain-based investment contracts that are subject to existing securities law. Many startups are switching from utility to security token issuances (Lambert, Liebau, & Rosenbloom 2021). Yet, there are also stock-tracking digital tokens (e.g., Binance's Tesla-tracking token) and even incumbent firms converting their existing stock to security tokens like ANEXIO.

What is driving the interest in security tokens? Smart contract technology features at least two major competitive advantages over existing financial technologies: interoperability and settlement speed. Interoperability is an essential weakness of incumbent technologies. For example, sending shares from E*TRADE to Realty Shares is impossible. Blockchain technology also reduces settlement times. Stock trades on the New York Stock Exchange (NYSE) take two business days to settle. In contrast, cryptocurrency trades automatically settle within a few minutes. Thus, interoperability and almost instantaneous settlement plausibly reduce frictions, such as transaction costs, making financial markets more efficient.

Notwithstanding the promise of security tokens, decentralized finance (DeFi) is still in its infancy and requires overcoming several challenges. For example, as token-specific case law evolves, regulators need to design a coherent set of principles to regulate cross-border activity. Several national authorities, such as the US Securities and Exchange Commission (SEC) and the Monetary Authority of Singapore (MAS), claim jurisdiction over security token offerings (STOs) of issuers not located in their jurisdiction. Yet, these issuers can affect residents or domestic operations. This situation illustrates the regulators' task of creating a legal framework that does not leave loopholes between jurisdictions, while ensuring that overregulation does not deter technological and economic progress. Further, the underlying blockchain technology must evolve to improve blockchain interoperability and scalability while reducing the degradation of natural resources (e.g., the energy use of the bitcoin blockchain).

The Economics of Security Tokens

The following outlines various aspects concerning the economics of security tokens and STOs. It discusses why security tokens may add value to the economy, such as 24/7 trading hours, fractional ownership, rapid settlements, reduced costs and compliance effort, and interoperability. It also outlines the STO process and provides an overview of the market for tokens.

The Economic Rationale for Security Tokens

Although academic research on security tokens is still rare, a consensus exists among practitioners about their benefits and costs. The consensus also tends to be that security tokens may replace traditional recording and trading ownership methods in various asset classes over time. The following subsection reviews the most critical elements of the debate based on McKeon's (2018) synthesis.

Around-the-Clock Trading Hours. Stock market exchanges have restricted trading hours. For example, the NYSE operates only on trading days between

9.30 a.m. and 4 p.m. Eastern Standard Time. The restricted trading hours delay incorporating new information into prices, reducing overall market efficiency. Further, trading hours at various locations, such as London, Frankfurt, and Tokyo, have little or no overlap. This situation creates a business case for 24/7 security token markets. A potential downside is that extended trading hours spread trading activity over a longer period, potentially reducing relative liquidity, resulting in higher bid–ask spreads (Barclay & Hendershott, 2004).

Fractional Ownership. Fractional ownership matters in various asset classes. For example, Binance's equity-tracking security token of Tesla's stock allows retail investors to purchase a fraction of a Tesla share. Similar equity-tracking tokens that allow fractional investing could interest owners of many high-cost equities. They could also apply to other asset classes, such as art and commercial real estate, which are typically too expensive for the average retail investor. Such assets are only accessible via intermediaries, such as real estate investment trusts, implying intermediary fees and portfolio choices that may not be fully aligned with an investor's interests. Fractional ownership may overcome these issues. Further, such ownership may increase trading activity, thereby counteracting the negative effect of decreased liquidity in 24/7 markets.

Potentially Instantaneous Settlement. Although stock market exchanges can execute trades almost as rapidly as blockchain technologies (McKeon, 2018), settlement takes longer. For example, a settlement at the NYSE takes two business days. Blockchain technologies might substantially reduce settlement time. However, the settlement of stocks is more complex than that of ether (ETH) or bitcoin (BTC) transactions, as different parties and dependencies exist between those parties. Therefore, the extent to which smart contracts can automate the dependencies between the players may determine the eventual improvement in settlement speed, drastically reducing securities settlements from two days to a few minutes.

Cost Economics. Security tokens may significantly reduce the costs associated with ownership administration, potentially leading existing companies with traditional outstanding shares to convert those to security tokens. ANEXIO is a famous example engaged in a stock-to-token conversion (Shen, 2018). For instance, substantial ownership reconciliation costs are associated with creating capitalization (cap) tables for an acquisition. Tokenized securities could lead to instantaneous and automated cap tables created by code.

Market Depth. Many asset classes lack marketability due to contractual provisions or relative illiquidity due to thin markets. No matter the source of illiquidity, research finds that illiquid assets trade at a substantial discount (Albuquerque & Schroth, 2015; Bernardo, Momtaz, & Welch, 2021). Security tokenization may mitigate the problems associated with asset illiquidity. In his blog, McKeon (2018) explains that:

> Tokenized funds allow the fund managers to invest in illiquid assets without fear of redemptions, while fund investors can access liquidity in the secondary market. A deeper market for the ownership interests and increased investor liquidity are expected to be accompanied by an increase in value.

Compliance. Security tokenization could further reduce regulatory compliance burdens by integrating various dimensions associated with asset class, investor class, and federal and state-level contingencies into smart contracts. McKeon (2018) notes that regulators may even start requiring security tokenization to reduce frictions. He cites the case of the SEC requiring electronic corporate filings via the Electronic Data Gathering, Analysis, and Retrieval system (EDGAR) in 1996 when internet adoption was at similar levels as blockchain adoption is now.

Interoperability. Interoperability is at the core of technological advancement. Standards facilitate interoperability, and blockchain's decentralized nature helps generate network effects for adopting standards, which, in turn, further promotes interoperability. Interoperability is the reason blockchain is hyped in financial markets. McKeon (2018) makes the following observation:

> Let's take a moment to address the question every blockchain skeptic loves to ask: "Do we need a blockchain for this? Couldn't this be done with a database?" The answer is yes, some of it could be done with a centralized database, but it begs the question "why hasn't it already been done?" The answer is that the current centralized solutions for electronic value transfer lack compatibility – they don't talk to each other. I can't send value from PayPal to Venmo, or from E*TRADE to RealtyShares. These layers aren't interoperable.

The fundamental promise of security tokens is that all tokenized assets could be self- custodied on the same platform and in the same wallet, resulting in an integrated global pool of all asset classes. The liquid nature of such an integrated global pool of all asset classes could also result in reduced cash holdings as working capital, thus potentially reducing economy-wide frictions from inefficient resource usage. Despite the promise, several issues, such as scalability, cross-chain interoperability, and natural resource degradation (i.e., mainly energy to operate decentralized networks), need to be resolved for security tokenization to become a sustainable alternative to traditional financial market infrastructure.

The STO Process

The STO process resembles utility token offerings (Momtaz, 2020b) but with additional regulatory components and different time frames. Figure 5.1 describes the steps from startup formation to security token listing, with the estimated time horizons described in Lambert et al. (2021).

1. *Startup formation.* This step concerns shaping the startup idea, developing the business case, assembling a core team and advisors, sketching the fundraising process and capital needs, and summarizing it in a whitepaper.
2. *STO design.* This step involves setting the proper parameters for the STO, such as developing the token distribution structure and governance rights, selecting the jurisdiction, appointing financial and legal advisors to help with

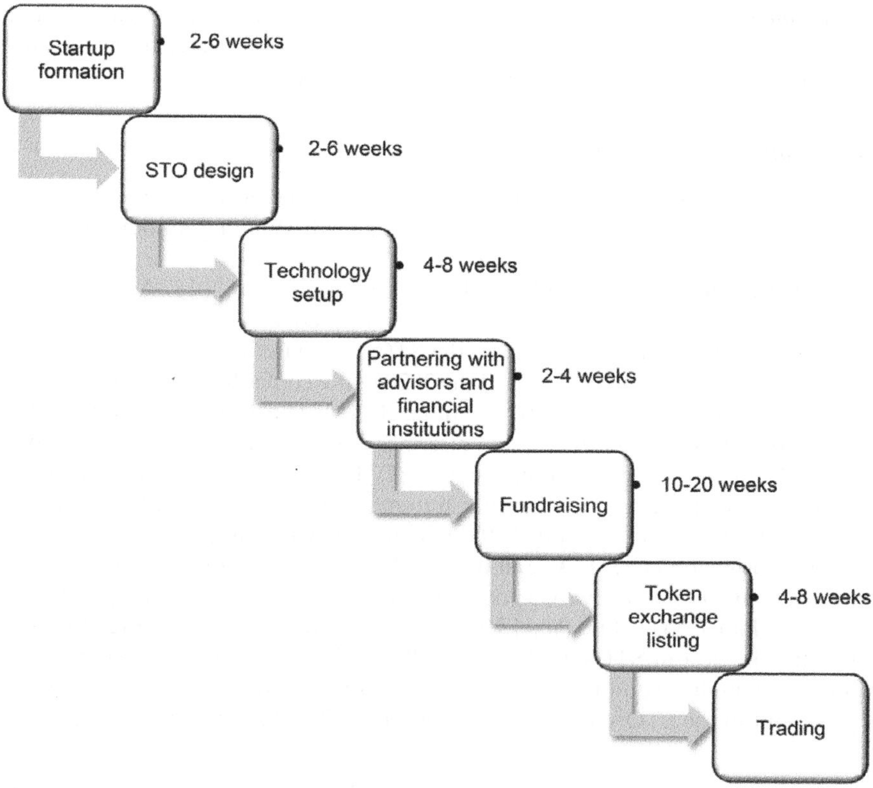

Figure 5.1. The STO Process. *Note*: This figure describes the steps from startup formation to security token listing with an estimated time horizon for each step. *Source*: Modified from Lambert et al. (2021).

the regulatory process and prepare required documents, such as a prospectus, and starting communication with the regulatory authority.

3. *Technology setup*. The third step focuses on the technological architecture, such as selecting the blockchain platform and coding the security tokens.
4. *Partnering with advisors and financial institutions*. This step requires coordinating with outside partners, such as security brokers and custodians.
5. *Fundraising*. This step is the actual STO, which takes longer than utility token offerings. Lambert et al. (2021) estimate that the typical STO takes 10–20 weeks. Reasons for this longer period are that investors require more time to review the prospectus and other offering documents. Additionally, many sophisticated investors need more traditional roadshow events.
6. *Token exchange listing*. This step establishes a liquid market for the security token by listing it on an exchange platform. The listing process for security tokens may also be longer than for utility tokens, with an estimated average of four to six weeks (Lambert et al., 2021).

7. *Trading*. The final step is trading the security token and the obligations that come with such trading, such as appointing a market maker to ensure sufficient liquidity and regulatory disclosure obligations.

Some Empirical Patterns

This section reviews token market activity, focusing on security, utility, and cryptocurrency tokens. It also examines differences in the funding amount in STOs vis-á-vis utility and cryptocurrency ICOs.

Market Evolution. The STO market gained traction in 2018. After the first five STOs in 2017, the following two years witnessed 71 and 107 STOs. Figure 5.2 illustrates the number of STOs by the STO start date. The 2017–2019 figures come from Lambert et al. (2021), and the 2020 figure comes from the Token Offerings Research Database (TORD) (Momtaz, 2021b). The 2020 figure for the STO market compares to 229 utility token offerings and 122 initial exchange offerings (IEOs). These numbers also come from the TORD. The STO market is also sizable in terms of the aggregate funding amount. Lambert et al. (2021) report that the 124 STOs between 2017 and 2019 raised an aggregate amount of $762 million.

Comparison of STOs, IEOs, and ICOs. How do STOs, IEOs, and ICOs compare? Here, ICOs are utility token offerings. Table 5.1 presents summary statistics for STOs (Panel A), IEOs (Panel B), and ICOs (Panel C). The average funding amount is highest in STOs, with $13.1 million, although the difference between IEOs ($12.6 million) and ICOs ($11.9 million) is not dramatic. The average funding amount in the STO sample of Lambert et al. (2021) is only $6.1 million. The

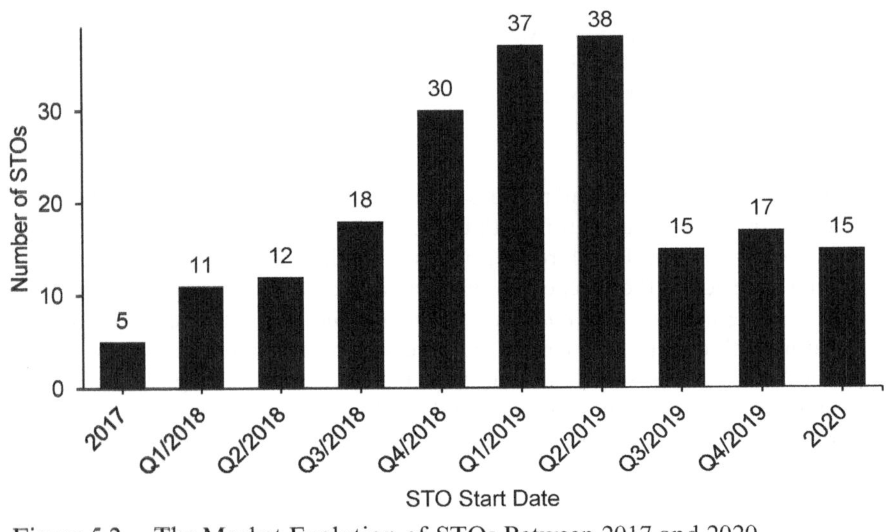

Figure 5.2. The Market Evolution of STOs Between 2017 and 2020.
Note: This figure illustrates the number of STOs by the STO start date. *Source*: The 2017–2019 figures come from Lambert et al. (2020) and the 2020 figure comes from the TORD.

fraction of distributed tokens is similar in STOs and ICOs (54 percent) and the lowest in IEOs (38 percent). This information indicates that token retention, often understood as a positive signal of firm quality (Leland & Pyle, 1977), is highest in IEOs.

The offering duration is a distinguishing feature of STOs, IEOs, and ICOs. The STO duration is the longest, plausibly reflecting the extra effort associated with regulatory compliance. STOs take an average of 113 days to complete, whereas IEOs and ICOs end on average after 45 and 70 days, respectively. Further, STOs and ICOs are equally likely to conduct a pre-sale (49 percent and 50 percent, respectively), while IEOs have fewer pre-sales (39 percent). Moreover, the project quality ratings of STOs and IEOs are similar, with ICO bench ratings of 3.32 and 3.28, respectively. These results are higher than the average rating in ICOs of 2.90. Finally, the average team size in STOs is slightly smaller (9.7) than in IEOs (10.2) and ICOs (10.8).

Table 5.1. A Comparison of Key Characteristics of STOs, IEOs, and ICOs.

N		**Mean**	**Standard Deviation**	**Q1**	**Q3**
Panel A. Security Token Offerings (STOs)					
Funding amount, in $ million	28	13.110	28.037	0.958	12.075
Fraction of distributed tokens	67	0.542	0.246	0.360	0.750
Offering duration, in days	83	113.422	218.066	32.000	115.500
Pre-sale (dummy)	89	0.494	0.503	0	1
Rating (1 = low, 5 = high)	13	3.315	0.836	3.000	3.800
# Team members, in # FTE	76	9.697	6.195	5.000	12.250
Panel B. Initial Exchange Offerings (IEOs)					
Funding amount, in $ million	141	12.628	84.446	0.576	5.240
Fraction of distributed tokens	369	0.384	0.239	0.200	0.600
Offering duration, in days	422	45.384	65.031	5.000	57.000
Pre-sale (dummy)	438	0.390	0.488	0	1
Rating (1 = low, 5 = high)	290	3.279	0.770	2.625	3.900

(*Continued*)

Table 5.1. (*Continued*)

	N	Mean	Standard Deviation	Q1	Q3
# Team members, in # FTE	331	10.190	7.375	5.000	14.000
Panel C. Initial Coin Offerings (ICOs)					
Funding amount, in $ million	2,000	11.934	45.082	1.000	12.503
Fraction of distributed tokens	4,508	0.541	0.211	0.400	0.700
Offering duration, in days	5,007	70.932	107.210	30.000	87.000
Pre-sale (dummy)	5,989	0.500	0.500	0	1
Rating (1 = low, 5 = high)	5,431	2.902	0.759	2.400	3.500
# Team members, in # FTE	4,298	10.780	7.259	5.000	15.000

Source: The data come from the TORD.

Notes: N = number of observations, FTE = full-time equivalent, and Q = quarter.

This table presents summary statistics for key variables by offering type. Specifically, Panels A, B, and C contain summary statistics for STOs, IEOs, and ICOs.

Amount Raised as a Proxy for Valuation. How do amounts raised differ in STOs, IEOs, and ICOs? This addition is relevant to the literature because Lambert et al. (2021) analyze STO success factors, but do not compare them to IEOs and ICOs. The present analysis adds to Lambert et al. (2021) as far as it compares the log funding amount (in $ million) across STOs, IEOs, and ICOs, not just within the STO sample. However, this analysis is more limited in terms of the scope of the control variables. Replicating all results reported in Table 5.2 is possible using Momtaz (2021b) TORD version 1 data available from https://www.paulmomtaz.com/data/tord.

Table 5.2 presents three separate regressions of the funding amount in $ million (log) on STO and IEO dummies. Model (1) controls only for the rating. Model (2) also controls for whether a pre-sale took place. Model (3) adds the number of team members as a control. The STO dummy is consistently negative across all models but only statistically significant at the 0.05 level in the third model. The IEO dummy is also consistently negative and statistically significant at the 0.01 level in all models. The models have ICOs as the base group. Therefore, the results suggest that both STOs and IEOs raise less relative to ICOs, conditional on the controls used in the regressions. Additional control variables could potentially change the results. Although this finding may be surprising, it plausibly reflects the trade-off between the benefits from certification in IEOs and investor protection in STOs and, on the other hand, lower compliance costs in ICOs. The negative STO and IEO dummies suggest that the regulatory compliance costs outweigh the various benefits of conducting STOs and IEOs in the sample.

For the other variables, the regression results suggest that (1) the project rating is statistically and economically positive, (2) the pre-sale dummy is statistically significantly negative, and (3) the number of team members is statistically significantly positive. These results are consistent with many empirical studies on ICOs (Adhami et al., 2018; An, Duan, Hou, & Xu, 2019; Ante & Fiedler, 2020; Bellavitis, Cumming, & Vanacker, 2020; Benedetti & Kostovetsky, 2021; Benedetti & Nikbakht, 2021; Boreiko & Sahdev, 2018; Boreiko & Vidusso, 2019; Drobetz, Momtaz, & Schröder, 2019; Fisch, 2019; Fisch & Momtaz, 2020; Giudici & Adhami, 2019; Howell et al., 2020; Lyandres, Palazzo, & Rabetti, 2019; Momtaz, 2020a, 2020c, 2021a; Perez, Sokolova, & Konate, 2020; Roosenboom, van der Kolk, & de Jong 2020).

Table 5.2. A Regression Analyses of the Amount Raised (Log in $ Million).

	Dependent Variable: Funding Amount, in Log $ Million		
	(1)	**(2)**	**(3)**
STO dummy	−1.256	−1.431	−2.960**
	(1.172)	(1.167)	(1.335)
IEO dummy	−0.748***	−0.759***	−0.877***
	(0.186)	(0.185)	(0.182)
Rating	0.471***	0.576***	0.254***
	(0.063)	(0.067)	(0.089)
Pre-sale		−0.438***	−0.319***
		(0.098)	(0.102)
# Team members			0.040***
			(0.007)
(Constant)	13.510***	13.403***	13.903***
	(0.205)	(0.205)	(0.272)
Observations	1,941	1,941	1,530
Adjusted R^2	0.033	0.042	0.053

Source: The data come from the TORD.

Notes: *, **, and *** indicate statistical significance at the 0.10, 0.05, and 0.01 levels, respectively. This table contains regression results for the amount raised (log, in $ millions) as the dependent variable. With ICOs as the base group, the STO and IEO dummies indicate the marginal effect on the amount raised associated with conducting an STO or IEO instead of an ICO, conditional on the control variables.

The Law of Security Tokens

This section focuses on US securities law and its application to tokens and STOs because SEC legislation has taken center stage in the academic and practical debate. The SEC regulation also serves as a blueprint for many other jurisdictions. This section draws on Mendelson's (2019) legal analysis.

Tokens as Investment Contracts

The Securities Act of 1933 (1933 Act) and the Securities Exchange Act of 1934 (1934 Act) are the legislative foundations for the nature of tokens and the regulation of token offerings. The 1933 Act regulates security issuances, while the 1934 Act regulates the subsequent trading of those securities. State-level blue sky laws are beyond the scope of this chapter. Paragraph 2(a)(1) of the 1933 Act provides a legal definition of what constitutes a security and includes the abstract term of an "investment contract."

The SEC claimed authority over token offerings by declaring STOs "investment contracts." A token classified as an investment contract requires registering its offering with the SEC unless specific exemptions apply.

The Devil's in the Details: The Howey Test

Determining whether a token qualifies as an investment contract and thus a security relies on the Howey test. It goes back to the 1946 US Supreme Court's decision in *SEC* v. *W.J. Howey Co*. A token passing the Howey test is a security. To pass the Howey test, the SEC uses four criteria (Momtaz, 2019, 2020b): (1) investment of money, (2) common enterprise, (3) profit expectation, and (4) efforts of others.

The SEC first applied the Howey test to tokens in the context of the Decentralized Autonomous Organization (DAO) hack. The SEC's investigation report is the "DAO 21A Report." The DAO was an autonomous, algorithm-operated company that raised $150 million from investors for DAO tokens. DAO used the tokens to fund novel startup projects. DAO investors could also resell them. Someone hacked the DAO and stole about one-third of investor funds. This incident led to an SEC investigation in which the SEC had to address whether tokens are subject to securities law. The SEC based its assessment on the Howey test, providing precedence for subsequent token status assessments. The investigation also provided initial guidance about applying the Howey test to token offerings. The SEC continues to refine these guidelines through further examinations of other tokenized projects.

Investment of Money. The first condition for a token to constitute a security is that investors must invest "money." The DAO investigation clarified that "money" does not necessarily refer to fiat currency. This view is relevant in the token context because many investors purchase tokens for other cryptocurrencies. As per *Majors* v. *South Carolina Securities Commission*, the critical condition is that whatever the contribution, it must put the investor at the risk of a financial loss. Therefore, token investors who risk a financial loss generally satisfy the first Howey condition.

Common Enterprise. The second Howey condition requires a common enterprise, typically given in the token context if a pooling of funds for investment purposes occurs. Mendelson (2019) discusses *Continental Marketing Corp.* v. *SEC* to point out that control is not strictly necessary for the typical enterprise condition. This ruling seems relevant as many tokenized projects rely on blockchain networks that provide investors with limited or no control. Therefore, Mendelson (2019, p. 75) concludes that "unless the underlying network for which the ICO is being held is purely a non-profit, open-source project, the common enterprise element is easily met."

Profit Expectation. The third Howey condition is the most critical parameter in practice. Profit expectation requires testing during a potential pre-sale and the actual offering. The distinction is important because the legal theories underlying the assessments differ.

For pre-sales, the SEC may revert to the "risk capital test," stipulating that affirmatively answering the profit expectation condition occurs if token investors' investment risk cannot be assumed to be fundamentally different in the pre-sale from the actual sale. For example, in *Silver Hills Country Club* v. *Sobieski*, the court ruled that the discounted sale of country club memberships at a soon-to-be-reopened establishment constitutes a security issuance. This ruling primarily occurred because potential membership benefits would only materialize if the construction would come to a successful end, no matter the name of the actual contract (i.e., "membership" in this case).

The SEC reverts to the "economic realities test for the actual token sale." This test focuses on whether a token is functional in its isolated network context only or whether its intrinsic value depends on the underlying startup's state and the ability of investors to trade it in liquid markets to realize profits of a potentially speculative nature. Although case law on the interpretation of the third Howey condition is still developing, Mendelson (2019, p. 79) summarizes helpful indications of when the SEC is likely to consider a token a security:

> If the motivation is focused more on investment, speculation, and creating a secondary market for token sales, rather than functional token use or "utility," it is likely that the token will be considered a security and subject to regulation. If the functional token sale is intended to build a market for the product and develop network participation, or in other words, to get people to use the tokens and thereby grow the network and demand for the digital products, it is less likely to be considered a security, taking on "kickstarter-like" characteristics. Whether the tokens appreciate in value due to scarcity, thus encouraging peer-to-peer, eBay-like trading, in and of itself should not affect this analysis. Whether the ICO is capped at a number of tokens or a dollar value may also have an impact on this analysis. [... A] token, in and of itself and based on its usage, may not constitute a security, but actively listing those tokens on an exchange creates a secondary market which may reverse the classification in the eyes of the SEC.

Efforts of Others. As Mendelson (2019, p. 80) notes, the final Howey condition assesses the "degree of managerial control over an enterprise," meaning the extent to which token investors may influence critical decisions related to allocating assets and other governance rights. The SEC is demanding, as it ruled in the DAO case that token investors' voting rights on DAO's investment decisions were insufficient. In principle, to negate the effort of others, token investors and miners may need to control the project's operations and the network's development and design.

Conducting STOs

If a token constitutes a security, issuers must register the token offering with the SEC unless a registration exemption applies. Regulations A, D, Crowdfunding, and S contain potential exemptions.

Regulation A. Regulation A is one of the options for small and medium-sized enterprises (SMEs) to sell securities without requiring SEC registration. Given that registration filings and fees are often associated with costs above \$1 million for legal and other advisors (Mendelson, 2019), foregoing registration can lower an essential barrier to acquiring growth financing. Regulation A allows SMEs to tap the pool of "unaccredited investors" subject to several restrictions. Unaccredited investors are those whose net worth is below \$1 million, excluding the value of their primary real estate, or net income of more than \$200,000 for singles and \$300,000 for married couples (SEC Rule 501, 17 CFR Paragraph 230.501, 2017).

The Jumpstart Our Business Startups Act (JOBS Act) amended Regulation A in 2021 concerning equity crowdfunding. All Regulation A offerings must be conducted on an equity crowdfunding platform or with an SEC-registered broker or dealer. The JOBS Act established two registration exemptions:

- *Tier 1.* Companies that raise up to \$20 million within 12 months are exempt from SEC registration but are not exempt from potential state-level requirements.
- *Tier 2.* Companies that raise up to \$50 million within 12 months are exempt from SEC registration and potential state-level requirements if they (1) have had their financial statements audited for at least the last two years, (2) file annual, semiannual, and event-related reports, and (3) do not raise more than 10 percent of each unaccredited investor's annual income or net worth per investor.

Regulation D. Private placements are also exempt from the registration requirement according to Section 4(a)(2) of the 1933 Act and Rules 504 and 506 of Regulation D. Bernardo et al. (2021) provide a more detailed discussion of private placement regulation.

- *Rule 504.* Private, non-reporting companies are exempt from the SEC registration requirement if they raise financing of not more than \$5 million via a private placement within 12 months while still subject to state-level requirements. Regulation D prohibits solicitation and advertising in Rule 504 placements, making it unattractive in the startup tokenization context.

- *Rule 506*. Companies raising any amount are exempt from the SEC registration requirement under Rule 506 if they do not raise financing from more than 35 unaccredited investors and disclose sufficient company and offering information to them. The number of accredited investors in Rule 506 placements is unlimited.

Both Rule 504 and 506 placements are subject to a one-year resale restriction.

In the token context, scholars and practitioners alike discuss the applicability of Rule 506(c) with some interest because it lifts the ban on solicitation and advertising. Filecoin is a prominent example that raised $257 million through a Rule 506 offering (Momtaz, 2020b).

Regulation Crowdfunding. Congress added Regulation Crowdfunding under Title III of the 2012 JOBS Act, coming into effect in May 2016. It requires conducting any financing on an SEC-registered crowdfunding portal. This legislation restricts campaigns to a maximum funding amount of $1.07 million within 12 months, with similar per-investor contribution restrictions as Regulation A.

Regulation S. Regulation S applies to offshore offerings. It relaxes registration requirements in the United States. However, it does not mean that laws in jurisdictions where projects are headquartered do not apply. Therefore, Regulation S offerings may be attractive for token offerings in low-tax jurisdictions, such as the Cayman Islands or the Isle of Man, to attract investors seeking US-regulated offerings.

Other Jurisdictions

Besides the United States, other jurisdictions have put forth regulatory frameworks for token offerings. Yet, others, such as China and South Korea, banned ICOs (Deng, Huang, & Wu, 2018).

Singapore. Singapore's regulation of token offerings is advanced. Security tokens fall under the Securities and Futures Act (SFA). STOs must be accompanied by a prospectus and registered with the MAS. Like the United States, exemptions to these requirements apply for STOs to accredited investors and/or institutional investors, for small-cap STOs not exceeding $5 million in any 12-months, or if the STO is a private placement to a group of not more than 50 investors over any 12-months.

The MAS also requires capital markets services licenses from token issuers or intermediaries and financial advisor's licenses under the Financial Advisors Act (FAA) from experts giving financial advice. It also requires token offering platforms to seek MAS's approval first. Further, the 2020 Payment Services Act (PS Act) requires businesses with cryptocurrency point-of-sales to obtain a specific license. The PS Act makes them subject to anti-money laundering and countering terrorism financing regulations.

The MAS partly claims extra-territorial jurisdiction. It has proclaimed that the SFA and FAA also apply to token exchange platforms outside Singapore and individuals abroad if they offer Singapore's citizens their activities.

Switzerland. The Swiss Financial Market Authority requires token issuers to legally assess their tokens themselves first. The assessment criteria resemble the "economic realities test" in the United States. Security tokens are subject to the Swiss Financial Market Infrastructure Act, the Stock Exchange Act, and the Stock Exchange Ordinance. These regulations also apply to "hybrid" tokens featuring some characteristics typical for security tokens and others typical for utility or cryptocurrency tokens, thus reflecting the ambiguous nature of many tokenized projects. Security and hybrid token offerings require a prospectus in compliance with the Swiss Code of Obligations.

The Swiss Banking Act can apply to debt-like tokens if investors contribute funds for a finite time horizon. Such a case requires a banking license from the issuer. The Collective Investment Schemes Act governs any form of intermediation. Anti-money laundering laws also apply to cryptocurrency tokens.

European Union. The European Commission declared that the European Securities and Markets Authority and the European Banking Authority have competencies to regulate token markets in the European Union (EU) when they published the Markets in Crypto-Assets Regulation in September 2020. Security tokens usually qualify as "financial instruments" according to the Markets in Financial Instruments Directive II, making them subject to several regulatory obligations, such as prospectus requirements. The EU grants its member states some discretion over applying and enforcing the rules. For example, member states may exempt STOs from the prospectus requirement if the issuance amount does not exceed EUR 8 million. Cryptocurrency tokens qualify as "electronic money" under the Payment Services Directive II, mandating issuers to obtain a license and meet other requirements, such as minimum capital, safeguarding, and consumer protection standards. Similarly, the Fifth Anti-Money Laundering Directive (5AMLD) mandates token exchange platforms to be registered, perform comprehensive know your customer processes, and monitor transactions to identify and report suspicious activities to the competent national authority.

United Kingdom. The Financial Conduct Authority (FCA) claimed jurisdiction over STOs in 2019. Security tokens are "specified investments" under the Regulated Activities Order. They are subject to a prospectus requirement, with a similar EUR 8 million exemption as in the EU that the FCA must review and approve. The FCA also must authorize STOs. Europe's 5AMLD has been transposed into British law and thus applies to cryptocurrency tokens. However, the FCA has not claimed jurisdiction over cryptocurrency and utility tokens.

The Technology of Security Tokens

The following section discusses security tokens from a technical perspective. That is, it characterizes security tokens as smart contracts. It also discusses the ERC-1400 technical standard for security tokens.

Security Tokens as Smart Contracts

Security tokens are, technically speaking, at the most basic level smart contracts. A *smart contract* automates contracting between two parties without a third (intermediary) party. At the most basic level, smart contracts have four stages (Subramanian, 2019): (1) rules, (2) events, (3) executables, and (4) settlement.

The following illustrates these stages with the example of a Simple Agreement for Future Equity (SAFE). In a SAFE, *rules* describe the triggering events, like financing, liquidity, and dissolution, and the determination of startup valuations and investor payments at these events. *Events*, such as financing, liquidity, and dissolution, trigger the execution of a smart contract. Events are not smart contract-immanent; they are exogenous. *Executables* are the steps that a smart contract takes to fulfill contractual obligations – if coded on Ethereum, then via the *Ethereum Virtual Machine*. Suppose a financing event occurs, and the SAFE investor wants to purchase equity. The smart contract would create additional equity tokens and send them to the investor's wallet. Suppose a liquidity event occurs, and the SAFE investor is entitled to a cash payment. The smart contract would contact a third party, such as a bank, to execute the cash transfer.

On-chain and off-chain settlements can be distinguished. The financing event that would trigger the transfer of equity tokens via the blockchain would typically be an *on-chain settlement*. In contrast, the liquidity event that would trigger a cash settlement would usually be an *off-chain settlement*. An external system, such as a bank system, is used to complete the execution.

The ERC-1400 Standard for STOs

ERC-1400 is the most prominent infrastructure for security tokens. It represents a library of standards on the Ethereum blockchain providing standard interfaces to operate security tokens by all relevant parties, including issuers, investors, and regulators. It includes standardized interfaces for issuing and redeeming security tokens, managing ownership and transfer restrictions, and informing token holders about their rights and balances.

ERC-1400 is open-source and made available by its authors – Adam Dossa, Pablo Ruiz, Fabian Vogelsteller, and Stephane Gosselin – at https://github.com/ethereum/EIPs/issues/1411. It is backward compatible with ERC-20, the most common standard for utility token offerings, and ERC-777, with advanced features extending ERC-20 to interact with a token. The suite contains the following four standards:

1. ERC-1594 (Core Security Token Standard) supports off-chain data injections into issuances, redemptions, transfers, and restriction checking and feedback via error messages. It also supports off-chain inputs and authorizations.
2. ERC-1410 attaches metadata to tokens, significantly increasing the functionality of security tokens, such as by defining lock-up periods.
3. ERC-1643 attaches documentation to tokens. It can apply to security token contracts, such as the mandatory offering prospectus. It also provides an interface to modify the documents *ex post*.
4. ERC-1644 enables forced token transfers, for example, if a regulator requires a reversed transaction in response to illicit activity.

Example: Binance

Crypto exchange platform Binance is among the leading players building an infrastructure for security tokens. Binance's approach is to track stock exchange-traded equity securities, such as *Tesla*. It allows investors to invest fractionally in these equity securities without any commission and with instant settlement during traditional exchange hours via the stablecoin Binance USD (BUSD).

Changpeng Zhao, Binance's chief executive officer (CEO), explains his vision of security-tracking digital tokens. According to Zhao (2021):

> Stock tokens demonstrate how we can democratize value transfer more seamlessly, reduce friction and costs to accessibility, without compromising on compliance or security. Through connecting traditional and crypto markets, we are building another technological bridge for a more inclusive financial future.

Binance still faces some regulatory concerns in the context of security-tracking digital tokens. In particular, the German financial market authority, BaFin, expressed a concern that Binance's security-tracking tokens may require a prospectus, which Binance currently does not offer.

Summary and Conclusions

This chapter reviews the emergent market for security tokens. It discusses the economics, law, and technology of security tokens and STOs. Security tokens are promising from an economic perspective. They enable automated and rapid settlement thanks to interoperability standards and higher market participation due to fractional ownership and potentially more liquid markets. Security tokens also offer higher market completeness due to the financial innovations expected from blockchain technology. The discussion of the economics of security tokens provides a basis for legislative efforts to reduce legal and commercial uncertainty around tokens and the required technological evolution of blockchain technology and token standards. This discussion is needed to address some remaining challenges to the pervasive adoption of security tokens across all industries.

Discussion Questions

1. Explain the difference between utility and security tokens.
2. List several advantages of security tokens over traditional securities.
3. Explain some regulatory challenges to the broader adoption of security tokens.
4. Explain the typical STO process.

References

Adhami, S., Giudici, G., & Martinazzi, S. (2018). Why do businesses go crypto? An empirical analysis of initial coin offerings. *Journal of Economics and Business*, *100*(C), 64–75.

Albuquerque, R., & Schroth, E. (2015). The value of control and the costs of illiquidity. *Journal of Finance*, *70*(4), 1405–1455.

An, J., Duan, T., Hou, W., & Xu, X. (2019). Initial coin offerings and entrepreneurial finance: The role of founders' characteristics. *Journal of Alternative Investments*, *21*(4), 26–40.

Ante, L., & Fiedler, I. (2020). Cheap signals in security token offerings (STOs). *Quantitative Finance and Economics*, *4*(4), 608–639.

Barclay, M. J., & Hendershott, T. (2004). Liquidity externalities and adverse selection: Evidence from trading after hours. *Journal of Finance*, *59*(2), 681–710.

Bellavitis, C., Cumming, D., & Vanacker, T. (2020, August 24). Ban, boom, and echo! Entrepreneurship and initial coin offerings. *Entrepreneurship Theory and Practice*, 104225872094011 4. https://doi.org/10.1177/1042258720940114

Benedetti, H., & Kostovetsky, L. (2021). Digital tulips? Returns to investors in initial coin offerings. *Journal of Corporate Finance*, *66*(C), 101786.

Benedetti, H., & Nikbakht, E. (2021). Returns and network growth of digital tokens after cross-listings. *Journal of Corporate Finance*, *66*(2), 101853.

Bernardo, A., Momtaz, P. P., & Welch, I. (2021). *The discount for lack of marketability in private investments in public equity*. Working Paper, University of California, Los Angeles.

Boreiko, D., & Sahdev, N. K. (2018, July 6). To ICO or Not to ICO – Empirical analysis of initial coin offerings and token sales. Retrieved from https://papers.ssrn.com/sol3/Papers.cfm?abstract_id=3209180

Boreiko, D., & Vidusso, G. (2019). New blockchain intermediaries: Do ICO rating websites do their job well? *Journal of Alternative Investments*, *21*(4), 67–79.

Deng, H., Huang, R. H., & Wu, Q. (2018). The regulation of initial coin offerings in China: Problems, prognoses and prospects. *European Business Organization Law Review*, *19*(3), 465–502.

Drobetz, W., Momtaz, P. P., & Schröder, H. (2019). Investor sentiment and initial coin offerings. *Journal of Alternative Investments*, *21*(4), 41–55.

Fisch, C. (2019). Initial coin offerings (ICOS) to finance new ventures. *Journal of Business Venturing*, *34*(1), 1–22.

Fisch, C., & Momtaz, P. P. (2020). Institutional investors and post-ICO performance: An empirical analysis of investor returns in initial coin offerings (ICOS). *Journal of Corporate Finance*, *64*(C), 101679.

Giudici, G., & Adhami, S. (2019). The impact of governance signals on ICO fundraising success. *Journal of Industrial and Business Economics*, *46*(2), 283–312.

Howell, S. T., Niessner, M., & Yermack, D. (2020). Initial coin offerings: Financing growth with cryptocurrency token sales. *Review of Financial Studies*, *33*(9), 3925–3974.

Lambert, T., Liebau, D., & Roosenboom, P. (2021). Security token offerings. *Small Business Economics*, *59*(1), 299–325. Retrieved from https://link.springer.com/content/pdf/10.1007/s11187-021-00539-9.pdf

Leland, H. E., & Pyle, D. H. (1977). Informational asymmetries, financial structure, and financial intermediation. *Journal of Finance*, *32*(2), 371–387.

Lyandres, E., Palazzo, B., & Rabetti, D. (2019). Do tokens behave like securities? An anatomy of initial coin offerings. Retrieved from https://papers.ssrn.com/sol3/papers.cfm?abstract_id=3287583

McKeon, S. (2018). The security token thesis. *Hackernoon*, May 22. Retrieved from https://hackernoon.com/the-security-token-thesis-4c5904761063

Mendelson, M. (2019). From initial coin offerings to security tokens: A U.S. federal securities law analysis. *Stanford Technology Law Review*, *22*, 52–94. Retrieved from https://law.stanford.edu/wp-content/uploads/2019/01/Mendelson_20180129.pdf

Momtaz, P. P. (2019). Token sales and initial coin offerings: Introduction. *Journal of Alternative Investments*, *21*(4), 7–12.

Momtaz, P. P. (2020a). Entrepreneurial finance and moral hazard: Evidence from token offerings. *Journal of Business Venturing*, *36*(5), 1–26.

Momtaz, P. P. (2020b). Initial coin offerings. *Plos One*, *15*(5), e0233018. Retrieved from https://journals.plos.org/plosone/article?id=10.1371/journal.pone.0233018

Momtaz, P. P. (2020c). Initial coin offerings, asymmetric information, and loyal CEOs. *Small Business Economics*, *57*(2), 975–997.

Momtaz, P. P. (2021a). CEO emotions and firm valuation in initial coin offerings: An artificial emotional intelligence approach. *Strategic Management Journal*, *42*(3), 558–578.

Momtaz, P. P. (2021b, June). Token offerings research database (TORD). Retrieved from https://www.paulmomtaz.com/data/tord

Perez, C., Sokolova, K., & Konate, M. (2020). Digital social capital and performance of initial coin offerings. *Technological Forecasting and Social Change*, *152*(March), 119888.

Roosenboom, P., van der Kolk, T., & de Jong, A. (2020). What determines success in initial coin offerings? *Venture Capital*, *22*(2), 161–183.

Shen, L. (2018). This firm just turned a company's stock into cryptocurrency. *Fortune*, May 18. Retrieved from https://fortune.com/2018/05/18/ico-coin-cryptocurrency-tokenization/

Subramanian, H. (2019). Security tokens: Architecture, smart contract applications and illustrations using SAFE. *Managerial Finance*, *46*(6), 735–748.

Zhao, C. (2021, April). Crypto exchange Binance launches tradable stock tokens, starts with Tesla. Retrieved from https://www.rt.com/business/520789-binance-stock-tokens-tesla/

Chapter 6

Utility Tokens

Hugo Benedetti, Christian Caceres and Luis Álvaro Abarzúa

Abstract

Utility tokens are digital currencies that serve as the only accepted means of payment for services and products provided through a blockchain-based platform. They finance the development of their product or service, reward and incentivize early adopters and network promoters, align economic incentives between supply, demand, and the marketplace, and enhance network effects among all participants. Their tokenomic design consists of the rules and regulations governing a token's issuance, distribution, allocation, and potential destruction. The chapter describes utility tokens, compares them with other types of cryptoassets, and discusses their value creation process and role in network economics. It also reviews common tokenomic designs, discusses different regulatory approaches, and provides examples of current utility token applications in decentralized applications such as decentralized finance and virtual reality platforms (metaverses).

Keywords: Cryptoassets; utility tokens; network effects; tokenomics; decentralized finance; metaverse

Introduction

An unknown person or group of people using Satoshi Nakamoto introduced bitcoin as the first cryptocurrency in 2008 (Nakamoto, 2008). Its purpose was to serve as open access, peer-to-peer (P2P), decentralized, and censorship-resistant digital currency. Several thousand cryptocurrencies are available using different configurations regarding transaction speed, data encryption mechanisms, validation process, degree of decentralization, transparency, and consensus algorithms (Blandin et al., 2020; Hileman & Rauchs, 2017). Despite these many variations,

The Emerald Handbook on Cryptoassets: Investment Opportunities and Challenges, 79–92

doi:10.1108/978-1-80455-320-620221006

all seek to provide the three roles commonly fulfilled by traditional currencies: to function as a medium of exchange, a unit of account, and a store of value.

The ability of bitcoin and cryptocurrencies to accomplish these roles has been widely criticized due to their lack of intrinsic value, price volatility, limited widespread adoption, presence of bubbles, potential price manipulation, and linkages to money laundering and crime (Atici, 2018; Baur & Dimpfl, 2021; Foley, Karlsen, & Putnins, 2019; Gandal, Hamrick, Moore, & Oberman, 2018; Griffin & Shams, 2020; Hazlett & Luther, 2020; Roubini & Byrne, 2018; Yermack, 2015). Users accept bitcoin and cryptocurrencies as a medium of exchange by freely and independently choosing to do so, but cryptocurrencies lack an intrinsic or fundamental value (Baur, Hong, & Lee, 2018).

Utility tokens are different. Besides users being able to use them as cryptocurrencies, they provide consumptive rights on services and products through a blockchain-based platform (Lambert, Liebau, & Roosenboom, 2021). For instance, the blockchain Ethereum (Buterin, 2013) incorporates its native utility token called ether. Users must pay ether to execute smart contracts (Fries & Paal, 2019; Szabo, 1996), which are pieces of code programmed on the Ethereum blockchain, such as creating new tokens, receiving funds, book building before the sale, executing the sale process, distributing tokens, applying restrictions or conditions on token transfers, among many others. Although ether and any blockchain-based asset can be used as a cryptocurrency, its primary purpose is to provide consumptive rights on executing programs in the Ethereum blockchain. Therefore, ether's intrinsic value is linked to the value of services offered by the Ethereum blockchain.

The consumptive rights granted by a utility token vary according to the different business models implemented by blockchain projects. In some instances, projects allow users and providers to freely determine the number of tokens required for a specific service, such as the number of tokens needed to store a gigabyte of data on a decentralized network for one month. Others have a predetermined amount of tokens for the service or a mixture containing a predetermined baseline plus an additional variable cost. Ethereum charges a marginally increasing transaction fee ("gas fee") determined by the amount of data required to process a transaction. Ethereum also allows users to include a priority fee on top of the base gas fee to increase the probability of a faster transaction.

Utility tokens are central to the functioning of a blockchain ecosystem. Additionally, the *tokenomic design* contains the rules and regulations that control their usage, issuance, distribution, allocation, and potential destruction. The tokenomic design's objective is to allow the token to enhance economic growth within the token issuer's ecosystem. Utility token issuers are usually subject to *network economics*, where the value received by network participants increases as the number of network participants increases (Benedetti & Nikbakht, 2021). The existence of network economics provides issuers with the opportunity to use token issuance and distribution as a mechanism to enhance network effects.

Regulating utility tokens has proven difficult. Many token issuers take precautions not to distribute tokens to parties under the jurisdiction of countries without clear rules and regulations. Given that a utility token can also be used as a cryptocurrency and, in some cases, grant users power over the issuer's business decisions, certain jurisdictions may consider a utility token as a security, others as a digital currency, and others as a utility token. Most regulations describe utility tokens by exclusion. A token is a utility token if it does not fall under the definition of other types of tokens or digital financial instruments. Under UK regulation, the Financial Conduct Authority (FCA) (2019, p. 14) defines utility tokens as "any token that does not meet the definition of e-money or provide the same rights as other specified investments under the Regulated Activities Order (RAO)." In Switzerland, the Swiss Financial Market Supervisory Authority (FINMA) (2018, p. 3) classifies utility tokens as "tokens which are intended to provide access digitally to an application or service by means of a blockchain-based infrastructure" and does not consider them securities. However, it recognizes that some utility tokens might also be a security if they grant access rights and connections with capital markets or provide an investment function. In France, Ministre de l'Economie et Finance (2019) regulates initial coin offerings (ICOs) of utility tokens, defined as intangible digital assets that may be issued, registered, stored, or transferred using a distributed ledger technology and do not qualify as financial instruments. The United States still lacks specific regulations defining utility tokens. Nevertheless, the Token Taxonomy Act of 2019 (United States Congress, 2019) proposes a definition for digital tokens and the characteristics required for them not to be considered a security.

Utility tokens enable different use cases, functions, tokenomic designs, and organizational models. There are simple models such as Filecoin (Protocol Labs, 2017), a decentralized storage network that uses its native token (Filecoin) to compensate storage providers and charge users for data storage. Another is Mana (Ordano, Meilich, Jardi, & Araoz, 2017), the native token used as the internal currency in all transactions of the Decentraland *metaverse,* a virtual world platform. More recently, ALEX (Automated Liquid Exchange, 2021), a decentralized finance (DeFi) platform, implemented a dual-token design, with one token (Alex) being freely tradable and transferable among users and another (APower) being neither non-tradable nor transferable. Alex serves as the monetary unit in the ecosystem, while APower grants access to specific DeFi instruments such as initial DEX offerings (IDOs), where *DEX* means decentralized exchange.

Utility tokens and their tokenomic design can also evolve and adjust to the changing needs of the ecosystem. Ether is a clear example (Buterin, 2013). Designers intended it to be the only means of payment for transaction processing on the Ethereum blockchain. Some also use ether as a cryptocurrency, given the widespread adoption of the Ethereum blockchain and the hundreds of thousands of applications built on its platform. The protocol has evolved to include a priority fee to increase the probability of faster processing and a burning rate that destroys a percentage of the transaction fee to reduce the overall token supply. It involves implementing a new mining mechanism based on token ether reserves instead of the current computation-intense mechanism. Although ether began with a simple tokenomic design based on linear issuance to miners, it has evolved into a more complex mechanism.

The chapter proceeds by developing the concept of utility tokens and their role in platform development. Next, it reviews the different tokenomic design components and mechanisms. The chapter then provides a brief overview of the regulatory approach taken by different jurisdictions and a set of utility token implementation examples. The final section offers a summary and conclusions.

Utility Tokens

Tokens are digital units of account issued on a blockchain-based platform. They are key elements in any blockchain ecosystem, as they provide the operational foundation for any transaction. Tokens consist of different categories according to their designed purpose and underlying applications. Although no universal definition is available, commonly accepted types include cryptocurrencies, utility tokens, security tokens, and tokenized assets and securities.

- *Cryptocurrencies* are digital units of account issued on a blockchain-based platform to provide open access, P2P, decentralized, and censorship-resistant functions commonly attributed to traditional currencies, such as serving as a medium of exchange, a unit of account, and a store of value.
- *Utility tokens* are digital units granting consumptive rights to services and products through a blockchain-based platform.
- *Security tokens* are blockchain-based instruments subject to existing securities law.
- *Tokenized assets and securities* are blockchain-based digital representations of assets and securities outside the blockchain infrastructure. As token functionalities and applications evolve and the use cases developed by network participants, a token can change categories or be classified in more than one category simultaneously.

Stablecoins follow a different classification dimension. They are tokens used as a means of payment consisting of cryptocurrencies, security tokens, or tokenized assets, depending on their underlying price stabilization mechanisms and reserves.

Like cryptocurrencies, utility tokens serve as a means of payment, a unit of account, and a store of value. However, their fundamental difference involves their creation for a specific use case. Utility tokens intend to enhance the value creation process of the issuers' ecosystem. As an analogy, utility tokens are merchant pre-paid cards. Pre-paid cards are tailored to an issuer's needs, such as a commercial retail chain. They are meant to be used within the issuer ecosystem, like physical stores, online stores, and affiliates. Users can create a secondary market for those pre-paid cards. If based on a common payment platform such as Visa or Mastercard, other merchants could also accept them as means of payment.

Still, utility tokens present many differences from pre-paid cards. Pre-paid cards are denominated in a specific monetary currency with a known value and redeemable for goods and services. Those goods and services can also be redeemed or paid for using the base monetary currency. In the case of utility tokens, no base monetary currency exists other than the token itself, which has a variable value. There is no certainty on the number of goods and services for which it can be redeemed. Moreover, the goods and services provided by the issuer's platform cannot be purchased using any other means of payment. Consequently, the issuer's platform is a closed payment system, accepting solely the issuers' token. The utility token is an open means of payment, allowing other platforms and consumers to use it if preferred. The latter feature enables utility tokens to be used as cryptocurrencies.

One reason projects choose to issue utility tokens, as opposed to adopting an existing cryptocurrency or utility, is to create an alternative source of early-stage funding (Adhami, Giudici, & Martinazzi, 2018; Bellavitis, Cumming, & Vanacker, 2020; Benedetti & Kostovetsky, 2021; Fisch, 2019; Momtaz, 2019, 2020). This mechanism is similar to crowdfunding but with global access, lower issuance cost, and fewer regulatory, legal, and operational constraints.

Another critical aspect of a project's long-term prospects is a token's programming capability, allowing issuers to design and tailor a token's technical and operational features to the platform's requirements. Technical features include transaction speed and size, level of transparency regarding transaction information, validation of user credentials such as know-your-customer requirements, compatibility with other blockchain applications, and compatibility with external non-blockchain applications. Operational features relate to a token's potential uses and the mechanics of its issuance, distribution, allocation, and possible destruction. The operational characteristics are often called *tokenomic design*, explored in detail in the following section.

Tokenomic Design

The *tokenomic design* contains the rules and regulations controlling a token's usage, issuance, distribution, allocation, and potential destruction. Its main objective is to enhance value creation within the token issuer's ecosystem. The cornerstone of the tokenomic design relates to allocating and distributing tokens across different stakeholders and through time. In addition, it controls the mechanisms for usage, rewards, penalties, destruction, and reallocation of tokens.

Utility tokens are frequently used as an early-stage funding mechanism. Thousands of projects have sold and distributed utility tokens through processes such as ICOs, initial exchange offerings (IEOs), and IDOs. During an ICO, the issuer sells tokens to a crowd of early adopters and investors using blockchain infrastructure, commonly without intermediaries (Adhami et al., 2018; Bellavitis, Cumming, & Vanacker, 2020; Benedetti & Kostovetsky, 2021; Fisch, 2019; Momtaz, 2019, 2020). An IEO is conducted through a cryptocurrency exchange platform that acts as a listing agent and can provide vetting services to the listed token and the potential investors. Lastly, an IDO is conducted on a DEX platform, which may or may not perform a decentralized vetting of the token and potential investors. Decentralized vetting usually takes the form of users voting on a token's quality and the conditions required for investor participation.

Besides token sales as a fundraising mechanism, token issuers frequently distribute tokens for free to foster network growth. Common distribution activities include social media contests requiring project mentions on tweets, blog posts, friend invites, and forum interaction. Other activities include token *faucets,* smart contracts that randomly send tokens to blockchain addresses that interact with them; *airdrops* that send tokens to all addresses in a network; and targeted *rewards* to users of partner projects and applications such as centralized exchanges, wallets, or custodians.

Utility tokens can also be distributed to project contributors as payment for services provided, including the founding team, advisors, promoters, influencers, and providers. Tokens distributed in this category are usually subject to a vesting schedule and a lock-up period. During the lock-up, the token owner cannot transfer the token to a third party but can commonly "stake" it in the platform and receive additional token rewards.

Staking programs are another mechanism for token distribution. Token issuers create smart contracts that allow users to deposit tokens for a period and receive additional tokens as a reward. When users deposit the issuer's token, it refers to *staking*. However, when users deposit a different token, such as a cryptocurrency, it is typically called *farming*.

Drains and burning determine how utility tokens are eliminated from the ecosystem. *Drains* are the activities that reduce tokens, while *burning* is the actual process of elimination. For example, a common drain in DeFi applications is participating in an IEO/IDO. To participate, users and investors must pay using a utility token. Instead of transferring the token to the application, it is burnt, thus reducing the total supply of tokens in the ecosystem. Burning consists of sending tokens to a cryptographically *unavailable blockchain address*, an address that cannot perform transfers, rendering unusable any tokens deposited to the account.

Investors also play a fundamental role in tokenomic design. According to Cong, Li, and Wang (2021), early adopters can function as investors, purchasing utility tokens before they are usable or the network is fully developed, expecting to capture part of the value creation. Such value can be captured by purchasing tokens at a price lower than their expected future value, intending to use the token as designed, or potentially selling it in secondary markets.

A project's tokenomics design also determines the allocation of value creation. Some projects are fully decentralized and open-source, with free entry of users and providers and no intermediation by the platform. In this setting, transactions are P2P, and the user transfers a token's full value to the provider. Other projects function as intermediaries and collect a fee on each transaction. Therefore, the platform captures part of the value and the provider the rest. Projects including drain and burning mechanisms reduce total token supply, potentially increasing each token's expected value and distributing value creation across all token holders.

The goal of decentralization and reduction of token concentration is usually present in the distribution and allocation mechanisms. This goal goes beyond fostering network growth and enhancing network effects by explicitly targeting the creation of a broad token holder base and limiting the ability of single entities to control a large portion of the circulating token supply. A large and fragmented token holder ecosystem can potentially limit the impact of token hoarding and dumping by large investors on the issuer's internal ecosystem market and the secondary trading market, disrupting and increasing a token design management's complexity.

Lastly, projects can implement different tokenomic designs over time, replace them, or include new mechanisms according to the ecosystem's needs. A token's characteristics and features are programmed in the blockchain protocol and can be modified according to that protocol's rules.

Forms of Utility Token Regulation

The flexibility granted by tokenomic design to utility tokens regarding potential use cases, features, attributes, and functions has resulted in a challenging regulatory environment. As of April 2022, there is no widely accepted classification methodology for cryptoassets, with different jurisdictions proposing and implementing their classifications and the applicable regulation. Due to inconsistencies among regulations, the same token can be considered a utility token, security token, digital currency, or digital asset, depending on the jurisdiction. Token issuers have avoided jurisdictions without clear definitions and regulations, limiting their network growth and preventing users and investors from participating. The following subsections provide examples of utility token definitions and the applicable regulation across jurisdictions.

United Kingdom

In January 2019, the FCA published "Guidance on Cryptoassets" (Financial Conduct Authority, 2019), establishing a reference framework for digital asset transactions. The report defines digital tokens as follows:

- *Exchange tokens.* These tokens serve as a medium of exchange and lack backing from any central authority. They are usually a decentralized instrument to buy or sell goods and services without involving traditional intermediaries, such as commercial banks. Buying and selling exchange tokens is not subject to FCA supervision. The FCA states that this type of token neither constitutes legal tender in the United Kingdom nor is it considered money, even when used for similar purposes. The FCA also highlights that even if a user acquires a token for financial speculation or obtains a gain from an increase in its value, this fact is insufficient to be considered a security. Therefore, exchange tokens are not subject to FCA's authority.
- *Security tokens.* These investment instruments bestow some or all the rights conferred to shareholders or holders of debt securities. Security tokens also refer to a device that grants an ownership position within an entity, creditor status, or other ownership or dividend rights. They grant certain rights usually associated with traditional securities and are classified accordingly.
- *Utility tokens.* These tokens grant holders a right of access to a current or future good or service. They do not meet the definition of e-money or provide the same rights as other specified investments under the Regulated Activities Order (RAO).

Switzerland

Swiss Financial Market Supervisory Authority (FINMA) (2018) provides guidelines related to the regulatory framework for issuing ICOs and defines the following classification of tokens:

- *Asset tokens* represent assets such as a credit or a right on the issuer's capital. For example, they denote a share in a company's future dividends. Tokens that allow trading physical assets on a blockchain also fall into this category. Under this modality, the investment or speculative purpose predominates. Unlike a payment token, asset tokens represent tangible physical assets off-chain.
- *Utility tokens* grant their holder a right to access a digital service or application provided by the blockchain. Depending on their form, they could be compared to vouchers for contractual services owed. Like asset tokens, utility tokens are based on a contractual relationship. They cannot be considered securities, unlike asset tokens. The issuer's purpose is primarily to raise funds, and the buyer's purpose is to invest in a project or speculate on the opportunity. For this reason, utility tokens are under the control of the stock exchange authority.
- *Payment tokens* serve as a means of payment to acquire goods or services without the purpose of investment or speculation.
- *Hybrid tokens* share characteristics common to asset and utility tokens. In such a case, the token may be required to comply with regulations as an asset and utility token.

France

The PACTE LAW (Ministre de l'Economie et Finance, 2019), implemented in May 2019, introduced a specific regulation for token issuers, ICOs, digital asset service providers, and targeted tax considerations for digital assets. The definition of digital assets describes two subcategories: utility tokens and cryptocurrencies.

- *Utility tokens* are intangible assets representing in digital form rights that may be issued, recorded, stored, or transferred digitally, enabling an owner's direct or indirect identification, and do not qualify as financial instruments.
- *Cryptocurrencies* are digital representations of value not issued or guaranteed by a central bank or public authority, not necessarily attached to a legal tender. They lack money's legal status but are accepted as a means of exchange and can be transferred, stored, or exchanged electronically.

United States

Legislators introduced the Token Taxonomy Act of 2019 (United States Congress, 2019) before the US Congress in April 2019 but still needed approval as of March 2022. The standard introduces the concept of digital tokens and their defining characteristics, highlighting their decentralized, censorship-resistant, and P2P transaction properties. According to the proposed taxonomy, digital tokens cannot represent a financial interest in a business or partnership, including ownership or revenue-sharing interest, and establishes that digital tokens are not securities under the Securities Act of 1933 and 1934.

The taxonomy also defines *digital currencies* as a digital representation of value used as a medium of exchange. According to Section 988 of the Internal Revenue Code, these currencies are not money. The bill also provides a tax exemption for exchanging digital currencies and establishes a non-taxable minimum for gains from the sale of digital currencies.

Examples of Utility Token Implementations

The following section presents examples of utility token implementations, describing the issuer's project, the rationale for using utility tokens, and the most relevant aspects of their tokenomic design. It begins with more straightforward implementations, such as the Filecoin blockchain and the Decentraland metaverse and their respective tokens, Filecoin and Mana. Following these examples are a more advanced dual-token implementation of Alex and APower, from the DeFi platform ALEX. Lastly, the section explores the evolution of ether, the native token of the Ethereum blockchain.

Filecoin

Filecoin is a decentralized storage network, managed using a blockchain marketplace and a native token, also named Filecoin (Protocol Labs, 2017). The cloud-based network rewards miners using Filecoin according to the active storage they provide to the network. Users pay for decentralized storage using Filecoin tokens purchased on the secondary market.

The token serves as an incentive and balancer in the ecosystem. As demand for decentralized, censorship-resistant, and encrypted data storage increases, Filecoin's price also increases, leading to higher income for miners and incentivizing storage capacity growth. If an excess supply of storage capacity occurs, rewards to miners do not compensate for their capacity contribution, leading to a decrease in supply.

The company conducted an ICO in August 2017, reaching over $200 million in public token sales and a private round of over $50 million. The project raised $257 million, becoming the largest ICO. The issuer used the ICO's proceeds to finance the project's development and launch. In August 2020, the issuer officially launched its blockchain after three years of development. Within two months from launch, the project's market valuation reached over $1 billion and continued to increase to an all-time high of $12.3 billion by April 2021. By March 2022, the market value had dropped to $2.3 billion.

Decentraland

Decentraland is a decentralized, shared virtual reality platform with a tokenomic design built on the Ethereum blockchain (Ordano et al., 2017). The project consists of a decentralized ledger for land ownership, a protocol for describing the contents and attributes of each land parcel, and a P2P network for user interactions, including monetary transactions.

The infrastructure allows the construction of a community-owned and developed virtual reality. This reality includes virtual land, goods, services, digital representations of users (*avatars*), and any programmable function or interaction. The native token, Mana, is the ecosystem's exclusive means of payment. A different type of token, a non-fungible token (NFT), represents virtual land. *NFTs* are tokens that uniquely identify an item, such as an image, a document, or a virtual plot. Mana is used for purchasing land NFTs, which grant the owner the right to design and create virtual environments on its virtual real estate.

The project launched an ICO in 2017, which sold out in 35 seconds and raised $24 million (Parker, 2017). The project retained 60 percent of the token issuance as a treasury to fund future developments. In 2020, after three years of development, Decentraland initiated the sale of virtual real estate NFTs, and its market cap hovered around $100 billion. In November 2021, a virtual plot sold for $2.3 million (Howcroft, 2021), and the market capitalization of Mana reached over $10 billion. By March 2022, it had fallen to around $4 billion.

ALEX

ALEX is a DeFi platform built on Stacks, a programmable blockchain secured by bitcoin (Automated Liquid Exchange, 2021). ALEX provides a comprehensive set of services based on blockchain financial infrastructures, such as a launchpad for early-stage projects in an initial decentralized offering platform, a decentralized token exchange, decentralized collateralized borrowing/lending mechanisms, and yield investing instruments. The project's innovation resides in a dual-token system. One tradeable utility token (Alex) serves as a monetary unit in the ecosystem, and another non-tradeable (APower) provides access to special features.

Alex's tokenomic design included an IDO conducted in the ALEX launchpad, a treasury to finance future developments and partnerships, team allocations, and a public reward issuance. The public supply of both tokens follows a predetermined schedule. It is distributed to users who contribute to the ecosystem by locking up Alex tokens (*staking*) or providing liquidity to the protocol's automated market maker pools (*farming*). Those receiving Alex tokens as a reward can trade them in the protocol's DEX for other tokens, *staked*, re-invested as liquidity, or saved to participate in future IDOs. Holders of the non-transferable APower token can only use them to participate in IDOs, in combination with the tradable Alex token.

The rationale behind the non-transferable token is to increase and reward retail investor and user participation. As the APower token is not transferable, someone can only receive this token directly from the protocol as a reward. It is unavailable in the secondary market. Therefore, only users who contribute to the ecosystem have access to it. This situation implies that only those users will have access to IDOs launched on the platform, creating an additional incentive to participate in the network. Lastly, ALEX set up a lottery-based IDO process, requiring users to burn an increasing amount of APower tokens in exchange for IDO lottery tickets. The more tokens a user purchases, the higher the marginal burn of APower per ticket. This process prevents large investors from dominating the IDO process, providing more participation from retail investors, and contributing to a more decentralized token distribution.

Ethereum

The Ethereum blockchain allows coding and executing any type of computation, including infinite loops and conditional functions. It enables developing blockchain-run applications such as financial instruments, smart property records, DEXs, P2P trading, gambling, identity, and reputation management, among many others (Buterin, 2013).

Ether is the native utility token of the Ethereum blockchain, the only means of payment for transaction processing on its blockchain. Another use of ether is as a cryptocurrency, given the widespread adoption of the Ethereum blockchain and the hundreds of thousands of applications built on its platform. According to the website www.coinmarketcap.com, at the end of March 2022, ether was the second most valuable cryptoasset by market capitalization, valued at over $400 billion; and the third most traded, with an average daily volume of $17 billion.

Ether is a *mined* token, meaning that it is continuously issued and distributed to *miners*. A *miner is* a contributor who processes and stores the transactions conducted in the Ethereum blockchain. It was *pre-mined*, with an initial number of tokens assigned to investors, early contributors, developers, and research projects. An ICO sold part of the pre-mined tokens. Ethereum's creators designed transaction fees to be a fixed factor of the amount of processing a transaction or program required. Together with mining rewards, such fees compensate miners for their contributions. The protocol has evolved to include a priority fee to increase the probability of faster processing and a burning rate, which destroys a percentage of the transaction fee to reduce the overall token supply. Ethereum plans to implement a new mining mechanism based on token ether reserves instead of the current computation-intense mechanism.

Summary and Conclusions

This chapter explores the concept of utility tokens, their relevant features and functionalities usually contained in the tokenomic design, some regulatory approaches to utility tokens, and examples of utility token applications. Utility tokens are cryptoassets that provide consumptive rights on services and products through a blockchain-based platform. They allow projects to finance the development of their product or service, reward and incentivize early adopters and network promoters, align economic incentives among supply, demand, and the marketplace, and enhance network effects among all participants. Although commonly compared to cryptocurrencies, utility tokens have distinct features, primarily involving usage and tailoring to a specific use case. These features relate to technical and operational elements. The technical elements involve processing capacity and speed, configuration mechanisms, interaction, compatibility with blockchain, and non-blockchain applications. The operational elements commonly refer to a project's tokenomic design and include details about a token's usage, issuance, allocation, distribution, and potential destruction. A project's evolving nature results in a potentially dynamic token design, with features modified according to its changing needs. This evolutionary component and the many combinations of token features and functionalities create a complex regulatory environment, with various jurisdictions lacking specific definitions of utility tokens. Some jurisdictions have resorted to describing utility tokens by exclusion because tokens do not fit in the description of cryptocurrencies, securities, or other financial instruments.

Utility tokens enable a range of different use cases, functions, tokenomic designs, and organizational models. Simple models like Filecoin or Mana use utility tokens as a means of payment for services provided within the ecosystem. Other projects, such as ALEX, use a dual-token design, with one token (Alex) as a means of payment and another (APower), non-tradable or transferable, as a special contribution reward providing access to specific features. Lastly, projects such as Ethereum launched with basic usage and a linear issuance model. It evolved to include advanced mechanisms of shared rewards, dynamic pricing, and new mining mechanisms.

The dynamic tokenomic design capabilities provided by the utility token's programmable nature enable the continuous creation of new features and functionalities. New business models, such as those based on decentralized autonomous organizations, DeFi applications, and metaverses, may require a flexible monetary element, driving the development and adoption of new and improved utility tokens and tokenomic designs.

Discussion Questions

1. Discuss the difference between utility tokens and cryptocurrencies.
2. Explain the concept of tokenomic design.
3. Describe three mechanisms token issuers use to raise funds using utility tokens.
4. Discuss the potential benefits of reward programs such as token farming.

References

Adhami, S., Giudici, G., & Martinazzi, S. (2018). Why do businesses go crypto? An empirical analysis of initial coin offerings. *Journal of Economics and Business*, *100*(C), 64–75.

Atici, G. (2018). Bitcoin and blockchain: A threat or opportunity for the financial system. *European Journal of Economics and Business Studies*, *4*(3), 95–101.

Automated Liquid Exchange. (2021). What is ALEX? Retrieved from https://docs.alexgo.io

Baur, D. G., & Dimpfl, T. (2021). The volatility of bitcoin and its role as a medium of exchange and a store of value. *Empirical Economics*, *61*(5), 2663–2683. https://doi.org/10.1007/s00181-020-01990-5

Baur, D. G., Hong, K. H., & Lee, A. D. (2018). Bitcoin: Medium of exchange or speculative assets? *Journal of International Financial Markets, Institutions and Money*, *54*(C), 177–189.

Bellavitis, C., Cumming, D., & Vanacker, T. (2020, August 24). Ban, boom, and echo! Entrepreneurship and initial coin offerings. *Entrepreneurship Theory and Practice*. https://doi.org/10.1177/1042258720940114

Benedetti, H., & Kostovetsky, L. (2021). Digital tulips? Returns to investors in initial coin offerings. *Journal of Corporate Finance*, *66*(C), 101786.

Benedetti, H., & Nikbakht, E. (2021). Returns and network growth of digital tokens after cross-listings. *Journal of Corporate Finance*, *66*(2), 101853.

Blandin, A., Pieters, G. C., Wu, Y., Dek, A., Eisermann, T., Njoki, D., & Taylor, S. (2020). 3rd global cryptoasset benchmarking study. Retrieved from http://www.jbs.cam.ac.uk/wp-content/uploads/2021/01/2021-ccaf-3rd-global-cryptoasset-benchmarking-study.pdf

Buterin, V. (2013, March). Ethereum white paper – A next generation smart contract and decentralized application platform. Retrieved from http://blockchainlab.com/pdf/Ethereum_white_paper-a_next_generation_smart_contract_and_decentralized_application_platform-vitalik-buterin.pdf

Cong, L. W., Li, Y., & Wang, N. (2021). Tokenomics: Dynamic adoption and valuation. *Review of Financial Studies*, *34*(3), 1105–1155.

Financial Conduct Authority. (2019, July). Guidance on cryptoassets. Retrieved from https://www.fca.org.uk/publication/policy/ps19-22.pdf

Fisch, C. (2019). Initial coin offerings (ICOS) to finance new ventures. *Journal of Business Venturing*, *34*(1), 1–22.

Fries, M., & Paal, B. P. (Eds.). (2019). *Smart contracts*. Tübingen: Mohr Siebeck. Retrieved from https://library.oapen.org/handle/20.500.12657/24858

Foley, S., Karlsen, J., & Putnins, T. (2019). Sex, drugs, and bitcoin: How much illegal activity is financed through cryptocurrencies? *Review of Financial Studies*, *32*(5), 1798–1853.

Gandal, N., Hamrick, J. T., Moore, T., & Oberman, T. (2018). Price manipulation in the bitcoin ecosystem. *Journal of Monetary Economics*, *95*(C), 86–96.

Griffin, J. M., & Shams, A. (2020). Is bitcoin really untethered? *Journal of Finance*, *75*(4), 1913–1964.

Hazlett, P. K., & Luther, W. J. (2020). Is bitcoin money? And what that means. *Quarterly Review of Economics and Finance*, *77*(2), 144–149.

Hileman, G., & Rauchs, M. (2017). Global cryptocurrency benchmarking study. Retrieved from https://www.jbs.cam.ac.uk/wp-content/uploads/2020/08/2017-04-20-global-cryptocurrency-benchmarking-study.pdf

Howcroft, E. (2021). Virtual real estate plot sells for record $2.4 million. *Reuters*, November 23. Retrieved from https://www.reuters.com/markets/currencies/virtual-real-estate-plot-sells-record-24-million-2021-11-23/

Lambert, T., Liebau, D., & Roosenboom, P. (2021). Security token offerings. *Small Business Economics*, *59*, 299–325.

Ministre de l'Economie et Finance. (2019). PACTE, Le Plan d'Action pour la Croissance et la Transformation des Entreprises. Retrieved from https://www.economie.gouv.fr/files/files/2019/PACTE_Juin2019/bro-a4-pacte.pdf

Momtaz, P. P. (2019). Token sales and initial coin offerings: Introduction. *Journal of Alternative Investments*, *21*(4), 7–12.

Momtaz, P. P. (2020). Initial coin offerings. *PLoS ONE*, *15*(5), e0233018.

Nakamoto, S. (2008, June). Bitcoin: A peer-to-peer electronic cash system. Retrieved from https://bitcoin.org/bitcoin.pdf

Ordano, E., Meilich, A., Jardi, Y., & Araoz, M. (2017). Decentraland: A blockchain-based virtual world. Retrieved from https://decentraland.org/whitepaper.pdf

Parker, L. (2017, August 20). *Decentraland raises $24 million in 35 seconds, leaving retail investors out in the cold.* Brave New Coin. Retrieved from https://bravenewcoin.com/insights/decentraland-raises-24-million-in-35-seconds-leaving-retail-investors-out-in-the-cold

Protocol Labs. (2017, July 19). Filecoin: A decentralized storage network. Retrieved from https://filecoin.io/filecoin.pdf

Roubini, N., & Byrne, P. (2018, March 5). *The blockchain pipe dream.* Project Syndicate. Retrieved from https://www.project-syndicate.org/commentary/blockchain-technology-limited-applications-by-nouriel-roubini-and-preston-byrne-2018-03

Swiss Financial Market Supervisory Authority FINMA. (2018). Guidelines for enquiries regarding the regulatory framework for initial coin offerings (ICOs). Retrieved from https://www.finma.ch/~/media/finma/dokumente/dokumentencenter/myfinma/1bewilligung/fintech/wegleitung-ico.pdf

Szabo, N. (1996). *Smart contracts: Building blocks for digital markets.* Extropy 16. Retrieved from https://www.fon.hum.uva.nl/rob/Courses/InformationInSpeech/CDROM/Literature/LOTwinterschool2006/szabo.best.vwh.net/smart_contracts_2.html

United States Congress. (2019). Token taxonomy act of 2019. Retrieved from https://www.congress.gov/bill/116th-congress/house-bill/2144/text

Yermack, D. (2015). Is bitcoin a real currency? An economic appraisal. In D. Lee (Ed.), *Handbook of digital currency: Bitcoin, innovation, financial instruments, and big data* (pp. 31–43). Amsterdam: Elsevier.

Chapter 7

Stablecoins

Ingo Fiedler and Lennart Ante

Abstract

This chapter introduces the concept of stablecoins such as Tether, DAI, or Ampleforth. It also provides a taxonomy of the different types of stablecoins consisting of (1) traditional asset-backed stablecoins, (2) crypto-collateralized stablecoins, and (3) algorithmic stablecoins and seigniorage shares. The chapter continues with a brief history of stablecoins, starting from BitShares as the first stablecoin implementation over tether and market-wide stablecoin adoption to Facebook-initiated Diem. Next, the chapter explains the impact of stablecoins on cryptocurrencies and other markets and discusses trends and challenges facing stablecoins. The chapter provides a basic understanding of stablecoins, their defining characteristics, challenges, and markets.

Keywords: Asset-backed stablecoins; crypto-collateralized stablecoins; algorithmic stablecoins; Diem; tether

Introduction

A major concern of cryptocurrencies is their price volatility, severely limiting their use as a medium of exchange (Dyhrberg, 2016; Katsiampa, 2017). One reason for launching stablecoins was to mitigate volatility risk. Users could also take advantage of digital currency's benefits, such as low-cost and immutable transactions, without exposure to possible strong price fluctuations (Moin, Sekniqi, & Sirer, 2020). These features potentially render stablecoins more useful as a means of payment, a store of value, and a more flexible alternative to fiat currencies.

Stablecoins are digital currencies with their value pegged to fiat currencies like the dollar or physical assets like gold. They share the considerable advantage of

The Emerald Handbook on Cryptoassets: Investment Opportunities and Challenges, 93–105

doi:10.1108/978-1-80455-320-620221007

cryptocurrencies of a 24/7 availability of immutable payments without delays (Kołodziejczyk & Jarno, 2020). Traditional banking still cannot compete with these features. The low transaction costs are particularly beneficial for cross-border transfers and remittances. The most popular stablecoins function as a means of payment in virtually any blockchain-based system. Presently, the prime use case of stablecoins is to serve as a substitute for fiat currencies on cryptocurrency exchanges and in decentralized finance.

The core characteristic of low volatility varies among types of stablecoins depending on their design. Although centralized entities based on the US dollar (USD) cash or equivalents manage the most popular stablecoins, digital assets like ether (ETH) also back some stablecoins. For other stablecoins, algorithms aim to achieve price stability. Stablecoins backed by digital assets and supported by algorithms tend to have higher price volatility (Jarno & Kołodziejczyk, 2021). They are also more decentralized and thus less prone to a single point of failure, bringing them closer to the original idea of cryptocurrencies. This situation avoids the need to trust a central entity that controls the process of minting and redeeming stablecoins.

The less volatile but more centralized fiat-backed stablecoins share a similar degree of pseudonymity to cryptocurrencies and, apart from extreme cases of crime, a similar degree of immutability. This feature tends to raise stablecoin's popularity among regular cryptocurrency users. It is also sufficient to keep away criminals who risk having authorities freeze their funds. Issuers also need to go through a know-your-customer (KYC) process once they redeem stablecoins for fiat currencies. The market-leading stablecoin provider Tether, for example, usually reacts to the emergence of hacks in the cryptocurrency ecosystem, quickly freezing funds (Stevens, 2021).

Early research on stablecoins focused primarily on their issuance (Ante, Fiedler, & Strehle, 2021b; Kristoufek, 2020; Wei, 2018), which tends to occur in the market's negative phases (Griffin & Shams, 2020). Another research area on stablecoins analyzes their applicability as a safe haven from volatility (Baur & Hoang, 2021; Wang, Ma, & Wu, 2020). A more recent research stream focuses on the different design mechanisms of stablecoins, especially algorithmic stablecoins (Zhao, Li, & Yuan, 2021). This chapter presents the current state of the literature on these topics, provides a taxonomy of stablecoin design options and a brief outline of the history of stablecoins, and discusses challenges and opportunities for their future.

Stablecoin Taxonomy

Stablecoins differ by their backing and design. They consist of the following subgroups: traditional asset-backed stablecoins, crypto-collateralized stablecoins, and algorithmic stablecoins with or without seignorage shares.

Traditional Asset-backed Stablecoins

Legal currency or physical assets back the most prominent stablecoins. For example, a third party collects the USD deposits and issues stablecoins linked to each dollar deposit. This form of stablecoin exists for various fiat currencies, such as USD, EUR, CHF, and CNH, with USD being the most popular option (e.g., USD Tether, USD Circle, and Paxos, including Binance USD). This form of stablecoins also exists for gold – Tether Gold and Paxos Gold – where one ounce of gold backs each token, and for Tether Gold, a uniquely identifiable ounce of gold.

For stablecoins in this category, the company operating the cryptocurrency obtains a reserve of some valuable asset like the US dollar or another sovereign currency, gold or another commodity, or a basket of multiple assets. It then issues digital tokens representing a unit of the underlying asset, which the holder can exchange online.

The idea of directly backed and redeemable currency predates cryptocurrencies. Liberty Reserve of e-gold provided a similar digital currency supposedly backed by assets held by the issuer (White, 2014). The difference was the centralization of the transactions but decentralization for blockchain-based stablecoins. Still, the token creation and redemption processes of stablecoins rely on a trustworthy entity. Hence, this type of stablecoin is more centralized than bitcoin but less than liberty reserve.

Crypto-collateralized Stablecoins

A sibling to traditional asset-backed stablecoins is those backed by digital assets, namely cryptocurrencies. BitUSD and Dai of MakerDAO belong to this group. Both aim to peg their token to the value of one USD. The backing can be a single cryptocurrency or a basket of cryptocurrencies. In the case of Dai, the key idea of this mechanism is to offer a redeemable token that holders can convert into $1 worth of ETH at the going USD/ETH exchange rate. Therefore, the ETH amount received grows or shrinks depending on the exchange rate. Because a blockchain has no inherent knowledge of exchange rates, this mechanism requires the so-called *oracles* trusted to write the exchange rate into the blockchain or take the consensus across a set of oracles (Brennecke, Schellinger, Guggenberger, & Urbach, 2022).

Stablecoins backed by traditional assets require a trusted centralized issuer. By contrast, crypto-collateralized stablecoins involve a *smart contract* – decentrally anchored scripts on blockchains or similar infrastructures that enable the transparent execution of predefined processes (Ante, 2021). That allows them to run trustless and independently from counterparty risks. The disadvantage is that the price peg lacks a direct tie to the value it aims to represent. Hence, from a theoretical perspective, the market price fluctuation will be higher, as empirical analyses (Jarno & Kołodziejczyk, 2021; Zhao et al., 2021), theoretical research (Clements, 2021), and market observations (Dale, 2021) suggest or show.

Algorithmic Stablecoins and Seigniorage Shares

Assets do not back algorithmic stablecoins. Instead, an *algorithmic stablecoin* is a type of cryptocurrency managed by algorithms anchored on the blockchain via smart contracts to dynamically minimize its price volatility relative to a specific form of asset, such as the USD. For example, Ampleforth increases the supply when the stablecoin's price rises and decreases the supply when the price falls.

An oracle provides the going exchange rate between the cryptocurrency and a stable-valued asset, such as the USD. When the cryptocurrency gains value, its supply increases; when it loses value, the supply decreases. At Ampleforth, the adjustment automatically occurs via a daily process called "rebasing," which intends to stabilize the stablecoin's price near a specific peg of $1. That creates the incentive to buy the token below the threshold of supply decrease, sell it above the threshold of supply increase, and, in turn, keep the price in line and around the target rate of, for example, $1. Allowing a cryptocurrency to expand its supply is easy. The challenge is to decide who must bear a balance reduction. In the case of Ampleforth, it is fully symmetric: any balance holder gets a balance expanded and reduced proportionally in case of a supply change (Kuo, Iles, & Cruz, 2019).

In contrast to pure algorithmic stablecoins or pure asset-backed stablecoins, fractional-algorithmic stablecoins emerged as a middle-of-the-road solution. Compared to asset-backed stablecoins, fractional-algorithmic stablecoins have fewer custodial risks and are more efficient in preventing over-collateralization. Additionally, a better comparison of enforcing the price peg is to purely algorithmic designs.

Frax is the first attempt to implement the partial-collateral protocol of stablecoins consisting of two tokens: FRAX, the stablecoin pegged to $1, and FXS as a governance token. A smart contract dynamically determines a collateral ratio (r) between 0 percent and 100 percent every hour, depending on FRAX's market price, to control the percentage of collateral required to stabilize FRAX's value (Frax, 2022; Zhao et al., 2021). For example, when r = 50 percent, the requirement is to provide 50 cents in collateral to mint a new FRAX. It becomes fully collateralized when r = 100 percent and a pure algorithmic stablecoin if r = 0 percent. Another example is Terra USD. It started as a seignorage share model and later introduced a capital backing of $1 billion in bitcoin after selling a respective amount of its governance token LUNA to a group of venture capitalists (Godbole, 2022).

The seigniorage share model for algorithmic stablecoins commonly introduces two types of cryptocurrencies: coins as a stablecoin and shares as ownership of seigniorage (Zhao et al., 2021). Arbitrageurs use seignorage shares to increase the supply of stablecoins when a coin's price is above its intended peg. Besides these two tokens, algorithmic stablecoins often offer bonds as an incentive for buyers when the price falls below the intended peg. For example, Basis Cash uses three tokens: Basis Cash (BAC) as the stablecoin, Basis Shares the seignorage token, and Basis Bond, a price dependent on BAC's price. The design aims to push BAC back to $1 when its price falls below $1. However, Basis Cash has consistently traded between $0.02 and $0.03 during January and February 2022, illustrating the complexity and challenges associated with seignorage shares (Coingecko, 2022a).

If they were stable, some would refer to algorithmic stablecoins as the "holy grail." They share the same immutability and decentralization of transactions, the protocol's decentralization, and do not require trusting the value of any backing, like any cryptocurrency. However, the price volatility of current implementations of algorithmic stablecoins does not yet render them a substitute for the more stable asset-backed stablecoins. Jarno and Kołodziejczyk (2021) find that existing complex stablecoins designs do not compete with simple designs in terms of volatility.

The History and Functioning of Stablecoins

Stablecoins have a shorter history than bitcoin. The following discussion involves the major steps in developing stablecoins from their early days to the current ecosystem.

Bitshares and BitUSD: The First Stablecoins

BitShares (BTS), formerly known as Angelshares, launched in 2014 as a delegated proof of stake blockchain platform with its native token BTS. The project also issued crypto-collateralized stablecoins such as BitUSD, BitEUR, or BitCNY, for which BTS functioned as the sole collateral. Accordingly, the price peg of the stablecoins depended entirely on the traded price of BTS, making a collapse in the BTS price, depending on the amount of collateral deposited, a liquidity and stability risk. In addition, no price oracle existed to provide the system with actual exchange rates, leading to vulnerability to various intentional or unintentional manipulations. For example, a user unintentionally traded BitUSD at $34 in the short term (Munster, 2019). The lack of a price stability mechanism and a reference to the real the USD in 2018 resulted in BitUSD losing its peg to the dollar due to under-collateralization and its inability to regain it (Cermak, 2019).

The rise and fall of BitUSD show the importance of the intention and scope of stablecoins' underlying mechanisms. The BitUSD mechanism aimed to protect the collateral's value (i.e., BTS). However, it did not correspond to a more appropriate mechanism that would directly affect the price of stablecoins.

BitUSD, as the first stablecoin, was a novel and unproven project and product backed by an equally novel, unproven, and volatile cryptoasset. Although the project or experiment effectively failed and experienced comparatively low adoption, BitUSD paved the way for other stablecoins. In 2017, the project team proposed a new stablecoin, SteemUSD, which had a price feed system based on previous learnings (Guidi, Michienzi, & Ricci, 2021). Today's successful crypto-collateralized stablecoin projects such as MakerDAO follow a similar conceptual approach and have mechanisms such as oracle price feeds and automated liquidations of collateral.

Tether, Crypto Exchanges, and Stablecoin Adoption

The wide adoption of stablecoins and the stablecoin Tether occurred in 2017. The reason was that cryptocurrency exchanges faced increasing difficulties in accessing banking services, including the on- and off-ramping of fiat currencies (Bitfinex, 2017). This situation led to much uncertainty for customers, explaining the adoption of USD-Tether (USDT) as a substitute for traditional currency on exchanges as a trading pair. All major cryptocurrency exchanges introduced USDT as a trading pair against cryptocurrencies such as bitcoin or ether within a short period. Using a USD-backed stablecoin enabled cryptocurrency exchanges to provide USDT trading pairs, even if an exchange had no banking partner. Accordingly, stablecoins also enabled creating new cryptocurrency exchanges and decentralized applications with no direct connection to the traditional financial industry but still offer fiat-like services.

Tether's success came with a controversial discussion about the extent to which the underlying collateral of Tether might not exist and could be used to manipulate bitcoin's price. These accusations have proven wrong after a lengthy investigation by the New York Attorney General ending in 2021. This investigation neither found a lack of assets backing outstanding Tether tokens nor their manipulative issuance. Instead, the results reveal that Tether informed its customers late that it had switched its reserve model from pure cash to a basket of assets. With a market capitalization of $80 billion in February 2022, Tether represents the third-largest cryptoasset by market capitalization and the asset with the highest trading volume in the cryptocurrency market (Coingecko, 2022b).

The Emergence of Tether Competitors

Attracted by the success of Tether, competing fiat-backed stablecoin projects emerged, such as USD Coin (USDC), Gemini USD, Paxos, and True USD. USDC is the second largest stablecoin and is like Tether, except USDC holds its reserves through the US-onshore banks. Tether has its reserves offshore. Centre, a consortium of companies, manages the project. These companies are Circle, the cryptocurrency exchange Coinbase, and the bitcoin mining company Bitmain, a Circle investor. On March 20, 2021, Visa announced its plans to adopt the USDC stablecoin to settle transactions on its network (Hussain, 2021).

The Emergence of DAI and Algorithmic Stablecoins

Besides the emergence of direct competition, Tether's high adoption and growth also led to spillover effects on other stablecoin projects, such as the crypto-collateralized stablecoin project MakerDAO, which issues the stablecoin DAI. DAI launched on the Ethereum platform and has since reached other blockchain infrastructures. It is a complex system that includes various money pools and possible stability mechanisms (MakerDAO, 2020).

A user can deposit Ethereum and, more recently, other cryptocurrencies for the multi-collateral DAI into asset pools serving as collateral for issuing new DAI stablecoins and managing the secure lifecycle of the stablecoins. Another term for these pools is a *collateralized debt position* (CDP). MakerDAO has a governance token called Maker (MKR). Its purpose is to allow investors and stakeholders to vote on the decentralized organization's various strategic decisions. An example is including new cryptoassets as underlying collateral for DAI. Furthermore, MKR is required as a form of payment of fees and the required collateral to generate a new DAI.

Market participants can transparently monitor the deposited DAI collateral and purchase it via open auctions in case of possible under-collateralization by issuing DAI. Dai provides collateral and purchases the collateral in an open auction by spending Dai. MKR token holders function as the final collateral authority in the system. Suppose the collateral in ether or other cryptocurrencies falls below 100 percent. In that case, an algorithm automatically creates and offers MKR on the open market to raise new funds that serve to bring the collateral ratio back to a predetermined level. Accordingly, MKR token holders have exposure to the system's liquidity risk, which receives protection via (1) the ability of CDP owners to liquidate their positions if DAI trades below $1 and (2) arbitrageurs creating new stablecoins if DAI trades above $1. Until today, DAI plays a significant role among stablecoins, with a market capitalization of around $9.9 billion in late March 2022.

TERRA-UST, an algorithmic stablecoin backed by the seignorage of the LUNA governance token, launched in October 2020. Its market capitalization rose to $2.5 billion by November 2021 before exponentially growing to $18.7 billion on May 9, 2022, before it failed in light of a "bank run" scenario on LUNA causing the price to fall below $0.01 per UST. Although UST was the most popular stablecoin based on the Terra protocol, others also exited, such as tracking the Korean Won. The number of such stablecoins was only limited by reliable price oracles. The Terra protocol relied on arbitrage traders keeping the peg between the stablecoin and its represented fiat currency. When a stablecoin's demand is high, Terra's price was supposed to increases, and arbitrage traders mint new stablecoins by burning LUNA at the rate of the price oracle, plus a 0.5 percent fee. The opposite occurs the stablecoin's price was below its peg. Sharing these conversion fees, any transaction fees for sending stablecoins, and fees to exchange one stablecoin for another (0.35 percent) as revenues occured with 130 validators who validated transactions in the proof-of-stake blockchain. LUNA's holders could delegate their tokens to one of these validators and receive a share of these revenues in staking income. This staking incentive and the prospective burning of LUNA when minting more stablecoins seemed to be the main drivers of LUNA's price. On April 04 2022, LUNA's market capitalization was $36.6 billion making it the eighth largest cryptocurrency at that time shortly before becoming worthless a month later.

Libra/Diem & Co.

Diem, formerly known as Libra, was a stablecoin project initiated by the American company Meta Platforms (then Facebook) and abandoned in January 2022. The project aimed to create a private cryptocurrency or private currency managed by a Swiss non-profit foundation, with the ability of various companies to participate as system validators. The intent was to create a financial infrastructure that people in developing countries could use without access to banking services (Diem Association, 2021).

To this end, Diem planned to secure the value of its currency with a basket of existing legal currencies as collateral. The announcement of the intention to create a private currency, only part-collateralized by the USD, led to wide-ranging discussion and criticism about such a solution's underlying motives, intentions, risks, and implications (Cecchetti & Schienholtz, 2019; Eichengreen, 2019; Iwashita, 2021). The Diem Foundation addressed public and private concerns and published an updated plan to implement the project. However, it continued to draw criticism, questions regarding regulatory hurdles, and institutional pressure (Rrustemi & Tuchschmid, 2020).

Amid regulatory concerns, developers abandoned the project abandoned. According to Zetzsche, Buckley, and Arner (2021), the most significant effect or impact of a private stablecoin like Diem would come not from the currency itself but from reactions to it by large tech companies, financial institutions, and governments around the world.

Market Impact of Stablecoins

Stablecoins represent an essential factor in cryptocurrency markets, which is why the question arises as to how stablecoins affect the overall market. Empirical studies benefit from the fact that anyone can monitor stablecoin transactions and accounts due to the inherent transparency of public blockchain infrastructures. Every issuance, transfer, and so-called *burn*, the process of destroying stablecoins and exchanging them into fiat currency, can be traced historically and in real time. Additionally, interested parties can easily retrieve pricing data to analyze, such as the deviation or stability of stablecoin prices over time.

Impact on Cryptocurrency Markets

Various studies have examined how stablecoins affect the cryptocurrency markets. A prominent stream of literature focuses on how issuing "new" stablecoins affects cryptocurrency markets. Wei (2018) finds that Tether issuances affect the trading volume of bitcoin but not the returns. The author also identifies falling bitcoin prices leading to higher trading volumes of Tether, which can indicate stablecoins being used as a safe haven. Other studies also examine this topic (Baur & Hoang, 2021; Wang et al., 2020). Still, other studies on stablecoin issuances identify that issuances are often related to previous market downturns and lead to significantly abnormal trading volumes and positive returns (Ante et al., 2021b; Griffin & Shams, 2020).

Related to stablecoin issuances are stablecoin transfers that can be observed transparently via so-called *block explorers*. A *cryptocurrency block explorer* is an online blockchain browser that can show the details of all transactions on a blockchain network. Ante, Fiedler, and Strehle (2021a) assess the effect of large stablecoin transfers and identify significant increases in trading volume before and after the transfers. They conclude that the real-time traceability of cash flows allows on-chain data analysis to provide cryptocurrency market participants with additional information, making markets more efficient.

Another significant literature stream deals with the price volatility of stablecoins and their relation to the volatility of other cryptocurrencies, namely bitcoin. Grobys, Junttila, Kolari, and Sapkota (2021) point out that while stablecoins generally track their peg, some recurring spikes exist in stablecoins' intraday volatilities. They find that volatilities of stablecoins are not Granger-causal for bitcoin volatility, while lagged bitcoin volatility exhibits Granger-causal effects on the volatilities of stablecoins. Thus, the authors conclude that bitcoin volatility is a fundamental factor driving the volatility of stablecoins.

Grobys and Huynh (2021) find that positive returns on Tether are related to and even predict negative price changes in bitcoin. Hoang and Baur (2021) find that stablecoin volatility and volumes correlate highly with the corresponding bitcoin time series. The authors also demonstrate that stablecoins increase bitcoin's trading volume and conclude that stablecoins play a key role in cryptocurrency markets. Hasan, Hassan, Rashi, and Alhenawi (2021) view Tether's emergence as a strong, new safe haven.

Potential Impact Outside Cryptocurrencies

Although the use of stablecoins occurs mainly in the sphere of cryptocurrencies, their application for other use cases continues to evolve. More businesses now accept bitcoin as a cryptocurrency payment and stablecoins. A prominent example is Bitrefill, which accepts various cryptocurrencies, including stablecoins, and allows users to buy gift cards or products. Another typical example of stablecoins is cross-border transfers for business and remittance payments. Although payments in bitcoin or other cryptocurrencies are cheaper and faster than international wire transfers, stablecoins have the added value of stability and are thus even more suited for these use cases.

Citizens of countries threatened with hyperinflation and instability in the financial markets also use stablecoins as a store of value and safe haven. Examples include the surge in the trading volume of the pair USDT to Turkish Lira and the premium Ukrainians paid during the first days of the war with Russia in March 2022. Recently, the Swiss city of Lugano made Tether USD a de facto legal tender for all public services. It also intends to integrate it as a payment method with local businesses. Such evidence shows the relevance of stablecoins outside cryptocurrency markets that might have implications for the broader economy and monetary policy.

Stablecoin Trends, Challenges, and Central Bank Digital Currencies

Speculating about future stablecoin trends is subjective. Nonetheless, their market capitalization and usage, especially outside the sphere of cryptocurrencies, are likely to continue growing. Li and Shen (2021) even speculate whether global stablecoins will lead to the dollarization of a country's monetary system.

An important challenge to overcome for stablecoins is the Financial Action Task Force's (FATF) travel rule. Currently, any acquisition or redemption of stablecoins at a centralized operator requires completing a KYC check. However, no additional check of on-chain transactions occurs and can be deemed immutable except involving crime. However, the travel rule requires the sender to identify the recipient and vice versa. Although this rule might be possible in transactions between cryptocurrency exchanges, it might be troublesome or even impossible for other transfers. Any frictions created around the travel rule could negatively affect stablecoin growth.

One type of stablecoin might, by design, have an easier time implementing the travel rule: central bank digital currencies (CBDCs). A *CBDC* is a legal tender provided by a central bank in addition to the cash or balances it holds. The ideas around CBDCs vary widely, and much depends on their actual design. For example, every citizen could have an account with the central bank or a few large banks. Managing the money supply could occur manually or by an algorithm. Smart contracts could be allowed or not. Transactions could entail a fee or be feeless. The account could pay interest and incentivize specific behavior. With all the different options, blockchains based on an open protocol are likely to play a small role.

The People's Bank of China has undertaken the most advanced CBDC project called digital currency/electronic payment (DC/EP). At the current stage, it is positioned for use in retail payment and does not pay interest on balances. DC/EP involves three stages: (1) a preparatory stage, (2) a steady development phase, and (3) an accelerated research and development (R&D) and launch of the pilot phase (Tong & Chen, 2021). The People's Bank of China follows the "no harm" principle. It does not interfere with or impede the ability of central banks to fulfill their responsibilities to maintain monetary and financial stability. DC/EP should coexist with existing cash and bank accounts. Finally, it should foster innovation and efficiency in society (Tong & Chen, 2021). Although innovation and efficiency for digital cash payments seem likely, some view using the DC/EP and CBDCs as surveillance and control mechanisms.

Summary and Conclusions

Stablecoins are blockchain-based tokens with limited price risk that play a vital part in today's cryptocurrency markets. They are almost immutable, cheap, and near-instant transactions that can trigger smart contracts. For cryptocurrency trading, USD Tether is the most relevant counter currency, exceeding even the role of the USD. Stablecoins also allow an easily accessible store of value for individuals excluded from the traditional financial system or who fear hyperinflation of their local currencies.

Stablecoins are likely to play a role in the broader economy when issued by central banks. With a simple design – one token equals $1 – the question arises concerning why so many different stablecoin projects exist. One reason is competition among different projects. Another is that the tokens differ, especially relative to (1) the type of asset they represent, (2) their technology, (3) whether a central counterparty exists, and (4) managing collateral and money supply regarding digital asset-backed or algorithmic stablecoins.

Discussion Questions

1. Explain the purpose of stablecoins.
2. Identify an application of stablecoins in traditional finance or banking.

3. Distinguish between the different forms of stablecoins.
4. Discuss the potentials and risks of CBDCs.

References

Ante, L. (2021, March). Smart contracts on the blockchain – A bibliometric analysis and review. *Telematics and Informatics*, *57*, 101519.

Ante, L., Fiedler, I., & Strehle, E. (2021a, September). The impact of transparent money flows: Effects of stablecoin transfers on the returns and trading volume of bitcoin. *Technological Forecasting and Social Change*, *170*, 120851.

Ante, L., Fiedler, I., & Strehle, E. (2021b, July). The influence of stablecoin issuances on cryptocurrency markets. *Finance Research Letters*, *41*, 101867.

Baur, D. G., & Hoang, L. T. (2021). A crypto safe haven against bitcoin. *Finance Research Letters*, *38*(2), 101431.

Bitfinex. (2017, May 18). Pausing wire deposits to bitfinex. Retrieved from https://www.bitfinex.com/posts/200

Brennecke, M., Schellinger, B., Guggenberger, T., & Urbach, N. (2022). The de-central bank in decentralized finance: A case study of MakerDAO. In *Proceedings of the Hawaii international conference on system sciences (HICSS)*, January.

Cecchetti, S., & Schienholtz, K. (2019, August 31). Libra: A dramatic call to regulatory action. *VOX CEPR Policy Portal*. Retrieved from https://voxeu.org/article/libra-dramatic-call-regulatory-action

Cermak, L. (2019, February 15). *BitUSD hasn't had its $1 peg for more than two months*. The Block. Retrieved from https://www.theblockcrypto.com/linked/11876/bitusd-hasnt-had-its-1-peg-for-more-than-two-months

Clements, R. (2021, October). Built to fail: The inherent fragility of algorithmic stablecoins. *Wake Forest Law Review*, *11*, Online 131. https://ssrn.com/abstract=3952045 or http://dx.doi.org/10.2139/ssrn.3952045

Coingecko. (2022a). *Basis cash price chart (BAC)*. Coingecko. Retrieved from https://www.coingecko.com/en/coins/basis-cash

Coingecko. (2022b). *Tether price chart (USDT)*. Coingecko. Retrieved from https://www.coingecko.com/en/coins/tether

Dale, B. (2021, April 7). *$1B Fei stablecoin's Rocky start is a wake-up call for DeFi investors*. Coindesk. Retrieved from https://www.coindesk.com/markets/2021/04/07/1b-fei-stablecoins-rocky-start-is-a-wake-up-call-for-defi-investors/

Diem Association. (2021, January 12). Diem whitepaper. Retrieved from https://www.diem.com/en-us/white-paper/

Dyhrberg, A. H. (2016, February). Bitcoin, gold and the dollar – A GARCH volatility analysis. *Finance Research Letters*, *16*, 85–92.

Eichengreen, B. (2019, September 8). Libra: The known unknown and unknown unkowns. *VOX CEPR Policy Portal*. Retrieved from https://voxeu.org/article/libra-known-unknowns-and-unknown-unknowns

Frax. (2022). Frax: Fractional-algorithmic stablecoin protocol – A new category of decentralized stablecoin with a novel mechanism. Retrieved from https://docs.frax.finance/

Godbole, O. (2022, February 23). *Terra's LUNA jumps 15% as UST stablecoin gets $1B bitcoin reserve*. Coindesk2. Retrieved from https://www.coindesk.com/markets/2022/02/23/terras-luna-jumps-15-as-ust-stablecoin-gets-1b-bitcoin-reserve/

Griffin, J. M., & Shams, A. (2020). Is bitcoin really un-tethered? *Journal of Finance*, *75*(4), 1913–1964.

Grobys, K., & Huynh, T. L. D. (2021, December). When tether says 'JUMP!' bitcoin asks 'how low?' *Finance Research Letters, 47*, 102644.

Grobys, K., Junttila, J., Kolari, J. W., & Sapkota, N. (2021). On the stability of stablecoins. *Journal of Empirical Finance, 64*(C), 207–223.

Guidi, B., Michienzi, A., & Ricci, L. (2021). Analysis of witnesses in the steem blockchain. *Mobile Networks and Applications, 26*(5), 2099–2110.

Hasan, Md. B., Hassan, M. K., Rashi, Md. M., & Alhenawi, Y. (2021). Are safe haven assets really safe during the 2008 global financial crisis and COVID-19 pandemic? *Global Finance Journal, 50*, 100668.

Hussain, N. Z. (2021). Exclusive: Visa moves to allow payment settlements using cryptocurrency. *Reuters*. March 29. Retrieved from https://www.reuters.com/article/crypto-currency-visa/exclusive-visa-moves-to-allow-payment-settlements-using-cryptocurrency-idINKBN2BL0XI

Iwashita, N. (2021). Facebook's libra is far from broad acceptance as a world currency. *Evolutionary and Institutional Economics Review, 18*(1), 335–339.

Jarno, K., & Kołodziejczyk, H. (2021). Does the design of stablecoins impact their volatility? *Journal of Risk and Financial Management, 14*(2), 1–14.

Katsiampa, P. (2017, September). Volatility estimation for bitcoin: A comparison of GARCH models. *Economics Letters, 158*, 3–6.

Kołodziejczyk, H., & Jarno, K. (2020). Stablecoin – The stable cryptocurrency. *Studia BAS, 3*(63), 155–170.

Kristoufek, L. (2020, December 4). On the role of stablecoins in cryptoasset pricing dynamics. Retrieved from https://ssrn.com/abstract=3672909 or http://dx.doi.org/10.2139/ssrn.3672909

Kuo, E., Iles, B., & Cruz, M. R. (2019, May 20). Ampleforth: A new synthetic commodity. Retrieved from https://drive.google.com/file/d/1I-NmSnQ6E7wY1nyouuf-GuDdJWNCnJWl/view

Li, C., & Shen, Y. (2021). The potential impacts and risks of global stablecoins. *China Economic Journal, 14*(1), 39–51.

MakerDAO. (2020). The maker protocol: MakerDAO's multi-collateral dai (MCD) system. Retrieved from https://makerdao.com/whitepaper/WhitePaper-TheMakerProtocol_MakerDAO's Multi-CollateralDai(MCD)System-FINAL-021720.pdf

Moin, A., Sekniqi, K., & Sirer, E. G. (2020). SoK: A classification framework for stablecoin designs. In J. Bonneau & N. Heninger (Eds.), *Financial cryptography and data security: 24th international conference, Kota Kinabalu, Malaysia, February 10–14, 2020*. Revised Selected Papers (pp. 174–197). Berlin: Springer.

Munster, B. (2019, August 19). *Why was 'dollar-pegged' stablecoin BitUSD trading at $34?* Yahoo Finance. Retrieved from https://finance.yahoo.com/news/why-dollar-pegged-stablecoin-bitusd-114939384.html

Rrustemi, J., & Tuchschmid, N. S. (2020). Facebook's digital currency venture 'diem': The new frontier … or a galaxy far, far away? *Technology Innovation Management Review, 10*(12), 19–30.

Stevens, R. (2021, February 5). *Tether freezes $1.7 million in profits from yearn finance hack*. Decrypt. Retrieved from https://decrypt.co/56779/tether-freezes-profits-yearn-finance-hack

Tong, W., & Chen, J. (2021). A study of the economic impact of central bank digital currency under global competition. *China Economic Journal, 14*(1), 78–101.

Wang, G. J., Ma, X.Y., & Wu, H. Y. (2020). Are stablecoins truly diversifiers, hedges, or safe havens against traditional cryptocurrencies as their name suggests? *Research in International Business and Finance, 54*(C), 101225.

Wei, W. C. (2018). The impact of tether grants on bitcoin. *Economics Letters, 171*(C), 19–22.

White, L. H. (2014). The troubling suppression of competition from alternative monies: The cases of the liberty dollar and E-gold. *Cato Journal*, *34*(2), 281–301.

Zetzsche, D. A., Buckley, R. P., & Arner, D. W. (2021). Regulating libra. *Oxford Journal of Legal Studies*, *41*(1), 80–113. https://doi.org/10.1093/ojls/gqaa036

Zhao, W., Li, H., & Yuan, Y. (2021). Understand volatility of algorithmic stablecoin: Modeling, verification and empirical analysis. In *International conference on financial cryptography and data security, FC 2021 international workshops*. Berlin: Springer.

Chapter 8

Tokenized Assets and Securities

Hugo Benedetti and Gabriel Rodríguez-Garnica

Abstract

Tokenization is a relatively new activity in digital finance. *Tokenization*, a process that creates a blockchain representation of the underlying instrument, can enhance the standard features and characteristics of assets and securities. Asset and security tokenization produces many benefits. These benefits include reducing issuance and trading costs, lessening dependency on intermediaries, facilitating more liquidity in markets, and providing greater transparency around an asset's lifecycle for all parties involved. This chapter synthesizes the key characteristics, benefits, processes, tools, and techniques of tokenizing real-world assets. It also provides several examples of current asset-backed token applications to help understand the rapidly growing industry and analyzes future expectations of this new technology.

Keywords: Tokenization; asset-backed tokens; asset tokenization; security tokenization; digital finance; blockchain

Introduction

Traditional asset classes include equities, fixed income, and cash. Alternative assets are other assets such as real estate, hedge funds, private equity, commodities, and infrastructure. As a result of blockchain technology, most traditional assets, both physical and digital, can be "tokenized." Therefore, a token can represent instruments such as stocks, bonds, real estate, consumer loans, and even art.

Tokenization is how public or private blockchain networks can digitally represent assets, services, or activities. The resulting tokens are identifiable, attributable,

The Emerald Handbook on Cryptoassets: Investment Opportunities and Challenges, 107–121

doi:10.1108/978-1-80455-320-620221008

immutable, transferable, and traceable in their native blockchain environment. Each token could have its programming code and internal rules and be subject to different legal regimes. Occasionally, tokens have a governance system established in the code, making them predictable, scalable, automatic, and adaptable to changes in the environment. Using transparent information sources based on blockchain technologies can generate efficiencies and improve liquidity, trust, and traceability. Although a token is a digital representation in a blockchain network, it can connect and interface with non-blockchain information through "oracles." An *oracle* is an application designed to extract, process, and incorporate external information onto a blockchain safely and reliably. Consequently, it allows smart contracts and tokens to use non-blockchain information on their programming.

Tokenized assets and securities are independent and fundamentally different from cryptocurrencies, utility tokens, and security tokens. The latter represents various forms of value generated within a blockchain network and inseparable from their digital representation. By contrast, tokenized assets and securities are digital representations of assets and securities outside the blockchain infrastructure. Tokenized instruments are linked and completely dependent on their off-chain underlying assets. Therefore, they maintain core intrinsic characteristics and gain new elements and features from blockchain technology.

Among the benefits of tokenizing traditional assets, the most salient are increased efficiency and reduced cost, enhanced transparency and security, better compliance and traceability, improved liquidity, and facilitated innovation. Some benefits, such as transparency, security, and traceability, derive directly from the underlying blockchain infrastructure. Others, like efficiency, compliance, liquidity, and innovation, arise from the possibility of creating smart contracts and building ecosystems using blockchain infrastructure.

Several industries have already implemented asset and security tokenization projects. The chapter discusses applications in the financial sector (Santander Bank/tokenized bonds), real estate (Reental/tokenized rental properties), and commodities (Agrotoken/grains).

Regarding the blockchain and distributed ledger technology (DLT) used for tokenizing assets, understanding the differences between blockchain-based tools and platforms is essential. Each blockchain platform, like Ethereum, Solana, Binance Smart Chain, Polygon, Terra, and Stellar, has different characteristics involving cost, security, speed of transactions, traceability, and accessibility. A tokenized asset's best fit with a platform depends on its tokenization purpose and objectives.

The tokenization of assets introduces a new system of representation and property registration and transmission. Therefore, understanding its legal framework, level of development, and future regulatory reforms is critical. The pilot regulatory framework to be implemented in Europe in 2022 and the existing financial sandbox in the United Kingdom, Spain, and other countries are promising initiatives to absorb these innovative global changes.

This chapter has the following structure. First, it describes the concept of tokenized assets and securities and discusses the similarities and distinctions between security tokens. Next, the chapter explores the potential benefits of tokenizing traditional assets and securities. Third, it presents the tokenization process, briefly explores some tokenization platforms, and then presents examples of current tokenized assets and securities projects. Lastly, it summarizes and concludes.

Tokenized Securities

According to Mougayar (2016, p. 24), a *token* is a "unit of value that an organization [or private entity] creates to govern its business model and give more power to its users to interact with its products or services." Tokens can have multiple purposes because they represent product usage rights or ownership rights tied to intrinsic value. They are identifiable, attributable, immutable, transferable, and traceable in the environments, ecosystems, and markets created for them. Each type of token has its programming code and applicable legal regime. Tokens respond to coding and consensus protocols between the parties. Occasionally, they have a governance system established in the code, making them predictable, scalable, automatic, and adaptable to changes in the environment. In contrast to centralized registries, tokens can generate high efficiencies, improve liquidity, trust, and traceability using transparent information sources based on blockchain technologies.

Tokenization is a process or system for storing, registering, and mobilizing tokens representing ownership rights over digital or physical assets or rights over the provision of activities. This process works through DLT systems, permissioned (private DLT) or not (public DLT or blockchain), which function as systems to transmit transparent and valuable information through tokens (Chen, 2018; Cong & He, 2019). Therefore, tokenization digitally represents assets, services, or activities in public or private blockchain networks. In other words, owning a token from a tokenized asset is owning all or part of the underlying asset registered on a DLT infrastructure of blockchain.

The owner or investor keeps the representation of the tokenized asset (token) in a private address (wallet). The investor owns the token and usually is its custodian unless a third party provides this contracted service. Investors can transact the token peer-to-peer (P2P) or through centralized or decentralized marketplaces if rules and regulations on the underlying asset allow.

Tokenization can occur with any asset.

- Traditional financial assets (Gan, Tsoukalas, & Netessine, 2021; Howell, Niessner, & Yermack, 2020; Khan et al., 2022; Tian, Lu, et al., 2020; Yermack, 2017).
- Real estate (Baum, 2021; Sazandrishvili, 2020; Smith, Manasi, Benedetti, Yoshida, & Vogel, 2019)
- Renewable energy, carbon emissions credits, and "green finance" through tokens such as "Climatecoin" (Dorfleitner & Braun, 2019, chapter 9; Neves & Prata, 2018; Schletz, Nassiry & Lee, 2020; Uzsoki, 2019).
- Space resources (Lucas-Rhimbassen, 2021).

Some use cases require blockchains to connect, receive, and send information to non-blockchain applications and systems. An oracle is a bridge connecting blockchains to other information environments, whether blockchain-based or not. An *oracle* is an application that monitors, manages, and verifies real-world information on events, people, and identities. This information constitutes off-chain data to which smart contracts initially lack access. Therefore, oracles function as an intermediary that provides a vital link between real-world data and blockchain ecosystems, providing a trusted data feed to smart contracts. The data feed supplied by oracles to smart contracts enables them to monitor any information affecting the adjacent assets or change of the tokenized asset. This situation allows the automatic and decentralized execution of the programmed code on smart contracts.

Oracles can make smart contracts robust, enabling their application to many different and complex scenarios. Examples of oracles and smart contract interaction include releasing flight insurance payments upon flight cancelation, permitting margin calls on tokenized asset loans upon price changes in traditional asset markets such as the New York Stock Exchange, and making payments on smart, automated betting contracts based on the result of sporting events.

For financial transactions, identity oracles can block transactions to and from non-accredited investors from those not subscribed in a *whitelist* (a list of previously vetted and approved investors) or belonging to a *blacklist* (a list of previously vetted and rejected investors). They can also block certain age groups, such as those younger than 18 and residents from specific countries. Oracles can even restrict transactions to ID-verified users meeting compliance requirements such as know your customer (KYC), general data protection regulation, and anti-money laundering (AML).

Although oracles can safely and reliably analyze real-world events, some threats exist. If the data source outside the blockchain is manipulated, altered, deleted, or flawed, the smart contract process would be incorrect due to inaccurate data, not a coding problem in the smart contract. This issue refers to *oracle risk*. Its resolution requires a transparent methodology and sources, an auditable data trail and smart contracts relying on consensus-based oracles instead of a single oracle. A consensus-based oracle consists of many distributed and connected oracles. Therefore, it compares many data sources to identify and eliminate outliers and reduce oracle risk.

Although many use the concept of tokenized securities and security tokens interchangeably, essential differences exist between them. Tokenized securities and security tokens are digital assets. Both offer benefits over traditional securities, but the difference relies on the underlying asset. Tokenized assets or securities are a digital blockchain-embedded representation of real-world assets or securities. By contrast, security tokens do not represent a pre-existing adjacent asset or security but constitute a newly created security.

Security tokens are blockchain-native tokens that do not exist outside of the blockchain (Smith et al., 2019). Security tokens, also called dative digital securities (Lambert, Liebau, & Roosenboom, 2021), are uniquely programmable. Each security token can work differently from others, depending on its programmed functions. For example, each can have unique characteristics and ownership rights. Given that security tokens are financial securities, they must initially satisfy

Table 8.1. Comparison of Security Tokens and Tokenized Securities.

Security Token	Tokenized Security
Is a digital blockchain-native asset	Digital and blockchain-embedded representation of real-world assets
Represents a newly created security	Represents a pre-existing underlying asset
Can have unique characteristics and ownership rights distinct from traditional asset classes	The underlying security maintains its traditional characteristics and receives additional blockchain-enabled features
Must comply with all securities laws in the jurisdictions where the security token is issued and marketed	If applicable, it must comply with existing regulations that apply to the underlying asset and additional regulations targeting the tokenized security

Source: Authors' elaboration based on Smith et al. (2019).
Note: This table compares the key characteristics and features of security tokens and tokenized securities.

stricter levels of regulatory compliance and approvals. Therefore, each security token must be issued, transacted, and processed by the relevant federal securities' laws in the jurisdictions where they are issued and marketed. Table 8.1 compares security tokens and tokenized securities.

Potential Benefits of Tokenizing Traditional Assets and Securities

Blockchain technology and tokenization offer great advantages (Chen, 2018; Garcia-Teruel, 2021; Garcia-Teruel & Simón-Moreno, 2021; Roth, Schär & Schöpfer, 2019; Tian, Lu, et al., 2020). Their key benefits include:

- *Increased efficiency*. A benefit of using blockchain technology is reducing the need for intermediaries by automating specific smart contract processes. The absence of intermediaries also reduces the time required for settlement and issuance, auditing, transitioning, trading, purchases, and sales. It can also lead to better product management control among other processes. These benefits are also due to the native tools that blockchain technology offers for speeding up business processes.
- *Reduced cost*. Automation, transparent record-keeping, and reliance on the public internet allow significant cost reductions. Statistics show that blockchain technology can reduce bond issuance costs by up to 90 percent and fundraising costs by up to 40 percent compared to traditional private placement (Cashlink, 2020).

- *Increased transparency and security*. Tokenization and blockchain systems offer high transparency. Recording all transactions in a public ledger, stored in a distributed manner worldwide, increases reliability and reduces potential information disputes. Furthermore, the transparent intrinsic nature of blockchain systems permits quick and complete auditing. Tokenization enables absolute traceability of each tokenized asset.
- *Better compliance*. Programming allows including complex compliance requirements into each token created. Smart contracts can automatically verify KYC, AML, age, or specific local requirements compliance on any transaction.
- *Improved liquidity*. Tokenization helps investors efficiently offer their previously illiquid or non-fractionable assets to investors worldwide. Markets allowing higher divisibility and lower prices per unit tend to be more liquid than markets of assets that trade only in large batches (Muscarella & Vetsuypens, 1996). Since tokens can represent a fraction of the tokenized asset, entry barriers for small investors with low investment power diminish (Chang, 2020).
- *Facilitated innovation*. Smart contracts are programmable and accommodate the specific requirements of different industries. For example, smart contracts used in tokenized assets can create fractionalized real estate, liquid revenue share agreements, dynamic exchange-traded funds, and other previously unmanageable offerings in the finance industry. Also, blockchain innovation has already proved the enormous potential of this technology in creating new financing methods such as initial coin offerings (ICOs), initial exchange offerings, and decentralized finance (DeFi).

Tokenization can transform the market, democratize and globalize investment options, and facilitate innovation opportunities (Blémus & Guegan, 2020; OECD, 2020; Tian, Adriaens, et al., 2020; Tian, Lu, et al., 2020; Yermack, 2017). Entrepreneurs and innovators realize they can now tokenize almost any scarce asset (Chen, 2018). They can now benefit from these innovations through tokens representing preorders in crowdfunding campaigns and ownership stakes in profit-sharing crowdfunding campaigns (Belleflamme, Lambert, & Schwienbacher, 2014; Mollick, 2014; Rodriguez-Garnica, Gutierrez & Tribo, 2022; Vismara, 2016). The combination of traditional crowdfunding settings with blockchain technology has made ICOs emerge (Adhami, Giudici, & Martinazzi, 2018; Campino, Brochado, & Rosa, 2022; Gan et al., 2021; Howell et al., 2020; Momtaz, 2019, 2020, 2021; Momtaz, Rennertseder, & Schröder, 2019; Yermack, 2017).

Table 8.2 presents the benefits of tokenized assets and securities over traditional assets and securities in different activities and industries. These benefits include increasing the potential investor base through the global distribution of tokens, including retail investors due to the fractionalization of tokenized instruments, enhancing traceability of the underlying instrument, and securely incorporating and storing additional information of the instrument into the token.

Table 8.2. How Tokenization Benefits Business, Stakeholders, and the Traditional System.

	Traditional Assets	Tokenized Assets
Fundraising	• Entrepreneurs may raise funds from angel investors or venture capitalists. • Entrepreneurs may raise funds from the public through crowdfunding	• Entrepreneurs can raise funds directly from any investor type worldwide. • Entrepreneurs can raise funds from the public through ICOs
Investing	• Average investors have few opportunities to invest in promising early-stage ventures. • Investors have limited liquidity with private company investments	• Average investors can have almost equal opportunities to invest in early-stage ventures worldwide through blockchain tokens. • Investors enjoy almost immediate liquidity with blockchain tokens. They can freely transfer tokens representing an asset
Real estate	• Low liquidity occurs after making the initial investment. • High entry barriers. Few investors have enough capital for the initial payment to acquire the property and then obtain a mortgage for the remaining capital	• Investors experience higher liquidity of traditionally illiquid investments. • Democratization occurs due to low entry barriers. A small initial investment is enough to acquire the whole or part of a token representing the real estate investment
Agro-Commodities	• Traceability of products along their lifecycle is complex and prone to falsifications, fraud, and errors. • Production loans are difficult to obtain. • Intermediaries are necessary to provide the commodity to the final user, and prices are opaque. • Preselling commodities occurs for complex security assets like futures	• Traceability of products is secure, unalterable, and efficient. For instance, livestock lifecycle events result in tracing and efficient pricing. • Asset-backed tokens collateralize or back production loans. Asset-backed tokens are publicly available in secondary marketplaces to any user and have transparent prices. • Investors can easily presell asset-backed tokens like a ton of wheat

(*Continued*)

Table 8.2. (*Continued*)

	Traditional Assets	**Tokenized Assets**
Law	• Any transaction or event registration requires a notary and registrar. • System costs are higher	• DLT is enough for registering an event to be certified and binding. • An oracle is cheaper than a notary or registrar for connecting the real world to the asset and token events
Community Building	• Platforms may appeal to users and third-party providers after achieving strong network effects	• Platforms can reward early adopters with tokens, compensating for the lack of network effects
Open Sourcing	• Open-source projects may fund their continued development through donations. • Open-source projects usually do not share their success with core developers	• Open-source projects can fund their continued development through token sales. • Open-source projects can share their success with core developers through tokens

Source: Authors' elaboration of Chen (2018, p. 569).
Note: This table summarizes the tokenization benefits of traditional assets across different use cases and industries.

The Tokenization Process

Although the tokenization process might look tedious and obscure, many tools and services facilitate issuers and businesses in the tokenization process. Examples include Polymath, Tokeny, Templum, Securitize, Swarm, Nivaura, Horizon, tZero, Paxos, LiquidShare, Setl.io, Zodia, and Custody. Therefore, the tokenization process becomes more straightforward and more intuitive due to new tools in this changing environment.

Tokenization processes differ based on the tools used and the tokenization goal or underlying asset (Sazandrishvili, 2020; Tian, Adriaens, et al., 2020). The following tokenization steps are common to most assets that a business may want to tokenize.

Ecosystem Assembly

The first step in the tokenization process is analyzing and planning the use or creation of a robust ecosystem of industry specialists for a specific token. Therefore, businesses interested in tokenizing assets should consider the digital asset lifecycle and ensure the proper fit of each piece of the ecosystem. Developers should plan the technical, legal, marketing, business, and financial aspects to satisfy participant needs and ensure the ecosystem is strong enough to cover unpredictable situations by following the smart contract coded rules.

Regarding ecosystem assembly, two potential approaches depend on the services provided by the ecosystem participants. Some token issuance platforms might offer end-to-end service, an "all-in-one" solution approach. Others follow a "modular approach," specializing in a few specific services. Issuers partnering with providers offering an "all-in-one" solution approach do not need to find other partners to cover further ecosystem needs. Issuers with particular requirements such as exponential scalability or high customization levels often prefer a modular approach, assembling an ecosystem of providers.

Examples of participants that can integrate a complete ecosystem follow.

- KYC/AML providers help issuers comply with securities regulation requirements in an automated instead of a traditional manual one.
- Legal service providers assist in submitting regulatory filings and structuring the token offerings.
- Advisory service providers facilitate the relationship between market agents such as buyers and sellers. They can assist in developing a business plan and launching a token offering, token custody, distribution, and the token payment process.
- Marketing service providers develop promotion actions, list the token offering on different platforms, and provide press releases.
- Token sale platforms facilitate primary and secondary token sales.
- Capitalization table management platforms manage company equity and holdings, offer an updated list of token owners, and provide regulatory compliance.
- Custodians safely keep funds and tokens and manage ownership rights attributed to investors. However, many jurisdictions still need to provide clear legislation to deal with the insolvency risks of crypto custodians (Haentjens, De Graaf, & Kokorin, 2020).

Security Token Creation

The next step after ecosystem assembly is to configure the token to represent the asset. Coding and programming a token's characteristics and the related smart contracts are critical in a successful tokenization process. The token configuration should be simple, intuitive, and transparent regardless of the technology or adjacent asset type. Therefore, tokenization should avoid introducing complexities but improve traditional processes using technology. Blockchain selection should consider technical capabilities and its provider and user network, especially an oracle's availability to integrate off-chain information and the existence of a user base compatible with the tokenized asset or security.

Compliance Set-up

Automating compliance is crucial to consider during the tokenization process. Enforcing token investors to comply with the changing and complex regulatory environment processes is notoriously costly and time-consuming. Each investor must comply with different securities regulation requirements depending on the jurisdiction where a token is issued and where an investor is domiciled.

Services dealing with meeting ownership and transfer restrictions, fulfilling KYC/AML obligations, and enforcing requirements for future transfers involve continuous development. Automating these compliance requirements is possible because blockchain technology maintains a clear record of procedures and compliance activities for each investor/user in a secure, immutable manner. Blockchain technology also reduces the risk of errors and oversights.

Oracles are essential for restricting token ownership by age, residency, and accreditation (KYC/AML) status, among other identity-based restrictions. KYC and AML providers are not only oracles but also other agents attaching attestations to "investors" identities. The blockchain includes off-chain information through oracles, becoming on-chain information. Therefore, smart contracts can automatically respond to this on-chain evidence checking and ensure that investors meet all requirements before transferring any token. Automating this process automatically allows investors to comply with all rules and conditions set in each jurisdiction. In summary, a smart contract should set systematic and automatic transfer and ownership restrictions by using previously selected trusted attestation providers.

Token Distribution

Token distribution is the process of transferring tokens to their intended recipients. This process is like a primary issuance and usually proceeds as follows. First, interested investors transfer funds to an entity in charge of the distribution process, usually a broker-dealer. Once the external broker-dealer receives the funds, it requests the custodian holding the tokens to transfer them to the investor's private wallet. Once the investor gets the token, the issuer instantly receives the payment of the retained funds by the broker-dealer. This process resembles the traditional distribution of securities but is cheaper and quicker. It is also more secure due to using a unique, immutable, and public transaction record through blockchain, which is the only source of truth against any agent's complaints. Therefore, the asset distribution process through blockchain technology provides automated, transparent, and reportable transactions during the initial and future token distribution processes.

The token distribution process offers issuers and stakeholders different pricing, minting, control, and custody opportunities. Token distribution allows issuers to set pricing tiers for their tokens depending on arrival orders and market demand. It also allows transferring tokens in exchange for funds in any currency – fiat and crypto – as determined by the issuer. In terms of minting the token, the issuer can pre-establish a list of requirements, such as intended recipients or selling restrictions. Record transparency and visibility give substantial control to token issuers and other stakeholders. Finally, issuers and investors can establish a custody service to hold tokens during the token distribution process.

Corporate Actions Execution and Management

Corporate actions are events initiated by public companies that can provoke changes in the securities issued by the company and hence affect stakeholders. Events considered corporate actions include rights issues, voting in annual or extraordinary general meetings, stock splits, coupon payments, dividend distributions, spin-offs, mergers, and acquisitions. These corporate actions are traditionally complex, costly, labor-intensive, and error-prone.

Using tokenization processes and blockchain technology can simplify these actions. They can also state clear and transparent information and rules on distributing dividends, transparency of token distributions among all stakeholders, and security, so no privileges or errors occur without stakeholders noticing. Therefore, establishing token distribution rules through coding is useful whether the business benefits are predictable (bond payments) or unpredictable (dividend payments. Blockchain technology also helps issuers publicly state announcements and notices on-chain to transmit information efficiently to any investor. It also provides faster report generation. Tokenized shares allow streamlining of the execution of stock options contracts, share splits, share exchanges, and other share agreements. Finally, investors can vote on-chain efficiently and transparently during annual meetings and motions.

Asset and Security Tokenization Platforms

Various tokenization platforms are available. Some platforms specialize in a particular service of the tokenization process, such as Polymath, offering highly customized services. Private businesses wanting to tokenize specific and heterogeneous asset types often use these companies and platforms. Other companies provide a full-service approach to the tokenization process, such as tZero, including token issuance to a secondary marketplace or exchange and post-trading services, such as custody, clearing, settlement, compliance, and reporting. These companies offer more standardized services, use permissioned technology, and focus on specific asset types. Some providers are a hybrid form, providing primary and secondary market services, such as Securitize. These companies tend to collaborate with partners providing post-trading services. Hence, financial institutions are the primary users of these services.

The following platforms provide services for asset and security tokenization.

- *tZero*. Created in 2014 in New York, tZero is one of the first companies to tokenize assets. It provides a marketplace where investors can buy and sell private asset-backed tokens. tZero uses Ethereum, Tezos, and Algorand blockchains.
- *ConsenSys Codefi*. Established in 2017 in New York, ConsenSys Codefi offers many blockchain applications for businesses. Its tokenization application, called Codefi Assets, operates a secondary marketplace. It uses Ethereum for the tokenization processes.

- *Securitize.* Starting in 2017 in San Francisco, the company offered full-service covering primary asset issuance to secondary exchange, market trading, and post-trading. It has a secondary market called Securitize Markets, where investors can buy and sell new asset-backed tokens. Securitize has over 200 issuers of crypto-asset and asset-backed tokens and more than 300,000 accredited investors. Furthermore, it is registered as an alternative trading system and performs as a licensed broker-dealer by the Securities and Exchange Commission and Financial Industry Regulatory Authority. Securitize uses Ethereum, Algorand, and Avalanche for the tokenization processes.
- *Polymath.* Founded in 2017 in Toronto, Polymath is an asset tokenization and issuance platform specializing in creating, issuing, and managing asset-backed tokens. In February 2022, it had tokenized over 200 assets on its platform, worth more than $2.4 billion. The company is developing a permissioned blockchain built for security tokens.

Many evolving options are available in blockchain infrastructure, classified as permissioned and permissionless infrastructure. Some companies prefer using private, permissioned blockchain infrastructure to maintain complete control over the activity. Examples of permissioned blockchain infrastructure are Polymesh and Quorum. Other companies favor using public, permissionless infrastructure, which is usually open-source and accessible to community developers. Therefore, companies can easily integrate innovations, creating and implementing new applications. Corporations prefer this option because it offers higher innovative tools, services, and applications. Ethereum, Solana, Tezos, and Cardano are permissionless blockchain infrastructures.

Current Tokenized Assets and Securities Projects

The following are examples of current tokenized asset projects worldwide.

Reental – Real Estate

High entry barriers and low liquidity characterize real estate investments. Investors usually require large down payments and high credit scores to obtain mortgage financing. In real estate markets, direct ownership cannot be fractionalized among many investors since it requires special investment vehicles with high intermediary and legal costs.

Reental, a Spain-based firm, uses the tokenization process of a participating loan to acquire a real estate investment, with a minimum amount of €100 (Reental, 2021). The company rents the property and distributes dividends to token holders every month. After two years, Reental sells the property, receiving capital gains and distributing them among token holders. Furthermore, Reental fractionalizes a real estate investment and increases its liquidity by combining multiple DeFi protocols. These protocols provide liquidity pools for the property-backed tokens so that investors can trade them at market value.

Santander Bank – Debt Issuance

In September 2019, Santander Bank issued the first bond issued end-to-end on a public blockchain (Santander Bank, 2019). The bond, valued at $20 million, offered 1.98 percent quarterly coupons, which Santander Bank also tokenized. Santander Securities Services functioned as the tokenizing agent and custodian. According to the bank, this process offers increased market transparency, shorter settlement time, increased security, and fewer intermediaries.

Agrotoken – Commodities

Agrotoken is a tokenization ecosystem providing commodities tokenization, trading, custody, wallet, and integration with oracles and third-party applications (Agrotoken, 2020). The company currently issues tokens backed by tradable commodities, such as a metric ton of wheat, corn, and soy. Grain producers deposit their product with a custodian, who generates a certificate of deposit and informs Agrotoken. Agrotoken issues or "mints" new tokens equivalent to the deposited amount of grain and transfers them to producers' wallets. Producers can trade the token in the internal market or P2P. Prices are set by the market and tracked by oracles that connect with commodities markets in the region. Token holders can claim the underlying grain from the custodian, which would lead to a token's destruction (burning).

Summary and Conclusions

Tokenizing real-world assets is a promising phenomenon that can enhance traditional business models from different industries, reducing inefficiencies and expanding value creation potential. This chapter reviews tokenization applied to traditional assets and securities. It also differentiates tokenized securities from security tokens, explores tokenization's potential benefits, describes steps in the tokenization process, discusses some involved stakeholders, and presents current business applications of tokenized assets and securities.

Discussion Questions

1. Explain the difference between tokenized securities and security tokens.
2. Describe some tokenization benefits of traditional assets.
3. Explain the steps of the tokenization process.
4. Discuss the importance of oracles in the asset tokenization process.

References

Adhami, S., Giudici, G., & Martinazzi, S. (2018). Why do businesses go crypto? An empirical analysis of initial coin offerings. *Journal of Economics and Business*, *100*(C), 64–75.

AgroToken. (2020). Retrieved from https://register.agrotoken.io/bundles/app/whitepaper_es.pdf

Baum, A. (2021). Tokenization: The future of real estate investment? *Journal of Portfolio Management*, *47*(10), 41–61.

Belleflamme, P., Lambert, T., & Schwienbacher, A. (2014). Crowdfunding: Tapping the right crowd. *Journal of Business Venturing*, *29*(5), 585–609.

Blémus, S., & Guégan, D. (2020). Initial crypto-asset offerings (ICOs), tokenization and corporate governance. *Capital Markets Law Journal*, *15*(2), 191–223.

Campino, J., Brochado, A., & Rosa, A. (2022). Initial coin offerings (ICOs): Why do they succeed? *Financial Innovation*, *8*(17), 1–35.

Cashlink. (2020, October 1). Cost disruption in the issuance market. Retrieved from https://cashlink.de/cost-disruption/

Chang, C. (2020). From securitization to tokenization. In A. Pentland, A. Lipton, & T. Hardjono (Eds.), *Building the new economy: Data as capital* (pp. 89–104). Cambridge, MA: The MIT Press.

Chen, Y. (2018). Blockchain tokens and the potential democratization of entrepreneurship and innovation. *Business Horizons*, *61*(4), 567–575.

Cong, L. W., & He, Z. (2019). Blockchain disruption and smart contracts. *Review of Financial Studies*, *32*(5), 1754–1797.

Dorfleitner, G., & Braun, D. (2019). Fintech, digitalization and blockchain: Possible applications for green finance. In M. Migliorelli & P. Dessertine (Eds.), *The rise of green finance in Europe* (pp. 207–237). Palgrave Studies in Impact Finance. Cham: Palgrave Macmillan.

Gan, J. R., Tsoukalas, G., & Netessine, S. (2021). Initial coin offerings, speculation, and asset tokenization. *Management Science*, *67*(2), 914–931.

Garcia-Teruel, R. M. (2020). Legal challenges and opportunities of blockchain technology in the real estate sector. *Journal of Property, Planning and Environmental Law*, *12*(2), 129–145.

Garcia-Teruel, R. M., & Simón-Moreno, H. (2021). The digital tokenization of property rights. A comparative perspective. *Computer Law & Security Review*, *41*(2), 1–16.

Haentjens, M., De Graaf, T., & Kokorin, I. (2020). The failed hopes of disintermediation: Crypto-custodian insolvency, legal risks and how to avoid them. *Singapore Journal of Legal Studies* (September), 526–563.

Howell, S. T., Niessner, M., & Yermack, D. (2020). Initial coin offerings: Financing growth with cryptocurrency token sales. *Review of Financial Studies*, *33*(9), 3925–3974.

Khan, N., Kchouri, B., Yatoo, N. A., Kräussl, Z., Patel, A., & State, R. (2022). Tokenization of Sukuk: Ethereum case study. *Global Finance Journal*, *51*(C), 100539.

Lambert, T., Liebau, D., & Roosenboom, P. (2021). Security token offerings. *Small Business Economics*, *12*, 1–27.

Lucas-Rhimbassen, M. (2021). On the dangers of enclosing the intangible: Applying Pistor's 'code of capital' critique to 'space 3.0' and DLT from an anti-monopoly perspective. In A. Froehlich (Ed.), *Outer space and cyber space* (pp. 29–54). Studies in Space Policy. Cham: Springer Nature Switzerland AG.

Mollick, E. (2014). The dynamics of crowdfunding: An exploratory study. *Journal of Business Venturing*, *29*(1), 1–16.

Momtaz, P. P. (2019). Token sales and initial coin offerings: Introduction. *Journal of Alternative Investments*, *21*(4), 7–12.

Momtaz, P. P. (2020). Initial coin offerings, asymmetric information, and loyal CEOs. *Small Business Economics*, *57*(2), 975–997.

Momtaz, P. P. (2021). Entrepreneurial finance and moral hazard: Evidence from token offerings. *Journal of Business Venturing*, *36*(5), 106001.

Momtaz, P. P., Rennertseder, K., & Schröder, H. (2019). Token offerings: A revolution in corporate finance? *Journal of Financial Transformation*, *49*, 32–41.

Mougayar, W. (2016). *The business blockchain: Promise, practice, and application of the next internet technology*. Hoboken, NJ: John Wiley & Sons, Inc.

Muscarella, C. J., & Vetsuypens, M. R. (1996). Stock splits: Signaling or liquidity? The case of ADR solo-splits. *Journal of Financial Economics*, *42*(1), 3–26.

Neves, L. P., & Prata, G. A. (2018). *Blockchain contributions for the climate finance: Introducing a debate*. Rio de Janeiro: FGV, International Intelligence Unit. Retrieved from https://www.kas.de/c/document_library/get_file?uuid=ea6109a2-7677-9bfa-d4d0-6cbae35ebcc7&groupId=252038

OECD. (2020). *The tokenisation of assets and potential implications for financial markets*. OECD Blockchain Policy Series. Retrieved from https://www.oecd.org/finance/The-Tokenisation-of-Assets-and-Potential-Implications-for-Financial-Markets.htm

Reental. (2021). Retrieved from www.reental.co

Rodriguez-Garnica, G., Gutierrez, M., & Tribo, J. A. (2022). *Signaling and herding in reward-based crowdfunding: Complements or substitutes?* Working Paper, University Carlos III, Madrid.

Roth, J., Schär, F., & Schöpfer, A. (2019). The tokenization of assets: Using blockchains for equity crowdfunding. In K. Wendt (Ed.), *Theories of change: Change leadership tools, models and applications for investing in sustainable development* (pp. 329–350). Cham: Springer Nature Switzerland AG.

Santander Bank. (2019). Retrieved from https://www.santander.com/en/press-room/press-releases/santander-launches-the-first-end-to-end-blockchain-bond

Sazandrishvili, G. (2020). Asset tokenization in plain English. *Journal of Corporate Accounting and Finance*, *31*(2), 68–73.

Schletz, M., Nassiry, D., & Lee, M.-K. (2020). *Blockchain and tokenized securities: The potential for green finance*. Working Paper 1079, Asian Development Bank Institute. Retrieved from https://www.adb.org/publications/blockchain-tokenized-securities-potential-green-finance

Smith, J., Manasi, V., Benedetti, H., Yoshida, K., & Vogel, Z. (2019). *Tokenized securities and commercial real estate*. Working Group Research Paper, MIT Digital Currency Initiative.

Tian, Y., Adriaens, P., Minchin, E., Chang, C., Lu, Z., & Qi, C. (2020). *Asset tokenization: A blockchain solution to financing infrastructure in emerging markets and developing economies*. Working Paper, Institute of Global Finance.

Tian, Y., Lu, Z., Adriaens, P., Minchin, R. E., Caithness, A., & Woo, J. (2020). Finance infrastructure through blockchain-based tokenization. *Frontiers of Engineering Management*, *7*(4), 485–499.

Uzsoki, D. (2019). *Tokenization of infrastructure: A blockchain-based solution to financing sustainable infrastructure*. International Institute for Sustainable Development. Retrieved from https://www.iisd.org/system/files/publications/tokenization-infrastructure-blockchain-solution.pdf

Vismara, S. (2016). Equity retention and social network theory in equity crowdfunding. *Small Business Economics*, *46*(4), 579–590.

Yermack, D. (2017). Corporate governance and blockchains. *Review of Finance*, *21*(1), 7–31.

Part III

Cryptoassets as Investment Opportunities

Chapter 9

A Comparative Review of Cryptoasset Products

Kristin M. Kalish, Kerem Proulx and Andrew C. Spieler

Abstract

Cryptoassets are an asset class recorded in a digital form that does not represent a financial claim or liability for an issuer or a custodian. This chapter provides a detailed review of various cryptoassets by comparing different characteristics, products, and listing exchanges and discusses criticisms of the crypto ecosystem. It also discusses cryptoasset features, methods of tokenization, and advances in decentralized, peer-to-peer exchanges. Another topic examined is the criticisms of cryptoasset exchanges and ongoing regulatory implications due to cryptocurrency's open-source nature. The chapter evaluates numerous types and trends of cryptoassets, including currency, utility, platform, and transactional tokens.

Keywords: Cryptoassets; cryptocurrency; tokenization; peer-to-peer exchanges; cryptoasset exchanges; open-source

Introduction

Cryptoassets are digital assets that leverage cryptographic methods to provide a medium of exchange, represent some form of rights, and give the holder some future benefit as defined in a decentralized network. Use cases of these assets range from financial transactions to facilitating an arbitrary mechanism or incentive design. For instance, a cryptocurrency exchange for goods or services operates like fiat currency. However, it requires clearing several technical hurdles during a cryptoasset transaction. Transactions in the cryptoasset ecosystem typically refer to a cryptographically signed packet of data sent from an account that affects

The Emerald Handbook on Cryptoassets: Investment Opportunities and Challenges, 125–139

doi:10.1108/978-1-80455-320-620221009

the state of a blockchain. A governance token could be minted and distributed to users of a decentralized application (Dapp) or platform to reward them for using and providing voting power to participate in future decision-making. Cryptoassets have also become popular financial instruments, with US dollars (USD) billions of cryptoassets trading on crypto exchanges. In addition, with services such as Synthetix or dYdX pioneering the crypto-derivative space, including a few financial institutions offering bitcoin, BTC, futures products), the proliferation of cryptoassets as viable trading instruments is still in its infancy.

Although the widespread use of cryptoassets has several implications for financial markets, this digital asset class has limitations that could hinder its adoption or pose hurdles to owners and users. For example, cryptoassets are not widely accepted or adopted as a viable medium of exchange. The properties traditionally associated with fiat currency remain. However, their use outside of finance or decentralized finance (DeFi) is limited. Services providing solutions to this problem, such as cryptocurrency credit cards, have technical and political limitations for using crypto as a traditional currency. The development of user-friendly crypto wallets by services such as MetaMask facilitates the ownership and exchange of cryptoassets between peers and mitigates technical issues. Enterprise solutions such as multi-signature wallets, also called multi-sig-wallets, also verify using cryptography so that a pre-defined portion of a wallet's owners approves a transaction before sending it to the blockchain network. Although these services exist, many enterprises are reluctant to accept cryptoassets due to policymakers' uncertainty surrounding potential regulatory restrictions.

Another limitation is that cryptoassets rely upon decentralized networks built on blockchain technology, providing all the fundamental strengths and technical advantages of cryptoassets over traditional assets. The primary limiting factor of these networks, however, is scalability. Recently, networks such as Ethereum (ETH) have made significant advances in this respect. However, transactions on blockchain networks are notoriously slow and can be expensive because of network transaction fees. Miners receive these fees and for the computing power of the ETH virtual machine (EVM). This scalability issue is why the BTC blockchain relies upon the Lighthouse layer two solution to facilitate more efficient transactions. *Layer two* is an application built on top of the base blockchain layer. ETH relies on services like Arbitrum or ZK-rollup to increase transaction throughput.

A final limitation is that cryptoassets suffer considerable scrutiny from policymakers and central bankers for potential use associated with criminal activity. Cryptoassets may cause environmental harm because of the tools needed to secure blockchains, typically mining blocks of transactions using large computer clusters made of parallelized graphics processing units (GPUs). Producing mining blocks could cause environmental damage, excluding the amount of electricity needed to run such clusters. This environmental scrutiny has led to frictions in the widespread adoption of cryptoassets and may further hinder their proliferation. However, with the development of new consensus mechanisms such as proof-of-stake (PoS), the need for GPUs, application-specific integrated circuits (ASICs), and other compute or proof-of-work (PoW)-based methods should decline in popularity and offset these environmental factors indirectly.

Cryptoasset Characteristics

Unlike other mechanisms facilitating a transaction, cryptoassets do not represent a financial claim or liability for an issuer or a custodian. Instead, cryptoasset protocols use open-source methodology freely available for redistribution and modification by all users. All cryptoasset transactions use timestamps in blockchain, creating chronological documentation of ownership and custody of the assets. In general, a cryptoasset must meet four characteristics:

- *Cryptography*. This practice is the basis for cryptoasset construction. Cryptography comes from the Greek syntax meaning "secret writing." It is a mathematics and computer science discipline focused on securely communicating messages or data. Algorithms such as the secure hash algorithm (SHA) and Keccak256 are used to sign transactions, generate public and private keys, and create unique deterministic hashes used in blockchains. Using cryptography offers the foundation for much of the security and attractive characteristics of cryptoassets.
- *Distributed ledger technology (DLT)*. A *blockchain* is a method of storing data on a distributed and decentralized network on a peer-to-peer (P2P) basis in a cryptographically secure way. Without such security, blockchain networks would not be socially or economically viable. In a traditional centralized system, a central authority validates legitimacy throughout the system. For instance, a central bank, such as the Federal Reserve in the United States, determines monetary policy and acts as the main point of trust and authority. This point of trust also serves as a central point of vulnerability. If a foreign attacker were to compromise the central bank, this attacker would effectively compromise the entire US financial system. Blockchains implement a mantra of "do not trust, validate." They provide the basis for a decentralized network among several participants, known as *nodes*, which can each individually validate and attest to the state of the blockchain and the data stored on it, creating a more robust system void of any single point of potential fault. The earliest blockchains used a PoW-based consensus algorithm to validate blocks and the linkages between blocks. This approach removes the need for trust in a central authority, as any node in the network can verify that these transactions occurred. Consensus algorithms also ensure the properties of immutability and security of blockchains and DLTs. Suppose one node is compromised in a network and attempts to make a malicious change to a previously mined block. In that case, the other nodes in the network can detect this issue by inspecting the block's header and hash, denying this change. A *hash* is a unique identifier of a block containing information about its content and linking it to previous blocks, known as *children*.
- *Exclusion of any third-party intermediaries*. In traditional finance, when a user conducts a transaction at a point of sale (e.g., at a local business with a debit card), the payment is routed through various third-party service providers to facilitate the transfer of funds from a user's bank account into a receiver's bank account. The crypto ecosystem criticizes this reliance on third-party

intermediaries. It places too much trust in centralized entities that could willingly conduct malpractice without a user's knowledge, taking advantage of the absence of transparency. The inability of users to act and process a single point of fault in the event of a system compromise undermines the robustness of the macro-system that relies upon these third parties.

- *Tokenization*. Tokens are the digital representation of an asset, utility, or some arbitrary form of data that facilitates secure storage, transfer, or verification. *Tokenization* is the process of storing information related to an asset in a digital format for use within a blockchain system. Tangible assets such as gold, art, and real estate can become tokens, along with intangible assets such as ownership rights and licenses. Tokenization predates the development of blockchains as advances in early cryptography allowed for converting sensitive client information such as social security and credit card numbers into an alphanumeric string that facilitated the secure transfer and storage of sensitive data. These tokenized data pass through a cryptographic decryption function to retrieve the data stored.

Tokenizing "real" assets offers several advantages. First, users exchange tokenized assets more frequently than tangible assets like art or real estate. Of course, tokens only represent an asset's ownership within a blockchain ecosystem. However, the modular nature of tokens allows their creators to design various functionalities and embed other desirable properties, such as non-fungible tokens (NTFs). NFTs are unique in that users cannot duplicate or mint each specific token. Use cases for NFTs range from tokenizing art to real estate. Some tokens have an "expiry" date wherein they must be spent or used by the maturity date. Afterward, the tokens are burned or effectively deleted. Tokenization also allows market participants to bypass intermediaries traditionally involved in selling assets as participants exchange tokens in a P2P setting. Finally, blockchain systems ensure provable authenticity and provide a transparent, auditable, and immutable transaction history.

Types of Cryptoassets and Tokens

Although various cryptoassets and tokens exchange on blockchain systems, ranging from BTC to ETH and other alternative coins such as DAI and Filecoin, there are broadly four main methods to tokenize assets. The implementations can differ. The features of one token may resemble those of another, as the specificity of any one token largely depends on its use and ecosystem.

Currency Tokens

Currency tokens are the most common and well-known class of tokens. Transactions combine into blocks in currency token protocols. The building blocks link together in a historical transaction record throughout the blockchain system. BTC and ETH are the two most notable currency tokens to be spent and exchanged, like the behavior of fiat currency. Although the currency token's value does not derive from an underlying asset, several asset-backed currency tokens aim to maintain a peg to the value of a unit of currency, such as $1 (USD). These tokens are "stablecoins." They are backed by exact reserves in USD, such as Gemini's GUSD, or maintain a ranged peg to the value of $1, such as MakerDAO's DAI token. Users utilize currency tokens as the base for an incentive mechanism in the context of various blockchain-based services and applications.

Platform Tokens

Platform tokens enable Dapp stacks and various mechanisms and use cases. Typically, these tokens are used in smart contracts or underlying networks to deliver arbitrary functionality through a blockchain infrastructure. Smart contracts are neither smart nor contracts. They consist of code allowing for the design of applications and services on top of blockchains and enabling interaction with these services by general users, typically by using a platform token. MakeDAO's DAI token is an example of a platform token designated as a stablecoin. It maintains a soft peg to the USD through arbitrage mechanisms built into the DAI smart contract stack. It is also the token of exchange on its platform, enabling other services to extend its functionality and build complementary services. Platform tokens provide rewards for users who use the platform and, in some cases, refund transaction fees.

Utility Tokens

Utility tokens represent a form of tokenized rights or access granted to a service on a blockchain network. They have several use cases typically tied to their implementation, the mechanism design of their service, and the network. Use cases include paying back transaction fees and providing voting rights and a governance framework to members of a decentralized autonomous organization (DAO). In some cases, utility tokens make up the incentive mechanism for a blockchain's consensus algorithm.

Transactional Tokens

Transactional tokens serve as units of account and typically resemble the properties of traditional currency. However, they can provide incremental benefits for blockchain infrastructure. For instance, no need exists for third-party intermediaries or central clearing authorities such as banks or clearinghouses when using transactional tokens. Another use of transactional tokens is to facilitate transactions such as cross-currency exchanges. Besides taking on the properties of traditional mediums of exchange, various industries, such as global supply chain logistics, use transactional tokens to leverage the characteristics and security advantages of blockchains and smart contracts to enhance their operations.

Cryptocurrency

A *cryptocurrency* is a tradeable digital asset and form of currency that uses blockchain technology and cryptography to facilitate transactions as a medium of exchange. Advanced coding practices allow storing and transmitting cryptocurrency data between user wallets and public ledgers, increasing security and safety through encryption. This section discusses prominent cryptocurrencies like BTC, litecoin (LTC), dogecoin, and dash.

Bitcoin

BTC was the first modern implementation of a decentralized cryptocurrency built on top of a distributed P2P blockchain infrastructure. Technically, several iterations of digital currency began with "e-gold" in 1996, which ended with a legal battle against the US Department of the Treasury. Satoshi Nakamoto is the name used by the presumed pseudonymous person or persons who developed BTC (Nakamoto, 2008). Much speculation exists about Nakamoto's identity. However, some prominent figures in the cryptocurrency space believe the identity is Hal Finney. This influential computer scientist, who contributed significantly to BTC's development, received the first transaction on the BTC network between Nakamoto and himself.

BTC removes the need for a trusted third party to facilitate online transactions. It improves upon the existing implementations of digital currencies, which lack a robust method of network consensus. The cryptographic PoW consensus mechanism, a method like an existing one implemented by Hashcash (Back, 2002), solves the problem of P2P verification. The assumption is that "if honest nodes control a majority of CPU power … the honest chain will outpace any competing chains" (Nakamoto, 2008, p. 3). PoW and other consensus algorithms have improved since their inception in 2008. However, the original BTC whitepaper laid the groundwork for the now $2 trillion cryptocurrency market (Ossinger, 2021). It also enabled creating several P2P electronic payment system solutions.

Although BTC has evolved since Nakamoto's premiere, the network has received widespread criticism from other cryptocurrency communities due to its performance constraints and high transaction costs. The bottlenecks affecting BTC often arise from its highly polarized developer community. BTC and most other cryptocurrencies are technically open-source projects. Cryptoassets are not developed or maintained by a sole organization or considered proprietary software. Any individual with software engineering skills can inspect the BTC source code. Such individuals can propose improvements to implement enough network participants to "upgrade" to the new version of the BTC protocol. The most widely adopted version of the BTC software is the BTC Core project, which uses forking from the original implementation by Satoshi Nakamoto. *Forking* is a term originating in the software development community, which loosely means to base a new version of software on an existing project, making up most of the BTC network's nodes.

The BTC network processes three transactions per second. Transaction fees range from a recent high on April 9, 2021, of $62.79 to $2.41 on February 8, 2022 (Blockchain.com Staff, 2021). This variability in transaction fees and speed is the main criticism facing the BTC network. Such criticism led to questions about its viability in replacing traditional currency and potentially limiting its use case, despite its rise to more than $60,000 in value per coin. Although BTC is popular with traders and other market participants as an alternative asset class, some cryptocurrency community members question the importance of BTC's price maximalist nature. Members of the traditional financial community often accuse BTC and cryptocurrency of being pseudo-pyramid schemes. They criticize the currency's ability to deliver on the utility promised by its mysterious creator.

Litecoin

LTC is a viable alternative to BTC and is a fork of BTC Core. LTC aimed to improve upon several criticisms of BTC by decreasing block generation time to 2.5 minutes versus BTC's 10 minutes, leading to a capacity for 56 transactions per second ("Litecoin – Litecoin Wiki", 2022). LTC additionally implements a different hashing algorithm for use in its PoW mechanism instead of SHA-256 used by BTC. Scrypt (pronounced "ess-crypt") is a *memory-hungry algorithm*, meaning the algorithm occupies a large amount of space in a computer's memory. Therefore, using it to perform large-scale custom hardware attacks is particularly costly. This algorithm makes the field-programmable gate array and ASIC hardware needed for mining LTC much more expensive to produce, creating a higher cost barrier for potential attackers. LTC also features lower transaction costs than BTC, with an average transaction fee of three to four cents (Statista.com Staff, 2021).

Dogecoin

Dogecoin's creation in 2013 was to deride the widespread speculation occurring in the cryptocurrency markets. Since its introduction, dogecoin has participated in several market frenzies, representing a market cap increase from about $500 million to more than $80 billion, rising more than 20,000 percent. The currency's original creators and current maintainers still enjoy mocking the cryptocurrency and broader financial ecosystem, maintaining the token's lighthearted nature. Little technical difference exists between dogecoin and BTC. Dogecoin is a fork of BTC, with the addition that it sports a mascot of a Shiba Inu breed of a Japanese dog, a homage to an online meme. Elon Musk helped popularize the coin through whimsical tweets that stoked a trading frenzy in the coin in early 2021. Although the coin originated as a joke, the sentiment of its developer community and creators harkens to the dissonant nature of much of the technical crypto community concerning their views of traditional finance. Some within the cryptocurrency community believe the financial industry's current state emphasizes speculation and price maximization, blatantly disregarding value or utility creation. A vocal critic of the financial system, Billy Markus avidly tweets tongue-in-cheek remarks and memes about his stance.

Dash

Dash is an alternative cryptocurrency, forked from the BTC protocol and launched in 2014 by Evan Duffield, originally as XCoin. Dash claims to process transactions in under 1.5 seconds (Luz, 2019) and relies upon the X11 cryptographic algorithm to secure its PoW mechanism. What makes dash novel compared to BTC and LTC is its governance model. Dash is a form of DAO run by master nodes. Master nodes facilitate many of a blockchain's same properties as vanilla, or common nodes. A *common node* is one the average users run and maintain. Thus, they do not require such ample resources or capital investments as a master node. However, a user must hold 1,000 dash coins to become a master node and participate in on-chain governance. This configuration has led to much criticism of the Dash network's decentralization. The master node architecture causes a large concentration of governance power in a small group of wealthy Dash holders. This situation creates a potentially vulnerable attack vector for malicious actors seeking to compromise the blockchain and increases the risk of collusion between a small group of master nodes.

Platform Tokens

Platform tokens use blockchain technology to support Daaps. Two notable features of platform tokens include providing higher security and facilitating transactional activity. This section discusses platform tokens such as ETH, Neo, and EOS.IO, with ETH viewed as the prominent platform token of the three.

Ethereum

ETH is a next-generation smart contract and decentralized application platform launched in 2015 by Vitalik Buterin and Anthony Di Iorio (Buterin, 2013). Its focus was to dramatically improve upon the utility aspect of cryptocurrencies by creating a platform-based ecosystem, allowing an open community of developers to develop decentralized services and applications to extend the use cases of ETH. This decentralized system creates a protocol with the ultimate *abstract foundational layer* (Buterin, 2013), a blockchain ecosystem with a built-in Turing-complete programming language enabling its users to build applications, services, and currencies to be used with their respective platforms. ETH enables its users to communicate with the EVM, allowing for arbitrary read and write operations on-chain. This protocol permits creating complex application protocols that leverage the P2P and cryptographically secure nature of distributed blockchain infrastructures without developers creating a distribution network.

Although individuals use ETH as a transactional token, its primary use cases are related to incentive and mechanism design for Dapps. The most prominent of which currently exists in DeFi. Dapps such as dYdX, UniSwap, and OpenSea extend the ETH protocol with many functionalities of traditional financial markets, augmented with many traits of a cryptographic blockchain ecosystem. For instance, UniSwap's community treasury currently commands over $4 billion in UNI tokens (Uniswap.org Staff, 2021). Platform users can vote on how to distribute these tokens to the open-source community of developers. Other Dapps variations include Sybil, which maps ETH wallet addresses to real-world identities for governance/voting delegation, and Gitcoin, which allows for retroactive funding of open-source projects and attempts to redefine the view on public goods/services.

The ETH protocol is a sufficiently modular and accessible ecosystem. Several implementations of the ETH client allow for a more diverse set of nodes and reduce the chance of a single point of failure. Vitalik Butern, ETH's co-founder, maintains a maximally secure blockchain. Regular end-users should have the ability to run nodes and validate new blocks or transactions (Buterin, 2021).

Finally, a stark difference between the ETH network and BTC or LTC is the use of a PoS consensus algorithm introduced with ETH 2.0. PoS is a version of a consensus mechanism that requires validators (vs miners) to stake, at most, a minuscule 32 ETH to become a validator. Validators secure the blockchain by performing transaction validation to create new blocks. If a new block verified by a validator turns out to be false, the validator's stake burns. This strategy creates a significant barrier to the majority attack vector. If an attacker wants to control most of the network, that person needs most of ETH's supply, which is an expensive endeavor. Advocates also praise PoS as a countermeasure to the environmental impacts of PoW-related consensus mechanisms. It serves to improve blockchain scalability (Buterin, 2020).

Neo

Da Hongfei and Erik Zhang initially launched Neo as AntShares in 2014. It is a Dapp platform and blockchain ecosystem that utilizes a Byzantine fault. A *Byzantine fault* is a condition of a computer system, mainly distributed computing systems, where components may fail, and imperfect information exists on whether a component has failed. Neo has evolved to become a prominent contender to the ETH ecosystem. It enables developers with native support for smart contracts and oracles, which allow for consensus/verification of externally provided data, name services, and support for interoperability with the global blockchain ecosystem. Like ETH's gas system, Neo's base asset is the non-divisible Neo token, which generates gas tokens used to pay for network transaction fees that can divide into the eighth decimal. One notable feature of Neo is using X.509 digital identities, enabling Dapp developers to map tokens and digital assets to real identities. This feature allows services built on Neo to be compliant with know your customer and anti-money laundering standards required by financial regulators.

EOS.IO

EOS.IO is an open-source blockchain protocol emphasizing enterprise-level digital infrastructure. EOS.IO enables system administrators and enterprise developers to leverage blockchain infrastructure and smart contracts to build cryptographically secure and deterministic digital infrastructure. Notably, EOS.IO permits the deployment of both public and private blockchain networks, allowing for highly customizable configurations making it an efficient choice for businesses looking to utilize a blockchain backend.

Utility Tokens

A *utility token* is a blockchain-based asset issued to fund the future development of cryptocurrency. Utility tokens hold a synergistic relationship with platform tokens. Platform tokens provide security for utility tokens, and utility tokens facilitate activity so that platform tokens can increase in value. This section describes utility tokens such as BABB Platforms, OMG Network, and Bancor.

BABB Platforms

BABB acts as a decentralized bank focused on helping underserved economies and enabling those affected by financial exclusion with all the benefits of banking services in a decentralized P2P system. BABB is built on top of ETH smart contracts. It is registered in the United Kingdom as a Financial Conduct Authority Authorized Small Payment Institution, enabling the platform to provide financial services to and stimulate micro-economies (Averroes, 2021). BABB utilizes tokenization to host fiat currencies on its platform and its native BAX token.

OMG Network

The OMG Network is an L2 (layer 2) scaling solution to the ETH Mainnet. It aims to optimize the ETH network by bundling ETH transactions and validating them on a *sidechain*, also known as a *child chain*, before sending them to the ETH Mainnet for confirmation. OMG does this task by leveraging Plasma's platform to create a child chain of the ETH Mainnet, compressing the bundle of transactions it creates into a single transaction and verifying this single transaction on the OMG child chain. This child chain then serves this verified transaction to the ETH Mainnet for confirmation and inclusion in the next block. As one of the initial L2 scaling solutions on ETH, OMG Network has contributed to solving the blockchain scalability issues that have hindered cryptocurrency's widespread adoption and achieved the transaction throughput of significant payment processors such as Visa and Mastercard. The OMG Network minted its OMG token to pay transaction fees on the ETH network and raise funds for its initial development.

Bancor

The Bancor protocol enables using automated market makers (AMMs). It also creates liquidity pools and mechanisms to facilitate the decentralized trading infrastructure of decentralized token exchanges (Hertzog, Benartzi, & Benartzi, 2018). Liquidity pools allow for the creation of liquid markets on a P2P basis and serve a similar function to traditional market makers. However, liquidity pools operate on an automated basis, allowing liquidity for the more obscure or illiquid crypto tokens on the market. According to a Bancor whitepaper, the Bancor Network uses smart contracts to build liquidity directly into tokens, making these tokens always available for sale or purchase. This process initiates by utilizing "connectors" with link tokens to other tokens in the network. These connectors hold a reserve of a linked token and establish a pricing relationship between the parent token and its linked tokens. These reserve balances provide liquidity for the parent token and its connected tokens algorithmically. All tokens must be ERC-20 compliant, a standard for ETH-based tokens. Allowing for a standardized approach to token creation enables a more diverse universe of tokens and interoperability between platform tokens. The Bancor token is used as a governance token for users to participate in decisions of the Bancor DAO to delegate on protocol improvements and changes.

Transactional Tokens

Transactional tokens function as units of account to be exchanged for goods and services, operating as a digital currency. These tokens allow participants using decentralized cryptocurrencies to complete transactions without a traditional intermediary or central authority. This section discusses transactional tokens such as Ripple, Stellar, and IOTA.

Ripple

Ripple is a blockchain system that enables the global payments industry with scalable blockchain solutions. Ripple boasts a roster of several large institutional clients building services on its platforms, such as Bank of America and Santander Bank. Ripple utilizes the XRP token to provide "on-demand liquidity" during transactions to avoid the need for pre-funding and facilitate easier cross-currency transactions between counterparties and potentially reduce the cost of foreign exchange transactions. In 2020, the US Securities and Exchange Commission (SEC) sued Ripple Labs for an unregistered sale of XRP tokens that the SEC classified as unregistered securities (U.S. Securities and Exchange Commission, 2020).

Stellar

Stellar is an open-source network built to facilitate the exchange of digital representations of multiple forms of currency, from USD to gold to cryptocurrencies. The Stellar platform allows users to create tokenized versions of physical or fiat assets. For instance, a user can create a "gold token" on the Stellar platform, allowing for the issuance of a "gold token" by the user to anyone who deposits gold with Stellar. The user agrees to exchange the gold token for the actual gold on a one-to-one basis. This process allows treating tokens as equivalent to traditional currency if the one-to-one exchange ratio holds. Stellar uses the Lumen native token to pay transaction fees and create accounts.

IOTA

IOTA is a platform to facilitate data transfer within an internet of things (IoT) ecosystem. It emphasizes low resource consumption such that low-power devices like sensors can leverage the technology. IOTA implements an acyclic directed graph instead of a blockchain-based distributed ledger system. This implementation means that IOTA has no miners and no blocks, which the developers hope will allow the network to overcome other blockchain cost and scalability limiting factors. Instead of PoW or PoS mechanisms, IOTA requires that users validate two prior transactions when sending a new transaction. Using this configuration, IOTA can provide fee-free transactions.

Cryptoasset Exchanges

Cryptoasset exchanges enable cryptotoken users to transact in centralized and decentralized ways while allowing for various price discovery mechanisms to determine the price of assets, like traditional exchanges. However, cryptoasset exchanges are typically fully automated and implement P2P transactions that remove the need for conventional intermediaries such as market makers. The following sections introduce various crypto exchanges and outline the differences between centralized exchanges (CEXs) and decentralized exchanges (DEXs).

Binance

Founded by Changpeng Zhao in 2017, Binance is one of the largest cryptocurrency exchanges in daily volume despite its lack of a US presence (Flitter, 2021). Binance offers several cryptoasset exchange services from traditional token trading, trading terminal solutions, crypto-backed loans, crypto derivatives, and similar financial services. Although once the most widely used crypto exchange, Binance has received criticism from the crypto community for its perception as too centralized and several regulatory bodies in the United States, Germany, and the United Kingdom. It is currently under investigation by both the US Department of Justice (DOJ) and the Internal Revenue Service regarding allegations of money laundering and tax offenses (Schoenberg, 2021).

Coinbase, Gemini, Kraken, Cex.io, and Bittrex

Besides Binance, several other implementations of centralized cryptocurrency exchanges are available. These exchanges act similarly to traditional exchanges that quote prices for purchasing securities, cryptoassets, and balances in custody. These exchanges are more suited for those looking to speculate on the price of various cryptocurrencies. They also benefit those who want to use crypto derivative products or manage stake programs. These programs include Kraken's crypto futures and Gemini's staking program. The latter allows users to "stake" a balance with Gemini. It then lends out those stake tokens to counterparties and kicks back a portion of the returns to the user. Although many CEXs offer crypto wallet services, these platforms typically do not directly own the cryptoassets. To use the cryptoassets for purchases or on other platforms, users must withdraw their tokens from their exchange account into an externally owned account (EOA) wallet using a service such as MetaMask, the most popular EOA wallet service. Further, CEXs typically utilize standard order matching protocols like traditional financial exchanges instead of automated market-making protocols implemented by DEXs. Due to their centralized nature, they cannot guarantee similar uptime or availability of trading as decentralized alternatives.

Decentralized Exchange

Cryptocurrencies exist on a decentralized, distributed P2P network. Creating a discerning method of a single currency unit without a form of numeraire remains challenging. As such, most cryptocurrencies use quotes in terms of USD. Before the development of DEXs, price discovery occurred through CEXs such as Binance, which now features DEX offerings and Coinbase. Although these solutions established a price discovery mechanism, they received widespread criticism from the cryptocurrency community as being too reliant on centralized infrastructure, a mortal sin in the crypto ecosystem.

In response to the advent of AMM technology pioneered primarily by the Bancor project, DEXs emerged with the promise of enabling users to trade cryptocurrency in a fully decentralized and P2P transaction without needing intermediary market makers. Projects such as UniSwap, Curve, and Balancer implemented Dapps, which offers DEX services for those looking to utilize a fully decentralized infrastructure for their trading needs. AMM-based DEXs allow users to create liquidity pools, staking their tokens in return for potential fees. They also enable instant bootstrapped liquidity and the availability of various trading pairs across the cryptoasset space. Trading occurs almost instantly and on a P2P basis rather than through an intermediary market maker.

The AMM model is not the only implementation of a DEX. Services such as "1 inch" use a limit-order book (LOB) protocol, like traditional stock exchanges, to price cryptoassets and facilitate trading. This approach is important to ensure the accuracy of AMM and LOB-based exchanges, as a diverse set of price discovery mechanisms typically leads to more accurate and robust pricing (Buterin, 2017). This situation is especially true for cryptoassets because several different exchanges all quote prices for similar pools of assets due to the ecosystem's distributed nature. DEXs provide users with several complex offerings, including the ability to perform flash swaps and flash loans. These enable users to take on practically uncapped amounts of instant debt and complete a transaction. Suppose the user pays back the fee owed for the flash loan. In that case, the transaction is submitted and mined. Otherwise, the transaction reverts, and no messages submit to the blockchain. This process led to notable flash loan-based attacks on insecure Dapp protocols (Qin, Zhou, Livshits, & Gervais, 2021).

Summary and Conclusions

Cryptoassets operate using a distributed database, with the ability to maintain a verifiable, accurate public record with no single individual in control. Cryptocurrencies, utility coins, platform tokens, and transactional tokens are different cryptoassets. Further, cryptoassets utilize cryptography encryption to secure financial transactions, build additional units, and verify the accuracy of asset transfers. Unlike fiat currency and central banking systems, cryptoassets use decentralized systems based on blockchain technology. The various cryptoassets differ, expanding the role of the prominent participants in the crypto-asset ecosystem. Nevertheless, criticism persists relating to the overreliance of some cryptoassets on centralized networks, pushing for the more widespread adoption of decentralized systems throughout the cryptoasset ecosystem. The decentralized nature of cryptoassets enables the assets to operate independently of governments and central authorities. Consequently, they efficiently transfer funds directly between two parties without a trusted third party to arbitrate the transaction.

Discussion Questions

1. Identify and describe four cryptoasset characteristics.
2. Explain the similarities and differences between the four main methods to tokenize assets.
3. List and describe the risks and criticisms of using cryptocurrency as an open-source project.
4. Summarize the benefits of cryptoassets on a DEX compared to a centralized infrastructure.
5. Describe the current limitations of cryptoassets as a digital asset class in financial markets and potential solutions to these issues.

References

Averroes, R. (2021). BABB Whitepaper. *Getbabb.com*. Retrieved from https://getbabb.com/wp-ontent/uploads/2021/03/BABB-Whitepaper.pdf

Back, A. (2002, August). Hashcash – A denial of service countermeasure. *Hashcash*. Retrieved from http://www.hashcash.org/hashcash.pdf

Blockchain.com Staff. (2021). Fees per transaction (USD). *Blockchain.com*. Retrieved from https://www.blockchain.com/charts/fees-usd-per-transaction

Buterin, V. (2013). Ethereum Whitepaper. Retrieved from https://ethereum.org/en/whitepaper/

Buterin, V. (2017, June 22). On path independence. Vitalik.ca. Retrieved from https://vitalik.ca/general/2017/06/22/marketmakers.html

Buterin, V. (2020, November 6). Why proof of stake. Vitalik.ca. Retrieved from https://vitalik.ca/general/2020/11/06/pos2020.html

Buterin, V. (2021, May 23). The limits to blockchain scalability. Vitalik.ca. Retrieved from https://vitalik.ca/general/2021/05/23/scaling.html

Flitter, E. (2021). The world's biggest crypto exchange still lacks U.S. footing. The New York Times, August 19. Retrieved from https://www.nytimes.com/2021/08/19/business/binance-cryptocurrency-exchange-ipo.html

Hertzog, E., Benartzi, G., & Benartzi, G. (2018, March 18). Bancor protocol. *Storage.googleapis.com*. Retrieved from https://storage.googleapis.com/website-bancor/2018/04/01ba8253-bancor_protocol_whitepaper_en.pdf

"Litecoin – Litecoin Wiki". (2022). *Litecoin.info*. Retrieved from litecoin.info/index.php/Litecoin. Accessed on February 14.

Luz, N. (2019). Digital is the cash. Retrieved from https://media.dash.org/wp-content/uploads/Digital_is_the_Cash-Nathaniel_Luz.pdf

Ossinger, J. (2021, August 15). Crypto market retakes $2 trillion market cap amid bitcoin gains. *Bloomberg.com*. Retrieved from https://www.bloomberg.com/news/articles/2021-08-15/crypto-market-retakes-2-trillion-market-cap-amid-bitcoin-gains?sref=uF9VgDwQ

Nakamoto, S. (2008). Bitcoin: A peer-to-peer electronic cash system. *Bitcoin.org*. Retrieved from https://bitcoin.org/bitcoin.pdf

Qin, K., Zhou, L., Livshits, B., & Gervais, A. (2021). Attacking the DeFi ecosystem with flash loans for fun and profit. In N. Borisov & C. Diaz (Eds.), *Financial cryptography and data security*. Lecture Notes in Computer Science (vol. 12674). Berlin: Springer.

Schoenberg, T. (2021, May 13). Binance faces probe by U.S. money-laundering and tax sleuths. *Bloomberg.com*.. Retrieved from https://www.bloomberg.com/news/articles/2021-05-13/binance-probed-by-u-s-as-money-laundering-tax-sleuths-bore-in?sref=uF9VgDwQ

Statista.com Staff. (2021). Mean transaction fee of litecoin from April 2013 to October 25, 2021. *Statista.com*. Retrieved from https://www.statista.com/statistics/1224417/transaction-fees-litecoin/

Uniswap.org Staff. (2021). Uniswap's year in review: 2020. *Uniswap.org*. Retrieved from https://uniswap.org/blog/year-in-review/

U.S. Securities and Exchange Commission. (2020, December 22). SEC charges ripple and two executives with conducting $1.3 billion unregistered securities offering. *Sec.gov*. Retrieved from https://www.sec.gov/news/press-release/2020-338

Chapter 10

Decentralized Finance

Kiran Pandian, Daniel Pfeiffer and Samson Qian

Abstract

One aspect of the opportunities and challenges for cryptoassets concerns decentralized finance (DeFi). DeFi is a growing area of cryptoassets that couples blockchain technology, digital assets, and financial services. DeFi is a publicly available system on a decentralized blockchain network, offering financial products and applications. This chapter provides an overview of the DeFi universe that has enormous potential in various industries in the global market. It also discusses the implications of DeFi's new wave and its applications involving initial coin offerings and stablecoins and specific challenges like the scalability trilemma in DeFi and financial markets.

Keywords: Cryptoassets; decentralized finance; blockchain; initial coin offering; stablecoins; scalability trilemma

Introduction

Decentralized finance (DeFi) refers to financial products and services that are open, global, and accessible to anyone with the internet. It does not have a central entity or an intermediary, eliminating traditional finance's opaque and tightly controlled characteristics. Service users own and maintain DeFi, giving them greater control and visibility over their money. DeFi eliminates intermediary fees of bank loans and exchange trades with no central authority. It contributes to creating an efficient market system by operating throughout the year.

DeFi's first application was in 2009 with the Bitcoin (BTC) peer-to-peer (P2P) system, allowing users to exchange assets without needing a financial intermediary. However, the idea surrounding DeFi dates to the late 1990s with the introduction of smart contracts by Nicholas "Nick" Szabo, a computer scientist, legal

The Emerald Handbook on Cryptoassets: Investment Opportunities and Challenges, 141–156

doi:10.1108/978-1-80455-320-620221010

scholar, and cryptographer known for his research in digital contracts and digital currency. Szabo frequently wrote about his predictions regarding the digital revolution and how humans make contracts. He believed that someone would develop algorithms for "smart contracts." According to Szabo (1997), smart contracts are a set of digital promises that include protocols within which the parties perform on the other promises without using artificial intelligence.

DeFi operates in a completely permissionless manner without third parties, such as companies or governments, blocking trades or collecting fees. This situation occurs via *smart contracts*, which are pieces of code that specify a trade's terms and then automatically execute a transaction according to those terms. These contracts and their outcomes exist transparently across a distributed blockchain that no single entity can control. That is, it is censorship resistant.

This chapter aims to provide an overview of DeFi and its current implementations. The chapter has the following organization. The next section provides a background on DeFi's characteristics, introduces the components of the DeFi stack, and compares DeFi to centralized finance (CeFi). Subsequently, the chapter reviews various use cases of decentralized projects and applications: (1) decentralized exchanges (DEXs), (2) stablecoins, (3) borrowing and lending, (4) asset management, (5) derivatives, (6) insurance, and (7) payments. Lastly, the chapter concludes by identifying DeFi's current limitations.

DeFi Characteristics

This section reviews DeFi's main characteristics.

Decentralization

Financial institutions operating under a CeFi system help reduce transaction costs by facilitating many transactions as intermediaries. Reduced transaction costs and faster processing time create a smooth and efficient system for system users. However, as the number of transactions increases, a high chance exists for the centralized financial institutions to become a behemoth and a monopoly leading to dominating the market. As a result, customers could pay a monopoly price rather than an optimal one based on the value offered to them. A DeFi system inherently solves the above problem through a P2P network model, ensuring no single entity dominates. A *peer-to-peer (P2P) network* is a decentralized platform whereby two individuals interact directly without a third party's intermediation. The network effect of DeFi helps keep the transactional cost low at an optimal level as determined by the market (Catalini & Gans, 2020).

Innovativeness

Centralized architecture promotes innovation with some degree of control by central institutions. By contrast, DeFi facilitates innovation without any central organization dictating the rules. It gives rise to combinatorial and permissionless innovation (Helliar, Crawford, Rocca, Teodori, & Veneziani, 2020). Third-party developers working on products in a centralized platform could have their permission revoked by a central entity. Since a decentralized platform does not have a central entity, developers can freely and openly develop products, facilitating the creation of innovative products at a higher rate and leaving the product's success to the market participants or customers. Centralized platforms use trademarks and patents to protect their competitive advantage, hampering the rate at which innovation happens in the market. With the help of open-source technologies, decentralized platforms facilitate combinatorial innovation, thereby accelerating innovation and product creation. Ethereum (ETH) and BTC are two examples of decentralized networks on which many can create applications.

Interoperability

Interoperability is the ability of different financial systems and institutions to work together seamlessly and efficiently without delay. DeFi uses interoperability to facilitate the transfer of higher financial capital across products, borders, and services. Traditional finance operates in silos, and information is a scarce quantity with value. Individual departments and organizations have their ledgers, creating a complex system hindering interoperability. DeFi could address these limitations with the help of open-source, public blockchains. Currently, complete interoperability is unavailable due to the difficulty in facilitating the transfer of value between applications built on different blockchains. However, the new system's implementation is not far away. Polkadot and Cosmos are two examples of blockchains trying to facilitate interoperability with other blockchain networks

Transparency and Borderlessness

Traditional or CeFi involves a central entity maintaining a central ledger to which it only has access. DeFi overcomes the lack of transparency by using public ledgers containing transactions secured by distributed consensus. It creates trust and transparency between the transaction participants even without a prior relationship. The ledger could be publicly viewed and verified for current or past financial mishaps. No tie exists between DeFi and any country's fiat currency, in sharp contrast to CeFi. Thus, it facilitates the smooth transfer of capital and value globally. DeFi is not subject to the oversight of any central government entity. It truly is borderless and facilitates the transfer of value at just the touch of a button without any intermediaries.

The DeFi Stack

The DeFi stack is a combination of layers of the DeFi ecosystem, allowing for the use of networks. The stack contains units of value, transaction layers, oracles, markets, and wallets. Different applications can interact with each other across layers of the DeFi stack and within any given layer because they are composable. *Composability* means that someone can use one building block's output as the input of another building block. This feature allows the various components to interact and build off each other, opening many creative possibilities. However, composability also means that each DeFi stack layer is as secure as the layer below. For example, if one layer is compromised, each subsequent layer will not be secure.

Units of Value. Units of value are the starting point of the DeFi process. Units of value typically involve *stablecoins*, cryptocurrencies with a price pegged to another cryptocurrency, fiat money, or exchange-traded commodities. Examples of stablecoins include Tether, USD Coin, Binance USD, Dai, and Pax Dollar. Other units of value may consist of cryptocurrencies such as BTC, ETH, and Litecoin.

Transaction Layers. A *layer 1 solution* is the underlying blockchain architecture of transaction layers that allow building smart contract applications on top of them. ETH was the first layer 1 solution to allow for smart contracts. Developers can create applications using a programming language and execute those applications using the ETH Virtual Machine (EVM). The EVM creates compatibility between the programming language and the executing machine, ensuring the separation of each application from the other and its host. ETH can manage up to 30 transactions per second and often has high *gas fees* (i.e., payments that users make to compensate for computing power required to validate transactions.

A layer 2 solution can be built on top of it, such as various types of rollups. Thus, a *layer 2 solution* is an overlaying network on top of the underlying blockchain. A *rollup* is a solution that performs transaction execution outside the main ETH chain (layer 1) but posts transaction data on layer 1. With these solutions, transactions would execute more quickly on layer 2 and only settle on layer 1 (ETH) later (Ethereum.org Contributors. Layer 2 rollups,`x` 2021). According to Haga (2021), DEX trading volumes reached more than $829.5 billion in the first nine months of 2021. More than 90 percent of the current DEX trading volume is through ETH. Another example of a layer 1 solution is Solana (SOL). SOL uses proof-of-history to verify the order and passage of time between events by timestamping each transaction so that the transactions can be stitched together later in the proper order (Yakovenko, 2017). The introduction of proof-of-history allowed SOL to decrease the buffering time for receiving transactions and process up to 65,000 transactions per second. Another example of a layer 1 solution is Cardano. Cardano uses proof-of-stake, a system where owners of a token put up their token as collateral in return for network fees, newly minted tokens, or other forms of reward. These owners are called validators. However, validators are only awarded when they confirm that a new block is accurate and follows the protocol's rules.

Oracles. An *oracle* is a third party providing on-chain smart contracts with the external off-chain information (real-world data) needed to execute those contracts. On-chain is the movement of value on the blockchain, whereas *off-chain* is the movement of value outside the blockchain. A smart contract's effectiveness rests heavily on its access to accurate information, and most oracles seek out data from many different sources to ensure accuracy. The most widely used decentralized oracle is Chainlink, a multi-chain network providing reliable, tamper-proof inputs and outputs for smart contracts.

Wallets and CeFi Versus DeFi. Crypto wallets keep digital assets safe by storing private keys. A hardware wallet allows cold storage. Hackers cannot access a hardware wallet because it is not connected to the internet. Online wallets involve storing private keys in an app or via software. CeFi and DeFi are both media in which individuals access cryptocurrency-related services. CeFi is another alternative to traditional finance. CeFi users trust a firm's management to execute the promised services responsibly. By contrast, DeFi users trust that technology performs as proposed by the source code. Table 10.1 shows the similarities and differences between CeFi and DeFi.

Decentralized Currencies

Traditionally, precious metals like gold backed a country's fiat currency. The system evolved. The trust of a country's citizens in a central bank, government, and

Table 10.1. Key Differences between CeFi and DeFi.

Characteristic	**CeFi**	**DeFi**
Underlying technology	Blockchain	
Asset focus	Digital assets	
Unit of account	Denominated in fiat currency	Denominated in digital assets or stablecoins
Execution	Financial intermediaries	Smart contracts
Clearing and settlement	Processed by service providers or clearinghouses	Writing transactions to the underlying blockchain
Governance	Dependent on the service organization and regulators	Managed by protocol developers or users with voting rights
Auditability	Third-party auditors	Open-source code and public ledger for all to access
Privacy	Identity checks and personal data are subject to national laws such as know your customer and anti-money laundering	Currently, no identity verification requirements
Security	Vulnerable to data breaches, hacks, and glitches	
Privacy	Government-mandated disclosures, consumer protection, and regulation	Users assume all risks

Notes: This table shows how CeFi and DeFi differ. CeFi users trust a firm's management to execute the promised services responsibly. By contrast, DeFi users trust that technology performs as proposed by the source code.

economy determines the value of most fiat currencies. *BTC* is a decentralized currency issued through technology with a fixed supply to control inflationary effects. It acts as a store of value in the decentralized world as gold did in the traditional finance world. BTC could be used to store and transfer value across the world without being subject to the control of any central entity. Its utility value is still a matter of concern. Other popular cryptocurrencies are ether and dash.

Decentralized Fundraising

Companies often raise funds in various ways. One method is through an *initial public offer* (IPO) when a private company becomes public by selling its shares on a stock exchange to institutional and retail investors. An IPO involves many hurdles, such as intermediaries like lawyers and banks and regulatory institutions like governments. It is heavily regulated and entails considerable pre-work. Paperwork requirements before an IPO usually take about four to six months.

A second fundraising method is *venture financing*. It requires investors to trust the project and thus relies on the network effect. The *network effect* refers to the value added to a network member by adding new members and exchanging information and capital. Leveraging the network effect requires access to connections and capital, causing a substantial burden to innovators with no connections.

A third approach is decentralized fundraising, which overcomes this hurdle with an *initial coin offering* (ICO). Startups often use this fundraising tool, especially involving blockchain projects.

A crowdfunder receives a new token or coin in exchange for popular cryptos like BTC or ether. A token resides on another blockchain, whereas a coin is a new native blockchain. An ICO allows a project to raise capital from investors worldwide, enabling the participation of smaller retail investors, unlike an IPO. ICOs are borderless due to open source and smart contracts. The distributed trust enabled by blockchain promotes entrepreneurship and innovation. A good ICO involves tokens having inherent value. The tokens issued can be utility-based or security-based. Other chapters in this book discuss tokens in detail.

Recently, a different form of ICO, namely an *initial exchange offering* (IEO), has emerged. An *IEO* is a way for startup companies to raise capital by selling utility tokens conferring preferred status with a company through a cryptocurrency exchange platform. It involves crypto exchanges analyzing the potential of blockchain startups before connecting them with investors. A company pays a listing fee and gives some of its tokens to the exchange. The exchange, in return, takes care of marketing, securing funds, and vetting investors. The token sale occurs through the exchange. The IEO facilitates instant liquidity and access to a prospect list. It gives better credibility compared to the normal ICO process. An example is when the Bitfinex exchange issued an IEO to shore up its reserve for tether tokens.

Decentralized Payment Services

Current payment services based on centralized networks, like Visa, charge high fees, especially cross-border payments. Decentralized networks solve this issue by facilitating payments at a low cost due to the decentralized networks' global nature while offering better security and transparency. BTC lightning network, for instance, uses payment channels maintained by a decentralized network of hubs, thereby enabling microtransactions at a low cost. Twitter and Square are among the many companies experimenting with decentralized payments as a service. As merchants move toward the service charging lower costs, the service fee should decline in the future, enabling merchants to offer products and services to consumers at a lower price. Similarly, Ripple facilitates large cross-border payments at a faster and lower cost.

Decentralized Contracting

Contracts require trust between the parties involved, which financial intermediaries usually facilitate. These contracts involve many costs, such as negotiating, drafting, enforcing, and renegotiating costs. Blockchain technology substitutes the financial intermediary with P2P smart contracts that automatically execute different contract stages as each of the stated rules in the protocols are met over time. It reduces a project's cost and complexity while adding trust, transparency, immutability, and automaticity. Such technology also leads to innovation. Lending and borrowing based on smart contracts are examples. These cost savings could be passed on to the end-users, thereby helping to improve a firm's profits.

Governance Mechanisms

DeFi does not have a central entity. Due to its distributed consensus mechanism, the governance mechanism shifts the control from a third party to active protocol users. The protocol's active users make critical decisions. A group of investors and developers creates a protocol. However, every active participant user of the protocol makes the choices for the protocol due to its decentralized nature, thus making it more transparent and reliable. The most favored governance mechanism for DeFi is liquid democracy, discussed below, along with other governance mechanisms.

Founder Control. Initially, founders controlled most DeFi projects. They control the project and scale it up as fast as possible.

Council Control. The power in the council control model rests with a core group of developers who set forth a project's roadmap and strategy, such as ETH and BTC developers in their respective projects.

Liquid Democracy. It is a governance mechanism allowing active network protocol users to have a say in the decisions. Members can vote by satisfying the minimum number of governance tokens requirement, which varies by the blockchain network. The number of governance tokens held determines a vote's weight. Investors favor this type of blockchain network for DeFi projects because they have a considerable say in the network protocol. Thus, governance tokens ensure DeFi's democratic and decentralized governance. Currently, networks give governance tokens depending upon the liquidity they stake or bring as collateral to the protocol through their participation.

Decentralized Projects and Applications

DeFi has many applications, including (1) DEXs, (2) stablecoins, (3) borrowing and lending, (4) asset management, (5) insurance, (6) decentralized insurance, and (7) payments.

Decentralized Exchanges

A *DEX* is a non-custodial exchange that connects crypto buyers and sellers. It employs smart contracts for a trade's execution instead of an intermediary. The non-custodial nature ensures the users keep their private keys and funds rather than a third party. Each transaction is secured on a blockchain, thus enabling the exchange to offer a new set of digital financial assets and products with trust and transparency. The absence of intermediaries, such as a clearinghouse, ensures lower fees for the traders for each trade. Thus, DEXs offer better privacy, security, and fees. DeFi's growth should eventually improve the liquidity of DEXs. Development is ongoing to address the scalability trilemma, discussed later, of BTC and ETH blockchain on which the smart contracts of DEXs are built. Examples of DEXs include Uniswap, Bancor, and Kyber.

Stablecoins

Cryptocurrencies are infamous for their high volatility and price swings, making using them for many applications, such as borrowing and lending, infeasible. Because of the unstable prices, government entities and other financial institutions are unlikely to back these cryptos. This instability is one of the most significant differences for financial transactions involving a cryptocurrency and a regular currency like the US dollar. In these instances, an asset should be a *store of value,* meaning an asset that would generally retain purchasing power into the future. This feature is vital because many applications in finance require stability and security of asset value to ensure fair transactions. Consequently, using crypto such as BTC for these purposes is problematic.

A solution to this problem lies in *stablecoins*, which are cryptos that maintain a steady and constant value over time. Stablecoins have little or no volatility, resulting in exceedingly low price risk. This feature makes stablecoins an attractive mechanism for specific finance applications. Brock Pierce, Craig Sellars, and Reeve Collins founded Tether (USDT), originally known as Realcoin, in July 2014. This cryptocurrency, commonly known as a stablecoin, aims to keep a fixed 1:1 exchange ratio with the US dollar. Since then, many new stablecoins have emerged, such as Dai, PAX Gold, and Binance USD. These coins trade less frequently than regular cryptocurrency, as their purpose is to keep the price steady in the long term, despite occasional small fluctuations.

Three main methods are available for implementing a stablecoin and maintaining its value over time. Stablecoins are usually matched to a commodity's price, such as the US dollar or gold.

- *Fiat-collateralized stablecoins*. The traditional and most popular method is a *fiat-collateralized stablecoin*, in which an independent institution manages the crypto's supply and circulation. Off-chain fiat currency backs these stablecoins, which have many compliance audits.

- *Crypto-collateralized stablecoins*. This method removes the need for an independent institution to regulate circulation and is gaining popularity. An on-chain cryptocurrency backs these stablecoins. Thus, a smart contract, not an institution, manages the supply and circulation. This way, users deposit cryptocurrency into a wallet and receive corresponding tokens equal in value.
- *Algorithmic or non-collateralized stablecoins*. Compared to the former two methods, this method uses algorithms to control the number of tokens in circulation and maintain a steady price. If the price decreases, the algorithm reduces the token supply, and if the price increases, the algorithm increases the supply. This approach removes the need to use another asset to back a stablecoin's value. However, a drawback is the volatility of the stablecoin supply, which may present issues in some financial transactions.

Although some confusion exists about which method works the best, no agreed-upon solution is available, as each has benefits and drawbacks. The type of stablecoin to choose mainly depends on its application, but each method has proven to give crypto a store of value.

Applications of stablecoins appear in various financial services that have become decentralized. They have become implemented in entities offering commercial banking, credit and lending, fixed income, and payment systems. Volatility in traditional cryptocurrencies makes using crypto for these services difficult. However, stablecoins enable creating smaller institutions that provide the same service as large central institutions, except with cryptocurrency as the form of payment. The stablecoin market had a value above $130 billion in 2021. It has gained popularity for those who want to invest money in the cryptocurrency market without putting the investment at high risk.

The stablecoin industry is still heavily unregulated in the United States and lacks backing from government entities, unlike regular currency. Thus, all cryptocurrency protocols currently involve risk because system loopholes could cause crypto to crash. For example, crypto protocols could be hacked, and scammers could jeopardize a project. Speculation and market trends could affect the system, potentially resulting in a crash. Such an impact would not occur with traditional currency and financial systems. Discussion exists on regulating stablecoins to reduce systemic risk and smoothly integrate it into the current financial system.

Borrowing and Lending

Borrowing and lending are essential functions of the DeFi system. Various protocols allow users to borrow and lend cryptoassets on decentralized platforms while remaining anonymous. Liquidity pools are the center of DEXs and reward users for pooling their capital while facilitating permissionless borrowing, lending, and trading activities for others.

On a DeFi platform, a borrower can take a loan while a lender receives a yield until the loan is returned. A lender sends tokens into a liquidity pool using a smart contract making the coin available for others to borrow. The interest that lenders receive and borrowers pay is calculated using the ratio of supplied and borrowed tokens in a particular market. DeFi's mechanics for borrowing and lending vastly differ based on whether the loans are collateralized or uncollateralized.

Loans Collateralized by Cryptoassets

When using cryptoassets as collateral, they are locked in a smart contract and released after repayment of the loan and interest. The two main categories of collateralized crypto loans are collateralized debt positions and pooled collateralized debt markets (Schär, 2021).

- *Collateralized debt position (CDP)*. A *CDP* is a smart contract that locks initial collateral and generates stablecoins. These stablecoins are loans backed by the initial collateral. For users to retrieve their collateral, they must pay back the generated stablecoins in the future.
- *Pooled collateralized debt markets*. This category of collateralized crypto loans is where one can borrow existing cryptoassets without creating new tokens by putting up collateral. DeFi credit protocols like Compound and Aave (Kim, 2021) facilitate broad categories of collateralized debt markets like P2P matching and pooled matching. P2P matching is when a person providing liquidity lends cryptoassets to a specific borrower. With P2P matching, both parties of the transaction agree on a maturity with a fixed interest rate. By contrast, pooled matching loans use variable interest rates based on supply and demand. Once lenders deposit capital into the pool, they immediately earn interest (Schär, 2021).

Uncollateralized Cryptoasset Loans

A *flash loan* is a form of decentralized lending that allows one to borrow without posting any collateral. The dynamics of flash loans is that if a borrower takes out a loan, it is paid back in the same transaction. However, since the loan is only valid within one blockchain transaction, if it is not paid back, the loan fails and is never granted (Qin, Zhou, Livshits, & Gervais, 2021). There are multiple use cases for flash loans that span from arbitrage to flash liquidation. According to Wang et al. (2021), traders can capitalize on an arbitrage opportunity without owning an asset with flash loans. If a trader discovers an arbitrage opportunity, the trader can instantly borrow the cryptoasset, convert it into another cryptoasset, sell the cryptoasset in a liquidity pool, and return the initial capital in one transaction while retaining a profit. Another use case for flash loans is flash liquidation. *Flash liquidation* is when one becomes a liquidator to make profits by buying uncollateralized assets at a discount and then reselling them in liquidity pools using a flash loan.

Since DeFi lending traditionally includes collateral while uncollateralized loans do not, some DeFi protocols are testing uncollateralized loans with a credit approval process assigned to a decentralized network of credit approvers. These credit approvers would receive a reward for accurate credit predictions (Birry & Duran, 2021).

Asset Management

Traditionally, asset management in the financial services industry encompasses allocating assets to reach various financial goals. However, individuals make decisions that leave room for error when allocating capital. Applying DeFi in asset management removes human decision-making because all decisions occur algorithmically. A primary use case for DeFi in asset management is yield aggregators. *Yield aggregators* are smart contract protocols that allocate cryptoassets per predefined rules, with the primary goal of maximizing yield while minimizing risk. They automate the process of staking on behalf of users to optimize strategy and risk tolerance (Jensen, Wachter, & Ross, 2021).

Many other DeFi protocols like Enzyme Finance and Set Protocol allow users to find investment funds or vaults with stakes in various DeFi projects and passively invest. For example, USF Fund I, the largest vault on Enzyme Finance, has a stake in four DeFi projects based on various risk parameters and has more than $105 million in assets under management (AUM) in November 2021. On the other hand, users can manage their own "vault" and create smart contract-based rulesets based on their risk/reward tolerance. As of November 2021, the Enzyme Network offered 894 vaults with more than $155 million AUM. Set Protocol offers semi-automated strategies with dynamic rebalancing triggered by threshold values and time clocks (Schär, 2021).

DeFi inherently increases transparency in asset management. On the other hand, traditional asset management encompasses long settlement times and releases financial reports monthly, quarterly, or yearly. Another aspect of DeFi's benefits, when applied to asset management, is its ability to make investing easier, cheaper, and more accessible. Due to its decentralized nature, DeFi removes many barriers in asset management, like expensive portfolio management fees and accredited investor status.

Investors usually have little independence, autonomy, and customization within traditional asset management. However, because DeFi asset management has decentralized technology at its core, increased transparency, customization, and automation allow for a great opportunity in the future.

Crypto Derivatives

Derivatives contracts are financial instruments in the secondary market that derive their value from a specific asset in the primary market, such as equity. Like equity markets where trading derivatives of stocks occurs, the crypto market also involves trading cryptocurrency derivatives. Cryptocurrencies, including BTC and ETH, have futures, calls, and puts, just like equities. These instruments allow investors to gain exposure to the cryptocurrency without holding any. Crypto derivatives also serve to hedge against risk for traders. Many platforms offer an exchange for these crypto derivatives to be traded. Three of the most notable ones are Binance, OKEx, and FTX.

Investors' trading strategies involve a long-short strategy, including long-term holding assets and short-selling overpriced assets. *Short selling* uses margin to borrow and sell an asset, hoping the price declines to earn a profit. However, unlike equities, shorting cryptocurrency like BTC is difficult. Thus, most crypto traders earn returns through long positions on their crypto. Crypto derivatives offer a way for traders to earn profit even if the underlying price declines. For example, a trader can buy a crypto put option, which is equivalent to taking a short position on that crypto. By the time the contract expires, the investor generates a return on that specific cryptocurrency if the price goes below the option strike price.

Like traditional derivatives markets for equities and fixed income, new crypto derivatives markets also offer a platform to match buyers and sellers with corresponding bid-ask spreads in the crypto options. Traders bet against cryptocurrency price trends. The crypto options exchanges match buyers with sellers, where they agree upon a specific strike price until the contract's expiration. This approach becomes a zero-sum game in which the losing bettor must pay the winning bettor.

Also, like traditional options markets, both American and European options for cryptocurrency are available. An investor can exercise an American option at any time up to the expiration, but a European option only at expiration. Therefore, many theoretical foundations of options pricing also apply to some crypto derivatives. The Black-Scholes options pricing model provides a formula for computing the price of a European equity option but is also applicable to a crypto option.

The main difference between secondary cryptocurrency and equity markets is that the former is open continuously, 24 hours a day, seven days a week. The latter runs typically from 9.30 a.m. to 4 p.m. Eastern Standard Time (EST). In the primary crypto and equity markets, cryptocurrency exchanges do not close. Therefore, transactions may occur throughout the day, unlike equities that close at 4 p.m. EST. Furthermore, crypto prices tend to be much more volatile than equity prices, resulting in large gains and losses for crypto options. Crypto prices tend to have a much higher deviation from the contract strike prices than equities. Overall, the crypto derivatives market is highly speculative, and some compare it to gambling. There is no way to predict what event may trigger sudden movements in crypto prices.

Insurance

Several issues caused by insurers and claimers plague the insurance industry. Major problems include delays in claims, false claims, fraud schemes, and human errors. Intermediaries claim considerable money as service fees. Additionally, efficiently identifying false claims is difficult because of data scattered among many issuers in redundant systems. The insurance industry's security, transparency, and efficiency are optimized with blockchain technology, decreasing payment times and streamlining insurance claims. Smart contracts, for example, are programmed to help execute or process a claim automatically if certain conditions are met, eliminating human intervention, improving claim and payment processes, and lowering transaction costs.

Decentralized Insurance

Investors have lost billions of dollars due to cyberattacks on smart contracts and DEXs. One notable cyberattack is the DAO hack. The DAO was a decentralized autonomous organization launched on the ETH blockchain. It launched in 2016 and raised about $150 million in ether through a token sale. Hackers took advantage of the DAO's code vulnerabilities and stole funds. The ETH blockchain had to be forked to restore the stolen funds. A *hard fork* refers to a radical change to a blockchain protocol, effectively resulting in two branches, one following the previous protocol and the other following the new version. Thus, a need exists to protect crypto deposits against theft and hacking. A new branch of insurers has emerged to help address the above issues and others caused by defects or errors. Some use cases of their products include the following.

Crypto Wallet Insurance. In August 2021, hackers stole around $600 million in tokens from the Poly Network, a DeFi project. Hackers exploited a flaw in Poly Network's code, allowing them to transfer the assets to their crypto wallets. Although hackers returned the money, this breach showcased vulnerabilities due to coding flaws (Browne, 2021). People might lose money from their wallets due to theft, fraud, hacks, lost keys, and other reasons. A survey by decentralized insurance company Etherisc confirmed the need for crypto wallet insurance (Etherisc, 2018). Etherisc and many other insurance companies thus started offering crypto wallet insurance covering a large sum of money.

Collateral Protection for Crypto-backed Loans. Decentralized insurance providers like Celsius, Etherisc, and Sweetbridge provide collateral protection for crypto-backed loans discussed in earlier sections. This insurance coverage protects borrowers whose collateral for crypto loans is destroyed, stolen, or hacked.

Smart Contract Cover. *Smart contract cover* is insurance coverage covering loss to investors caused by hacking and manipulating a smart contract. If someone hacks a smart contract and manipulates its code to transfer funds, resulting in a loss to an investor, a smart contract handles this situation. Thus, investors can operate on DEXs without worrying about security. Nexus Mutual is one such company offering this service.

Payments

Current payment systems involve money flowing through banks, central banks, or both since the 1970s and 1980s. Also, a lack of omnichannel banking experience exists for customers, especially Gen Z and millennials who expect faster and easier ways to conduct transactions. Studies show that banks receive about 40 percent of their total revenue from payments (Bruno, Denecker, & Niederkorn, 2020). Thus, streamlining this process is imperative. DeFi helps execute global payments in real-time while offering security against fraud in real-time with the help of blockchain. It brings more transparency and helps reduce administrative and operational costs by operating 24/7. Ripple blockchain protocol developers state that its service helps banks reduce operating costs by about 33 percent through its real-time gross settlement system, remittance network, and currency exchange (Kharpal, 2016). Ripple's service eliminated the intermediaries and helped pass on the benefits received by the banks to their customers. Visa has adopted a smart contract based on the ETH blockchain protocol due to the proprietary nature of Ripple's blockchain network.

Limitations of DeFi

Currently, interoperability and scalability are two main factors limiting DeFi's growth.

Interoperability. DeFi still must address some inherent issues that hinder siloed blockchains from establishing inter-blockchain communication. Without a third-party intermediary, transferring value, data, and assets across different blockchain networks is challenging. Interoperability is necessary to enable clients to scale their businesses on a large scale.

Scalability Trilemma

People often expect three characteristics in technology before adopting it on a large scale: (1) ability to scale, (2) decentralization, and (3) security offered. The scalability trilemma claims that blockchain systems can perform well in only two properties. Improving the third property decreases one of the factors. New companies propose various methods of achieving an optimal level on all three factors. For now, however, transactions based on DeFi protocols are expensive and slow due to the inherent issues in the protocol. Under the lens of the scalability trilemma, the current banking industry performs well on the scalability and security criteria but is highly centralized. People felt the ill effects of centralization in the financial crisis of 2007–2008, also called the global financial crisis, eroding trust in central entities like governments and banks. DeFi based on blockchain puts the responsibility on users to secure their keys for funds and assets. With no intermediary and a lack of industry regulation, DeFi becomes difficult for users to reclaim their assets in an unlikely event.

Summary and Conclusions

DeFi is evolving and has advantages and limitations. However, the drawbacks could be overcome by customizing protocols according to the needs. In the test phase, some next-generation blockchain protocols can overcome issues like the scalability trilemma and interoperability. Investment and confidence in DeFi are increasing at an exponential rate. Loans on DeFi platforms increased by 650 percent to $86 billion in about seven months in May 2021 (Chavez-dreyfuss, 2021). With such benefits as lower transactional and operational costs, automaticity, transparency, decentralization, and immutability, DeFi is here to stay.

Discussion Questions

1. Identify and explain the five stages of the DeFi stack.
2. Explain the main challenge to DeFi scalability.
3. List several DeFi business models.
4. Explain whether stablecoins backed by the government and Federal Deposit Insurance Corporation are a form of currency and payment.
5. Discuss the government regulations on stablecoins.
6. Discuss whether equity option pricing models work on cryptocurrency options and the possibility of accurately pricing crypto options and developing a crypto hedging strategy.

References

Birry, A., & Duran, C. (2021, September 16). *DeFi lending | set to disrupt traditional systems – But not until constraints are lifted.* S&P Global. Retrieved from https://www.spglobal.com/_assets/documents/ratings/research/100495247.pdf

Browne, R. (2021). Hacker behind $600 million crypto heist returns final slice of stolen funds. CNBC, August 23. Retrieved from https://www.cnbc.com/2021/08/23/poly-network-hacker-returns-remaining-cryptocurrency.html

Bruno, P., Denecker, O., & Niederkorn, M. (2020, October 1). *The 2020 global payments report.* McKinsey & Company. Retrieved from https://www.mckinsey.com/industries/financial-services/our-insights/accelerating-winds-of-change-in-global-payments

Catalini, C., & Gans, J. S. (2020). Some simple economics of the blockchain. *Communications of the ACM, 63*(7), 80–90. Retrieved from https://cacm.acm.org/magazines/2020/7/245703-some-simple-economics-of-the-blockchain/fulltext

Chavez-dreyfuss, G. (2021). Largest decentralized finance venture cap firm raises $100 Mln for 2nd fund. *Reuters.* May 14. Retrieved from https://www.reuters.com/business/finance/largest-decentralized-finance-venture-cap-firm-raises-100-mln-2nd-fund-2021-05-14/

Ethereum.org Contributors. Layer 2 rollups. (2021). ethereum.org. Retrieved from https://ethereum.org/en/developers/docs/scaling/layer-2-rollups/

Etherisc. (2018, December 7). *The ideal crypto wallet insurance should cover hacks, theft, and fraud; survey.* Etherisc Blog. Retrieved from https://blog.etherisc.com/the-ideal-crypto-wallet-insurance-should-cover-hacks-theft-and-fraud-survey-ee57a6fa0d4f

Haga. (2021). Monthly DEX volume grouped by year. *Dune Analytics.* Retrieved from https://dune.xyz/queries/4424/8622

Helliar, C., Crawford, L., Rocca, L., Teodori, C., & Veneziani, M. (2020). Permissionless and permissioned blockchain diffusion. *International Journal of Information Management, 54*(October), 102136. Retrieved from https://www.sciencedirect.com/science/article/abs/pii/S0268401219314586?via%3Dihub

Jensen, J., Wachter, V., & Ross, O. (2021). An introduction to decentralized finance (DeFi). Complex Systems Informatics and Modeling Quarterly, *26*(March/April), 46–54. Retrieved from https://csimq-journals.rtu.lv/article/view/csimq.2021-26.03

Kharpal, A. (2016). Google backed blockchain startup ripple raises $55 million from big banks. CNBC, September 15. Retrieved from https://www.cnbc.com/2016/09/15/google-backed-blockchain-start-up-ripple-raises-55-million-from-big-banks.html

Kim, S. (2021). New crypto-secured lending system with a two-way collateral function. Ledger, *6*, 1–16. Retrieved from http://ledger.pitt.edu/ojs/ledger/article/view/215/206

Qin, K., Zhou, L., Livshits, B., & Gervais, A. (2021). Attacking the DeFi ecosystem with flash loans for fun and profit. In N. Borisov & D. Claudia (Eds.), *Financial cryptography and data security*. Lecture Notes in Computer Science (vol. 12674, pp. 3–5). Berlin: Springer.

Schär, F. (2021). Decentralized finance: On blockchain- and smart contract-based financial markets. Review, *Federal Reserve Bank of St. Louis*, *103*(2), 153–174. Retrieved from https://files.stlouisfed.org/files/htdocs/publications/review/2021/04/15/decentralized-finance-on-blockchain-and-smart-contract-based-financial-markets.pdf

Szabo, N. (1997). The idea of smart contracts. Retrieved from https://www.fon.hum.uva.nl/rob/Courses/InformationInSpeech/CDROM/Literature/LOTwinterschool2006/szabo.best.vwh.net/idea.html

Wang, D., Wu, S., Lin, Z., Wu, L., Yuan, X., Zhou, Y., … Ren, K. (2021). Towards a first step to understand flash loan and its applications in DeFi ecosystem. Association for Computing Machinery. Cornell University. arXiv:2010.12252v3.

Yakovenko, A. (2017). Solana: A new architecture for a high performance Blockchain v0.8.13. Retrieved from https://solana.com/solana-whitepaper.pdf

Chapter 11

Blockchain and Crypto Exchange-traded Funds

Philip C. Sookram

Abstract

This chapter examines the current state of crypto exchange-traded funds (ETFs). It focuses on issues preventing wider implementation and specific products. ETFs have become a popular investment vehicle that investors use to help achieve their long-term goals. A recurring theme is that regulators protect individual investors from direct exposure to cryptocurrency, which many view as highly speculative investments. Pressure from institutions and investors for a bitcoin-based ETF made progress in 2021 when Proshares, an ETF specialized investment company, debuted the first-ever bitcoin futures ETF in the United States. This event is the first-time investors could buy a fund on the New York Stock Exchange that tracks derivative futures contracts of bitcoin. This occurrence pushed this digital asset's spot price to all-time highs, serving as a breakthrough in cryptocurrency history.

Keywords: Bitcoin; exchange-traded fund; bitcoin futures; cryptocurrency; financial reporting; marketplace

Introduction

An *exchange-traded fund* (ETF) is an investment product that tracks the performance of a particular asset or group of assets. ETFs must register with the Securities and Exchange Commission (SEC) under the Investment Company Act of 1940 (the Investment Company Act or Act) as an open-end investment company (fund) or a unit investment trust (Securities and Exchange Commission, 2012).

The Emerald Handbook on Cryptoassets: Investment Opportunities and Challenges, 157–169

doi:10.1108/978-1-80455-320-620221011

An ETF is a pooled investment vehicle, enabling investors to diversify their investment portfolios at a lower cost than mutual funds. ETFs allow investors to gain exposure to an asset or basket of assets without owning the assets (Securities and Exchange Commission, 2017).

Nathan Most and Steven Bloom introduced the first ETFs in 1993. These two American Stock Exchange (AMEX) executives designed and created Standard and Poor's Depository Receipts (SPDRs) (ticker symbol SPY). Because of its acronym, the SPDR instrument is called a "spider." SPDRs are units of an ETF that holds the principal stocks in the Standard & Poor's 500 Composite Stock Price Index (S&P 500®). Thus, this fund tracks the S&P 500 stock market index. These two executives started a market that holds over $9 trillion in net assets. In 2020, the 7,602 ETFs worldwide used many different strategies (Statistica, 2021).

The SPDR® S&P 500 is still the world's largest ETF, with about $402 billion of assets under management (AUM) as of January 27, 2022. This fund was the first to expose investors to an index following the S&P's performance without individually buying those companies' stocks. It seeks to provide investment results that, before expenses, generally correspond to the price and yield performance of the S&P 500® Index. The committee selects these stocks based on market size, liquidity, and industry.

By 1998, sector ETFs gave investors a first-time opportunity to invest in a specific industry within the S&P 500®, such as energy or technology. These securities bundles often appeal to bullish investors in specific sectors but do not want to buy those companies' stocks individually. In 2003, the SEC also approved its first alternatively weighted ETF. These funds perform better than a regularly weighted index but with higher costs. As the demand for the ETF market increased, institutions' styles and strategies also increased. In 2019, AUM for US ETFs reached an all-time high of over $4 trillion. Worldwide AUM topped $6 trillion, which exceeded the gross domestic product of all countries except the United States and China in 2020. Since 2013, institutions have expressed interest from their investors in the blockchain network and digital assets.

Bitcoin is a digital asset relying on blockchain technology. The Securities and Exchange Commission (2021a) also refers to bitcoin as a virtual currency or a cryptocurrency. In 2008, an unknown person or group of people using Satoshi Nakamoto sent a nine-page paper to some cryptographers outlining a new form of "electronic cash" called bitcoin (Nakamoto, 2008). In January 2009, the bitcoin network came into existence with Satoshi Nakamoto mining the genesis block of bitcoin. Thus, bitcoin started during an economic recession as a peer-to-peer cash system.

Rejection has not stopped institutions from reapplying and flooding the SEC with S-1 registrations. *SEC Form S-1* is a registration filing form for companies to complete the registration of a securities offering under the Securities Act of 1933. The next big step for institutions was to get an ETF approved that holds bitcoin or closely follows the asset's spot price rather than a speculative derivative-based index. Since bitcoin's emergence in 2009, investor and organizational interests have rapidly grown regarding blockchain technology and cryptocurrencies. Bitcoins limited supply as a hedge against inflation, and the decentralized fund protection offered by cryptography appealed to a large market across the globe, especially during the Covid-19 pandemic. Recent bitcoin futures ETFs constitute a significant step in the right direction for cryptocurrencies and their incorporation into US stock exchanges.

The SEC's main issue with cryptocurrencies, especially bitcoin, is that most of the circulating supply is in offshore markets. The SEC has not entirely determined how to tax or regulate these non-traditional assets. Efforts are underway to regulate the marketplace as equivalents to traditional equity securities, with mixed results achieved so far.

This chapter provides an analysis and examination of the current state of crypto ETFs. The remainder of the chapter discusses the regulators, attempts to get a crypto ETF approved, why the SEC has failed to approve more crypto ETFs, and potential market and regulatory framework changes.

The Regulators

The SEC enforces US securities laws and acts to provide investors with a fair and honest trading experience. The Investment Company Act of 1940 plays a significant role in providing accurate information to investors about funds. Lastly, the Commodities Futures Trading Commission (CFTC) mainly enforces rules and regulations within the derivatives markets.

A remaining obstacle toward more widespread development of crypto products and services available to individual and institutional investors is the regulatory ambiguity in the United States and other markets. As discussed below, several US regulatory agencies oversee different aspects of the cryptoasset ecosystem. Given the evolution of the cryptoasset space and the lack of a global regulatory framework, the slower than forecasted proliferation of crypto products is unsurprising.

Securities Exchange Commission

The Securities Act of 1933 and the Securities Exchange Act of 1934 created the US Securities Exchange Commission (SEC or the Commission) in 1934. These acts were in response to the stock market crash of 1929, partially caused by a lack of investor confidence in the securities market. The SEC is an independent government agency responsible for maintaining a fair securities market and protecting investors from fraud and manipulation in the securities market. These acts aim to provide investors with better transparency.

The SEC has five commissioners. The President of the United States nominates a chairperson, and the US Senate confirms the nomination. Gary Gensler became the 33rd SEC chairperson in April 2021. His prior experience includes serving as the US CFTC chair between 2009 and 2014, leading the Obama Administration's reform of the $400 trillion swaps derivative market. Substantial documentation is available on Gensler's support of blockchain technology. He instructed a course called Blockchain and Money at the Massachusetts Institute of Technology in the fall of 2018. Yet, this expertise has not always led him to be a proponent of the space. For example, recent commentary reveals that the SEC under Gensler is to emphasize compliance and regulation by edict versus a more hands-off approach.

Cryptos face competition like other assets. Thus, regulation by edict can have a chilling effect on future investment plans. Due to their global and decentralized nature, blockchain and cryptoassets have no native jurisdiction. No country has the advantage of serving as a "hub" for the sector. In that context, a rationale and market-driven regulatory approach would seem to be more sensible versus a top-down approach that some commentary suggests is the trend in the United States.

Investment Company Act of 1940

The Investment Company Act sets the standards and regulations that investment companies, also called funds, must follow. Funds regulated under this Act must provide important investor protections. For example, they must comply with legal requirements regarding the valuation and custody of fund assets and liquidity (Securities and Exchange Commission, 2021a). More than 100 million Americans have invested $25 trillion in mutual funds and ETFs regulated by the Act, making funds the predominant investment vehicle in the United States (Weiner, 2020). The SEC enforces that investment companies follow the established rules and act in the investor's best interest. This Act aims to protect investors by focusing on the regulatory framework for funds.

Commodity Futures Trading Commission

The Commodity Futures Trading Commission Act created the CFTC in 1974. THROUGH SOUND REGULATION, the CFTC aims to promote the US derivatives markets' integrity, resilience, and vibrancy (Commodity Futures Trading Commission, 2021). Future contracts fall under the derivatives market. A *bitcoin futures contract* is a standardized agreement to buy or sell a specific quantity of bitcoin at a specified price on a particular date in the future. In the United States, bitcoin is a commodity, and authorities require commodity futures trading to occur on futures exchanges regulated and supervised by the CFTC (Securities and Exchange Commission, 2021a). The Chicago Mercantile Exchange is the largest marketplace for global derivatives.

Attempts to Get a Crypto ETF Approved

Since 2013, many financial institutions such as Winklevoss Capital Management, Grayscale Investments, Fidelity Investments, VanEck, and Proshares have expressed interest in offering ETFs with exposure to cryptoassets. The demand from investors for a bitcoin ETF skyrocketed in the past decade. The SEC is unsure how to regulate, tax, and manage these decentralized intangibles, so it delayed or rejected all attempts to date. Although the SEC denied authorizing a crypto ETF on multiple occasions, investors could gain access to crypto products via trust vehicles. Hundreds of millions of dollars are in trusts waiting on the SEC's approval. Until approval, most institutions treat these digital assets as over-the-counter (OTC) securities traded via a broker-dealer network.

Winklevoss Capital Management

In 2013, Cameron and Tyler Winklevoss, founders of Winklevoss Capital Management, filed an S-1 form for the first-ever securities offering bitcoin as the underlying asset. A company must file an S-1 form with the SEC to sell shares on a national stock exchange. If the SEC approved, the Winklevoss Bitcoin Trust could easily allow investors to purchase shares representing units of fractional undivided beneficial interest in and ownership of the trust consisting of bitcoins. Investors can buy the shares in blocks of 50,000 or more, also called a *basket trade*. The initial offering was $20,090,000. The SEC reviewed this exchange-traded product proposal but did not decide until almost four years later.

In 2017, the SEC officially rejected the Winklevoss Bitcoin Trust ETF, with concerns about the digital assets' high volatility and properly regulating it on US exchanges. The SEC commented, "When the spot market is unregulated – there must be significant, regulated derivatives markets related to the underlying asset with which the exchange can enter into a surveillance-sharing agreement" (Securities and Exchange Commission, 2018a). According to the SEC, this form of communication has yet to be feasible on offshore exchanges. After having its application rejected, Winklevoss filed a petition to have the decision reviewed by a delegated authority, but the SEC quickly denied the request. The Winklevoss Bitcoin Trust registration form had more risk factors than benefits, resulting in a 3 to 1 vote against the petition.

In July 2018, the Winklevoss brothers met with the SEC about the initial 2013 registration. The SEC again rejected the application with many similar concerns about offshore markets holding bitcoin as the underlying asset. The issue is that decentralized exchanges are unregulated, therefore, highly susceptible to market manipulation and fraud.

> A decentralized exchange is a peer-to-peer marketplace that connects cryptocurrency buyers and sellers. In contrast to centralized exchanges, decentralized platforms are non-custodial, meaning a user remains in control of their private keys when transacting on a DEX platform. (Cryptopedia Staff, 2021, para. 1)

The Commission also added concerns about investor protection concerning The Gemini Cryptocurrency Exchange owned by the Winklevoss brothers. CBOE Global Markets made comments to the SEC stating:

> bitcoin is too decentralized for fraudsters to manipulate the price of the asset and that they could monitor trading on the Gemini Exchange to see if the price of bitcoin has been manipulated. (Securities and Exchange Commission, 2018a)

The SEC replied by commenting on Gemini Exchange's small size and how it could not provide assurance about an effective surveillance program with the Commission (Michaels, 2018).

Grayscale Bitcoin Trust

The world's largest bitcoin trust is the Grayscale Bitcoin Trust (GBTC), formed in 2013 shortly after Winklevoss' first attempt to register the Winklevoss Bitcoin Trust shares. The GTBC fund consists of 654,885 bitcoins, about 46 percent of the 1.4 million bitcoins currently held by publicly traded companies in early 2022. Grayscale trades its shares OTC but prefers the visibility and share liquidity offered on US exchanges. This majority owner filed an S-1 in 2016, but the SEC has rejected it multiple times. Grayscale continues to fight with the SEC to convert its trust into an ETF but must overcome many major concerns with the underlying assets within the fund. Following the approval of the ProShares ETF, the management team of Grayscale made several public comments about plans to convert existing trust instruments to ETF products as soon as possible.

VanEck SolidX Bitcoin Trust

In 2018, VanEck, an ETF and mutual fund manager, partnered with Solidx Partners Inc, a financial services company focusing on digital assets. These two organizations started the VanEck SolidX Bitcoin Trust earlier in 2016, consisting of bitcoins and small amounts of cash to pay trust expenses. Both companies made many S-1 filings independently and as a partnership, but the SEC rejected all, noting the same concerns about investor safety. The two companies parted ways in 2020 because of matters of bad faith between themselves. Due to the SEC's constant delays and rejection, VanEck and Solidx decided to offer a limited version of their ETF to institutional investors such as hedge funds and banks.

Fidelity Investments

In 2021, Fidelity Investments launched a fund named Wise Origin Bitcoin Trust, aimed at following an internally constructed made index to track bitcoin's price. As explained in its S-1 filing in March 2021, "the index is constructed using price feeds from eligible bitcoin spot markets and a volume-weighted median bitcoin price" (Securities and Exchange Commission, 2021b, para. 1). The trust intends not to hold and trade bitcoins directly but to acquire them to pay for certain trading expenses. Fidelity raised over $100 million (Nelson, 2021) in its first eight months of 2021 and is ready to convert the trust into an ETF to meet investor demand if the SEC approves this proposal. Four months after filing the registration, the SEC rejected Fidelity's fund for public offering. In September 2021, Tom Jessop, Fidelity Investments President, met with the SEC to discuss its recent share registration application. Fidelity also claimed that the number of investors holding bitcoin and similar funds globally surged in 2021 (Namcios, 2021, para. 2).

The SEC's Failure to Approve a Crypto ETF

Before approving a fund's registration, the SEC must become comfortable with the derivatives market and how it will regulate, tax, and protect investors' funds. The new crypto market still involves many risks, making the SEC hesitant to approve direct investments in digital assets.

SEC Mission and Strategic Goals

The SEC's mission is to protect investors, facilitate capital formation, and maintain fair, orderly, and efficient markets. It has three strategic goals: (1) focus on the long-term interests of main street investors; (2) recognize significant developments and trends in evolving capital markets and adjust the SEC's efforts to ensure they are effectively allocating resources; and (3) elevate the SEC's performance by enhancing analytical capabilities and human capital development (Securities and Exchange Commission, 2018b). The SEC must protect investors from risky investments. One initiative is to facilitate a vibrant public securities market that offers a growing array of investment choices. Another initiative is to identify outdated SEC rules and approaches.

Risks

The SEC once argued that the crypto space is unregulated, potentially leading to price manipulation and insufficient liquidity. The SEC says the crypto space is risky, citing extreme price volatility. Bitcoin's returns for 2018, 2019, and 2020 were a 74 percent loss, followed by gains of 95 and 305 percent, respectively (Greifeld, Hajric, & Bain, 2021). Bitcoin's closing price on January 1 in 2018, 2019, 2020, and 2021 was $10,221.10, $3,457.79, $9,350.53, and $33,114.36, respectively. Additionally, the SEC questioned whether funds would have the information necessary to value cryptocurrencies or related products adequately. Other concerns are validating coin ownership by funds and the threat from hackers. Yet, these arguments and positions did not prevent the SEC and other regulators from approving collateralized debt instruments. This situation led to public commentary by crypto advocates that regulatory agencies have a built-in bias against the crypto industry.

Security Issues

The risks associated with blockchain technology and cryptocurrency platforms regarding the security of investors' digital assets have been a significant concern worldwide. Like physical bank robbers, hackers on the web are constantly looking to steal money virtually. However, a critical difference between traditional bank robberies and crypto hacks is the information asymmetry that continues to exist in the marketplace. Even as cryptoassets have become more widely discussed in the market, cryptoassets are still an emerging asset class. Many vendors lack the disclosures that security investors expect to protect them. They illegally obtain wallet keys using different hacking techniques such as phishing, routing attacks, and URL hijacking. Hackers usually target *hot wallets*, a form of digital storage connected to the internet accessible by computer or phone. A blockchain's heavy monitoring makes hacking difficult and expensive. Hackers usually find vulnerabilities in platforms and exchanges to steal users' personal information. The first cryptocurrency fund security breach occurred in 2011, and these attacks continue to happen regularly.

Mt. Gox, a Japan-based cryptocurrency exchange, was once known as the largest marketplace for bitcoin, overseeing over 70 percent of bitcoin transactions globally. In 2011, a hacker accessed an auditor's credentials, allowing the hacker to transfer coins to separate wallets, known as a cold wallet, whose private key was inaccessible to Mt. Gox officials. A *cold wallet* is an offline and external storage device that is highly effective when private keys or passwords are secure. Hackers steal personal information daily, using access to users' wallets connected to these big exchanges. Mt. Gox shut down in 2014 after a series of security breaches from hackers. The exchange lost a cumulative 850,000 bitcoins between 2011 and 2014. In late 2021, that amount was worth more than $45.2 billion.

Much controversy surrounds the shutdown and subsequent investigation of QuadrigaCx during 2018 and 2019, leaving 17,000 open claims seeking lost funds. In 2018, Gerald Cotten, founder of The Quadriga CX trading platform, died, leaving about $180 million in bitcoin cold storage. *Cold storage* is a way to hold cryptocurrency coins offline, making them unhackable unless a hacker has physical possession and private access keys. Unfortunately, cold wallets have flaws. To operate as advertised as an effective offline crypto storage solution, the owner must have a safe place to hide them and a high level of trust in the organization. Cotton had the passwords and digital keys. Months before his death, someone secretly stole most of the coins out of the wallet, with a majority still not found. Although many made claims to recover lost funds, most are still waiting for a response. This situation includes efforts by a Big Four accounting firm brought in to address the issue, only to accidentally send millions in funds to an account that it was subsequently unable to be access again.

Another incident regarding wallet security took place in 2019 when hackers stole over $40 million worth of assets from Binance wallets. Binance is the largest cryptocurrency exchange making it a target for cyber-attacks. In the first three months of 2019, hackers stole more than $256 million worth of crypto. In May 2019, they stole 7,000 bitcoins from Binance wallets and some users' two-factor authentication codes and API tokens. Zhao Changpeng, Binance's CEO, explained, "The hackers used a variety of techniques, including phishing, viruses, and other attacks. The hackers had the patience to wait and execute well-orchestrated actions through multiple seemingly independent accounts at the most opportune time. The transaction is structured in a way that passed our existing security checks" (Barrett, 2019, para 3). *Phishing* is when hackers send emails to others pretending to be a reputable person or company looking for personal information. Binance reimbursed all users affected by the breach and warned its users to be careful when sharing their information.

Coinbase, currently the largest cryptocurrency exchange in the United States, was also a victim of a phishing attack in March 2021, with more account breaches than Binance. Hackers bypassed the multi-factor authentication on 6,000 accounts, leaking personal information. Coinbase claims that a third party, such as through an email, stole the information. The hackers phished users to steal email passwords and phone numbers, enabling them to access accounts using short message service (SMS) text authentication. Upon investigation, Coinbase indicated that it had no evidence that it was the source from which these third parties obtained this information. Instead, Coinbase suggested that the information originated from phishing and social engineering campaigns (Ikeda, 2021). These events leave investors questioning cryptocurrency's safety.

Another large cryptocurrency hack happened on August 10, 2021, on the Poly Network, a decentralized finance platform where investors trade crypto and non-fungible tokens (NFTs). A *non-fungible token* is a non-interchangeable unit of data stored on a blockchain, a form of digital ledger, which can be sold and traded. The Poly Network suffered a $611 million hit when hackers exposed a flaw in its source code. It offered the thief $500,000 and a job as its chief security advisor. The "white hat" hacker soon returned the money but questioned Poly Network's security. A *white-hat hacker* uses personal capabilities to damage an organization, but only hypothetically. The real purpose is to uncover security failings in a system to help an organization safeguard its business from dangerous hackers. This example illustrates that some networks are desperate to upgrade their systems and adequately protect their users' funds.

People worldwide are interested in investing in cryptocurrencies. However, price volatility and security concerns often scare investors. Exchanges try to mitigate these risks by alerting users to reset passwords frequently and question emails seeking personal information, but generally, it is too late. Since the internet's introduction in the early 1980s, the public has struggled to stay ahead of hackers. Crypto hacks and breaches often make headlines. However, investors should view such events as part of crypto's evolution.

Although crypto hacking, social engineering, and phishing are illegal acts in virtually every country, few laws prevent crypto miners from conspiring to take over 50 percent of a network's mining power. This situation is known as a *51 percent hack*. Although such a hack has not yet occurred, it remains a risk even for public/permissionless blockchains. This threat creates a significant risk for investors who store large amounts of value in cryptocurrency (Makarov & Schoar, 2021).

The following list shows the 10 largest crypto hacks based on currency prices when the theft occurred.

- PolyNetwork 2021 ($611 million).
- CoinCheck 2018 ($547 million).
- Mt.Gox 2014 ($480 million).
- Kucoin 2020 ($285 million).
- PancakeBunny 2021 ($200 million).
- Bitmart 2021 ($196 million).

- BitGrail 2018 ($170 million).
- Cream Finance 2021 ($130 million).
- BadgerDao 2021 ($120 million).
- CoinBene ($105 million).

Potential Changes

Regulators and others create new rules as the market evolves. These changes keep frameworks modernized and reasonably efficient. When a person or entity makes an important decision, a dissenting statement user offers an alternate opinion. This section provides examples of such views.

SEC Rule Approval (Rule 6c-11)

In 2019, Jay Clayton, acting SEC chairman, and the Commission approved a new rule (Rule 6c-11) to modernize the regulatory framework for ETFs. This rule established a clear and consistent framework for most ETFs to come directly to market without the cost and delay of obtaining an *exemptive order*, providing a green light from the SEC to move forward on a new initiative. The SEC has issued over 300 exemptive orders between 1992 and 2019, allowing ETFs to operate under the Investment Company Act (Securities and Exchange Commission, 2019). The proposal's goal was to facilitate more innovation and competition in the ETF marketplace to diversify choices for investors.

A Dissenting View

After the SEC had repeatedly rejected numerous bitcoin ETF proposals, SEC Commissioner Hester M. Peirce issued a dissent statement in February 2020. A *dissent statement* explains non-agreement against the majority ruling (Bhagat, 2020). In the statement, Commissioner Peirce explained that the Commission's actions impeded institutionalization and innovation. She stated that instead of regulators impeding investor choice, they should ensure that investors have access to accurate disclosures about the range of available products, including their risks.

This situation was not the first time Peirce has criticized regulators for stifling markets' economic freedom and creativity. She expressed similar thoughts about the regulations involving the Dodd-Frank Act in 2008. Peirce started as SEC Commissioner in January 2018 and received a term extension through June 2025. Her dissent statement against the SEC's decision to reject the bitcoin ETF championed by Winklevoss made her popular among the online cryptocurrency community, who gave her the nickname "Crypto Mom."

A Breakthrough Moment in History

On October 18, 2021, Proshares launched a bitcoin ETF consisting of derivative futures contracts for bitcoin. The Proshares Trust is the first of its kind that authorities approved for trading on the New York Stock Exchange (NYSE). This N-1A form allows Proshares to sell shares of its open-end ETF publicly. The SEC has not formally approved the registration, but that is not officially necessary. According to the SEC ruling, the Commission can allow an application to become effective rather than make a formal announcement.

ProShares CEO Michael L. Sapir said (Hewes, 2021, para. 3),

> We believe a multitude of investors have been eagerly awaiting the launch of a bitcoin-linked ETF after years of efforts to launch one. BITO will open up exposure to bitcoin to a large segment of investors who have a brokerage account and are comfortable buying stocks and ETFs, but do not desire to go through the hassle and learning curve of establishing another account with a cryptocurrency provider … or are concerned that these providers may be unregulated and subject to security risks.

This fund is the first-ever bitcoin futures ETF on a public US exchange. The exposure this futures ETF gives to bitcoin and cryptocurrencies is a significant step in the right direction for the blockchain network. Crypto advocates greeted the announcement of this approval via public commentary and media appearances as a watershed moment for crypto innovation in the United States. Nonetheless, this instrument does not allow investors to obtain exposure to bitcoin directly but instead tracks the price of bitcoin futures.

On October 19, 2021, the initial public offering (IPO) of Proshares Bitcoin Strategy ETF (BITO) on the NYSE opened at $40 per share and did not show much volatility throughout the day. Thus, 2021 represents a milestone because it enables other institutions to introduce a bitcoin futures ETF to the market.

Fund providers like VanEck, Invesco, and Valkyrie Investments already have bitcoin futures ETFs waiting for SEC approval. Although the SEC did not formally accept Proshares ETF registration, the company waited until its expected IPO date, hoping for no SEC interference.

Grayscale hinted at converting its bitcoin trust into a spot ETF. The demand from investors and institutions for more bitcoin future ETFs and the first spot ETF is at an all-time high, putting much pressure on the SEC to make timely decisions. The release of Proshares Bitcoin Strategy ETF helped push the spot price of bitcoin over $64,000. Bitcoin's market capitalization at the end of 2021 was over $1.3 trillion. This cryptocurrency giant has made significant progress since its creation in 2009.

CNBC interviewed SEC Chairman Gary Gensler on October 19, 2021, to discuss the recent approval of the first bitcoin future ETF. The Commission must protect investors. The CFTC exercised oversight of the ProShares Bitcoin ETF product for four years, following the regulations of the Act of 1940. This ETF trading on the CFTC for four years increased confidence in avoiding market manipulation. Gensler clarified that the SEC is technology-neutral, not policy-neutral. He emphasized that these types of investments are still a highly speculative asset class (CNBC, 2021). Unlike previous cryptocurrency ETF proposals that the SEC rejected, the ProShares proposal is based on futures contracts and filed under mutual fund rules, providing significant investor protections.

Summary and Conclusions

This chapter reviews the history of ETFs and the journey of getting approval for the first crypto ETF. Since the first ETF's inception in 1993, the market has experienced many advancements. This progress indicates that investors still have a high demand for this fund type. Many S-1 applications remain pending. Instead of making timely decisions, the SEC attempts to regulate via enforcement measures versus constructive dialogue. A breakthrough moment occurred in October 2021, when the SEC decided to allow investments in crypto ETFs based on future derivative contracts that bet on bitcoin's price fluctuations rather than the underlying crypto. SEC Commissioners Gensler and Peirce played instrumental roles in this outcome. Investors can now invest in transparent crypto products regulated by a US agency and offer customary functionality. This situation is a positive step forward for the industry.

Discussion Questions

1. Explain the concept of pooled fund investing and its advantages and disadvantages.
2. List several different regulators involved in the ETF approval process.
3. Identify two major benefits of investing in an ETF rather than individual stocks.
4. Explain the difference between a hot and cold wallet.
5. Explain why Proshares received approval to list its bitcoin ETF on a national exchange.

References

Barrett, B. (2019). Hack brief: Hackers stole $40 million from Binance Crypto Exchange. *Wired*, May 8. Retrieved from https://www.wired.com/story/hack-binance-cryptocurrency-exchange/

Bhagat, D. (2020, September 29). *Ruth Bader Ginsburg & dissents: What's a dissent?* Boston, MA: Boston Public Library. Retrieved from https://www.bpl.org/blogs/post/ruth-bader-ginsburg-dissents-whats-a-dissent/

CNBC. (2021). SEC Chair Gary Gensler speaks with CNBC's "Squawk on the Street" today. CNBC, October 19. Retrieved from https://www.cnbc.com/2021/10/19/cnbc-transcript-sec-chair-gary-gensler-speaks-with-cnbcs-squawk-on-the-street-today.html

Commodity Futures Trading Commission. (2021). *About the commission*. Washington, DC: CTFC. Retrieved from https://www.cftc.gov/About/AboutTheCommission

Cryptopedia Staff. (2021, March 25). *What is a decentralized exchange (DEX)?* Gemini. Retrieved from https://www.gemini.com/cryptopedia/decentralized-exchange-crypto-dex.

Greifeld, K., Hajric, V., & Benjamin B. (2021, October 15). *SEC set to allow bitcoin futures ETFs as deadline looms*. Bloomberg. Retrieved from https://www.bloomberg.com/news/articles/2021-10-15/bitcoin-futures-etf-said-not-to-face-sec-opposition-at-deadline

Hewes, T. (2021). ProShares to launch the first U.S. bitcoin-linked ETF on October 19. Business Wire, October 18. Retrieved from https://www.businesswire.com/news/home/20211018005280/en/

Ikeda, S. (2021). Coinbase hack attributed to a multi-factor authentication flaw that allowed scammers to steal cryptocurrency from 6,000 accounts. *CPO Magazine*, October 14. Retrieved from https://www.cpomagazine.com/cyber-security/coinbase-hack-attributed-to-a-multi-factorauthentication-flaw-that-allowed-scammers-to-steal-cryptocurrency-from-6000-accounts/

Makarov, I., & Schoar, A. (2021, October 13). *Blockchain analysis of the bitcoin market*. MIT Sloan Working Paper 6479-21. MIT Sloan School of Management, Cambridge, MA. Retrieved from https://mitsloan.mit.edu/shared/ods/documents?PublicationDocumentID=7981

Michaels, D. (2018). SEC rejects winklevoss Bitcoin ETF proposal. The Wall Street Journal, July 27. Retrieved from https://www.wsj.com/articles/sec-rejects-winklevoss-bitcoin-etf-proposal-1532641106

Nakamoto, S. (2008, October 31). Bitcoin: A peer-to-peer electronic cash system. Retrieved from https://nakamotoinstitute.org/bitcoin/

Namcios – Bitcoin Magazine. (2021, September 17). Fidelity survey: 52% of institutional investors hold Bitcoin, Cryptocurrency. Retrieved from https://www.nasdaq.com/articles/fidelity-survey%3A-52-of-institutional-investors-hold-bitcoin-cryptocurrency-2021-09-17

Nelson, D. (2021, May 26). *Fidelity Bitcoin fund attracts $102M in first 9 months*. Coindesk. Retrieved from https://www.coindesk.com/business/2021/05/26/fidelity-bitcoin-fund-attracts-102m-in-first-9-months/

Securities and Exchange Commission. (2012, August). *Investor bulletin: Exchange-traded funds (ETFs)*. SEC. Retrieved from https://www.sec.gov/investor/alerts/etfs.pdf

Securities and Exchange Commission. (2017, January). *Mutual funds and exchange-traded funds (ETFs) – A guide for investors*. SEC. Retrieved from https://www.sec.gov/reportspubs/investor-publications/investorpubsinwsmfhtm.html

Securities and Exchange Commission. (2018a, July). *Self-regulatory organizations; Bats BZX Exchange, Inc.; Order setting aside action by delegated authority and disapproving a proposed rule change, as modified by Amendments No. 1 and 2, to list and trade shares of the Winklevoss Bitcoin Trust*. SEC. Retrieved from https://www.sec.gov/rules/other/2018/34-83723.pdf

Securities and Exchange Commission. (2018b, October). *Our goals*. SEC. Retrieved from https://www.sec.gov/our-goals#goal1

Securities and Exchange Commission. (2019, September 26). *SEC adopts new rule to modernize regulation of exchange-traded funds*. SEC. Retrieved from https://www.sec.gov/news/press-release/2019-190

Securities and Exchange Commission. (2021a, June). *Funds trading in Bitcoin futures – Investor bulletin*. SEC. Retrieved from https://www.sec.gov/oiea/investor-alerts-and-bulletins/ib_fundstrading

Securities and Exchange Commission. (2021b, March 24). *Wise origin bitcoin trust form S-1 registration statement*. SEC. Retrieved from https://www.sec.gov/Archives/edgar/data/1852317/000119312521092598/d133565ds1.htm

Statistica. (2021). Number of exchange traded funds (ETFs) worldwide from 2003 to 2020. Retrieved from https://www.statista.com/statistics/278249/global-number-of-etfs/

Weiner, M. B. (2020). A historical analysis of the investment company act of 1940. Michigan Business & Entrepreneurial Law Review, *10*(1), 67–93. Retrieved from https://repository.law.umich.edu/mbelr/vol10/iss1/4

Chapter 12

Approaches to Cryptocurrency Valuation

Arman Eshraghi

Abstract

Cryptocurrencies are notoriously difficult to value from a fundamental perspective. This valuation challenge is rooted in various debated issues in academia and the investments industry. For example, do cryptocurrencies and other cryptoassets have intrinsic value in the conventional sense? Can one appropriately regard cryptocurrencies as digital fiat currencies? What distinguishes cryptocurrencies such as bitcoin and ether from precious metals like gold from a financial perspective? How do cryptocurrencies compare to other cryptoassets in terms of pricing and valuation? This chapter aims to provide responses to these questions, discuss approaches to cryptoasset valuation, and identify areas for future research.

Keywords: Cryptocurrencies; cryptoassets; valuation; pricing; intrinsic value; bitcoin; ether

Introduction

Many market participants wonder about the valuation of cryptocurrencies and other cryptoassets. Valuing cryptocurrencies is highly challenging from a fundamental angle. Unlike stocks, cryptocurrencies do not generate income or pay dividends that one can discount back in time. Of course, many stocks do not pay dividends, such as high-growth stocks, so similarities in valuation may exist in that respect with cryptocurrencies. Because no universally agreed approach is available for valuing cryptocurrencies, this chapter examines several possible methods, including their pros and cons. The valuation process is slightly less complex for some cryptoassets, such as security and utility tokens. This chapter also discusses valuing these lesser-known cryptoassets.

The Emerald Handbook on Cryptoassets: Investment Opportunities and Challenges, 171–184

doi:10.1108/978-1-80455-320-620221012

An important caveat is that valuation involves subjectivity and is sensitive to a model's underlying assumptions. Even when the valuation assumptions are transparent and widely agreed upon, measurement noise is present. Noise is a concern in cryptoasset valuation since no centralized databases are available to impose registering, filing, and reporting requirements in the cryptoasset ecosystem. Unlike equity markets, the crypto market does not have financial regulators equivalent to the Securities and Exchange Commission (SEC) and databases comparable to EDGAR, the Electronic Data Gathering, Analysis, and Retrieval system. The few market intelligence databases available in the crypto space occasionally show disparities when reporting statistics on a given token. This situation may indicate different underlying assumptions, definitions, and measurement errors.

This chapter has the following organization. The next two sections provide a typological overview of cryptoassets and examine whether cryptoassets have intrinsic value. The chapter then focuses on valuating security and utility tokens and then discusses approaches to valuing exchange tokens. The final section provides a summary and conclusions.

Overview of Cryptoassets

Cryptoassets comprise three broad categories: (1) security tokens, (2) utility tokens, and (3) exchange tokens. This section provides an overview of these three classes.

Security Tokens

A *security token* is a digital, liquid contract representing an economic interest in the entity or business issuing the security. These tokens amount to a specified investment representing the crypto equivalent of ordinary equity securities. Security tokens may provide rights such as ownership, repayment of a specific sum of money, or entitlement to a share in future profits. They may also be transferable securities or financial instruments under the European Union's Markets in Financial Instruments Directive II. From a valuation perspective, security tokens are more straightforward than other cryptoassets.

In general, security tokens are subject to strict regulation from financial regulators. The regulatory framework for security tokens has become increasingly transparent, leading to a worldwide boom in security tokens. For example, in July 2020, Arca, an American asset management firm, began trading its digital security token, ArCoin, registered with the SEC and representing shares in Arca's US Treasury Fund. In September 2020, the SEC registered an $85 million security token offering from INX, a foreign crypto trading company. This offering became the first security token initial public offering qualified by the SEC. In April 2021, the SEC qualified a Reg A+ token offering for Exodus, a digital asset management company, marking the first digital asset security conferring equity in a US-based issuing company. Exodus subsequently raised $75 million from 6,800 individual investors.

Whether certain transactions qualify as investment contracts by financial regulators can be subject to some well-known tests. For example, the SEC has historically applied the so-called "Howey Test" and its alternatives to make such determinations. The Supreme Court created the "Howey Test" to determine whether certain transactions qualify as "investment contracts." If so, the Securities Act of 1933 and the Securities Exchange Act of 1934 consider those transactions securities and subject to specific disclosure and registration requirements. Whether a regulator authority considers an investment a security is critical because this designation means that the investment is subject to specific registration requirements.

Utility Tokens

A *utility token* is a token that the holder can redeem for access to a specific product or service typically provided using a distributed ledger technology (DLT) platform. Issuing a utility token involves developing a distributed organization designed to share some resource (product or service) in a peer-to-peer format. The utility token's creator effectively creates a small economy where the utility token is the exclusive medium of exchange. The microeconomy's developer funds the venture by selling the tokens upfront. In principle, the market can value utility tokens by assessing a token's performance in attracting and retaining user demand. The market determines the token at the intersection of variable demand for and finite supply of tokens offered.

Exchange Tokens

An exchange token, also called cryptocurrency, is the most popular form of cryptoasset. An *exchange token* is based on blockchain technology and designed to serve as digital money or a medium of exchange. Examples include bitcoin, ether, and several hundred other cryptocurrencies. These exchange tokens use a DLT platform and are not issued or backed by a central bank or other central body. They do not provide the types of rights or access offered by security or utility tokens but serve as a means of exchange or investment. As discussed later, cryptocurrencies are the most challenging type of cryptoasset to value from a fundamental perspective.

Do Cryptocurrencies Have Intrinsic Value?

The question of intrinsic value is highly relevant in valuing cryptocurrencies and cryptoassets more generally (García-Monleón, Danvila-del-Valle, & Lara, 2021). According to the *Oxford Handbook of Value Theory*, *intrinsic value* often refers to "what is valuable for its own sake, in itself, on its own, in its own right, as an end, or as such. By contrast, some characterize extrinsic value as what is valuable as a means, or for something else's sake" (Rønnow-Rasmussen, 2015, p. 29). Many economic scholars consider cryptocurrencies devoid of intrinsic value (Baur, Hong, & Lee, 2018; Cheah & Fry, 2015; Tirole, 2017).

The parallels between cryptocurrencies and precious metals such as gold are relevant to this debate. Those who believe that gold has intrinsic value often refer to its industrial and cosmetic applications, such as jewelry. However, the perceived value of gold resets on longstanding subjective and historical beliefs often rooted in cultural values. This debate highlights the complexity of creating a clear-cut distinction between intrinsic (value "as such") and extrinsic value (value as a "means to an end"). Some contend that using gold as a "store of value" or "means of exchange" or even as jewelry constitutes extrinsic rather than intrinsic value. Some contend that the widely agreed beauty of gold jewelry signals wealth or acts as a store of wealth. In addition, one might also maintain that gold's perceived value rests so deeply in human psychology that an abrupt loss in appreciation seems to be highly unlikely. Still, this appreciation is not necessarily an intrinsic characteristic of gold.

In a similar vein, those arguing that bitcoin has no intrinsic value since it has no use for industrial purposes may confuse extrinsic and intrinsic value. Treiblmaier (2021, p. 7) takes a philosophical stance on this question and posits that intrinsic value is "a vague concept and obfuscates rather than illuminates the properties of cryptocurrencies." He further maintains that some may view the intrinsic value of cryptocurrencies as the total of all properties, making them suitable as a means of exchange. The total cost of mining hardware and energy investments is a proxy to estimate their intrinsic value.

Valuation Approaches: Security and Utility Tokens

This section presents standard valuation approaches used for various cryptoassets. The discussion begins with security tokens, which are less challenging to value, and moves to utility tokens and exchange tokens (cryptocurrencies). The insights presented here draw upon academic papers and industry reports such as Johnson, Bufton, and Daniel (2019) and Athey, Parashkevov, Sarukkai, and Xia (2016).

Security Tokens

The nature of the decision-making and distribution rights associated with the ownership of different security tokens varies. However, one fundamental characteristic common to all security tokens is the right to receive future distributions. This right enables using traditional valuation methods under the market and income approaches.

Market Approach. The valuation method adopted for a given token under the market approach depends on its liquidity and stage of development. Relevant scenarios range from a token at the launch point (i.e., one with no liquidity and no directly observable price) to a token with continuously updated prices in a direct trading pair against a fiat currency. Secondary trade pricing of tokens is a relevant reference point in assessing market value. Typically, no principal market exists for security tokens because they may trade on various exchanges. However, at least one active market is usually available.

Considering liquidity and the depth of trades is critical. However, such factors are a matter of judgment regarding the threshold to apply and the means of assessment. For example, a particular token may be readily exchangeable only into another cryptoasset, a liquid cryptocurrency such as bitcoin or ether, or directly into a fiat currency. If a token exhibits sufficient liquidity in a direct trading pair against a fiat currency, a reasonable approach would be to adopt a quoted price as the token's market value. The volatility in token and cryptocurrency prices illustrates that market value may differ from *intrinsic value*, a security's perceived value.

When one cannot reliably and directly exchange a token for fiat currency (i.e., where such a realization requires one or more intermediate conversions, or "hops," into more readily convertible cryptoassets), or when liquidity is low, analysts should consider adopting a discount for lack of liquidity. When no secondary trade pricing is available or liquidity is too low to place reliance on the price, analysts can extend the market approach to compare the subject token to a recently launched token or one with liquid pricing. Adopting a valuation multiple is challenging, as financial metrics such as revenues or earnings are typically not sufficiently comparable between assets. Liquid security tokens are scarce. Yet, comparisons to quoted or recently sold companies give rise to conceptual issues resulting from the different maturity and risk of the sources of the income streams.

An alternative approach is to consider the token market capitalizations achieved in recent, comparable ICOs as a proxy for the subject tokens' total value (Catalini & Gans, 2018). This approach is like benchmarking when valuing early-stage companies raising venture capital (VC) funding rounds. Analysts could assess comparability based on a scorecard approach, often undertaken by VCs investing in early-stage businesses. Potential scorecard items include the stage of a project's technological and commercial development, the team's quality and experience behind the project, the addressable market's size, and the project's uniqueness. This approach could yield a broad and indicative value range.

Income Approach. Based on cash flows to a security token's holder, an income approach is conceptually the best approach when assessing fundamental value. It can help inform investment decisions when inefficiencies, sentiment, and speculation heavily influence market prices. However, this approach may be consistent with the bases of value required by financial reporting and tax valuation standards, which generally directly emphasize market-based measures.

Traditional startups tend to demonstrate excessive optimism in their forecasts and are associated with high failure rates. Yet, a high degree of optimism persists among many committed cryptoasset supporters. Therefore, analysts should rigorously analyze the market size targeted by each project and the amount of market share they want to capture. They need to appropriately factor in a coherent view of the market's development into a scenario analysis and its probabilities.

Discount rates are critical assumptions under the income approach. However, their estimation for investments in early-stage ventures is highly subjective. Adopting the traditionally accepted capital asset pricing model (CAPM) is challenging in determining an appropriate discount rate. This situation occurs because market data such as betas are unobservable, comparable quoted companies do not exist, and judgmental alpha risk premia assumptions are required (Liu & Tsyvinski, 2021; Schilling & Uhlig, 2019). One solution is to estimate a discount rate based on VC investors' hurdle rates from survey data or published returns. A large volume of return data is available from some large US pension funds. Such data may be unrepresentative of the total market. Also, alternative investment performance indices often rely on self-reported data and may thus contain inherent biases such as survivorship bias.

Another adaptation of the scorecard method uses scorecard items like those cited under the market approach. Typically, analysts apply this technique as a direct determinant of the value placed on a stake in a company at an early stage of development. This logic may apply equally well to estimating a discount rate within the broad range observed in the market. The range of discount rates implied by VC investors' hurdle rates can be a starting point.

Analysts can then assess qualitative factors that may increase or decrease a project's risk profile compared to a typical VC investment. One factor is funding risk. Is the project fully funded over its expected life cycle, or could it require further financing rounds? If so, what is the risk around achieving the required funding? A second factor is intellectual property risk. Is there clear ownership and protection around any intellectual capital developed? A third consideration is upfront participant commitments. Analysts should consider the upfront involvement of participants to reduce a project's commercial risk. They can determine a narrower discount rate range in assessing these qualitative factors more reflective of a project's specific risk.

An alternative approach is to adopt a scenario-based structure to model future cash flows. This approach allows separating a project's exposure to risks in the industry and the broader environment from the probability of extreme situations, such as a failure or a unicorn birth (e.g., achieving a valuation above $1 billion). One of CAPM's uses is to derive a normal discount rate, reflective of the risk associated with investing in a quoted company exposed to the same geographies and end markets.

Utility Tokens

Holders can redeem their utility tokens to access a specific product or service. The fact that utility token holders have no right to any future income streams presents unique challenges from a valuation perspective. For example, discounted cash flow models and traditional applications of the market approach are inappropriate in these settings. This situation, however, does not mitigate quantitative analysis.

Tokens Versus Platforms. The token utility concept highlights how to consider splitting value between a cryptoasset and its underlying platform. This issue is also relevant to security tokens. A token reflects an ownership share in an enterprise, and the platform reflects an enterprise's intangible asset. Thus, the analysis is more complex for utility tokens. A utility token's value depends primarily on the demand for goods or services transacted on the platform and the number of tokens in circulation. Tokens are divisible. Furthermore, the prices of goods or services in terms of tokens can require adjustment. A token's price in fiat currency terms can move independently of the price of a particular good or service transacted on the platform. The users typically enjoy a token's value and not necessarily the platform's operator.

A platform's value to its operator is a function of how the operator extracts benefits (income less costs) from the platform on an ongoing basis and the sustainability of such benefits over time. This value extraction, whether by the original platform developer or any party to which it was to sell the right to operate the platform, is limited by the opportunity cost of available alternative means of delivering the service provided by the token platform.

Market Approach. As in the case of a security token, the valuation method adopted for a given utility token under the market approach depends on its liquidity and stage of development. The range of scenarios and liquidity considerations for utility tokens mirrors those already discussed for security tokens.

Cost Approach. If no secondary trade pricing is available or liquidity is too low to place reliance on the price, opportunity costs can still provide an observable proxy for value. The function of a utility token as a medium of exchange creates the first such proxy: the opportunity cost of utility. Participants in a utility token network quote prices for goods or services they offer for sale, denominated in a utility token. Therefore, one can compare these quoted prices to the fiat currency prices paid for alternative means of acquiring the same quantity of goods or services. From these two inputs, one can estimate a unit value for the token based on the reasoning that rational users would not use the utility token network if the same goods or services were available elsewhere at a lower cost.

For example, consider a utility token system designed for hard drive storage sharing, such as Storj. Users offering hard drive space on the platform will accept payment in Storj tokens. Thus, a Storj-denominated price per gigabyte-month (GB-Mo) will be observable. Concurrently, the large technology companies that provide cloud storage services to the public quote fiat currency-denominated prices per GB-Mo of storage space. Because the measure of utility, GB-Mo, constitutes a common denominator, dividing the latter price by the former yields the fiat currency price of a Storj token.

Mineable cryptoassets require considering the cost of their generation using a proxy for a range's lower bound based on assuming rational miners would not mine at a loss. However, utility tokens typically that are not mineable make this consideration more relevant to the valuation of cryptocurrencies, such as bitcoin.

The Quantity Theory of Money. A utility token functions as a medium of exchange. It represents the only "legal tender" within its network, creating meaningful parallels with fiat currencies. The miniature economy metaphor is instructive in that it enables viewing a utility token's price level through the prism of the quantity theory of money (QTM), which states that:

$$MV = PY \tag{12.1}$$

The formula states that money supply (M) times velocity of money (V) equals price level (P) times the volume of goods and services transacted in the economy (Y), often proxied by gross domestic product (GDP).

One can consider the money supply within a utility token system as a combination of two quantities. The first is a long-run fixed M^* (i.e., the total number of tokens determined by the developer upon issuance. The second quantity is a float factor (F), equal to one minus the issuer's percentage of tokens retained in reserve. The issuer's short-run reaction function, and thus the behavior of F, requires further study, but this quantity should converge to 100 percent over the long run. A simplifying assumption treats M as constant for valuation purposes.

The public nature of the distributed ledgers underpinning utility token systems makes money velocity an observable quantity (i.e., the inverse of the average period for which someone holds a token at one address). Although the market must value any given token before its issuance (i.e., before its velocity becomes observable), a reasonable approach is to estimate velocity by referencing comparable tokens.

One could establish comparability by analyzing the nature of the service accessible through the utility token system. The size and frequency of potential purchases made in the network constitute more obvious comparison points. One might also consider how the system caters to unmet needs as a proxy for its ability to attract user demand. Strong demand could increase token liquidity and easier convertibility into fiat currency. A temptation might be to argue that transactions in utility tokens can and do occur outside of the ledger (e.g., when two customers of a centralized crypto exchange transact). Such transactions are unobservable and not captured in the observed velocity. However, including such transactions in the velocity measure would not ultimately measure a token's fundamental role as a transaction medium within its system. Thus, deriving velocity solely from on-chain transactions seems appropriate.

Estimating the volume of goods and services transacted (i.e., the "GDP term" of the QTM) constitutes the critical area of estimation. In a utility token system, this term equals the overall value of the services rendered through the system during a specified period. To illustrate, consider a utility token system designed for hard drive storage sharing. Such a system would effectively meet part of the global demand for remote file storage. Further, the overall market size for remote file storage and the share of that demand met by the system would determine the value of the services rendered. That is, decomposing the GDP term, Y, into two further terms – market size (D) and market share (s) – is useful. This valuation approach for a utility token focuses on deriving reasonable estimates of these quantities. Of course, such estimation involves considerable judgment and complexity.

Market size, for example, is likely to be further influenced by macroeconomic growth and the sensitivity of demand for the service to that growth. Some services may be normal, and others inferior. Moreover, adopting a probabilistic approach to estimating D, either a distribution or discrete scenario, would be desirable. Market share estimation would have to be probabilistic to be meaningful. Indeed, this estimate could be the key avenue for modeling the relatively high risk of failure inherent in early-stage ventures, including utility token initial coin offerings (ICOs). This dynamic introduces the additional complexity of modeling a non-normal distribution. Utility token systems benefit from the external reference point of fiat currency prices. The volume of goods and services transacted can be input as a fiat-denominated quantity, leaving the remaining unknown variable *P* also denominated in fiat currency terms.

Practical Application of the QTM for Utility Tokens. The discussion has ignored the question of time, which is important from a valuation perspective. Focusing on long-run equilibrium effectively visualizes a future state of the utility token system once operational and successful. Such development is likely to take several years. The first option for reflecting the time value of money would be to discount the output of the QTM formula, calculated at a particular time horizon, to its present value, using an appropriate discount rate. Deriving such a discount rate involves considerable judgment. Two choices are available: (1) adjusting the probability distribution and (2) using Monte Carlo or similar approaches. One would have to carefully consider the consistency of either choice with one's approach to modeling the probability of failure.

Regarding the first option, suppose the time value of money was to be reflected in the probability distribution of the market share term of the QTM. In that case, the discount rate should only reflect a normal risk level associated with the type of service rendered through the given utility token system and no additional risk relating to the early-stage nature of the venture. Such a discount rate could be determined using the CAPM. Alternatively, if the probability distribution did not incorporate the risk of failure, the discount rate applied would have to be much higher. One could derive it from the hurdle rates adopted by VCs to ensure appropriate returns on their funds.

The second option involves using Monte Carlo simulation. This approach requires identifying all relationships among variables in the model and specifying probability distributions for all input variables. It would also entail discounting at the risk-free rate. The two options should yield a similar result.

Valuation Approaches: Exchange Tokens (Cryptocurrencies)

As of January 2021, CoinMarketCap.com reports the global crypto market capitalization (cap) close to $2 trillion, with this value spread over 7,680 cryptocurrencies. However, most tokens are obscure and have an extremely small market cap. A few exceptionally large tokens dominate the cryptocurrency market. Bitcoin is the prime example, with a market cap above $1 trillion.

Cryptocurrency valuation methods constitute three broad categories: (1) the income approach, (2) the market approach, and (3) the cost approach. The income approach considers the cryptoasset features of medium of exchange and storage of value and applies QTM and network effects such as Metcalfe's law. *Metcalfe's law* states that a network's impact is the square of the number of nodes in the network. For instance, if a network has 10 nodes, its inherent value is 100 (10 × 10). The price/earnings (*P*/*E*) ratio, widely used in conventional equity market valuations, is the inspiration for the market approach. This approach emphasizes the transaction value and token utilities, with metrics such as the network value-to-transaction ratio and the price-to-utility ratio. Finally, the cost approach calculates mining costs as a lower bound for valuations.

Returning to the income approach and the QTM, the GDP term (*Y*) is almost impossible to estimate because cryptocurrencies are not confined to a limited-purpose network providing a specific service for which demand that one can reasonably model. For a cryptocurrency, D represents the aggregate demand in the global economy, and *s* is the cryptocurrency's "market share" among various media of exchange, including fiat currencies. Thus, a token's price (*p*) effectively becomes a function of market participants' expectations of the share of global GDP to be transacted through the given cryptocurrency. Such expectations are highly subjective and very difficult to assess with any degree of accuracy. Considering this realization, the QTM's value as an analytical tool diminishes greatly.

Bitcoin as Digital Gold

Taking a historical view, the technology behind online payments improved with the emergence of a series of gold-based digital currencies (Nica, Piotrowska, & Schenk-Hoppe, 2021, chapter 1). These currencies were essentially asset-backed payment systems (Nian & Chuen, 2015, chapter 1). Of these gold-standard digital currencies, the most popular was E-gold which, before its closure in 2008, processed more than $2 billion per year. E-gold's popularity decreased as the currencies faced attacks from hackers and cases of internet fraud. It shut down because it did not comply with the legal requirements imposed by the US authorities.

An emerging consensus among market participants is that bitcoin, due to technological limitations, will not become a large-scale replacement for fiat currency in payments. Proponents of this view typically contend that bitcoins will instead serve only as a store of value – the sort of safe-haven asset for the third millennium that gold has been for millennia. Unfortunately, that conceptualization violates QTM's most fundamental assumption of using bitcoin as a medium of exchange. QTM's application for valuation purposes would become invalid if one did not expect bitcoins to be used to fulfill a transaction motive. This situation would leave no fundamental basis for deriving bitcoin's price, making it like collectibles such as fine wine or art. Thus, bitcoin would demand a "trophy asset" premium that is not readily quantifiable. Some quantitative analysis might still be possible based on the analogy to non-interest-bearing safe-haven assets that do not constitute media of exchange.

Attention now turns to technical analysis, the algorithmic analysis of historical price, trading volume, and other statistical market data to identify trading opportunities, notably used by quantitative hedge funds. This type of analysis appears possible regarding cryptoassets. Given the market's sentiment-driven nature and high retail investor participation, technical analysis could even be profitable. Like those operating in the traditional financial markets, quantitative hedge funds also operate in cryptoasset capital markets. However, technical analysts and quantitative funds are likely to have short investment horizons because their methods are unlikely to be useful for a fundamentals-driven long-term investor.

Metcalfe's Law and Other Network Effects

Robert Metcalfe, an early internet pioneer and co-inventor of Ethernet, stipulated that a network's value is proportional to the square of the number of its users (Briscoe, Odlyzko, & Tilly, 2006). This relationship is because the number of unique connections in a network of *n* nodes can be expressed mathematically as $n(n-1)/2$, which is asymptotically proportional to n^2.

This logic similarly applies to cryptocurrencies. Suppose that the number of unique bitcoin addresses proxies is the number of bitcoin users. Metcalfe's law captures a token's long-term value by measuring the number of its users. Nevertheless, the validity of Metcalfe's law for cryptocurrencies is questionable in the short run. Besides the difficulty of quantifying a network's value, the mathematical justification for Metcalfe's law measures only the potential number of contacts. However, a network's social utility depends on the number of nodes in contact. In addition, the law simplistically assumes that all nodes are of equal value or benefit (Briscoe et al., 2006). Others, such as Liu, Sheng, and Wang (2021), propose considering the transaction volume per unique address. This modification would make Metcalfe's law-based models more suitable for token valuation analyses. One explanation is that the number of users reflects a token's long-run value, while the transaction volume per unique address mirrors a token's daily usage. Consequently, analysts should factor in the transaction volume per unique address when estimating the short-run price variation. Based on this logic, the network-value-to-transactions (NVT) ratio is related to velocity in the following way. Metcalfe's model only factors in a cryptocurrency's value as a medium of exchange and overlooks its function as a store of value. Equation 12.2 shows the NTV ratio:

$$\begin{aligned}\text{NVT Ratio} &= \text{Network Value/Transaction Volume}\\ &= (\text{Token Price} \times \text{Token Supply})/(\text{Token Price} \times \text{Transacted Token})\\ &= \text{Token Supply/Transacted Token} = 1/\text{Token Velocity}\end{aligned} \tag{12.2}$$

Similarly, Cong, Li, and Wang (2021) use the S-curve to clarify the roles of tokens on platform adoption. They compare platform adoption's endogenous S-curve with and without tokens. Without tokens, user adoption is often below the socially optimal level for a promising platform with improving productivity. Tokens can increase welfare because agents foresee token price appreciation and adopt more. Embedding tokens on a promising platform front-loads future growth. Notably, tokens may also lead to over-adoption in the very early stage. Similarly, for a bad platform with expected deteriorating productivity, tokens can precipitate its demise, which again can be welfare-improving.

Valuation Discounts

Market participants should consider the appropriateness of applying liquidity discounts to observable value benchmarks in determining a cryptoasset's value. When discussing varying liquidity levels using the market approach, such discounts may be appropriate in certain circumstances.

For a cryptoasset traded in a liquid market in a direct pair against a fiat currency, a discount is unlikely to be warranted from commercial valuation considerations or financial reporting standards. Adopting a discount for lack of liquidity is applicable in specific cases: (1) where someone cannot reliably and directly exchange a cryptoasset for fiat currency, and (2) where a liquid cryptoasset's valuation comes from the observable price of a comparable liquid cryptoasset. The amount of this discount could be determined similarly to when considering the liquidity discounts for traditional financial instruments such as private equity stakes.

An analyst should also consider liquidity in valuations performed under the income approach. In this case, the analyst needs to use consistent assumptions when determining the discount rate by referring to VC investors' hurdle rates. Additionally, the analyst should note that such rates already reflect the required returns of fund investors, given the illiquid nature of the underlying VC investments. Therefore, no need exists to apply a further discount for lack of liquidity. This approach contrasts with the alternative method of deriving a discount rate based on the market pricing of liquid financial instruments and modeling failure risk separately.

An analyst should also consider blockage discounts. One can characterize these discounts as a specific type of liquidity discount relevant to large holders of a particular asset. Financial reporting standards typically prohibit their adoption. Nonetheless, these discounts may represent an important commercial consideration. For example, suppose a utility token issuer retains a large token reserve relative to market trading volume. Assuming the issuer would sell a large volume of tokens without depressing the market price may be unrealistic.

Summary and Conclusions

Some contend that cryptocurrencies share certain features with *private money*, which is money issued by a private party rather than a central government (Athey et al., 2016). Some examples of private money include local currency usable within a network of merchants, notes issued by private banks whose value links to a government-backed currency, and notes issued by banks whose value floats. In many cases, uncertainty exists in the future value of private currencies. Additionally, some criticize private money for various reasons, including the exchange rate fluctuations and associated inefficiencies it brings, the lack of control over the money supply that it engenders, and the uncertainty due to the possibility of bank runs.

Private currencies also share attributes with complementary currencies. A *complementary currency* refers to a diverse group of currencies used for profitable commercial purposes and social/community exchanges. Many communities worldwide have adopted such currencies. Examples include Bristol/Brixton/Exeter/Lewes/Stroud Pound (UK), Calgary/Toronto Dollar (Canada), Eco-Pesa (Kenya), and Fureai Kippu (Japan). According to García-Corral, de Pablo-Valenciano, Milán-García, and Cordero-García (2020, p. 1), complementary currencies recognize that "social groups have something they can contribute and offer to the market to promote the well-being of an area. The inhabitants who participate in these currency schemes find in their use values such as equality, reciprocity, trust, and voluntariness, an activity which in the past has been underused." As outlined in Blanc and Fare (2018), complementary currencies often have four fundamental principles: (1) strengthening social links through exchange; (2) encouraging local consumption by engaging with providers in geographical proximity to a consumer; (3) encouraging initiatives, autonomy, and entrepreneurial responsibility, and (4) refusing speculation.

Cryptocurrencies typically do not face the same issues arising in fractional reserve banking (Athey et al., 2016). Thus, one can view them as private money or a complementary currency with unique characteristics such as immunity from bank runs. Approaches to their valuation are similarly unique. This chapter discussed some methods and provided thoughts on their limitations and underlying assumptions.

Discussion Questions

1. Discuss whether cryptocurrencies and other cryptoassets have intrinsic value.
2. Explain the common approaches to valuing the main types of cryptoassets.
3. Discuss the primary challenges in valuing cryptocurrencies.
4. Discuss the leading network effects in cryptocurrency valuation.

References

Athey, S., Parashkevov, I., Sarukkai, V., & Xia, J. (2016). *Bitcoin pricing, adoption, and usage: Theory and evidence*, Working Paper No. 17-033. Institute for Economic Policy Research, Stanford University.

Baur, D. G., Hong, H., & Lee, A. (2018). Bitcoin: Medium of exchange or speculative assets? *Journal of International Financial Markets, Institutions and Money*, *54*(C), 177–189.

Blanc, J., & Fare, M. (2018). Pathways to improvement. Successes and difficulties of local currency schemes in France since 2010. International Journal of Community Currency Research, *22*(Winter), 60–73.

Briscoe, B., Odlyzko, A., & Tilly, B. (2006). Metcalfe's law is wrong – Communications networks increase in value as they add members – But by how much? *IEEE Spectrum*, *43*(7), 34–39.

Catalini, C., & Gans, J. S. (2018). *Initial coin offerings and the value of crypto tokens*. Working Paper 24418, National Bureau of Economic Research.

Cheah, E.-T., & Fry, J. (2015). Speculative bubbles in bitcoin markets? An empirical investigation into the fundamental value of bitcoin. *Economics Letters*, *130*(C), 32–36.

Cong, L. W., Li, Y., & Wang, N. (2021). Tokenomics: Dynamic adoption and valuation. *Review of Financial Studies*, *34*(3), 1105–1155.

García-Corral, F. J., de Pablo-Valenciano, J., Milán-García, J., & Cordero-García, J. A. (2020). Complementary currencies: An analysis of the creation process based on sustainable local development principles. *Sustainability*, *12*(14), 1–22.

García-Monleón, F., Danvila-del-Valle, I., & Lara, F. J. (2021). Intrinsic value in crypto currencies. *Technological Forecasting and Social Change*, *162*(C), 120393.

Johnson, R., Bufton, J., & Daniel, J. (George). (2019). *The valuation of cryptoassets*. EY Financial Services Report.

Liu, Y., Sheng, J., & Wang, W. (2021). Technology and cryptocurrency valuation: Evidence from machine learning. Retrieved from https://papers.ssrn.com/sol3/papers.cfm?abstract_id=3577208

Liu, Y., & Tsyvinski, A. (2021). Risks and returns of cryptocurrency. *Review of Financial Studies*, *34*(6), 2689–2727.

Nian, L. P., & Chuen, D. L. K. (2015). Introduction to bitcoin. In D. L. K. Chuen (Ed.), *Handbook of digital currency* (pp. 5–30). Amsterdam: Elsevier.

Nica, O., Piotrowska, K., & Schenk-Hoppe, K. R. (2021). Cryptocurrencies: Concept and current market structure. In S. Goutte, K. Guesmi, & S. Saadi (Eds.), *Cryptofinance: A new currency for a new economy* (pp. 1–28). Singapore: World Scientific.

Rønnow-Rasmussen, T. (2015). Intrinsic and extrinsic value. In I. Hirose & J. Olson (Ed.), *The Oxford handbook of value theory* (pp. 29–43). New York, NY: Oxford University Press.

Schilling, L., & Uhlig, H. (2019). Some simple bitcoin economics. *Journal of Monetary Economics*, *106*(C), 16–26.

Tirole, J. (2017). There are many reasons to be cautious about bitcoin. Financial Times, November 29. Retrieved from https://www.ft.com/content/1c034898-d50f-11e7-a303-9060cb1e5f44

Treiblmaier, H. (2021). Do cryptocurrencies really have (no) intrinsic value? In Electronic markets (pp. 1–10). https://ssrn.com/abstract=3927924

Chapter 13

Cryptoassets in a Portfolio Context

Robinpreet Dhillon and Ehsan Nikbakht

Abstract

Since the inception of modern portfolio theory, traditional asset classes have been the standard investment products for portfolio construction. With the introduction of cryptoassets such as cryptocurrencies, tokenized securities, smart contracts, and blockchain-based token assets, the crypto "revolution" has created a new asset class for consideration in a modern portfolio. This chapter explains cryptoassets in a portfolio, including their limitations and parameters as an asset class in a diversified portfolio. Finally, it reports an improvement in a new portfolio's reward/risk ratio using the Sharpe ratio when adding cryptoassets to simulated equity, bonds, and real estate portfolios. A caveat is that a cryptoasset's contribution to a well-diversified traditional portfolio differs from the performance of investing in a single and isolated cryptoasset.

Keywords: Cryptoassets; portfolio theory; cryptocurrencies; Sharpe ratio; smart contracts; reward/risk ratio

Introduction

A *cryptoasset* is a new asset class for possible inclusion in a portfolio belonging to the general category of digital assets. Anything of potential economic value, tangible (e.g., real estate and commodities) and intangible (e.g., information including data, news, the right of ownership, and patents), could be an underlying asset that derives a new digital asset's value. Exchanging values through coins and tokens, utility functions (e.g., utility services such as using virtual games), and services related to financial instruments (e.g., trading settlements for stocks, bonds, and derivatives) are all candidates for creating digital assets capitalizing on one or some of their properties. A new product takes the creative imagination

The Emerald Handbook on Cryptoassets: Investment Opportunities and Challenges, 185–198

doi:10.1108/978-1-80455-320-620221013

of a cryptoasset developer or a technology entrepreneur. The market primarily influences a product's ultimate use, value, and popularity.

In the financial technology world, cryptoassets maintain a strong position as growing innovative financial instruments. Major applications in the blockchain and financial technology (FinTech) space are various tokens, peer-to-peer (P2P) lending, robo-advising, marketplace lending, and numerous decentralized finance (DeFi) products. The main outcome of these initiatives is the emergence of a new asset class known as cryptoassets, in which cryptocurrency is a subset challenging the financial markets and participants at global levels. The media contain reports claiming that traditional asset classes like stocks, bonds, and cash, in conjunction with cryptoassets, will be the future or the central part of modern portfolio applications. Initiating various types of cryptoassets occurs through an *initial coin offering* (ICO), a form of fundraising whereby blockchain-related ventures raise public capital in exchange for newly issued digital tokens.

This chapter examines cryptoassets in a portfolio context. The remainder of the chapter consists of the following sections: (1) ICO implications for portfolio construction, (2) cryptos' value-added contribution to portfolios, (3) factors to consider in a portfolio containing cryptoassets, (4) the future performance of cryptocurrencies in a portfolio, (5) other related issues, (6) crypto hedge funds and regulatory regimes, (7) digital assets and estate planning, and (8) a summary and conclusions.

ICO Implications for Portfolio Construction

An ICO's contribution to investments stems from a relatively low correlation between cryptoassets and traditional portfolios of stock and bonds, leading to a higher Sharpe ratio, a measure of risk-adjusted return. The following discussion examines an IC0's role, which involves creating a cryptoasset that an investor can add to a portfolio. A traditional initial public offering (IPO) is the standard way a corporation raises capital for future business opportunities. Although an ICO for cryptoassets is like an IPO for stocks in various ways, the main difference is that investing in an ICO does not secure an ownership stake in the crypto project or company. IPOs have existed since the beginning of stock exchanges.

An ICO has become a disruptor because buying a "token" enables its holder to use a private blockchain-based P2P network that an advertiser plans to develop with the token holder's funding. One could view an ICO as a crowdfunding campaign that sells new tokens to investors and others for fiat money. However, the primary difference between ICO fundraising and crowdfunding is the reward form. Investors in fiat currencies or any cryptocurrency get a reward in a tokenized form (Isha, 2021). In an ICO, a token's value is a matter of supply and demand. In an IPO, the holder expects a stock's share price to increase in value due to factors related to a firm's cash flows, growth, required rate of return, and news. For an ICO, suppose a hypothetical product X. Every time product X makes a sale, the ICO backing it registers the deal digitally through cryptography. Software, called a smart contract, streamlines the digital cryptoasset's functionality (Cohney, Hoffman, Sklaroff, & Wishnick, 2019). A *smart contract* is a computer program or a transaction protocol intended to execute, control, or document legally relevant events and actions automatically according to a contract's terms.

In an ICO, investors bear the full risk of a token's underlying issuer. With few financial regulations for tokenized coins, the issuers place their complete faith in the system's software and coding. A primary issue in an ICO smart contract is that investors do not typically read the contract's terms to become thoroughly familiar with them due to the "coding," which may not show all the details because it covers standardized clauses and is not specific to a document. Companies issuing ICOs are selling their "digital footprint," incentivizing the sale of their products with the assistance of smart contracts. An ICO provides an alternative for startup companies publicly issuing debt or equity. Thus, a firm can raise capital using an ICO. Investors benefit by having a platform to interact with a firm. Whether this feature appeals to a traditional portfolio manager is hard to assess. The instrument could be attractive to a portfolio manager seeking a higher return willing to bear more risk or of no value to others due to uncertainty and a client's low-risk tolerance.

Although an ICO is a new phenomenon, it has become a topic of discussion among portfolio managers. An ICO is a method for entrepreneurial firms to raise capital for their new cryptocurrency/business projects. After issuance, the issuer either takes fiat currency or cryptocurrency by encouraging investors to buy the startup firm's cryptographic coin. For example, a robust smart contract acts as authorizing software operating through the Ethereum coding machine that uses a specialized coding method known as a solidity code (Cohney et al., 2019).

ICOs do not require a firm to disclose the usage of investor funds, which is another limitation or caveat for some traditional portfolio managers in considering cryptos as viable products. Yet, ICOs give a competitive advantage over IPOs such that the funding achieved is almost covenant-free. As the ICO market exploded, so did the argument for scrutiny and regulations. In the traditional IPO context, securities regulators enforce rules and regulations restricting an issuer's activities. These regulations apply to all types of securities transactions, including IPOs. Either no or a limited transparent regime exists for ICOs. Instead, they opt to use a more informal document consisting of industry white papers (Cohney et al., 2019).

The ICO also relies heavily on cryptographic byte coding to create a coin supply. Unlike the Federal Reserve (Fed) system, where several means are available for controlling and managing the money supply, an ICO's supply can be virtually unlimited with no central authority monitoring the money creation and flow. An ICO smart contract has various supply effects. For instance, it has a code to limit the amount of cryptocurrency that each address can send to a smart contract. This parameter can modulate supply at any time. However, many cryptoassets do not require an absolute cap. For example, Ethereum has no specified supply cap, but bitcoin does. At best, "burning" (i.e., taking out of circulation) is the only mechanism to curtail monetary supply, subject to specific provisions in the crypto space. Thus, ICOs have radically changed the whole asset creation system, resulting in substantial challenges for all parties involved with critical implications for portfolio managers interested in adding those assets to their portfolios.

The rise of blockchain technology and the temptation to include cryptos in portfolios have raised financial regulators' concerns about accepting such products for portfolios. Some countries have implemented or are currently implementing ICO regulations. Others are still working on their white papers and proposals. Given recent changes in the US Securities and Exchange Commission (SEC) management, some still debate the rules of approving cryptoassets for portfolios. Yet, the SEC is gradually imposing restrictions. An example is the SEC scrutiny of new crypto exchange-traded funds (ETFs) proposals, such as GrayScale Trust (Wang, 2021).

Cryptos' Value-added Contribution to Portfolios

Table 13.1 shows the optimal asset allocation of a simulated portfolio with and without bitcoin using monthly data between 2015 and 2021 and a software program called Solver. The table also contains each portfolio's *Sharpe ratio*, measuring the risk-adjusted return of a financial portfolio. Analysts often view a Sharpe ratio of less than 1.00 as bad. They consider a Sharpe ratio from 1.00 to 1.99 as adequate/good, 2.00 to 2.99 as very good, and greater than 3 as excellent (Perez, 2021). The higher a portfolio's Sharpe ratio, the better its risk-adjusted performance. Calculating the Sharpe ratio follows:

$$S = \left(\frac{R_p - R_f}{\sigma_p} \right)$$

where *S*, the Sharpe ratio, R_p, the expected portfolio return, R_f, the risk-free return, and σ_p, the standard deviation of the portfolio's excess return. As Table 13.1 shows, the portfolio's Sharpe ratio without bitcoin is 0.85, indicating that the portfolio provides 0.85 units of excess return relative to the portfolio's standard deviation. Adding bitcoin increases the Sharpe ratio to 1.10, meaning that the portfolio now has more excess return per unit of portfolio risk.

Although these examples use simulated data, the results highlight that adding cryptoassets may improve a portfolio's reward/risk ratio as measured by the Sharpe ratio. These simulated results are consistent with a report from the CFA Institute (Hougan & Lawant, 2021) showing that when the bitcoin asset allocation increases from zero to 10 percent, the average Sharpe ratio improves from 0.68 to 1.54, or 2.26 times.

Factors to Consider in a Portfolio Containing Cryptoassets

A portfolio manager should consider several factors before adding a specific asset to a portfolio (Hougan & Lawant, 2021).

- Total money supply related to crypto as measured by the total market capitalization.
- A cryptoasset's speed or velocity (i.e., how fast a cryptoasset is used or spent in a currency's flow).

Table 13.1. A Portfolio With and Without Bitcoin.

Asset Class	**Percent**	
Stock market (S&P 500 ETF or SP&)	45.2	44.8
Bond portfolio (Invesco)	34.4	24.8
Real estate index (Jones Jones)	20.4	24.5
Bitcoin	0.0	5.9
Sharpe ratio	0.85	1.10

Notes: This table shows the optimal asset allocation with and without bitcoin using Solver. This example uses annualized monthly data between 2015 and 2021.

- The average volume of each transaction using crypto. The higher the average volume, the more popular the cryptoasset, leading to a more pronounced network effect. In other words, the size of transactions shows the intensity and degree of participation in the crypto space, known as the *network effect*.
- The number of cryptoasset transactions.

Investors and analysts could also use a commodity analogy method, better known as the stock-to-flow approach to value crypto in a portfolio. This approach views a crypto asset like a commodity, pricing it like a precious metal where supply and demand mainly determine its value. Pricing is a significant factor in investment decision-making before adding crypto to a portfolio. In the stock-to-flow approach, a commodity's value appreciates over the long run due to its scarcity. Supply and demand are the cornerstones of valuation in the absence of cash flow. Thus, the limited supply of bitcoin and its rising demand may increase its value. Based on the stock-to-flow approach, some investors may value cryptos following the bitcoin model in terms of supply and demand (i.e., how much demand chases a limited supply). This perspective values crypto in a portfolio based on its "store of value" expectation. Cryptos like bitcoin represent the first digital store value item. Based on this concept, a cryptocurrency's value could increase despite the absence of cash flows as one expects from a traditional asset, such as a stock or bond.

Investors and analysts use stock-to-flow statistics in pricing commodities like gold, silver, and other precious materials. Non-fungible assets in the crypto space might even be more of a suitable candidate for applying the stock-to-flow model in deciding if that specific crypto is worth including in a portfolio or selling if it is already in the portfolio. A *non-fungible asset* is unique and not exchanged in kind. For example, a non-fungible token (NFT) is a collectible digital asset that holds value, just like how physical art holds value.

Empirically evaluating the validity of the factors in a portfolio containing cryptoassets is beyond this chapter's scope. However, at the conceptual level, they represent a plausible set of measurable variables that portfolio managers should consider when adding crypto to a portfolio.

Future Performance of Cryptocurrencies in a Portfolio

Are cryptocurrencies headed for another asset bubble in the intermediate or long run? Although the answer to this question is unknown, having a sense of direction about the future of cryptos may guide investors in their strategic asset allocations. In the absence of any information about fundamentals, such as earnings, growth, dividends, and other cash flows, the price discovery process for cryptos is complex. For example, one may argue that the intrinsic value of bitcoin is almost zero (Chen, Després, Guo, & Renault, 2019). Determining a fair value is needed to manage a portfolio. So how is a crypto's value derived? A plausible attribute for valuing cryptos concerns liquidity imbalances (i.e., bids and asks at different levels).

Shichou (2021) provides empirical evidence involving liquidity imbalances. He shows that in the short run, traders and portfolio managers may get a sense of direction for cryptoassets by monitoring level 2 data where the total supply (ask prices at all levels) and the total demand (bid prices at all levels) interact, creating liquidity imbalances. Level 2 data show the best bid price and the best ask price. These data also show all bids and asks at different prices and the total available supply and total. One can visualize the imbalances (i.e., the differences between total supply and demand) by examining a "heatmap" (mainly graphical bids-asks) along with volume dots, bars, and other related microstructure and technical indicators (BookMap, 2021). Various social blogging websites, such as Reddit, host ideas and rumors for speculative investments in FinTech.

The basis of democratization in financial markets begins with retail investors sharing their information advantages to outperform institutional investors. Investors may detect a trend (signaling) by examining average retail investors' sentiments about the market, but information and data from social media may be biased. According to asset pricing theory, asset prices should move around the trajectory of their fundamental values. Eventually, they should return to their corresponding latent value (Chen et al., 2019). The concept of fundamental value typically comes from equity asset valuation. A stock's future cash flows are projected with a specific growth rate and discounted back to present value at the weighted average cost of capital or an equity discount rate based on the capital asset pricing model.

The same framework, including three-, four-, and five-factor models extending beyond a single market index, may not readily apply to cryptoassets. A significant reason is that, unlike equity, where the index is well-diversified, only a few giant cryptocurrencies, such as bitcoin and ether, disproportionally dominate crypto indices. Therefore, investors and analysts often use statistical and probability tools to predict future crypto prices based on the changing flow of supply and demand, which heavily affects them. The advantages of the cryptocurrency market are clear: it is decentralized, has a hard-to-quantify fundamental value, and is intangible. It also lacks a well-established institutional regulatory framework in which to operate. Therefore, speculative trading could lead to bubble formation, a risk that some portfolio managers and clients may choose to bear in exchange for possible higher yields. The bottom line is that risk tolerance is the main criterion if cryptos are suitable for portfolio managers and their clients over the long run.

Market participants should not ignore history. With the financial crisis of 2007–2008, also known as the global financial crisis, many investors looked for more decentralized financial institutions. In such institutions, their capital would be less vulnerable to risk, leading to new ideas, including DeFi products, and eliminating or reducing intermediates. Crypto's decentralized nature enables stakeholders to verify and record transactions securely. Crypto usage enables cross-border payments through virtual wallets. Its decentralized nature may make it a better alternative to paper-based transactions, creating a fair value premium and increasing its appeal to money managers.

Among cryptocurrencies, ether is second only to bitcoin in market capitalization. Ether is the native cryptocurrency of the Ethereum platform. Ethereum takes the concepts of bitcoin and builds upon them. The Ethereum platform allows alternate cryptocurrencies (altcoins) to operate. The blockchain hashing miners produce a byproduct called ether, providing resources for other altcoins to use blockchains. Ethereum also acts as a platform to execute smart contracts, perhaps another source of value and premium for cryptos. Its goal is to create more robust and secure products than traditional financial services.

As an added value for considering cryptos for a portfolio, blockchain's decentralized applications (dApps) have a robust infrastructure. The dApp creators may cater to investor demand for any product or service in the market. The task of portfolio construction with these dApps can also be simplified. Money managers and investors may use dApp creator algorithms to optimize their asset allocation through blockchain-based dApp. The dApps run on a distributed smart contract platform, and their main benefit is the ability to enable anyone to use them without any single institution or body controlling them (Harvey, Ramachandran, & Santoro, 2021).

For instance, Ethereum users can control their addresses through an external account or a unique smart contract code (Harvey et al., 2021). When a contract account receives data, the code is used for execution. A single transaction begins with an end-user who can interact with many dApps. Already sensitized and approved, clauses are a critical feature of smart contracts. They facilitate funds moving between multiple contracts without requiring the parties to spend time reviewing and accepting the terms repeatedly. These features may add value to a crypto's fair price that a portfolio manager may consider for investing. Although cash flows may be the primary determinant of a traditional asset's value, the novel technological features of cryptos and their network effects affecting growth help explain why some portfolio managers are eager to add cryptos to their assets under management.

Various regulatory initiatives in different countries may enhance the speed and accuracy of trades and payments of the securities bought and sold in a portfolio. Trading, payments, and managing the flow of funds when selling assets may go through a wholesale payment system and a payment system, enabling the transfer of funds directly from a buyer to a seller at the retail level. The term *wholesale payment system* involves various clearing and settlement systems, foreign exchange and derivatives clearinghouses, and central securities depositories (Awrey & van Zwieten, 2017).

A *retail payment system* is a type of electronic payment system enabling various forms of payment on a smaller scale for retail investors. The storage function has two main components: (1) protecting customer funds from theft, destruction, and loss and (2) transferring funds to third parties safely and securely. Although a bank vault exemplifies a mechanism for keeping funds secure, most financial institutions now use electronic accounting systems to store funds. With the usage of cryptocurrencies, the concept of shadow payment systems, which are P2P payment systems, has accelerated the possibility of higher liquidity and operational risk.

Compared to traditional methods, the new system has several advantages, including automation and quick settlement due to smart contracts and blockchain versatility. The system could work seamlessly with other systems with a more straightforward cross-platform operation. It can manage more participants and transactions at a higher speed and lower transaction costs, leading to more efficient and value-added features for the participants, including money managers and clients.

The new system also has limitations. Differences in investment laws create jurisdictional or legal risks when disputes arise. Although some portfolio managers want to enter the crypto space, they should be educated about the implications of the transfer payments of the securities they buy or sell, and the trade settlements involved. This book discusses trade settlements and their underlying technologies in a separate chapter.

Other Related Issues

For diversification, a portfolio may include sub-portfolios across different cryptoasset types. Alternatively, or additionally, a portfolio may include cryptocurrencies across global markets. Regardless of the overall strategy used to construct a portfolio, a portfolio manager should know how to buy and sell cryptos. Confirmation is the most critical component of any transaction. Crypto miners provide confirmation by adding blocks to the blockchain. The miner retrieves transactions from a previous step and cumulatively adds them to the next one, including the last hash. A cumulative immutable process occurs whenever someone buys or sells a security.

The concept of cryptocurrency trading consists of three main aspects: (1) the object, (2) the operation mode, and (3) the trading strategy. The *object* is the digital form of a physical item or asset. The *operation* mode is the process of transferring money in cryptocurrency. The *trading strategy* is the process of buying and selling cryptocurrencies. Under the crypto framework, miners who verify transactions in a blockchain network receive cryptocurrency for their computational work. They sell their assets to the secondary market, in which liquidity forces work to create an equilibrium price for the individual cryptocurrency. The interdependent network creates an ecosystem where a store of value and information occurs (Fang et al., 2021).

Cryptocurrency benefits include anonymity, P2P capabilities, programmable functions, and a 24-hour market. Additionally, cryptocurrencies do not involve intermediaries, reducing transaction costs and avoiding relying on banks, possibly leading to more efficiency and higher expected yields. Another advantage of cryptocurrency trading over traditional trading is less or no price manipulation due to the cryptographic confirmation required. Institutional investors may send block orders to sell out the market (dumping effect) in traditional markets, creating an unfavorable situation. In cryptocurrency markets, democratizing trading with decentralized blockchain trading platforms may minimize such manipulations. The lack of market manipulators makes favorable conditions for all parties involved, including global portfolio managers and retail traders. Why are market manipulators unable to influence a cryptocurrency? A plausible reason is that the blockchain network prevents irregularities in its code. Given its huge volume, the market size is so large that a price manipulator would have to take over the entire network to manipulate the price.

Cryptocurrency trading strategies can have deviances within their structure. A trading strategy that has received increasing attention is the quantitative approach. This strategy uses quantitative data to make buying or selling decisions based on the information gathered by the exchanges. Cryptocurrency markets are different from traditional markets due to their characteristics. Market participants have implemented high-frequency algorithmic trading systems. A cryptocurrency trading system is software based, enabling users to perform various transactions. It collects and processes customer information and transactions. Cryptocurrency trading systems intend to overcome the multiple problems associated with price manipulation, cyber-criminal activities, and delays (Fang et al., 2021). Investors can easily access various cryptocurrency trading systems.

Due to cryptoasset volatility, an intelligent analyst would consider high variance parameters. Suppose a quantitative portfolio manager could determine volatility or price swings or patterns. In that case, the manager could potentially achieve a high portfolio *alpha*, referring to an investment's excess returns above a benchmark return. Algorithmic trading systems, including machine learning (ML) technology, are becoming increasingly popular in the crypto space. *ML* is a computer algorithm that learns to improve itself by finding patterns in data. The system can understand and interpret data relationships that experienced analysts often ignore, improving portfolio construction and trading of various cryptocurrencies. *Input features* often refer to the multiple features of data sources, including economic, social, and technical indicators (Fang et al., 2021).

ML and artificial intelligence (AI) technologies have advanced coding that works with blockchain network platforms, expanding the FinTech space frontiers. For example, traditional accounting tasks and profit and loss reports of trading in a portfolio may be reformed or outdated and replaced with machines that can complete the accounting and trading cycles backed by blockchain networks in seconds. Speed and efficiency provide the rationale for new adoptions of ML and AI systems in the context of blockchain.

Crypto Hedge Funds and Regulatory Regimes

The emergence of financial systems and cryptocurrency portfolios created much interest among traditional investors (Mokhtarian & Lindgren, 2018). The trend generated many cryptocurrency-focused funds catering to this growing demand. Regulators are slowly establishing a framework to manage cryptocurrency activities. Hedge funds are high-risk investments using different strategies to seek high returns. They are not subject to the same regulations as traditional funds in this market. Hedge funds usually contend that cryptos are one of the most secure methods of payment using blockchain networks and more dependable than the process in a fee-charging credit institution. Using security and non-security cryptocurrencies attracts the attention of financial institutions searching for higher yields in crypto portfolios. Abnormal returns lead to growing crypto investment activity and the formation of special hedge funds chasing trading techniques and strategies focused on cryptocurrencies (Mokhtarian & Lindgren, 2018). The reason portfolio managers consider different types of cryptos, rather than a specific crypto, in constructing a portfolio is the expectation that not all cryptos are perfectly correlated.

Table 13.2 shows the correlation between several types of crypto assets. It identifies a less-than-perfect correlation (+1.0) to support diversification among cryptocurrencies. Bitcoin and ether have a correlation coefficient of around 0.73, providing an opportunity for better diversification because the returns of the two assets do not move perfectly together. The Gray Scale GBTC trust has a correlation coefficient of about 0.62 with bitcoin. A GBTC trust is a fund that holds bitcoin and operates like a closed-end mutual fund. As a caveat, these statistics should not be generalized beyond a five-year sample of monthly data, as reported in Table 13.2.

Due to a correlation of less than +1.0 between cryptos and the explosion in crypto usage, hedge funds and retail wealth management clients may allocate part of their investment capital to cryptoassets. The most significant advantage of crypto hedge funds is that they involve less compliance costs and fewer trading restrictions. Some hedge funds focus on liquidity imbalances (i.e., market depth, comparing supply and demand), macro (i.e., a function of global economic indicators), quantitative, and pattern recognition. Cryptoassets may seem risky to risk-averse investors.

Yet, many hedge funds are absolute return seekers. An *absolute return fund* aims to deliver a positive (absolute) return to investors regardless of whether the broader market in which it invests rises or falls. These funds offer an alternative to more traditional stock, bond, or balanced funds. An absolute return strategy is independent of traditional benchmarks such as the Standard & Poor's index (S&P 500). Such funds invest in various securities and use different strategies to hedge specific types of risk. Consequently, they may exhibit lower volatility over time and operate independently of market direction.

The SEC regulations on *security tokens*, a digital contract for a fraction of an asset's value, are minimal. The SEC shuns adopting a one-size-fits-all solution for all cryptos. This federal agency is developing and proposing regulations with the idiosyncratic features of each cryptoasset. A cryptocurrency differs from a traditional banknote. Some cryptocurrencies can perform specific tasks, such as proxy voting and automating contracts through smart contracts. They may also be used to raise funds for companies. Using cryptocurrencies for crowdfunding has also

Table 13.2. Regression Results.

Regression Statistics
Correlation coefficient of GBTC versus BTC = 0.62
Correlation coefficient of BTC versus ETH = 0.73

Source: Bloomberg terminal.

Notes: This table summarizes regression results for ETH/USD versus BTC/USD and GBTC/USD versus BTC/USD using monthly data between 2006 and 2001. The correlation is less than perfect (+1.0), implying room for diversification between these two cryptocurrencies.

caught the SEC's attention. In its guidance, the SEC refers to cryptocurrencies as securities, requiring the approval of federal securities laws. However, the SEC classifies bitcoin as a virtual currency.

The distinction between non-security tokens and security-oriented cryptocurrencies has become important to financial institutions seeking to profit from the cryptocurrency market (Mokhtarian & Lindgren, 2018). Cryptocurrencies' rapid emergence and success led to forming many new hedge funds. The SEC has historically been flexible about cryptoassets due to their decentralized nature and the absence of a regulatory authority. In this context, a hawkish view is that someday investor and consumer dependence on cryptoassets could lead to a potential financial crash if the status quo of a few regulations continues.

New hedge funds called "crypto funds" have emerged. These funds want to enhance returns by allocating part of their capital toward cryptoassets. Due to the nature of their operations and lack of regulations, crypto funds cater to clients with a high-risk tolerance and create a satellite fund, supplementary to the main fund, to maximize the absolute return.

However, using hedge funds to invest in cryptoassets has disadvantages, such as higher fees and greater disclosure requirements. Unlike traditional hedge funds, crypto funds are not subject to the same regulations. Although crypto funds are not subject to US tax laws, they face more complex tax concerns. For example, they may distribute returns in-kind, namely, payout in cryptos rather than fiat money. The SEC has been largely silent about this practice. Instead of protecting the public from fraudulent activities involving cryptocurrencies, some compliance professionals believe the agency has focused narrowly on protecting the public from exchanges operating in this area (Mokhtarian & Lindgren, 2018).

According to the SEC, a cryptocurrency is considered a virtual currency or a security for investment purposes, but not both. This distinction has investing implications but is not simple. A security is subject to federal securities laws. All cryptocurrencies bear features of both currencies and securities (Mokhtarian and Lindgren, 2018). The SEC has tried to create boundaries within which cryptocurrency investors must operate. In the past, similar cases occurred when a new asset class emerged. The market experienced euphoria, followed by a bubble that eventually burst. Examples include the internet or dot.com bubble between 1998 and 2000 and the housing and credit crisis of 2007. After the bubble crashed, regulators stepped in to do damage control mainly through public funds. Yet, the same cycle of correcting a situation may not easily be feasible with cryptoassets due to their decentralized technology.

Digital Assets and Estate Planning Applied to Portfolios

Estate planning and individual portfolios go together. Many people store various types of digital assets on their computers. These include business letters, photos, and videos. Since these types of investments are not formally valued and not considered assets, they are part of estate planning. With the rise of digitization, estate planning has become more complex to navigate when digital assets are involved. A *digital asset* is an online account that someone owns, or any document stored on a computer or in the cloud (Beyer & Nipp, 2011). The inheritors of an individual's wealth (assets) pass it on to the next of kin. Investors with intelligent online habits tend to make different passwords and multiple usernames to prevent the theft of sensitive information. An estate planner must determine which assets to remit due to privacy protection issues and pass to the beneficiaries. Investors who leave their portfolios to the next of kin should indicate their public and private keys in their will. If one enters information about digital assets in a will, it becomes public once the will goes into probate. Also, suppose a client wants to pass on a digital asset. In that case, that person should specify the full information about the asset in the will. For example, Leonard Bernstein, an American conductor, composer, pianist, music educator, author, and humanitarian, died in 1990, leaving the manuscript for his memoir entitled Blue Ink where no one could retrieve its contents (Beyer & Nipp, 2011).

When considering the legal aspects in the estate planning of digital assets, contracts should also move toward a digitized process, including cryptography for security. Cryptoassets work under the framework of smart contracts, which use blockchain technology. Smart contracts should use the same technology to streamline the legality of the process. Drafting documents such as wills or trusts would become automatic with smart contracts. The coding would immediately release the cryptoassets to the next of kin upon the passing of the initial owner should the smart contract permit such transfer. The possibilities of smart contracts and their applications in cryptoasset portfolios and estate planning are unlimited.

Although a cryptosystem portfolio for any purpose, including estate planning, may not be susceptible to hacking, the loss and theft of the passwords are a serious risk of using cryptoassets in a portfolio. Hot and cold wallets are needed to alleviate such concerns. A *hot wallet* is connected to the internet and could be vulnerable to online attacks, leading to stolen funds. However, it is faster and makes trading or spending crypto easier. A *cold wallet* is typically not connected to the internet. It has the advantage of being more secure, but it is less convenient. Hot wallets keep passwords on the internet; cold wallets are on local drives. Funds like Grayscale have products that may be more conveniently used to manage portfolios with cryptoassets, especially for individual portfolios. A drawback of using a crypto trust, rather than adding crypto directly to a portfolio, is the expensive fee involved in using such products.

Summary and Conclusions

Today's investment management is shifting from centralized financial systems to more democratized and transparent decentralized platforms. The natural order of any paradigm shift begins with innovations. Blockchain and decentralized technology through dApps are such innovations. The dApps hold the forefront of decentralized approaches, creating opportunities to capitalize on instantly verified information. DeFi, dApps, and smart contracts are inextricably interrelated, furthering applications and broadening the spectrum of their use in various investment areas, including portfolio management. Using byte coding (i.e., ERC-20 Ethereum software), DeFi can broaden its grasp in the crypto space. ERC-20 provides a standard for fungible tokens where stocks/tokens can be exchanged in kind, pushing the portfolio management toward a new horizon.

Cryptoassets may take different forms. They are not perfectly correlated, permitting diversification. Researchers should conduct more tests using different periods with diverse assets. However, this chapter shows that the Sharpe ratio increases by adding bitcoin to a portfolio of stocks, bonds, and real estate.

Understanding cryptoassets involves knowing its underlying technology: blockchain, a permanently irreversible and unalterable distributed ledger. The decentralized nature of such technology enables participants (buyers and sellers) to verify their transactions and keep track of them. Data integrity is essential in any trade. For that reason alone, trading assets with more security and trust appeals to investors and portfolio managers. Blockchain's core is its ability to store and record transactions. The network's decentralized property in the crypto space adds more safety and privacy for the traded assets, which some view as a premium. The unique security feature of cryptoassets providing higher yields through cryptography is one reason for adding cryptos to traditional portfolios.

Financial institutions and regulatory regimes face considerable challenges as they gradually adopt new asset classes. Imposing regulations is burdensome considering the different international and domestic laws as demand grows for crypto products from various market sectors. Decentralized mining and mining pools provide economies of scale where miners can efficiently pool their resources to block transactions in a chain. Crypto funds using quantitative strategies and high-frequency trading for cryptoassets are on the rise and becoming increasingly popular.

The field of cryptoassets is ever-growing and dynamically changing. Researchers are conducting more research on the use, value-added features, and associated risks of using blockchain in a portfolio. P2P systems may come forth in trading securities in a portfolio using fungible assets; namely using crypto to buy another crypto, leading to more fungible assets in the crypto space. A small data sample example shows that cryptoassets are not perfectly correlated, providing portfolio managers with an incentive to use various cryptos in a modern portfolio.

Discussion Questions

1. Explain an ICO's attributes.
2. Identify and discuss the factors to consider in a portfolio containing cryptoassets.

3. Describe the stock-to-flow method and its use in valuing crypto.
4. Discuss how crypto hedge funds operate and their usage in blockchain networks.

References

Awrey, D., & van Zwieten, K. (2017). The shadow payment system. *Journal of Corporation Law*, *43*(4), 101–142.

Beyer, G. W., & Nipp, K. G. (2011, July, 1–8). *Estate planning for digital assets*. Estate Planning Studies. Retrieved from https://papers.ssrn.com/sol3/papers.cfm?abstract_id=1879950

BookMap. (2021). Heatmap. Main Chart. Retrieved from https://bookmap.com/knowledgebase/docs/KB-SettingUpAndOperating-HeatmapMainChart

Chen, C. Y.-H., Després, R., Guo, L., & Renault, T. (2019). *What makes cryptocurrencies special? Investor sentiment and return predictability during the bubble*. IRTG 1792 Discussion Papers 2019-016, Humboldt University of Berlin, International Research Training Group 1792 "High Dimensional Nonstationary Time Series."

Cohney, S., Hoffman, D. A., Sklaroff, J., & Wishnick, D. (2019). Coin-operated capitalism. *Columbia Law Review*, *119*(3), 591–694.

Fang, F., Ventre, C., Basios, M., Kong, H., Kanthan, L., Martinez-Rego, D., … Li, L. (2021). *Cryptocurrency trading: A comprehensive survey*. London: Turing Intelligence Technology Limited, U.K. Kings College London.

Harvey, C. R., Ramachandran, A., & Santoro, J. (2021). *DeFi and the future of finance*. Working Paper, Duke University Fuqua School of Business and National Bureau of Economic Research (NBER). Retrieved from https://papers.ssrn.com/sol3/papers.cfm?abstract_id=3711777

Hougan, M., & Lawant, D. (2021). *Cryptoassets: The guide to bitcoin, blockchain, and cryptocurrency for investment professionals*. Charlottesville, VA: The CFA Institute Research Foundation. Retrieved from https://www.cfainstitute.org/-/media/documents/article/rf-brief/rfbr-cryptoassets.ashx

Isha, M. A. (2021, August 12). *ICO fundraising vs crowdfunding: Top 20 core differences!!!* dbtask. Retrieved from https://www.bdtask.com/blog/ico-fundraising-vs-crowdfunding#:⊠:text=The%20main%20difference%20between%20ICO,reward%20as%20a%20tokenized%20form

Mokhtarian, E., & Lindgren, A. (2018). Rise of the crypto hedge fund: Operational issues and best practices for emergent investment industry. *Stanford Journal of Law, Business, and Finance*, *23*(1), 112–158.

Perez, L. (2021). What is the Sharpe ratio? How investors use it to analyze an asset's risk. *Business Insider*, August 18. Retrieved from https://www.businessinsider.com/sharpe-ratio

Shichou, V. (2021, February 9). *Price impact of order book imbalance in cryptocurrency markets*. Toronto: Towards Data Science. Retrieved from https://towardsdatascience.com/price-impact-of-order-book-imbalance-in-cryptocurrency-markets-bf39695246f6

Wang, N. (2021, October 19). *Grayscale files with SEC to convert its bitcoin trust into an ETF*. CoinDesk. Retrieved from https://www.coindesk.com/business/2021/10/19/grayscale-files-with-sec-to-convert-its-bitcoin-trust-into-an-etf/

Chapter 14

Protection of Portfolios and Financial Consumers from Cryptoasset Frauds

Ibrahim E. Sancak

Abstract

This chapter introduces the fundamentals of portfolio and financial consumer protection from frauds in the cryptoasset space. Cryptoassets pose new risks to portfolios and financial consumers: idiosyncratic risks stemming from their unique features and systematic risks arising from transitioning from centralized to decentralized finance. Market experience indicates that these risks threaten every portfolio and financial consumer holding cryptoassets. In the consumer protection framework, cryptoasset risks are higher than traditional asset risks. Cryptoassets fall outside the regulatory domain in many jurisdictions. Moreover, their decentralized nature, technological attributes, and the momentum of financial technology cause asymmetric technology, disarming system-based portfolio and consumer protection mechanisms against frauds and abuses. Hence, the idiosyncratic and systematic risks of cryptoassets highlight the importance of developing more vigilant self-protection mechanisms.

Keywords: Cryptoassets; asymmetric technology; fraud; consumer protection; idiosyncratic risk; systematic risk

Introduction

Cryptoassets are new instruments for portfolio managers and financial consumers, offering opportunities and challenges. Both parties should understand the risks and threats of cryptoassets, the new investment environment, changing market conditions, and even market infrastructures.

The Emerald Handbook on Cryptoassets: Investment Opportunities and Challenges, 199–215

doi:10.1108/978-1-80455-320-620221014

Cryptoassets and their underpinning technologies, such as cryptography and blockchain, are frequently used with technical trust terminology, such as unhackable, immutable, and fraud-proof, implying that these assets are associated with a high degree of safety (Castonguay & Stein Smith, 2020). However, analyzing existing research on initial coin offerings (ICOs), security offerings, blockchain hacks and thefts, and data breaches of blockchain-based platforms and digital wallets, Castonguay and Stein Smith conclude that blockchain and cryptocurrencies are more prone to malfeasance, fraud, and manipulation than is commonly understood.

According to a popular view, economies and their regulatory and supervisory structures have fundamental investor protection technologies and mechanisms in each jurisdiction. This widespread assumption might be invalid in the cryptoasset world, considering the nature of these assets. Many economies still lack well-designed supervisory technology (SupTech) and financial supervision. The lack of a well-designed SupTech system leaves markets and financial consumers unprotected in financial technology (FinTech) (Zeranski & Sancak, 2021). Furthermore, FinTech players often fall outside the applicable regulatory and supervisory framework, creating an uneven playing field and increasing regulatory and supervisory risks (Berg, Guadamillas, Natarajan, & Sarkar, 2020). Financial supervisors with capacity constraints may be ill-equipped to address this challenge (Berg et al., 2020). Therefore, investor protection comes to totally new shores and requires new protection strategies.

This chapter focuses on the distinctive features of cryptoassets and their markets. It also introduces the fundamentals of portfolio and financial consumer protection from frauds in the cryptoasset space. The chapter comprises three sections. The first section concerns the main dimensions of portfolio and investor protection in the cryptoasset space, addressing the first step in protection – "know the investor protection environment." The following section discusses various types of cryptoasset fraud, citing real fraud cases worldwide. It also examines the second step in protection – "know the major types of cryptoasset frauds." The last section identifies core portfolio and consumer protection strategies for portfolio managers and financial consumers in the cryptoasset world with a concluding suggestion – "develop your protection strategy."

Portfolio and Investor Protection

Cryptoassets include a broad spectrum of instruments with different risk and return profiles. Some cryptoassets are like fiat money in the digital world. For example, central bank digital currencies (CBDCs) are cryptoassets, but they function as digital fiat money.

The cryptoasset experience, frauds, and failures focus on native cryptocurrencies. However, whether they are a CBDC or native cryptocurrency, cryptoassets share advanced technological features, such as blockchain and cryptography, having many implications for portfolio and consumer protection. Moreover, in many jurisdictions, cryptoassets are not entirely under the regulatory and supervisory realm, including in developed economies.

Furthermore, distributed ledger technology (DLT) or blockchain addresses revolutionary change in financial markets infrastructure, namely the transition from traditional finance or centralized finance (CeFi) to decentralized finance (DeFi). New instruments, technologies, infrastructures, unregulated domains, and a drastic transition period pose multiple threats to portfolios and financial consumers.

As an International Monetary Fund (IMF) and World Bank's joint policy paper points out (IMF–World Bank, 2019), many frauds in the cryptoassets space have raised significant consumer and investment protection issues. Catastrophic cryptoasset cases worldwide in the last decade reveal that financial consumers are vulnerable to scams involving cryptoassets. Hence, the core approach is not about whether portfolios and financial consumers need protection from fraud. Instead, it is about the content of the committed and probable scams and protection strategies against them.

Regulatory and Supervisory Domains in Consumer Protection

To realize the potential of technology, consumers need to trust it and know that their privacy is protected and their wealth is secure (Adams et al., 2016). An IMF study indicates that cryptoassets face more significant regulatory gaps than other FinTech-related developments and should address the magnitude of vulnerabilities to frauds in a regulatory protection context (Cuervo, Morozova, & Sugimoto, 2019).

Some extreme reactions exist to the emergence of cryptoassets, such as the banning approaches of Turkey and China. However, many countries and economies have tried to regulate cryptoassets and crypto-related activities or allow them under their current regimes without any further regulation. Among the latter group, the core theme of investor protection policies is warning financial consumers. The biggest economies' regulators and supervisors fall into this category, such as the United States and the European Union's regulatory and supervisory agencies. For example, in February 2018, the European Securities and Markets Authority (ESMA), the European Banking Authority (EBA), and the European Insurance and Occupational Pensions Authority (EIOPA) (three European Supervisory Authorities or ESAs) warned consumers about the high risks of buying and holding so-called cryptocurrencies or virtual currencies (VCs) with the following notes (ESMA, EBA, & EIOPA, 2018, p. 1):

> They are highly risky, generally not backed by any tangible assets and unregulated under EU law, and do not, therefore, offer any legal protection to consumers. Three ESAs are concerned by the fact that an increasing number of consumers buy VCs particularly with the expectation that the value of VCs will continue to grow but without being aware of the high risk of losing their money invested.

The ESAs have been publishing warning messages and opinions on cryptocurrencies since 2013 (ESMA, EBA, & EIOPA, 2018). In March 2021, three ESAs reminded the same warnings referring to the February 2018 messages summarized above (EBA, 2021).

The US authorities also follow suit by clarifying investor protection capabilities in the cryptoasset space. In the framework of testimony in September 2021, the chair of the US Securities and Exchange Commission (SEC) stated (Gensler, 2021, Par. 36):

> Currently, we just don't have enough investor protection in crypto finance, issuance, trading, or lending. Frankly, at this time, it's more like the Wild West or the old world of "buyer beware" that existed before the securities laws were enacted. This asset class is rife with fraud, scams, and abuse in certain applications.

The UK's approach to cryptoassets, mainly cryptocurrencies, is like that in the United States. In the context of cryptocurrencies, the governor of the Bank of England states that "Buy them only if you are prepared to lose all your money" (Browne, 2021, Par. 4).

The UK's Financial Conduct Authority (FCA) warns financial consumers parallelly (Financial Conduct Authority, 2021, Par. 1):

> The FCA is aware that some firms are offering investments in cryptoassets, or lending or investments linked to cryptoassets, that promise high returns. Investing in cryptoassets, or investments and lending linked to them generally involves taking very high risks with investors' money. If consumers invest in these types of products, they should be prepared to lose all their money.

In some countries, cryptoassets are regulated or embedded into regulatory realms. For example, in Germany, since 2013, the Federal Financial Supervisory Authority's (BaFin) general administrative practice has been to qualify payment tokens, such as bitcoin, as units of account, hence, as financial instruments under the German Banking Act for supervisory and consumer protection purposes (Tochtermann, Weinberg, & Weiß, 2019). On September 18, 2019, the German government adopted a blockchain strategy. In line with the strategy, Germany's parliament enacted two cornerstone proposals to regulate its financial markets and enable cryptoasset markets proliferation. Hence, Germany started a transition to decentralized markets (Sancak, 2021).

The nature of cryptoassets can eliminate regulations in specific jurisdictions since cryptoassets can be offered to every consumer globally. Therefore, although the regulations play significant roles in consumer protection, the nature of cryptoassets requires strong financial literacy and consumer vigilance. For example, Germany has consumer protection regulations for cryptocurrencies, but the country's regulatory power does not apply to criminal cases that originated in another country. For example, a scam ICO can be initiated in any continent or country and might sell so-called cryptocurrencies in Germany. Germany's financial authority cannot protect German financial consumers from that fraud in such a case.

In a similar vein, supervisory agencies often face asymmetric technology issues. For example, their supervisory technology (SupTech) might not be compatible with cryptoasset domains since their supervisory models are designed primarily for centralized financial structures. The low pace of digital transformation of financial supervisors and the high speed of technological advancements increase the gaps between supervisors and their responsibility areas and result in a new phenomenon named asymmetric technology. This transition period's lagged and foggy atmosphere might be conducive to potential white-collar fraudsters who plan to abuse their technology to experience financial advantages (Zeranski & Sancak, 2020). Considering the asymmetric technology risk, financial supervisors face higher investor protection challenges, and financial consumers stay under the exposure to higher cryptoasset risks.

Misunderstandings and Misperceptions in Blockchain

The risks of blockchain may be less prevalent than traditional databases and ledgers (Castonguay & Stein Smith, 2020). However, contrary to the common perception and understanding, blockchain technology can be vulnerable under certain conditions (Orcutt, 2019). The most significant risk might not be about the pure technological background. It might be about the treatment and definition of blockchain-related projects and products with zero-risk features, such as "tamper-proof," "immutable," and "unhackable" in connection with cryptoassets. Blockchain technology has unique security features, but it also has unique vulnerabilities. In other words, marketing slogans and headlines calling the technology "unhackable" are false (Orcutt, 2019). The industry experience indicates hacking blockchain transactions, exposing private blockchain networks, and stealing digital wallets. Additionally, cryptocurrency offerings might be fraudulent and outright shams (Castonguay & Stein Smith, 2020).

Blockchain design is bound to a complex series of human or machine-created codes that determine how the blockchain operates, how consensus occurs, and what users can or cannot post to the blockchain (Castonguay & Stein Smith, 2020). Hence, neither blockchain technology nor cryptography-based assets are immune to fraud. Their names do not necessarily guarantee direct trust.

Blockchain has unique weaknesses, as shown in some real-world cases. For example, the Ethereum-based decentralized autonomous organization (DAO) launched in 2016 and raised $150 million worth of ether (ETH). Hackers stole $60 million in ether three months after its launch (Cryptopedia, 2021). The Ethereum blockchain on which the DAO was built was later controversially forked to restore the stolen funds and later returned to investors. This case indicates the DAO's vulnerability to fraud (Cryptopedia, 2021).

Furthermore, a kind of manipulation known as a "51% attack" is a reality. It refers to the abusive control power of a participant or group of participants acting in concert in a blockchain network. Such an attack might disrupt the integrity of blockchains. This attack could enable intruders to prevent new transactions from gaining confirmations and give them the power to stop payments between some or all users or double-spend coins (Ossinger, 2021). In 2019, a crypto exchange

(Gate.io) confirmed such an attack, reporting that a 51 percent attack occurred on the Ethereum Classic (ETC) blockchain (Huillet, 2019). Cryptocurrency Bitcoin SV reported another such attack that inflicted at least some damage to the blockchain network in 2021 (Ossinger, 2021).

Although the cryptoasset space experienced significant vulnerabilities under hacks and attacks, the zero-risk impression has continued to permeate the popular press and academic platforms (Castonguay & Stein Smith, 2020). Such an impression might fuel irrational exuberance. As Shiller (2015, p. 2) points out, "the psychological basis of a speculative bubble" might skyrocket some cryptocurrency prices and attract unsophisticated investors and financial consumers.

Implications of the Innovation Abuse Hypothesis

Some mention FinTech with "innovation" and "disruption," adding allure to FinTech companies (Pell, 2020). FinTech, as a buzzword, can induce financial investors to irrationally invest in FinTech-related companies and assume that their performance exceeds market returns (Zeranski & Sancak, 2020).

Moreover, blockchain-based assets might be overpromoted as new miracle instruments, which might fuel the irrational exuberance of financially illiterate consumers (Sancak, 2021). The case can be more dangerous because fraudsters tend to go where the money is, as in the cryptoasset cases involving cryptocurrency and ICO, the Financial Industry Regulatory Authority warns (FINRA, 2021). Hence, innovations might be a new window for fraud and give nefarious actors robust tools in the cryptoasset space. Financial innovations are also the materials, and transformation periods are the perfect time frames for potential white-collar fraudsters (Zeranski & Sancak, 2020). New financial instruments and products were a major type of innovation that facilitated or triggered dubious business practices. Innovation outcomes are highly uncertain, indirectly leading to questionable financial practices (van Driel, 2019). One of the causes of the global financial crisis was the abuse of innovative financial instruments. Recent evidence shows the world has a similar risk. The risk is much more than the previous ones in multiple dimensions (Zeranski & Sancak, 2020).

Transition periods are perfect time frames for potential white-collar fraudsters. Financial supervisors often do not keep pace with market developments because of their governmental natures (Zeranski & Sancak, 2020). In other words, FinTech moves faster than regulation or internal risk governance (Pell, 2020). Hence, white-collar fraudsters get the benefit of

- fragmented and disorganized financial structures,
- legacy supervisory systems,
- new trends and irrational exuberance,
- their experience in their area,
- their international network,
- weak international cooperation among national financial supervisors,
- a perfect story, true or false, to lure potential victims,

- inexperienced entrepreneurs and financial consumers,
- distorted statistics or data,
- positive reports from third parties, including audit firms, and
- their convincing ability with extraordinary self-confidence (Zeranski & Sancak, 2020).

The cryptoasset space perfectly fits these conditions. Thus, fraudsters attempt to exploit the rising popularity of digital assets to lure retail investors into scams (Securities and Exchange Commission, 2021). According to FINRA (2018, Par. 2),

> Even when legitimate companies begin to emerge within a hot, new sector, fraudsters almost always await the unwary, mimicking the most successful business models as a ruse to steal investors' money.

Fraudsters exploit the news to launch their latest frauds without business fundamentals and transparent financial reporting to back up their claims (FINRA, 2018). Castonguay and Stein Smith (2020, p. 17) support the "innovation abuse hypothesis" of van Driel (2019), Zeranski and Sancak (2020), and Pell (2020) in the context of blockchain-related frauds by stating that:

> Whenever there is a new product, platform, or instrument that is generating hype and financial interest, there will invariably be opportunistic actors looking to take advantage of the hype, uninformed investors, and information asymmetry before the new item obtains wider adoption.

The recent frauds in the cryptocurrency market, especially recent ICOs, strongly support the hypothesis.

Types of Cryptoasset Frauds

A prerequisite for protection from fraud is to know their types, primary fraud tactics, potential fraud attacks, and the risk magnitude of being defrauded. According to a recent report, the world witnessed a 40 percent year-over-year increase in crypto-related scams to over 400,000, and for 2021, a more than 75 percent increase is expected (Bolster, 2021). Fraudsters deploy a wide variety of fraud techniques. A recent report classifies cryptocurrency scams into four categories: (1) fake prizes, giveaways, and sweepstakes, (2) investment-related scams, (3) advance-fee schemes, and (4) celebrity impersonations (Bolster, 2021).

Furthermore, cryptoasset frauds are not economy or country-specific; instead, they are global. For example, 58 different countries of 396 hosting providers have hosed crypto scams since January 2020 (Bolster, 2021). Bolster observed a direct correlation between increases in individual cryptocurrency trade volumes and value and phishing and scam-related activity worldwide. As a particular cryptocurrency experienced an uptick in value or hype, fraudsters and scammers launched fraudulent websites. Once fraudsters develop a fraud tactic and digital fraud model in the crypto space, others can easily apply it to multiple cryptoassets in many jurisdictions and languages. In other words, the ease of replicating a scam allows bad actors to target multiple cryptoassets worldwide (Bolster, 2021).

Hackers stole hundreds of millions from various platforms for many years. In 2014, in the MtGox case, hackers stole $450 million of mostly bitcoin, collapsing the Japanese exchange. In 2016, hackers pocketed $60 million of ether from the DAO three months after its launch. In 2018, BitGrail users lost $146 million. In the Coincheck case, hackers absconded with $534 million from the Japanese exchange. In 2020, hackers stole $281 million from KuCoin (Cryptopedia, 2021; Tidy, 2021). In August 2021, hackers took more than $600 million in cryptocurrency from Poly Network, a DeFi platform operating on the Binance Smart Chain, Ethereum, and Polygon blockchains; the heist, estimated at $611 million in various cryptoassets, including hundreds of millions of dollars' worth of ether and Binance coins, is one of the largest in crypto history (Murphy, 2021). Poly Network reports that it regained all the assets except for $33 million in stablecoin tether (Reuters, 2021). Self-reportedly, the hackers attacked for fun to expose a vulnerability in the platform's digital contracts (Reuters, 2021).

Deception and fraudulent tactics are also pervasive in the cryptocurrency startup markets. *The Wall Street Journal* studied nearly 3,300 crypto offerings, finding about 16 percent of them, or 513, showing signs of plagiarism, identity theft, and promises of improbable returns (Shifflett & Jones, 2019). About 60 percent of them included luring terms, such as "nothing to lose," "guaranteed profit," "return on investment," "high return," "highest return," "funds profit," "no risk," and "little risk" (Shifflett & Jones, 2019). Another analysis based on over 1,000 ICO white papers shows that many ICOs provide inadequate disclosure. More than two-thirds of the ICO whitepapers are silent on the issuing entity, initiators, and backers or fail to provide contact details (Zetzsche, Buckley, Arner, & Föhr, 2019).

Unregulated ICOs have a high incidence of scams and theft (Benedetti & Kostovetsky, 2021). For example, in June 2016, the DAO case resulted in the theft of approximately $60 million in cryptocurrency. In July 2017, the CoinDash/Blox case resulted in $7 million stolen in just half an hour.

In some cases, the ICO organizers are scammers. In a Vietnamese pyramid scheme case, scammers used an ICO to raise $650 million and then disappeared with the money (Benedetti & Kostovetsky, 2021). According to Castonguay and Stein Smith (2020), regulatory gaps and blurred lines between ICOs and investors' understanding of initial public offerings (IPOs) created an opportunity for unethical actors to exploit the ICO market and create fraudulent or materially inaccurate offerings. Their findings support the *innovation abuse hypothesis*, positing that fraudsters always strike in the transition periods of new technologies.

Cryptoasset investors are vulnerable to new types of fraud and manipulation for many reasons. Various cases and studies indicate that cryptoasset markets are operating with frauds, scams, and business failures (Su, 2021). For example, a study of ICOs finds that about 78 percent were scams, about 4 percent failed, 3 percent became defunct, and 15 percent went on to trade on an exchange (Dowlat & Hodapp, 2018). In a similar vein, a recent study indicates that 44 percent of publicly traded coins resulted in abandonment, and 71 percent of them were later resurrected, leaving 18 percent of coins to fail permanently in four years (Gandal, Hamrick, Moore, & Vasek, 2021).

Every year, the cryptoasset space faces new cryptoasset fraud cases, indicating the horrifying capacity of fraudsters. In September 2021, the US Securities and Exchange Commission (SEC) announced that the agency brought charges in a $2 billion bitcoin-related investment scam in one of the largest bitcoin-related Ponzi-like schemes. In this case, the defendants reportedly collected about 325,000 bitcoins from retail investors worldwide through a platform that encouraged them to lend their bitcoins to BitConnect, luring investors with false promises of profits (Securities and Exchange Commission, 2021).

In 2021, another severe case involving cryptoassets occurred in Turkey, an economy in which financial consumers are highly interested in cryptocurrencies. According to a Turkish survey, 96 percent of 715 respondents own at least one cryptocurrency. The respondents are mainly university-educated male respondents in their 30s (Azmi, 2021). In April 2021, a cryptocurrency fraud hurt thousands of Turks, who filed criminal complaints against the defrauding company, alleging that they had been scammed and could not access their accounts (Kucukgocmen, Sezer, & Tuncay, 2021). The fraudsters had speculative amounts of collected money, ranging from $100 million to $2 billion, just for an exchange. Since there is no designated regulatory and supervisory agency for cryptocurrency exchanges, victims do not have a place to submit their complaints. Turkey's judicial system is an ineffective avenue to solve such cases quickly, making the case an unsolvable puzzle for many years.

A typical financial services regulation includes entry barriers for managers and operators, as well as accounting, reporting, and electronic infrastructure standards. Such standards let regulatory and supervisory bodies monitor the service providers and prevent fraud attacks. Some Turkish media outlets report that the recent scandal involves a $2 billion fraud. However, authorities can neither deny nor accept such an allegation since no solid evidence and reliable data exist to clarify the case. Starting and operating even a small broker-dealer requires strict regulatory restrictions in Turkey. Yet, operating a crypto exchange in the country is free from regulatory standards and entry barriers, such as having previous experience and professional qualifications. Hence, anyone can establish and operate a cryptocurrency exchange in Turkey, even someone with a primary school diploma. The Turkish cryptocurrency market, like many other cryptoasset markets, addresses the notion of *caveat emptor* or let the buyer beware.

Although cryptocurrencies might be considered the most abused cryptoassets, others can also be the objects of fraud, such as stablecoins. According to Tether's web portal, "Tether converts cash into digital currency, to anchor or tether the value to the price of national currencies like the US dollar, the Euro, and the offshore Chinese yuan." Its web portal also declares that every Tether token is always 100 percent backed by reserves (Tether, 2021). However, as part of an investigation, the Office of the New York Attorney General announced that "Tether's claims that its virtual currency was fully backed by U.S. dollars at all times was a lie" (New York State Office of the Attorney General, 2021). Moreover, the Office of the Attorney General reports that iFinex – the operator of Bitfinex – and Tether made false statements about the backing of the "tether" stablecoin and the movement of hundreds of millions of dollars between the two companies to cover up the truth about massive losses by Bitfinex (New York State Office of the Attorney General, 2021). The Tether case indicates that native cryptocurrencies and other cryptoassets, including stablecoins, can be used to defraud financial consumers.

The evidence indicates that fraud tactics and methods are not limited. White-collar fraudsters appear exceptionally talented. They can invent new tools and develop new tactics with engaging stories or techniques. Moreover, cryptoasset frauds can happen everywhere and hurt every consumer without respecting borders and jurisdictions.

Portfolio and Consumer Protection Strategies for Cryptoassets

The first step in involving cryptoassets as a portfolio manager and financial consumer is to know that these assets have new characters and different idiosyncratic risks. Hence, consumers should understand these assets, the risks associated with investing, and applicable regulatory protections (Financial Conduct Authority, 2021). Considering the warnings of regulators and supervisors and the unique risks and transition risks, portfolio managers and financial consumers should consider the following protection dimensions in their cryptoasset-related financial decisions:

- *Skyrocketing prices and high volatility*. Prices do not always indicate whether an instrument is a good or bad investment opportunity. Cryptoassets might have dynamic markets driven by irrational exuberance. Only emotions without proper fundamentals might drive up prices. Irrational exuberance is the psychological basis of a speculative bubble. According to Shiller (2015, p. 2), a speculative bubble is:

> A situation in which news of price increases spurs investor enthusiasm, which spreads by psychological contagion from person to person, and, in the process amplifies stories that might justify the price increase, and brings in a larger and larger class of investors, who, despite doubts about the real value of the investment, are drawn to it partly through envy of "others" successes and partly through a gambler's excitement.

Bubbles are doomed to collapse eventually. High price volatility is a phenomenon of cryptoassets, especially cryptocurrencies, indicating that prices change significantly. The volatility of cryptoasset prices and inherent valuation difficulties pose a high risk of losses for consumers (Financial Conduct Authority, 2021). Financial consumers should not make investment decisions by looking only at soaring prices and price dynamics.

- *Fancy technical terms*. Some technology terms sound attractive in financial investments, such as FinTech, blockchain, cryptography, bitcoin, and ether. Such buzzwords might directly induce investors to choose cryptoassets irrationally. In some cases, fraudsters might intentionally use these terms in their fraud tactics to attract attention. Many entrepreneurs are attracted to cryptoassets due to the lure of buzzwords connected with new technologies, such as blockchain. In fact, instead of blockchain, fraudsters produce typical technology domains, such as ordinary databases (Ito, Narula, & Ali, 2017). Fancy technical terms cannot guarantee any return or indicate the trustworthiness of instruments.
- *Misunderstandings and misperceptions*. Contrary to the common perception and understanding, blockchain technology can be vulnerable under certain conditions (Orcutt, 2019). More specifically, blockchain, the core technology of cryptoassets, does not eliminate all types of fraud. The infrastructure may leave back doors open to vulnerabilities, allowing unauthorized access and tampering (Mauri, 2017). The case is more dangerous because the biggest risk might not be about the pure technological background. Instead, it might be about the treatment and defining of blockchain-related projects and products with zero-risk features, such as "tamper-proof," "immutable," and "unhackable" in connection with cryptoassets. Financial consumers and portfolio managers should check the strengths and weaknesses of such technologies to avoid misunderstandings.
- *Improper and improbable return promises*. Hundreds of cryptocurrency startups used deceptive and even fraudulent tactics to lure investors into searching for quick riches in the market (Shifflett & Jones, 2019). One tactic is to include tempting phrases in marketing or disclosure documents, such as "nothing to lose," "guaranteed profit," "return on investment," "highest return," "no risk," and "little risk." Financial consumers should be wary if someone pressures them to invest quickly or promises returns that sound too good to be true. Additionally, portfolio managers and consumers should consider such promises as a strong warning signal of fraud. In an unregulated world, firms may overstate the returns of products or understate the risks involved (Financial Conduct Authority, 2021).
- *Regulatory gaps*. Cryptoassets might be unregulated in some jurisdictions. Therefore, regulators and supervisors frequently and insistingly warn financial consumers against cryptoasset risks. For example, the UK's Financial Conduct Authority (2021, Par. 1) announced the following warning: "If you invest in cryptoassets you should be prepared to lose all your money." Although the United Kingdom has one of the most advanced financial systems, its system does not guarantee any protection in cryptoasset investments. Other economies are similar in this respect. Financial authorities publish investor protection tips and newsletters against cryptoasset frauds in many jurisdictions worldwide.

For example, FINRA has web pages on "How to Avoid Crypto Stock Scams," and the FCA has web pages on "Cryptoasset Investment Scams." Moreover, financial regulatory and supervisory authorities in some jurisdictions reveal lists of unauthorized firms to protect financial consumers. Before making their decisions, consumers should check investor protection web portals, such as the websites of financial regulators and supervisors.

- *Financial services compensation.* Some financial instruments have compensation mechanisms. However, cryptoasset-related investments might not have such compensation schemes.
- *Charges and fees.* Marketing materials might not disclose the actual transaction costs and fees in unregulated jurisdictions. Cryptoasset transactions are not always costless for financial consumers. Hidden charges and astronomic fees diminish returns over time. The impact of charges and fees on such investments might be more than those for regulated investment products (Financial Conduct Authority, 2021).
- *Cross-border nature of transactions.* Cryptoassets inherently have cross-border natures, connecting their participants to parties in multiple jurisdictions. This situation can disable fully regulatory and supervisory protections in a particular jurisdiction and investor protection, even in regulated environments.
- *Decentralization.* Cryptoassets pave the way for DeFi. DeFi's working mechanism dysfunctions many currently deployed regulatory and supervisory protection tools and defense lines upon which current centralized financial systems rely. Furthermore, DeFi does not eliminate well-known fraud risks, such as market manipulation, distortionary incentives, Ponzi schemes, and money laundering (Chohan, 2021). Cryptoassets might be offered in a decentralized environment, making many standard protective features unavailable. For example, know your customer practices can barely be enforced in the DeFi space (Amler et al., 2021).

> In some cases, consumers might not find a contact to get information about their investments. Hence, introducing cryptoassets in an economy and enabling DeFi, namely the transition period from CeFi to DeFi, presents multiple challenges involving market integrity and investor protection risks. Such transition risks are only manageable by deploying personally-own protection shields, namely financial literacy.

- *Anonymity.* Anonymity increases the vulnerability of cryptoassets to some criminal acts, such as money laundering and financing terrorism. When a group of cryptoasset owners or cryptoasset markets faces criminal investigations, governments or governmental agencies might freeze assets and take other severe measures, making all investor assets, including standard assets and cash accounts, untouchable.
- *Two sides of innovations.* Innovation brings new economic values, and cryptoassets involve revolutionary aspects. However, not all cryptoassets and cryptoasset-related activities are trustworthy. The cryptoasset marketplace is a

target for fraud and scams (Financial Conduct Authority, 2021). The innovation abuse hypothesis suggests that nefarious actors can use innovation as a new window for fraud, giving them strong tools in the cryptoasset market.

- *Actors in cryptoasset businesses.* Existing statistics about cryptoasset businesses reveal many red flags for financial consumers. ICOs involve a high rate of fraud and scams. Before considering such products, consumers should check the main actors of cryptoasset businesses behind such developments.
- *Asymmetric technology risks.* Financial consumers and even portfolio managers might assume that their jurisdiction has a well-functioning financial supervisory system and financial supervisors have a good enough supervisory protection capacity (Zeranski & Sancak, 2020). Such assumptions might not hold in the cryptoasset world. When systematic protection shields do not work correctly, consumers should deploy more robust personal protection, such as checking legal documents thoroughly or getting legal advice before placing their money in this domain.
- *Product complexity.* Cryptoassets rely on new technologies. Their pricing methods also are tied to their inherent technological features and networks. The complexity of some products and services in the cryptoasset space can make understanding the risks difficult for consumers (Financial Conduct Authority, 2021). Consumers should have some fundamental digital literacy to understand the nature of products for pricing and self-protection.
- *Financial literacy requirement.* Financial literacy helps protect financial consumers from fraud attacks. A recent study's findings indicate that fraud tactics are becoming more complex. Better financial knowledge provides the sophistication necessary to detect fraud rather than basic money management skills (Engels, Kumar, & Philip, 2020). Cryptoasset requires special vigilance and understanding of the digital asset space. Financial consumers should understand the nature of products and services before deciding. Many confirmation and checking mechanisms enable consumers to understand investment instruments or the current financial system setup environment. For example, in many cases, financial consumers rely on audit firms' and rating agencies' reports before making financial decisions. Audit firms and rating agencies provide stakeholders and consumers with some confirmation or technical views for firms. Yet, many consumers enter the cryptoasset space without having reliable reports and technical opinions. This situation occurs despite cryptoassets relying on advanced technologies, such as blockchain and cryptography, that an average financial consumer can hardly understand. Placing money in an area without understanding the nature of instruments or getting reliable advisory services or technical views is like gambling. On the other hand, financially knowledgeable individuals have a greater ability to detect fraud. According to Engels et al. (2020), a one standard deviation increase in financial knowledge increases fraud detection probabilities by three percentage points.

Statistics indicate that cryptoasset frauds are not declining or under control. Instead, they are dramatically increasing. Regulatory and supervisory agencies worldwide frequently warn financial consumers about cryptoasset risks. However, given the attractiveness of cryptoassets and ICOs, warnings seem ineffective (Zetzsche et al., 2019). Nonetheless, regulatory and supervisory agencies currently do not have more instrumental options against cryptoasset frauds. The core concept for portfolio managers and financial consumers is self-protection, so let the buyer beware.

Summary and Conclusions

Cryptoassets are a novel asset class emanating from their underlying technology. Since they may not have any underlying assets, cryptoassets could be volatile and risky instruments, creating various challenges in traditional financial consumer protection systems. In some jurisdictions, governments have partly or wholly banned or restricted cryptoassets as an unorthodox method of investor protection. However, decentralization capacity and global accessibility to these assets or markets can evade regulatory restrictions.

Moreover, financial supervisory systems are mainly designed for CeFi and have limited effectiveness in the cryptoasset space. Private sectors move faster than government sectors and supervisory agencies. Hence, keeping up with the private sector technology seems complicated in a short period, raising questions about asymmetric technology and its outcomes. Therefore, financial systems' protective power and capacity are lower than in previous decades in the current transition period. This situation occurs since asymmetric technology is a reality in many economies, leaving portfolios and financial consumers more vulnerable to cryptoasset frauds. In addition to systematic risks, unique features of cryptoassets pose new risks to portfolios and financial consumers. Combined risks require new consumer habits and extraordinary vigilance to protect portfolios and personal wealth.

Economies have different consumer protection approaches, ranging from outright banning to internalizing cryptoassets. The mainstream reactions of regulatory and supervisory agencies worldwide in the cryptoasset domain have been strongly signaling a let the buyer beware policy for portfolios and consumers, particularly for individual financial consumers. Consequently, buyers or consumers need to increase their financial literacy on cryptoassets.

Discussion Questions

1. Identify the primary differences between traditional financial assets and cryptoassets in terms of portfolio and consumer protection.
2. Define asymmetric technology and explain how it changes the effectiveness of financial supervision.
3. Define the innovation abuse hypothesis and explain its relevance to the cryptoasset market.
4. Discuss how regulators and supervisors view consumer protection in the cryptoasset domains.
5. Explain who can protect portfolios and financial consumers most effectively.

References

Adams, V. "Tori", Casey, M., Gronager, M., Hinkes, A., Knight, B., Koonce, L., … Zeldin, M. (2016). *Protecting consumers in the digital currency economy*. Washington, DC: Consumer Research, CoinStructive, Microsoft, Bloq.

Amler, H., Eckey, L., Faust, S., Kaiser, M., Sandner, P., & Schlosser, B. (2021, January 14). *DeFi-ning DeFi: Challenges and pathway*. Ithaca, NY: Cornell University. https://arxiv.org/pdf/2101.05589.pdf

Azmi, E. (2021, March 8). *Cryptocurrency awareness in Turkey 2021*. CoinGecko. Retrieved from https://www.coingecko.com/buzz/cryptocurrency-awareness-in-turkey-2021

Benedetti, H., & Kostovetsky, L. (2021). Digital tulips? Returns to investors in initial coin offerings. *Journal of Corporate Finance*, *66*(C), 101786. https://doi.org/10.1016/j.jcorpfin.2020.101786

Berg, G., Guadamillas, M., Natarajan, H., & Sarkar, A. (2020). *Fintech in Europe and Central Asia: Maximizing benefits and managing risks*. Fintech Note, no. 4.World Bank, Washington, DC. Retrieved from https://openknowledge.worldbank.org/handle/10986/33591

Bolster. (2021). *Cryptocurrency scam report*. Los Altos, CA: Bolster.

Browne, R. (2021). Cryptocurrency investors should be prepared to lose all their money, bank of England governor says. *CNBC*, May 7. Retrieved from https://www.cnbc.com/2021/05/07/bank-of-englands-bailey-crypto-investors-risk-losing-all-their-money.html

Castonguay, J. "Jack", & Stein Smith, S. (2020). Digital assets and blockchain: Hackable, fraudulent, or just misunderstood? *Accounting Perspectives*, *19*(4), 363–387. https://doi.org/10.1111/1911-3838.12242

Chohan, U. W. (2021, January 26). *Decentralized finance (DeFi): An emergent alternative financial architecture*. Critical Blockchain Research Initiative (CBRI) Working Papers.

Cryptopedia. (2021, April 27). *What was the DAO?* Gemini. Retrieved from https://www.gemini.com/cryptopedia/the-dao-hack-makerdao

Cuervo, C., Morozova, A., & Sugimoto, N. (2019). *Regulation of crypto assets*. Washington, DC: International Monetary Fund.

Dowlat, S., & Hodapp, M. (2018, July 11). *Crypto-asset market coverage initiation: Network creation*. Research.bloomberg, pp. 1–30. Retrieved from https://research.bloomberg.com/pub/res/d28giW28tf6G7T_Wr77aU0gDgFQ.

EBA. (2021, March 17). *Crypto-assets: ESAs remind consumers about risks*. European Banking Authority. Retrieved from https://www.eba.europa.eu/financial-innovation-and-fintech/publications-on-financial-innovation/crypto-assets-esas-remind-consumers-about-risks

Engels, C., Kumar, K., & Philip, D. (2020). Financial literacy and fraud detection. *European Journal of Finance*, *26*(4–5), 420–442. https://doi.org/10.1080/1351847X.2019.1646666

ESMA, EBA, & EIOPA. (2018, February, 1–3). ESMA, EBA and EIOPA warn consumers on the risks of virtual currencies. Retrieved from https://www.eba.europa.eu/sites/default/documents/files/documents/10180/2139750/313b7318-2fec-4d5e-9628-3fb007fe8a2a/Joint%20ESAs%20Warning%20on%20Virtual%20Currencies.pdf?retry=1

Financial Conduct Authority. (2021, January 11). FCA warns consumers of the risks of investments advertising high returns based on cryptoassets. Retrieved from https://www.fca.org.uk/news/news-stories/fca-warns-consumers-risks-investments-advrtising-high-returns-based-cryptoassets

FINRA. (2018, September 6). Here's how to avoid crypto stock scams. Retrieved from FINRA – For investors. Retrieved from https://www.finra.org/investors/insights/avoid-crypto-stock-scams

FINRA. (2021, October 4). *Initial coin offerings (ICOs)—What to know now and time-tested tips for investors*. FINRA – Investor Alert. Retrieved from https://www.finra.org/investors/alerts/icos-what-know-now

Gandal, N., Hamrick, J. T., Moore, T., & Vasek, M. (2021, June 18). The rise and fall of cryptocurrency coins and tokens. *Decisions in Economics and Finance*, *44*, 981–1014. https://doi.org/10.1007/s10203-021-00329-8

Gensler, G. (2021, September 14). Testimony before the United States Senate Committee on banking, housing, and urban affairs. U.S. Securities and Exchange Commission. Retrieved from https://www.sec.gov/news/testimony/gensler-2021-09-14

Huillet, M. (2019). Crypto exchange Gate.io confirms 51% attack on Ethereum classic, promises refunds. *Cointelegraph*, January 9. Retrieved from https://cointelegraph.com/news/crypto-exchange-gateio-confirms-51-attack-on-ethereum-classic-promises-refunds

IMF–World Bank. (2019). *FinTech: The experience so far*. Washington, DC: International Monetary Fund–World Bank Group.

Ito, J., Narula, N., & Ali, R. (2017). The blockchain will do to the financial system what the internet did to media. Harvard Business Review, March 8. Retrieved from https://hbr.org/2017/03/the-blockchain-will-do-to-banks-and-law-firms-what-the-internet-did-to-media

Kucukgocmen, A., Sezer, C., & Tuncay, E. (2021). Police search cryptocurrency trading firm after turks say they were scammed. *Reuters*, April 22. Retrieved from https://www.reuters.com/world/middle-east/turkish-crypto-traders-file-complaints-after-access-accounts-frozen-lawyer-2021-04-22/

Mauri, R. (2017, July 12). *Blockchain for fraud prevention: Industry use cases*. IBM. Retrieved from https://www.ibm.com/blogs/blockchain/2017/07/blockchain-for-fraud-prevention-industry-use-cases/

Murphy, M. (2021). Poly network pleads for hackers to return assets after $611 million crypto heist — and they start to do so. *Marketwatch*, August 11. Retrieved from https://www.marketwatch.com/story/poly-network-pleads-for-hackers-to-return-assets-after-611-million-crypto-heist-11628650932

New York State Office of the Attorney General. (2021, February 23). Attorney General James ends virtual currency trading platform Bitfinex's illegal activities in New York. Letitia James – NY Attorney General. Retrieved from https://ag.ny.gov/press-release/2021/attorney-general-james-ends-virtual-currency-trading-platform-bitfinexs-illegal

Orcutt, M. (2019). Once hailed as unhackable, blockchains are now getting hacked. MIT Technology Review, February 19. Retrieved from https://www.technologyreview.com/2019/02/19/239592/once-hailed-as-unhackable-blockchains-are-now-getting-hacked/

Ossinger, J. (2021, August 4). *Crypto coin bitcoin SV appears to have faced a '51% attack*. Bloomberg. Retrieved from https://www.bloomberg.com/news/articles/2021-08-04/crypto-coin-bitcoin-sv-appears-to-have-suffered-a-51-attack

Pell, G. (2020). Wirecard fraud is risk management lesson for Fintech companies. *Forbes*, July 14. Retrieved from https://www.forbes.com/sites/gideonpell/2020/07/14/wirecard-fraud-is-risk-management-lesson-for-fintech-companies/

Reuters. (2021). Crypto platform poly network says hacked funds returned. *Reuters*, August 23. Retrieved from https://www.reuters.com/technology/crypto-platform-poly-network-says-hacked-funds-returned-2021-08-23/

Sancak, I. E. (2021). Implications of Germany's electronic securities act for supervisory technology. *Journal of International Banking Law and Regulation*, *36*(12), 531–536. http://dx.doi.org/10.2139/ssrn.3936211.

Securities and Exchange Commission. (2021, September 1). *Digital asset and "crypto" investment scams – Investor alert*. Retrieved from https://www.sec.gov/oiea/investor-alerts-and-bulletins/digital-asset-and-crypto-investment-scams-investor-alert

Shifflett, S., & Jones, C. (2019). A flood of questionable cryptocurrency offerings. *The Wall Street Journal*, January 19. Retrieved from https://www.wsj.com/graphics/whitepapers/#methodology

Shiller, R. J. (2015). *Irrational exuberance*. Princeton, NJ: Princeton University Press.

Su, E. (2021). *Digital assets and SEC regulation*. Washington, DC: Congressional Research Service. Retrieved from https://sgp.fas.org/crs/misc/R46208.pdf

Tether. (2021, October 20). *Digital money for a digital age; global, fast, and secure*. Tether. Retrieved from https://tether.to

Tidy, J. (2021). The real victims of mass crypto-hacks that keep happening. *BBC News*, August 26. Retrieved from https://www.bbc.com/news/technology-58331959

Tochtermann, M., Weinberg, M., & Weiß, H. (2019, March 28). *Crypto tokens remain a risk for consumers*. BaFin. Retrieved from https://www.bafin.de/SharedDocs/Veroeffentlichungen/EN/Fachartikel/2019/fa_bj_1902_kryptowaehrung_en.html

van Driel, H. (2019). Financial fraud, scandals, and regulation: A conceptual framework and literature review. *Business History*, *61*(8), 1259–1299. https://doi.org/10.1080/00076791.2018.1519026

Zeranski, S., & Sancak, I. E. (2020). *Does the 'Wirecard AG' case address FinTech crises?* Wolfenbüttel: ZWIRN-Research Center. Retrieved from https://www.ostfalia.de/cms/de/zwirn/.content/documents/Public-Wirecard-AG-Working-Paper-ZS-FINAL-UPDATE-17082020-GRP.pdf

Zeranski, S., & Sancak, I. E. (2021). Prudential supervisory disclosure (PSD) with supervisory technology (SupTech): Lessons from a FinTech crisis. *International Journal of Disclosure and Governance*, *18*, 315–335. Retrieved from https://link.springer.com/content/pdf/10.1057/s41310-021-00111-7.pdf

Zetzsche, D. A., Buckley, R. P., Arner, D. W., & Föhr, L. (2019). The ICO gold rush: It's a scam, it's a bubble, it's a super challenge for regulators. *Harvard International Law Journal*, *60*(2), 267–315. Retrieved from https://harvardilj.org/wp-content/uploads/sites/15/3_ICO_60.2.pdf

Part IV

Trading, Reporting, and Technical Aspects

Chapter 15

General Institutional Considerations of Blockchain and Emerging Applications

Peter C. Earle and David M. Waugh

Abstract

This chapter examines institutional investors' considerations while investing or otherwise engaging in the cryptocurrency sector, whether exclusively in bitcoin or the broader universe of crypto or decentralized finance assets. Given the rapid change in legal and regulatory oversight and cryptocurrency and blockchain innovation, offering inviolable advice about due diligence and compliance during commercial engagement is exceedingly difficult. However, general guidelines and rules of thumb are available.

Keywords: Bitcoin; cryptocurrencies; bitcoin; due diligence; compliance; legal; regulatory

Introduction

Unlike virtually every other wave of innovation over the last half-century, the blockchain and cryptocurrency initiatives began almost entirely within the realm of individual coders and inventors. For that reason, financial institutions are arriving at a more advanced stage of technological and economic development than they typically do. As the market capitalization and use cases of blockchain and cryptocurrencies increase, the call for involvement in the space by banks, hedge funds, private equity firms, venture capitalists, and other commercial entities has increased. Similarly, small enterprises and innovators with new or untested blockchain or crypto products and services need the financial wherewithal and economies of scale among financial institutions.

The cryptocurrency and blockchain ecosystem present familiar investment risks associated with prior technological revolutions and some new and

The Emerald Handbook on Cryptoassets: Investment Opportunities and Challenges, 219–232

doi:10.1108/978-1-80455-320-620221015

unanticipated risks, challenges, and opportunities. The following discussion involves the most critical concerns and countermeasures to esoteric sources of risk discussed in this chapter.

Legal Counsel

All crypto managers should ensure they retain the proper legal, accounting, and technical expertise to advise on issues a firm or fund is likely to face during its operation.

Legal Resources

Even if the proprietor, manager, or partner of a cryptocurrency-focused enterprise has a legal background, the emergent nature of regulation and legislation in this space necessitates a firm or operator to hire or retain legal resources to succeed. Legal practitioners must also understand the underlying technology of cryptocurrencies because how each cryptocurrency operates affects tax, regulatory, and legal issues. Cryptocurrency regulation is currently undergoing a period of significant engagement from federal agencies, but formal rulemaking is still in its infancy.

At the federal level, the Internal Revenue Service (IRS), Securities and Exchange Commission (SEC), and Commodity Futures Trading Commission (CFTC) oversee the regulatory activity surrounding cryptocurrency. In the future, the Federal Trade Commission, Financial Crimes Enforcement Network (FinCEN), and Office of the Comptroller of Currency may increase their engagement in regulating this space.

Legal practitioners should also pay attention to the federal government. For example, the Biden administration recently signed an executive order that:

> lays out a national policy for digital assets across six key priorities: consumer and investor protection; financial stability; illicit finance; U.S. leadership in the global financial system and economic competitiveness; financial inclusion; and responsible innovation. (The White House Briefing Room, 2022, p. 1)

Executive orders such as President Biden's have a trickle effect on how other federal agencies regulate cryptocurrencies. Most agencies publish updated guidance on their websites to aid legal practitioners seeking to monitor regulatory guidance at the national level. Further, practitioners can track regulatory activity using the *Federal Register*. The Law Library of Congress also maintains a guide on federal regulations.

The National Conference of State Legislatures maintains a guide to state-level cryptocurrency legislation for practitioners seeking to keep abreast of state-level legislation. Stanford University publishes the *Journal of Blockchain Law & Policy* concerning recent legal research on cryptocurrency; CoinTelegraph.com and CoinDesk.com are good resources for updates on cryptocurrency policy and regulations for practitioners seeking reputable cryptocurrency news sources.

Current cryptocurrency regulation often occurs at the state level, with most regulation coming from state legislatures. Categorizing state-level regulation occurs in two ways: (1) favorable legislation seeking to promote cryptocurrency technology and (2) unfavorable legislation seeking to deter cryptocurrency investment in the state. For example, Wyoming passed 26 blockchain-friendly bills, one of which is a new charter for bitcoin banks. According to Avanti Financial CEO Caitlin Long,

> What Wyoming did was create a welcoming legal environment, just clarifying that the industry is lawful and does exist in a recognized manner .... In other states, most of the industry is just in a legal and regulatory grey area. (Nasdaq, 2021, p. 1)

In Wyoming, this charter allows crypto banks to act in a custodial and fiduciary capacity and hold digital assets for clients safely and legally.

Iowa and New York have issued restrictive laws, unlike Wyoming. The Attorney General of New York issued alerts in "response to the 'extreme risk' posed to New Yorkers investing in virtual or 'crypto' currencies" (James, 2021, p. 1). Further, there is no formal, standard legal definition of "cryptocurrency," "virtual currency," "digital asset," or "digital token." Due to the industry's ever-changing nature, most states have used broad definitions for this asset class.

States regulate cryptocurrency sales if the sale

> constitutes the sale of a security under state or federal law, or if it is considered money transmission under state law or conduct otherwise making the person a money services business ("MSB") under Federal law. (Dewey, 2021, p. 1)

Futures, options, swaps, and other contracts are subject to regulation by the CFTC. The CFTC may increase its role in regulating cryptoasset derivatives contracts as exchanges like the Chicago Board Options Exchange (CBOE) and the Chicago Mercantile Exchange (CME) offer more bitcoin and other crypto futures. A bitcoin spot exchange-traded fund would have a similar effect if approved.

The SEC maintains regulatory authority over the issuance or resale of tokens or digital assets deemed a security at the federal level. In the United States,

> every offer and sale of a security is required to either be (a) registered with the Securities and Exchange Commission (SEC); or (b) subject to an exemption from registration under the Securities Act of 1933. (American Bar Association, 2017, p. 1)

The SEC uses the Howey Test to determine if something is an "investment contract" and, therefore, a security. The test has four parts: (1) it is an investment of money; (2) there is an expectation of profits from the investment; (3) the investment of money is in a common enterprise; and (4) any profit comes from the effort of a promoter of a third party (United States Supreme Court, 1946). SEC regulation over securities is critical to initial coin offerings (ICOs) and crypto exchanges that offer interest-bearing accounts.

Further, if authorities consider tokens a security, the token's seller must be an SEC licensed broker-dealer and a member of the Financial Industry Regulatory Authority. Additionally, a security "can only trade on a licensed securities exchange or alternative trading system ('ATS') approved by the SEC" (Dewey, 2021, p. 1). Exchanges and entrepreneurs involved with the issuance and sale of digital assets should pay attention to current SEC cases and statements to ensure compliance with federal regulations.

Another consideration for legal practitioners is money transmission, anti-money laundering (AML), and know your customer or client laws and regulations. In the United States, the Financial Crimes Enforcement Network (FinCEN) regulates money services businesses (MSBs). Per FinCEN guidance,

> an administrator or exchanger that (1) accepts and transmits a convertible virtual currency or (2) buys or sells convertible virtual currency for any reason is a money transmitter under FinCEN's regulations, unless a limitation to or exemption from the definition applies to the person. (Dewey, 2021, p. 1)

Concerning cryptocurrency companies, if they are classified as an MSB, they must maintain a written AML program to prevent themselves from being used to launder money or finance terrorism. Currently, stablecoin issuers and decentralized finance (DeFi) are contention points for regulators regarding AML laws. Some DeFi exchanges and products, such as Uniswap, are designed without customer identification processes, enabling circumventing AML laws.

Besides AML, taxation considerations are essential for legal practitioners to deliberate. IRS taxes virtual currency such as bitcoin and other cryptocurrencies as "property." It also requires individuals and businesses to maintain records of purchases and sales and pay taxes on gains from the sale and on mined cryptocurrency. For individuals holding cryptocurrency for investment purposes, the IRS refers to them as "capital assets." IRS form 8949 requires individuals to report the sales and other dispositions of capital assets. Maintaining the records for this form is challenging for individuals who use cryptocurrency to make multiple purchases.

Ownership and licensing requirements are significant for cryptocurrency fund managers. They must "register as a commodity trading advisor (CTA) and commodity pool operator (CPO), with the CFTC and with the National Futures Association (NFA) or satisfy an exemption" (Dewey, 2021, p. 1). The future uses of cryptocurrencies such as bitcoin will involve estate planning and generating future rules and regulations for estate planning.

Accounting

Preparing financial statements is among the most critical tasks of accounting firms. These functions include conducting payroll services, preparing tax statements for regulatory reporting, and generating statements for shareholders or investors. The designation of a tax year may be of strategic importance depending on the business model or strategy chosen.

With public companies such as Tesla and MicroStrategy adding large amounts of bitcoin to their balance sheets, the financial reporting of digital assets is increasingly important for accountants. The Financial Accounting Standards Board provided no clear standards for digital assets. New concepts such as key management and custody practices are essential for accountants in the cryptoasset space.

The firms that make up the "Big Four" are taking note, with several accepting bitcoins as a payment method. Further, KPMG launched a Digital Ledger Services program in 2016, and PwC recently announced it would offer a blockchain auditing service. Critical concerns for accounting firms within the digital asset space include changes in value, reporting intangible assets, recording losses, handling vendor payments, recording mining activity, reporting digital asset trading, and determining which crypto transactions are taxable or non-taxable events.

Determining a cryptocurrency's fair value is challenging because US authorities do not consider it a legal tender. Further, digital assets change value significantly, sometimes in short periods. Therefore, public companies account for digital currencies as indefinite assets with an indefinite life. Companies place digital currencies on their balance sheets on a cost basis. If a digital currency's price falls below its cost basis, the owner must recognize the loss. Since the owner only records unrealized losses and not gains in the United States, current reporting standards for digital assets may create misleading information regarding the value of those assets on company balance sheets. For example,

> MicroStrategy Incorporated, currently the public company with the most Bitcoin holdings, owned 70,469 BTC on December 31, 2020. Its holdings had a fair market value of $2 billion at the time, but its balance sheet showed only $1.1 billion at year-end because only unrealized losses were recorded. This creates a clear misalignment between the economic realities of a company's holdings, and how accounting standards reflect those holdings. (Jacob, 2021, p. 1)

Cryptocurrencies represent a unique asset that presents challenges for accounting practitioners. However, the fundamental accounting principles still apply to them. Businesses that purchase cryptocurrencies should recognize the asset on their balance sheets when they buy them and remove them from their balance sheets when they sell them. Regarding vendor payments, businesses should currently record transactions as if they were selling the cryptocurrency. Therefore, they must recognize the capital gain or loss. This situation complicates firms seeking to use cryptocurrencies for vendor payments, but accountants must know how to report these transactions.

Accounting rules for financial statements and taxes are closely linked but not uniform. Certain crypto transactions, such as mining income, crypto staking, hard forks, airdrops, and interest earnings, are taxable events. Others, such as buying crypto with fiat currency, giving or donating crypto, or transferring cryptoassets between exchanges, are non-taxable events.

In sum, cryptoassets create unique challenges for accounting practitioners. They also necessitate clarification from regulators so that accountants can be aware of what principles to follow when preparing financial and tax statements that include digital assets.

Compliance

Compliance obligations fall within two broad categories: formal and voluntary. Within the formal compliance rubric are regulatory and legal/legislative requirements. In the United States, agencies promulgate regulatory obligations. Legislative bodies include the US Congress and state securities agencies.

Internal Versus Outsources Resources

The choice as to whether to hire ("build") versus engage consultancies ("buy") to acquire cryptocurrency compliance services is partly a business consideration. Decision-makers need to balance overall cost and the projected intensity of legal and regulatory interactions. Any firm seeking to solicit, acquire, and service customers – the retail (non-institutional) population – will require more regular and intensive engagement regarding compliance issues. On the other hand, while not bereft of compliance considerations, businesses dealing primarily with qualified institutions or accredited investors tend to see the difference in implied sophistication reflected in less demanding requirements.

Two aspects of the crypto space set it apart from more traditional securities and investment management oversight. The first is the rapid change and need for compliance officers to stay abreast of legal and regulatory changes. Additionally, a vast patchwork of regulatory and governmental entities, domestic and international, oversee cryptocurrency-related businesses. Although streaming this Balkanized oversight structure is likely, vigilance is now the most reliable legal and regulatory compliance option.

Due Diligence

Some interpret due diligence as a legal obligation to exercise reasonable care before entering into an agreement with another individual or party, especially when evaluating the appropriateness of a business relationship. However, the obligation can go beyond explicit legal stipulations. The amount of information needed to assess a commercial agreement's propriety may fall short of or surpass regulatory requirements. Thus, most serve as guidelines. The best advice is to conduct such investigations according to the spirit and not merely the letter of the law.

Besides the required elements, which typically take the form of questionnaires, financial disclosures, and other documentation, due diligence assessments should consider the risks, benefits, and tradeoffs of crypto enterprises. Two issues that continue to plague investors and other commercial relationships follow.

Rug Pulls

A *rug pull* refers to various cryptocurrency scams. A fraudulent crypto developer promotes a new project – a coin, platform, or another asset – to investors, pumping up the price and then pulling as much value out of the project as possible before abandoning it as the price drops. In the dot com era, the media referred to similar swindles as vaporware or "not com" projects. Several factors exacerbate the ability to trick investors: (1) the secrecy customarily attending technology projects and (2) the enthusiasm surrounding early-stage investment opportunities. Thus, the fear of missing out has played a role in many successful rug pulls.

Illicit activity evolves alongside the markets they prey upon, but several broad protective measures may forfend all but the craftiest of hustles and hustlers. First, there are few substitutes for a face-to-face meeting with purveyors of a new investment opportunity. Both formal and informal networking creates a powerful information-based deterrent for active and repeat con artists. Although most experienced business professionals would not imagine doing so, refusing to provide financing before drawing up agreements and outlining responsibilities is essential, regardless of prospective or hypothesized rewards.

Projects led by unknown or anonymous developers or teams, DeFi projects offering yields vastly above those available in the broader market, guaranteed returns, and onerous lock-up requirements are just a handful of intimations requiring closer inspection if not outright skepticism. Entrepreneurs and technological innovators tend to be inexhaustible and motivated. However, a measured approach – one of the less quantifiable or qualifiable aspects of sagacious due diligence – tends to prevail over the long run.

New Issues

ICOs are an ongoing morass for investors in new projects and require a particularly energetic investigative approach. Factors influencing whether and what type of registration is required include an issue's characteristics, functionality, and jurisdiction in which the offer is undertaken.

Some issuers have promoted coin offerings employing the description "utility" as necessarily exempt from registration. An experienced attorney should only make that determination. The safest and most appropriate assumption is that a new issue is a security, with any exemptions verified by a legal professional.

Because crypto projects tend to be international, an affirmative determination regarding the legal domicile, applicable securities, and other laws in advance is highly recommended.

Even if not soliciting funds, businesses operating platforms enabling transactions in offerings that require regulation may violate the Securities Exchange Act of 1934 by effectively operating an unregistered securities exchange. Thus, using software platforms or other technological means of distributing coins is advisable to determine if they act in a national securities exchange capacity. Again, a securities industry attorney specializing in such matters can often make such a determination.

Operations

A critical but often overlooked step in initiating a cryptocurrency-related business is preparing an operations manual. As a firm or fund grows in size and complexity, guidelines are essential to maintain orderly and predictable internal procedures and provide a foundation to address unanticipated circumstances. A business needs to update such a document periodically and after exceptional circumstances or major internal changes, such as a change of custodian. This update should include at least three major sections: trading guidelines, cash management, and human resources.

Governance

Governance describes the rules for managing an organization or entity. In the corporate world, the orientation of competing governance structures is toward maximizing shareholder value while guarding stakeholder interests. They primarily do so through arrangements informally described as "checks and balances." A characteristic of effective governance is establishing a clear institutional framework that makes decisions and the discharge of responsibilities, reciprocities, and the allocation of resources clear to all relevant external and internal stakeholders.

This section refers to governance within cryptocurrency structures. Financial institutions, like investment banks, hedge funds, venture capital firms, and private equity firms, put considerable resources into planning and executing their corporate structures and extra corporate relationships. This section examines considerations of the internal governance challenges of cryptocurrencies using bitcoin and decentralized autonomous organizations (DAOs) as implicit and explicitly structured entities. A large body of academic literature discusses the purpose, types, and tradeoffs of forms of governance, but most are beyond this chapter's scope. However, contracts are a regular fixture that appears and reappears throughout tangible and virtual organization structures.

A *contract* is a legally enforceable agreement that sets forth some terms of performance, often mutual rights and obligations. Among the benefits of contracting are the alignment of incentives, clarity of performance expectations, and greater predictability of outcomes, all of which increase the ability of agents to plan. Contracts may be explicit, in the case of a written agreement, or implicit, as described by interrelated, complex behaviors of individuals in various organizational roles.

DAOs and Governance

A *DAO* is a member-owned community without central leadership facilitating collaboration and funding functions within a "trustless" schema. Most DAOs feature characteristics of more familiar corporate entities, including C- and S-sub election corporations, limited liability companies, partnerships, non-profits, or cooperatives. They differ in their expression of organizational and task organization and control and how to accomplish this. Smart contracts govern DAOs. DAOs monitor the performance and execution of smart contracts by algorithms and limit adjudication of disputes to the extent possible to those algorithms.

DAOs may represent a new paradigm upon or from which organizations plan and manage their undertakings. Alternatively, the determination may be made that they are utilitarian in organizations with strictly delimited purposes and scales. In any event, certain governance pitfalls of DAOs require discussion.

To the extent that specific duties or functions cannot easily be expressed algorithmically or coded, like implicit expectations and tacit understandings, trustless mechanisms for ensuring fulfillment may be difficult or impossible. Nevertheless, the design of smart contracts within a DAO may trigger or otherwise signal a need for third-party human mediation.

In the context of the "concrete" business and financial world, functional shortcomings linger. Although recent developments demonstrate the basic commercial viability of DAOs, the execution of specific fundamental tasks remains thorny, including such mundanities as opening corporate bank accounts. Where DAOs are employed in industries with high degrees of regulatory scrutiny, like in securities brokerage or transportation, regulators are likely to require representations or documentation attesting to satisfactory adherence to compliance requirements, mainly concerning licensed supervisory roles.

The same applies where DAO stakeholders are dispersed in terms of political geography. Certain jurisdictions, intra- or international, may harbor different views on the nature of decentralized work or the nature of "virtual" employment. Most importantly, establishing a DAO should ideally provide categorizable or quantifiable benefits over legacy organizational structures. Suppose initiating or transferring a firm's or project's operation from the corporeal world to networks of smart contracts adds no value. In that case, the resulting enterprise may prove fascinating, innovative, and wasteful.

Traditional Cryptocurrencies and Governance

Using bitcoin as a template for basic cryptocurrency governance makes comparisons more comprehensible. It is not stakeholders, developers, or miners but users at the helm of bitcoin's decentralized peer-to-peer (P2P) network.

To participate in bitcoin's governance, users may run nodes and thus participate directly in the emergent consensus, determining the protocol in use, which in this case, is proof of work (PoW). In what may be the ultimate embodiment of voice and exit, a user may build off the open-source software and create a hard or soft fork, incorporating that user's vision of what bitcoin may be or how it operates. A bitcoin user may begin using another cryptocurrency in the evolving complex.

Reporting

The pace at which crypto regulatory and tax reporting requirements change renders a conclusive review of best reporting practices futile. Yet, the growth of cryptocurrencies as money substitutes and the emergence of DeFi as an alternative to legacy financial markets have drawn the IRS and its foreign/international equivalents to scrutinize transactions closely. High levels of fraud and significant revenue opportunities from legitimate businesses are additional incentives for government oversight.

Basic accounting principles cover most facets of cryptocurrency reporting. An exception is the monetary unit assumption, which holds that transactions should be recorded in the same currency. Few legal jurisdictions permit paying taxes using cryptocurrencies. Thus, as a matter of sound recordkeeping, transactions should be recorded in their cryptocurrency terms and the prevailing currency terms. In November 2021, sections 6045 and 6050l of the Infrastructure Investment and Jobs Act provided clarity by defining such terms as "digital asset," "brokers," and "specified securities." Additionally, digital assets being among the specified securities requires their inclusion on Form 1099-B,

Most regulatory focus on cryptocurrency reporting focuses on AML requirements. But with the increased permeation of cryptocurrency ownership and usage, attention will necessarily expand to include customer on- and off-boarding, retail compliance, and other such areas.

Acknowledging the rapidity with which the cryptocurrency space is evolving, Deloitte provides the following four recommendations concerning reporting requirements.

1. *Applicability*. The trajectory over which regulatory and tax requirements tend to be codified and promulgated may lead managers and executives to question whether they fall within the scope of new rules. Where questionable, a safe approach is to include inclusion until clarity.
2. *Requirements*. Owners/managers should employ an integrated team, as necessary, to understand and ensure compliance with new reporting obligations.
3. Disruption. Owners/managers must understand that tradeoffs will inevitably occur between the customer experience and additional reporting requirements. Navigating that challenge is essential, but preparation can ease friction.
4. *Operations*. A disproportionate element of complying with new reporting requirements, whether regulatory or tax-based, is infrastructural, specifically,

technological. Assessing the internal ability to create, merge, and otherwise manipulate data is key to confirming new reporting stipulations and making the customer experience as innocuous as possible.

Although sometimes confusing and exasperating, new levels of regulatory compliance, such as recordkeeping and official reporting, are among the most visceral signs of the growing acceptance and evolution of the cryptocurrency space. The maturation of the industries developing, embracing, and deploying cryptocurrency assets is at times slow and painful but vindicates the innovations now in their second decade.

DeFi Considerations

DeFi is a growing field within the cryptocurrency space. It emerged in 2015, creating a new cryptocurrency network, or platform, known as Ethereum. According to Ramachandran, and Santoro (2021, p. 16),

> smart contracts – which are code that lives on a blockchain, can control assets and data, and define interactions between the assets, data, and network participants. The capacity for smart contracts defines Ethereum as a smart contract platform.

Although smart contracts predate blockchain technology, successful implementation did not occur before the advent of blockchain networks such as Ethereum. Nick Szabo (1997) conceptualized the smart contract:

> The basic idea behind smart contracts is that many kinds of contractual clauses (such as collateral, bonding, delineation of property rights, etc.) can be embedded in the hardware and software we deal with, in such a way as to make breach of contract expensive (if desired, sometimes prohibitively so) for the breacher. (p. 1)

Smart contract platforms such as Ethereum allow entrepreneurs to create decentralized applications, known as dApps. *A DApp* is an application built on smart contract platforms that use smart contracts to allow users to transact P2P without a central intermediary. Although other dApps are available, such as social media, prediction markets, and charities, the most popular use case for dApps is financial applications known as DeFi. DeFi is a new financial infrastructure built on blockchains using smart contracts. Most DeFi focuses on building and improving upon the current financial structure. DeFi applications provide individuals with new ways to exchange, lend, and save.

Entrepreneurs and companies seeking to engage in the DeFi space face critical risks. Carter and Jeng (2021, p. 1) state that the risks "stem from the decentralized nature of blockchains. The goal of automating the delivery of financial services and reducing human dependencies also has the congruent effect of reducing oversight and control."

DeFi Risks

DeFi users and entrepreneurs face a risk built into the DeFi space – smart contract risk. DeFi is built using code via software. Although this approach removes some counterparty risk of traditional finance, it opens up DeFi to hacks and malpractice. As Harvey, Ramachandran, and Santoro (2021, pp. 131–132) note,

> Smart Contract risk can take the form of a logic error in the code or an economic exploit in which an attacker can withdraw funds from the platform beyond the intended functionality.

Numerous smart contract hacks have occurred since DeFi's inception. The most famous was the DAO hack in 2016, resulting in losing $60 million of ether (Cryptopedia Staff, 2021). The Ethereum blockchain, on which the DAO was built, was later controversially forked, resulting in returning the stolen funds to investors. Businesses seeking to enter the space must consider smart contract risk. Their applications reduce counterparty risk, but they are not without the risk inherent to traditional computer programs.

Not all DeFi applications rely solely on autonomous computer code, or smart contracts, to operate. Some protocols use a human-controlled governance process to manage protocol risk actively. In these cases, users and investors acquire governance tokens to participate in the governance process and vote on changes to the protocol. This situation introduces a new risk called *governance risk*. If a malicious actor acquires 51 percent of the tokens, this person can implement a proposal that would benefit the bad actor while hurting other token holders. This situation is yet to occur on an Ethereum DeFi project. However, if the benefits outweigh the costs of an attack, malicious actors may seek to target a project through a governance attack. Practitioners entering the DeFi space should consider the threat of governance and programming hacks.

Besides governance risk, DeFi protocols also face oracle risk. According to Harvey et al. (2021, p. 137),

> Fundamentally, oracles aim to answer the simple question: How can off-chain data be securely reported on-chain? Without oracles, blockchains are completely self-encapsulated and do not know the outside world other than the transactions added to the native blockchain.

Therefore, DeFi protocols rely on data feeds to ensure reporting of the off-chain data, such as asset prices, so that the protocol functions. Oracle risk is an essential factor to consider. If the cost of corrupting the oracle to front-run transactions or some other form of profit is less than the potential profit, an oracle may be corrupted. Until someone devises robust solutions to oracle risk, it represents a systemic threat to the current DeFi landscape. DeFi presents opportunities for investors and consumers, but it also introduces new risks to consider.

Summary and Conclusions

Since bitcoin's implementation in 2009, adoption rates of blockchain and cryptocurrency outpace adoption rates of the internet. Cryptocurrency is here to stay, and mainstream financial institutions mainly play "catch up" when participating in the space. The cryptocurrency industry continues to grow in volume and importance. Financial institutions such as banks, hedge funds, private equity firms, and venture capitalists are increasingly active within the crypto ecosystem. This situation necessitates both mainstream financial institutions and policymakers to become familiar with the risks, challenges, and opportunities that the cryptocurrency industry presents. Practitioners and investors must develop a high degree of knowledge concerning the cryptocurrency industry's legal, compliance, accounting, due diligence, and other concerns. This chapter highlights the risks presented by DeFi, as currently understudied in academia.

Discussion Questions

1. Identify the test the SEC uses to determine if something is a security and the components making up the test.
2. Define a smart contract and explain its main use cases.
3. Discuss the advantages and disadvantages of internal versus outsourced compliance resources.
4. Identify the four general guidelines for reporting cryptocurrency and blockchain transactions accurately and adequately.
5. Explain the main risks inherent to DeFi in contrast to traditional finance

References

American Bar Association (2017, April 27). *What constitutes a security and requirements relating to the offer and sales of securities and exemptions from registration associated therewith.* American Bar Association (ABA). Retrieved from https://www.americanbar.org/groups/business_law/publications/blt/2017/04/06_loev/

Carter, N., & Jeng, L. (2021). DeFi protocol risks: The paradox of DeFi. *SSRN Electronic Journal*, 1–35. https://doi.org/10.2139/ssrn.3866699

Cryptopedia Staff (2021, March 2022). *The DAO: What was the DAO and how was it hacked?* Gemini.com. Retrieved from https://www.gemini.com/cryptopedia/the-dao-hack-makerdao

Dewey, J. (2021, October 21). *Blockchain & cryptocurrency laws and regulations 2022.* Global Legal Insights. Retrieved from https://www.globallegalinsights.com/practice-areas/blockchain-laws-and-regulations

Harvey, C. R., Ramachandran, A., & Santoro, J. (2021). *DeFi and the future of finance.* Hoboken, NJ: John Wiley & Sons, Inc.

Jacob, A. (2021, August 23). *A quick guide to accounting for cryptocurrency*. Taxbit. Retrieved from https://taxbit.com/blog/a-quick-guide-to-accounting-for-cryptocurrency

James, L. (2021, March 1). *Attorney General James warns investors about 'extreme risk' when investing in cryptocurrency, issues additional warning to those facilitating trading of virtual currencies*. New York State Office of the Attorney General. Retrieved from https://ag.ny.gov/press-release/2021/attorney-general-james-warns-investors-about-extreme-risk-when-investing

Nasdaq (2021). *Favorable regulation, abundant energy turning Wyoming into a Bitcoin hub*. Nasdaq.com. Retrieved from https://www.nasdaq.com/articles/favorable-regulation-abundant-energy-turning-wyoming-into-a-bitcoin-hub-2021-08-13

Szabo, N. 1997. *Formalizing and securing relationships on public networks*. Satoshi.nakamotoinstitute.org. Retrieved fromhttps://nakamotoinstitute.org/formalizing-securing-relationships/

The White House Briefing Room (2022, March 9). *Fact Sheet. President Biden to sign executive order on ensuring responsible development of digital assets*. Whitehouse.gov. Retrieved from https://www.whitehouse.gov/briefing-room/statements-releases/2022/03/09/fact-sheet-president-biden-to-sign-executive-order-on-ensuring-responsible-innovation-in-digital-assets/

United States Supreme Court (1946). *Securities and Exchange Commission* v. *W. J. Howey Co*. Caselaw.findlaw.com. Retrieved from https://caselaw.findlaw.com/us-supreme-court/328/293.html

Chapter 16

Custody, Provenance, and Reporting of Blockchain and Cryptoassets

Rocher Cyrus

Abstract

Although few fully understand the evolving science of blockchain technology, many agree that such technology promises countless crypto innovative applications. However, institutions using blockchain and cryptoassets face issues. Since more institutions are beginning to explore various private, public, and hybrid blockchains and their related cryptoassets, an increased need exists to understand and anticipate implementation problems. Such problems include contractual issues, privacy concerns, tax implications, jurisdictional issues, financial fraud, and data theft. Others involve intellectual property rights, money laundering, accounting and financial reporting, fork management and governance, and compliance and regulatory obligations. This chapter reviews and analyzes the various problems facing institutions in using blockchain and cryptoassets as financial instruments and mediums of exchange. It focuses on these aspects concerning custody, provenance, and reporting. This chapter also discusses the compliance, disclosure, and regulatory reporting of cryptoassets.

Keywords: Cryptoassets; blockchain; custody; provenance; compliance; reporting

Introduction

In recent years, blockchain technology and cryptoassets have become attractive options for institutions (Pratt, 2021). A blockchain creates trust between different entities where it is unproven or nonexistent. Institutions are more willing to engage in business dealings with one another involving data sharing or transactions without needing an intermediary. Blockchains also help institutions

The Emerald Handbook on Cryptoassets: Investment Opportunities and Challenges, 233–248

doi:10.1108/978-1-80455-320-620221016

minimize costs because of more efficient transaction processing and reducing the need for manual tasks involving aggregating and amending data. Another benefit of blockchains is immutability. Transactions recorded on a blockchain cannot be altered or erased. These are only a few of blockchain and cryptoasset's benefits for institutions.

Despite these benefits, institutions face concerns when using blockchain technology and cryptoassets. The failure to resolve these issues can lead to institutions facing challenging problems that adversely affect business dealings, practices, and operations. This chapter discusses blockchain technology and cryptoassets. It also examines potential custody, provenance, and reporting issues.

Understanding Cryptoasset Custody

This section provides an overview of cryptoasset custody by explaining what it is, why it is important, and how it works. As part of understanding cryptoasset custody, this section examines self-custody, third-party custody, and key storage. Institutions should understand cryptoasset custody because it is an essential aspect of trading. Investors need to know that they are safe and digital asset custody protects their assets.

What are cryptoassets? According to the International Monetary Fund, cryptoassets are digital assets denominated in their units of account and exist virtually (Smith & Srivastava, 2020). Thus, their transfer can occur from peer-to-peer (P2P) without an intermediary. Although cryptoassets are also intangible, many have become increasingly linked to real-world assets in recent years. Securing custody has become crucial with advances in blockchain technology and the more widespread acceptance of cryptoassets.

So, what is cryptoasset custody? *Cryptoasset custody* is a generalized term that includes various methods of storing and protecting an individual or institution's cryptoassets. Custodians can play a pivotal role in looking after cryptoassets on behalf of their owners. In many ways, cryptoasset custody is like the custody of financial assets because custodians are responsible for storing an investor's cryptoassets securely and safely.

Cryptoasset custody is more critical than traditional financial asset custody due to a cryptoasset's nature. Owners of cryptoassets like cryptocurrency receive cryptographic keys that prove their ownership of a digital asset. Investors and owners of cryptoassets use these keys to transfer ownership and buy goods and services.

The transfer of cryptoassets occurs between owners through cryptography and a blockchain. If an institution does not safeguard its keys, it risks losing its digital assets, so custodians are essential. A custodian stores an institution's cryptographic keys and not its digital assets. Storing all transactions and data takes place on a blockchain.

Without cryptoasset custodians, the widespread adoption of digital assets would slow. If institutional investors trust the security of their digital assets, more institutions may consider blockchain technology. With the advent of many crypto custody services, more institutions are dabbling in digital assets and beginning to place significant amounts of cryptocurrency on their balance sheets.

According to a report released by Blockdata (2022), digital assets under custody grew exponentially between January 2019 and January 2022, from $32 to $223 billion. Institutions that manage hedge funds, investment banks, family offices, and pension funds can access a digital asset custody partner proven to manage assets safely and securely. In that case, they are far more likely to invest in crypto. This number may increase as more institutions trust crypto custody services.

Self-storage

Most institutions do not choose self-storage when managing their cryptoassets because of their risks. *Self-storage* is when an institution or individual personally holds the key or keys to its crypto wallet. If an institution opts for self-storage, it is the only entity that can prove ownership of funds and has access to the funds in the wallet. The most significant risk with choosing self-storage is that if an institution loses the physical device (cold wallet), forgets its private key, or has it stolen, the institution has almost no chance of recovering its cryptoassets.

Third-party Custody

Third-party custody is a better choice for institutions that do not want the sole responsibility of managing their accounts. Additionally, a third-party custodian is also best for organizations that do not fully comprehend blockchain's technical aspects and the legalities surrounding cryptoasset storage.

Suppose an institution chooses a third-party custodian. In that case, it chooses a registered and regulated financial institution that has completed the requirements to acquire a national or state-level license allowing it to function as a custodian. Institutions are often more inclined to use a third-party custodian because it assumes the responsibility of ensuring the security of its clients' keys and holdings.

When an institution chooses a third-party custodian, it must complete a series of steps, including undergoing anti-money laundering (AML) and know-your-customer (KYC) checks to ensure no one acquires their cryptoassets illegally. Institutions may choose among three custodians: exchanges, custodial banks, and digital asset managers. Each option has positives and negatives. For example, a custodian can limit withdrawals, freeze assets, and block access to a wallet in certain instances. Additionally, a third-party custodian can be hacked or go bankrupt.

Exchanges

An exchange is a popular way that businesses and institutions can store their crypto funds, but it is not the safest option. When an institution signs up for a centralized cryptocurrency exchange, it allows an exchange to take responsibility for its cryptoassets.

Notably, a few exchanges outsource their security needs, meaning an external custody provider faces the task of safeguarding an institution's digital assets.

Unfortunately, exchanges are fallible and are at risk of hacking. Thus, an institution could encounter significant losses because the exchange is responsible for managing its private keys.

Custodial Banks

As of July 2020, authorities granted custodial banks in the United States the legal right to offer custody of cryptoassets. This move came after the Controller of the Currency declared that all nationally chartered banks could provide custody services. After this decision, numerous custody giants like Citibank, Fidelity, and BNY Mellon entered the cryptoasset custody market. However, many third-party custodial banks like Fidelity only offer custody services to institutional investors.

Digital Asset Managers

Since the crypto sphere is rapidly expanding, the need for digital asset managers has increased. Digital asset managers act similarly to banks. These managers act like banks for cryptoasset holders, and these institutions are regulated and licensed to offer customers cryptoasset custody.

Storage Keys

Crypto custodians store the private keys of individuals, businesses, and institutions. Those tasked with holding private keys can do so in four ways: hot storage, cold storage, smart contract wallet storage, and multi-signature wallet storage.

With hot storage, an investor's cryptoassets and private keys are stored online, allowing for online custodianship. Hot storage is not the preferred method, especially when large sums of money are in play, because it is the most vulnerable to hackers. In contrast, cold storage focuses on storing an investor's private cryptoasset keys offline. Unlike hot storage, cold storage is a safer alternative because it uses a private key to access an offline digital wallet that is less prone to hacking.

A smart contract wallet is a more complex custodial service offered to investors. A smart contract wallet manages custody via coded instructions. It proves ownership through online custodianship, making it unique. When using a smart contract wallet to store cryptoasset private keys, an investor also has a master account and special control by a code feature.

A newer but increasingly popular custodial service offered to investors is a multi-signature wallet. This wallet addresses many issues associated with storing cryptoassets. A multi-signature wallet requires multiple signatures to approve transactions and online custodianship. This cryptoasset custody solution allows institutions to have multiple users access a decentralized wallet.

Understanding Cryptoasset Provenance

Many believe that blockchain provenance is the future of record keeping but proving cryptoasset provenance is not straightforward. Since anyone can create a cryptoasset address anywhere and anytime, institutions face challenges determining ownership of certain assets. Fortunately, businesses and institutions can take advantage of underlying blockchain technology and third-party data to examine and establish the provenance of a customer's cryptoassets (Caruso, 2018).

Although analyzing cryptoasset provenance with blockchain technology is complicated, third-party data provider information (i.e., KYC data) can help. For example, many exchanges have begun sourcing a collection of KYC information to identify a significant percentage of addresses for certain cryptoassets. Although KYC data are invaluable at proving a cryptoasset's provenance, many addresses have no KYC data to aid in establishing provenance.

A need exists to realize and acknowledge that a degree of anonymity does not automatically classify transactions as illegal or malicious. Nevertheless, anonymity presents a significant challenge for KYC programs. These challenges result from the requirement for organizations to maintain the ability to pin down and keep track of the provenance of customers' cryptoassets, a crypto transaction's history, and the history of customer transactions.

Blockchain technology and KYC data can enable traceability of cryptoassets and identify if specific cryptoasset addresses participated in illegal actions. With blockchain technology and third-party data, institutions can determine the legitimacy of cryptoassets. If specialized data analytics are used, they can be determined if cryptoasset transactions are flagged for further investigation. These data analytics can establish provenance by assigning a risk rating to transactions to aid institutions and businesses in their cryptoasset dealings.

Many consider blockchain provenance the future of record keeping because any sector required to track data across different sources accurately can use blockchain provenance. Since a blockchain is immutable, distributed, and public if dealing with a public blockchain, it is ideal for data exchanges. As blockchain technology becomes more accepted, a shift in record keeping will occur with data stored on shared ledgers. Various indications suggest that blockchain provenance is becoming the norm. For example, a judge in China recently ruled that blockchain authenticated evidence is admissible in court, so a more comprehensive community across sectors should emerge using blockchain provenance.

Blockchain Provenance Uses

Multiple real-world examples are available of using a blockchain to prove provenance. One of the biggest niche industries using blockchain technology to prove provenance is the art industry (ELEV8, 2019). This industry is a global leader in blockchain adoption because numerous digital artists and collectors use the technology to record and track an artwork's provenance. They use a blockchain for auditing where an artwork originated and who had previously owned it to authenticate it.

Besides the art industry, large enterprises often use blockchain technology to prove provenance and audit almost any type of data ownership. For example, multiple businesses like Walmart, IBM, and DNV GL use blockchain provenance to improve supply chains. They employ blockchain technology to prevent item tampering and fraud and better track goods along a specific supply chain. They also use it to trace defects back to their primary sources and reduce the need for intermediaries in a multi-organizational process.

IBM encourages others to use its blockchain platform to prove the provenance of intellectual property and houses. Additionally, a provenance company called Provenance provides a blockchain framework for the origin of certain financial products. Moreover, the reputable Centers for Disease Control and Prevention is testing various blockchain solutions to monitor diseases. Blockchain technology is one of the best resources available to institutions that want to prove provenance.

Tax Compliance

Increased cryptoasset adoption rates affect disclosure, regulatory compliance, and reporting. As traditional financial institution participation increases in cryptoassets, United States and federal regulators are intensely focusing on the regulatory obligations of crypto businesses.

When cryptoassets become institutionalized, they are more likely to be tradable in other markets like other commodities. Thus, different classes of cryptoassets will have various regulators like the Securities and Exchange Commission (SEC), Commodities and Futures Trading Commission (CFTC), and Financial Industry Regulatory Authority (FINRA) (KPMG, 2020).

The current patchwork of US state and federal regulations governing the cryptoasset industry has created significant regulatory challenges for crypto businesses. Several current regulations apply to different crypto businesses. For example, the SEC has determined that certain cryptoassets that have been issued as part of initial coin offerings require registration with the Commission. This requirement applies to securities falling under the Securities Act of 1933 and the Securities Exchange Act of 1934. The CFTC considers certain cryptoassets as commodities. Thus, crypto futures, options, swaps, and other derivative contracts fall under the same regulatory protocols as physical assets.

Moreover, the Internal Revenue Service (IRS) requires treating certain cryptoassets as property. Thus, those cryptoassets seen as property must be disclosed and are subject to tax upon exchange or sale. Crypto businesses or institutions investing and trading in cryptoassets must consider various tax implications. Various regulators are trying to stay on top of crypto innovation while protecting the investing public.

Security Token Regulatory Challenges

Cryptoassets identified as securities create regulatory challenges because they are a vital part of the emerging tokenized economy. Investors often must trade the cryptoassets deemed securities through a registered broker-dealer. This situation is because they could fall under various securities laws and regulatory requirements. Institutions trading cryptoasset securities should be aware of this situation to meet all rules and regulations set out by the different governing bodies.

Unfortunately, the lack of clear regulatory and reporting guidance makes implementing the applicable processes and controls difficult. Additionally, the electronic trading of digital securities faces unique challenges. For example, authorities might require broker-dealers to establish electronic trading platforms to continue trading security tokens in an electronic environment because they are natively digital.

Disclosing Cryptoassets to Avoid Criminal Prosecution

Since disclosure and regulatory reporting of cryptoassets are murky, the IRS has implemented a new IRS form revision to help with avoiding criminal prosecution. Changes to the revised Form 14457 include an expanded reporting section and comprehensive instructions surrounding reporting virtual currency and other cryptoassets (Bonner, 2022).

Taxpayers can use this form to make a preclearance request to the IRS when they want to establish their eligibility to use the voluntary disclosure practice. This practice is a set of procedures that helps taxpayers avoid criminal prosecution if authorities find them willfully violating tax laws if they provide the IRS Criminal Investigations with complete and timely disclosure.

However, institutions and cryptoasset investors need to know that voluntary disclosure is not a free pass. It does not guarantee immunity from criminal prosecution, but the IRS can recommend against prosecution depending on an individual case's circumstances. Additionally, a taxpayer must initiate a disclosure before the IRS undertakes a criminal investigation or civil examination.

On the revised form 14457, taxpayers can now identify a new schedule of virtual currency where they can disclose each type of cryptoasset they own. On the form, taxpayers can identify each asset by name, number, date acquired, disposal date, whether they held it domestically or offshore, and the various account holders. Taxpayers also must disclose to the IRS if they use a "mixer" or "tumbler." These services are used to mix the cryptoassets of several users with the intent of laundering money or hiding the crypto owner's identity. Lastly, if taxpayers have had their preclearance application approved, they must write a "non-compliance narrative." Suppose the cryptoasset is a digital currency. In that case, they may need to describe the exchange, host wallet, customer ID, private wallet, account number, user ID, and how they acquired the virtual currency.

Tracking these transactions can be extremely difficult for individuals and institutions as most do manual tracking or use traditional tools such as excel. Several tools, such as Gilded, capture these transactions electronically and assist with their automated accounting.

The Infrastructure Act

As of November 2021, there were five key regulatory reporting changes for cryptoassets in the United States according to the Infrastructure Act signed into law by President Biden. This Act requires reporting the IRS Form 1099-B gross proceeds and cost basis tax for US sales of cryptoassets, including cryptocurrencies. This form comes into effect for returns needing to be filed in 2024. The five critical regulatory reporting changes follow.

- More details will be forthcoming for the potential treatment of digital asset market participants as brokers because, at present, the legalities surrounding this situation are controversial.
- The definition of digital assets subject to tax reporting is comprehensive and highly likely to include the reporting of non-fungible tokens (NFTs).
- A new type of IRS tax return will only apply to certain cryptoasset transfers completed by brokers to non-brokers.
- Distinct tax reporting rules will be allocated to different cryptoassets, depending on their tax classification. For example, crypto exchange-traded funds, options, and futures are already subject to Form 1099-B reporting because they are deemed securities according to tax reporting purposes.
- Although an issuer's classification is unclear, issuers must report organizational actions that affect a holder's basis in a cryptoasset.

Three pages of the new 1,039-page Infrastructure Act add new reporting requirements for select cryptocurrency transactions (Beringer, Biben, & Day, 2021). These pages are likely to have potentially significant and dramatic implications for millions of US consumers and businesses embracing cryptocurrency.

This Act extends traditional reporting requirements for certain cryptoassets or digital asset transactions, including cryptocurrencies involving more than $10,000. Thus, businesses must not report transactions involving different digital assets. Much confusion exists surrounding this new reporting obligation. Depending on its interpretation and implementation, authorities could require companies investing and trading in cryptoassets to collect further information, unlike the information needed for cash purchases, to the IRS.

If businesses fail to report this still to be determined information, they could face severe criminal penalties. In numerous instances, authorities could require them to pay up to $3 million annually in civil penalties. This sum could exponentially rise if the failure to comply with the new reporting requirements resulted from "intentional disregard." In addition, authorities consider the willful violation of these requirements under Section 6050I a federal felony, meaning violators face up to five years imprisonment. Moreover, corporate violators could face the same amount of jail time and fines of up to $100,000. This new reporting requirement could have unintended consequences for the cryptocurrency industry. For example, it could force businesses to complete crypto transactions with unregulated services or with private wallets, which would defeat the purpose of reporting digital asset transactions of more than $10,000.

IRS Enforcement

With businesses and organizations failing to be tax compliant, the IRS has taken steps to enforce tax laws in the crypto industry. Unfortunately, because no centralized institution is responsible for recording every transaction on the blockchain, tracking transactions is incredibly challenging for the IRS. Due to the severe implications surrounding tax evasion and cryptoassets, the IRS created a task force. This task force investigates cases of potential tax fraud surrounding the underreporting of income earned through cryptocurrencies. Additionally, the IRS's Large Business & International Division decided to add virtual currency to its list of compliance campaigns (Polizzano, 2018). Yet, the IRS urges compliance concerning cryptoasset reporting, but it does not provide much-needed guidance on virtual currencies. The IRS released a list of civil penalties applicable to non-compliant taxpayers who fail to declare income from cryptocurrencies as part of enforcing punishments. Some of these penalties follow.

- The civil fraud penalties under Section 6651(f) or 6663 amount to 75 percent of the unpaid tax on earned income.
- When taxpayers fail to file a comprehensive tax return for income earned through cryptocurrencies, they face paying 5 percent of the unpaid tax monthly. Still, this percentage could go up to 25 percent monthly under Section 6651(a)(2).
- An accuracy-related penalty under Section 6662 amounts to between 20 and 40 percent.
- When a failure to pay taxes appears on a return under Section 66651(a)(2), the monthly amount is between 0.5 and 25 percent.
- When a taxpayer fails to file Form 8938, the base penalty is $10,000 per failure to report an applicable asset. If the failure continues, an additional $10,000 is added and payable for each month the failure occurs.

Contractual Issues

The most valuable features of cryptocurrencies and blockchain technologies are their self-executing "smart contracts." A *smart contract* is a set of predetermined promises specified in a digital format. These promises function as the basis upon which the parties involved in a transaction fulfill their predetermined promises. A smart contract automatically pays a party once it completes its contractual duties. Since smart contracts are unique and incredibly complex, establishing whether they fit into the general framework of legal contract law is challenging.

Unfortunately, the United States does not have a federal contract law that applies to the nation. This means that contract law varies by state. Additionally, no federal law or specific guidance explicitly defines smart contracts or their legal validity. This situation is particularly concerning to businesses because the legality of smart contracts is unclear. Thus, smart contracts may result in lengthy litigation processes. The only exception is the Electronic Signatures in Global and National Commerce Act of 2000, providing limited legal validity to smart contracts.

Privacy Concerns

In the cryptocurrency space, privacy concerns are intertwined closely with data theft. A primary reason for introducing cryptocurrencies was to ensure individual and institutional users had the option of anonymity about transactions between users. However, as blockchain technology has continued to transform and adapt in recent years, analysts state the continuous improvement in blockchain analytic tools threatens anonymity. An excellent example is how KYC data and underlying blockchain technology are used to prove the provenance of digital assets.

Firms like Chainalysis demonstrate that they have access to blockchain analytic tools enabling them to trace most Dash and Zcash transactions (Kipilkov, 2020). This development has made using "privacy coins" the opposite of private, which concerns many. Furthermore, the United States does not have a comprehensive federal data protection framework, another privacy concern for those owning cryptoassets. Instead of a comprehensive framework, the United States has sector-specific privacy and data security laws and regulations. The existing US privacy and data security laws do not address the many privacy concerns resulting from blockchain technology. For example, a common belief is that P2P network architecture contradicts the California Consumer Privacy Act (CCPA) approach to a centralized controller-based processing system. The CCPA's controller-based processing system does not apply to cryptocurrencies because it is decentralized.

Tax Implications

Since cryptoassets like cryptocurrencies have become major players in the investment marketplace, numerous legal and regulatory questions appear worldwide. Indeed, cryptocurrencies and their innovative technologies can drastically change business processes, but blockchain's inherently decentralized nature can lead to sinister activity. This less than savory behavior challenges those tasked with upholding compliance with the law.

The IRS is cracking down on those non-compliant taxpayers who do not declare their income earned through cryptoassets. Additionally, the IRS is also investing other significant resources to combat what it believes will be potentially astounding levels of tax non-compliance surrounding the reporting of income associated with cryptoassets. The summons for account holder information from the American branch of the cryptocurrency exchange Coinbase highlight this move to more severe consequences for the individual and business crypto traders and investors.

Moreover, according to US federal income tax purposes, cryptocurrencies and other cryptoassets are not classified as currency but as property. Unfortunately, American taxpayers cannot use cryptocurrency as a functional currency for IRS code purposes. However, this does not mean that taxpayers should not report their transactions involving cryptocurrencies. According to the IRS, US taxpayers must report crypto transactions on their annual tax returns by determining the fair market value on each transaction date. Taxpayers often struggle with this compliance rule because correctly reporting various cryptoassets is burdensome since taxpayers must report each cryptoasset at the price they bought and sold it.

Furthermore, in the United States, authorities classify cryptocurrencies as capital assets. Consequently, individual investors must pay capital gains taxes on all profits they gain through cryptocurrencies. Unfortunately, this obligation applies regardless of whether someone purchased cryptocurrency from the United States or a foreign country. Nevertheless, the most significant issue surrounding tax reporting for institutions and investors is the lack of clarity about further reporting requirements when filing taxes.

Tax Accounting

Sizable tax liabilities exist on the sales or exchanges of cryptoassets. Still, many do not realize that they could bear significant tax accounting burdens associated with their holdings. The severity of these tax accounting burdens depends on the number and frequency of crypto transactions in which someone engages.

Since taxpayers must calculate and report gains or losses each time they complete a crypto transaction, reporting for tax purposes can quickly become convoluted and challenging. For example, those taxpayers who complete transactions at high volumes using a trading bot will need to account for each transaction. Likewise, those buying different products, like a cup of coffee or groceries with a crypto debit card, will quickly incur significant amounts of taxable income that they will need to report individually. Taxpayers must identify transactions relating to when a sale or exchange has been completed with crypto for a good or service because it is likely taxable. They will also need to report crypto transactions merely transferred into an account they control, like their wallet, because these transactions might not be taxable.

Moreover, each taxpayer may need to determine the dollar value for each transaction they complete, whether taxable or not taxable. Usually, determining the specific dollar value for the sales of cryptoassets for fiat currency is straightforward. However, the issue occurs when taxpayers need to establish the dollar value for exchanging crypto for other property.

Jurisdictional Issues

The primary concept behind blockchain technology that supports cryptocurrencies is that there is no way to pinpoint a ledger's location precisely. Thus, transactions completed on a blockchain offer greater privacy than those conducted on traditional platforms. Although this advantage may benefit many users, it presents a complex jurisdictional problem. Since a crypto transaction's location node usually appears in different jurisdictions, they could be conditional to various conflicting legal frameworks. In addition, determining a residence country for various cryptocurrency software is incredibly difficult because a ledger lacks a physical location.

Lastly, determining the applicable laws alongside the correct jurisdiction concerning blockchain disputes is increasingly difficult because of a blockchain's transnational nature. Ultimately, enforcing laws among blockchain users and crypto projects and transactions is difficult for most national regulators because of the cross-border reach of blockchain technologies.

Financial Fraud and Data Theft

Two issues facing institutions wanting to use cryptoassets are financial fraud and data theft. Institutions frequently find adopting blockchain technology and cryptoasset trading challenging because the blockchain promises anonymity and apparent freedoms surrounding regulations. Institutions may not want to risk trusting a financial partner using blockchain technology because of the illegal activities undertaken with cryptocurrencies, particularly financial transactions.

Two real-world examples of financial fraud and data theft in the cryptoasset space have heightened institutional concerns surrounding the use of cryptoassets. First, in 2017 a researcher at Cornell University identified a significant security flaw in the Ethereum blockchain. This security flaw placed $250 million at risk of theft. Second, the crypto wallet maker Ledger recently compromised about 1 million email addresses when a data security breach occurred. During this breach, hackers stole the postal addresses, full names, and phone numbers of the company's 9,500 customers. Whether existing data laws can address financial fraud and data theft concerning cryptoassets remains unclear.

Money Laundering

Another critical issue facing institutions wanting to use cryptoassets is money laundering. Numerous experts suggest that cryptocurrencies provide criminal and disreputable organizations with the means to commit money laundering, fraud, and other financial crimes. This criticism stems from a cryptocurrency trader's unique ability to remain anonymous. Dark market sites use cryptocurrency advancements. These sites are where criminals buy and sell illegal goods and services anonymously with minimal chance of being identified. Various governmental agencies label drug dealers exchanging drugs for cryptocurrencies as the "new generation" of criminals.

Unquestionable proof shows criminal entities using cryptocurrencies to complete nefarious transactions. In 2019, the analytics firm Chainalysis specializing in blockchains, estimated about $2.8 billion in transactions on bitcoin exchanges by criminals (Chainalysis Team, 2020). Previously, criminals had to convert their cryptocurrency earnings into liquid cash, and the exchange's uses for this purpose have strict AML in place. These rules require firms to identify their clients. Unfortunately, according to Chainalysis, criminals could use over-the-counter trading to bypass these AML rules. This situation presents a unique problem that experts may not resolve soon.

The Legal and Regulatory Concerns for Cryptoasset Investors

Cryptoasset investors face a multitude of legal and regulatory concerns. Bitcoin and other prominent cryptocurrencies are usually permitted in the United States and most other developed nations like Japan, Canada, and the United Kingdom. Nevertheless, despite their legal status and the IRS considering bitcoin and most other digital currencies legal, concerns still surround their legal validity. Their legal validity is in question because no centralized issuing authority backs them. Additionally, intrinsic goods like gold or silver do not back virtual currencies. Thus, nothing underlies a cryptocurrency's value. Most institutional investors find investing in cryptoassets difficult because their value depends on the value investors ascribe to them. Moreover, investors often do not want to risk investing in cryptoassets, given the lack of backing from a centralized authority. They also have few, if any, legal resources readily available to them. Consequently, investors could face substantial problems if any complications arise regarding ownership and transactions.

Fork Management and Governance

An unresolved area is the tax treatment and other issues involving cryptocurrency forks. *Bitcoin cash* is a cryptocurrency created in August 2017 from a fork of bitcoin. *Bitcoin gold* is a cryptocurrency also resulting from a hard fork of bitcoin. For example, does a taxpayer declare earning bitcoin cash or bitcoin gold as income? Most believe that bitcoin cash would be taxable as income, but bitcoin gold is a gift, so would that be taxable?

Moreover, what about the timing surrounding when income is recognizable? Whether cryptocurrency income is taxable depends on a cryptocurrency's exercise and control before the fork. Many wonder whether they realize income from blockchain splits. The IRS needs to provide more guidance and governance on this topic because cryptocurrency forks may become more common.

Foreign Asset Reporting

Institutions are often partial to holding foreign assets. One of their key concerns is the issue surrounding foreign asset reporting. Currently, taxpayers who possess cryptocurrency on a foreign-based exchange could be subject to filling out the Financial Crimes Enforcement Network (FinCEN) Form 114, the sometimes-confusing Report of Foreign Bank and Financial Accounts (FBAR), or Form 8938. The confusion is that a taxpayer may not know which form to submit.

This situation is even more confusing because, according to FinCEN regulatory guidance associated with FBARs, no requirement exists for investors to report virtual currency accounts on an FBAR. However, FinCEN states that such accounts might require reporting in the future. Moreover, considering the IRS's continued efforts in international tax enforcement and the various severe penalties, taxpayers should exercise caution. An exception is if an investor holds cryptoassets alongside other financial assets in a reportable account under 31

CFR 1010.50. Taxpayers will ultimately benefit by reporting foreign exchange accounts unless the IRS indicates explicitly that reporting such accounts is unnecessary.

Financial Accounting and Reporting

Finally, institutions face the issue of dealing with financial accounting and reporting requirements. The American Institute of Certified Public Accountants, Public Company Accounting Oversight Board, authorized by the United States Security and Exchange Commission (SEC), or the International Financial Reporting Standards issued limited nonauthoritative guidance on cryptoassets.

To understand the financial accounting and reporting issues with cryptoassets, management and auditors need to analyze the underlying blockchain technology that affects custody, provenance, and reporting. If an institution uses a third-party service provider as its custodian, management and the auditors would want to obtain a Service Organization Compliance Report Type I or Type II. These reports should focus primarily on procedures and controls regarding the handling of public and private keys and the confidentiality, integrity, and availability of data. In addition, the reports should provide knowledge on procedures, controls, and transactions that affect the financial statements. Should the cryptoasset be reported on the institution's balance sheet if held by a custodian? Management and auditors should determine who controls the digital asset by asking probing questions and reviewing the agreements of the custodian and institutions. The answer to these questions will determine if these assets should appear on the balance sheet of the institution or custodian.

Cryptoassets use cryptography for registration on a distributed network such as a blockchain and are immutable. Often immutability is mistaken for what is true. A transaction registered on a blockchain reflects that this transaction exists without providing evidence for the underlying rationale. For example, if a blockchain transaction reflects payment for acquiring a building, the institution and auditors should verify that a notarial deed substantiates this transaction. Such audit verification techniques should be applied for most transactions where institutions use cryptoassets as a medium of exchange. Careful consideration should be given to the underlying type of transaction (i.e., the cryptoasset involved) to determine the correct validation steps substantiating provenance. What underlying event triggered this transaction to be recognized and recorded on the blockchain? This should be a critical question toward establishing provenance for blockchain transactions.

Various types of cryptoassets are available, such as cryptocurrencies, NFTs, stablecoins, and central bank digital currencies. Regarding reporting, identical or similar cryptoassets must be processed and reported consistently. This task can be challenging as new cryptoasset variants often enter the market and existing constructions expand or change. Under current nonauthoritative guidance, most cryptoassets are reported as intangible assets. However, the specific type of cryptoasset and industry in which the institution operates, like an investment company, can trigger other classifications. Therefore, professional skepticism requires determining the best accounting treatment based on specific facts and circumstances.

Summary and Conclusions

This chapter reviewed various issues faced by institutions wanting to use cryptoassets, including custody, provenance, and reporting. Furthermore, it examined various regulatory reporting concerns and tax compliance issues institutions could encounter when using cryptoassets as a medium of exchange or financial intermediary. By understanding these fundamental concerns, such as the contractual issues, tax implications, and foreign asset reporting issues discussed, an institution can determine if investing in cryptoassets is a viable option. Although these issues are complex and are unlikely to be resolved shortly, the IRS, governments, and other regulatory bodies are taking steps to address them and provide guidance. Blockchain technology could play an instrumental role in numerous industries and acquire higher adoption rates among institutional users if these entities take appropriate action.

Discussion Questions

1. Summarize the issues around institutions using cryptoassets in custody, provenance, and reporting.
2. List the key takeaways from the Infrastructure Act coming into effect in 2024.
3. Explain the best custody option for institutions holding cryptoassets.
4. Identify three issues institutions wanting to use cryptoassets face and explain why they are important.
5. Identify several financial reporting issues institutions face to account for cryptoassets.

References

Beringer, A., Biben, M. L., & Day, M. K. (2021, November 18). *Infrastructure bill's new reporting requirements may have sweeping implications for cryptocurrency ecosystem*. Gibson Dunn. Retrieved from https://www.gibsondunn.com/infrastructure-bills-new-reporting-requirements-may-have-sweeping-implications-for-cryptocurrencye-cosystem/

Blockdata. (2022). Crypto custody: The gateway to institutional adoption. Retrieved from https://download.blockdata.tech/BLOCKDATA-Crypto-Custody-The-Gateway-to-Institutional-Adoption-VF.pdf

Bonner, P. (2022, February 15). Revised voluntary disclosure form highlights cryptoassets. *Journal of Accountancy*. Retrieved from https://www.journalofaccountancy.com/news/2022/feb/revised-voluntary-disclosure-form-highlights-cryptoassets.html

Caruso, J. (2018, October 29). *KYC and cryptoasset provenance*. KPMG. Retrieved from https://home.kpmg/us/en/home/insights/2018/11/kyc-cryptoasset-provenance.html

Chainalysis Team. (2020, January 15). *Crypto money laundering: How criminals cash out billions in bitcoin and other cryptocurrencies*. Chainalysis. Retrieved from https://blog.chainalysis.com/reports/crypto-laundering/

ELEV8 (2019, September 19). Blockchain provenance—tracking everything from art to disease. Retrieved from https://www.elev8con.com/blockchain-provenance-tracking-everything-from-art-to-disease/

Kipilkov, M. (2020, June 8). *Chainalysis can now track your ''privacy coins' Zcash & Dash*. CoinTelegraph. Retrieved from https://cointelegraph.com/news/chainalysis-can-now-track-your-privacy-coins-zcash-dash

KPMG. (2020, November). *Institutionalization of cryptoassets*. KPMG White Paper. Retrieved from https://assets.kpmg/content/dam/kpmg/us/pdf/2018/11/institutionalization-cryptoassets.pdf

Polizzano, B. (2018, October 1). *Cryptocurrency: Compliance challenges and IRS enforcement*. The Tax Advisor. Retrieved from https://www.thetaxadviser.com/issues/2018/oct/cryptocurrency-compliance-challenges-irs-enforcement.html

Pratt, M. K. (2021, June 2). *Top 10 benefits of blockchain technology for business*. TechTarget. Retrieved from https://www.techtarget.com/searchcio/feature/Top-10-benefits-of-blockchain-technology-for-business

Smith, P., & Srivastava, N. (2020, June). *A market overview of custody for digital assets*. Digital Custodian Whitepaper, Deloitte. Retrieved from https://www2.deloitte.com/content/dam/Deloitte/xe/Documents/finance/me_Digital-Custodian-Whitepaper.pdf

Chapter 17

Tokenized and Non-tokenized Assets: Legal Considerations

Brett Cotler

Abstract

This chapter discusses legal considerations relating to digital assets. The legal aspects of tokenized and non-tokenized assets are evolving. Although some states have enacted specific laws or regulations for digital assets, Congress and federal agencies have been slower to craft specific rules and regulations for such assets. As a result, regulators, such as the Securities and Exchange Commission, Commodity Futures Trading Commission, and Internal Revenue Service, and market participants must apply existing guidance to digital assets. This chapter examines applying specific aspects of federal securities and tax law to digital assets. It also discusses general business law considerations for blockchain and cyber enterprises. The discussion of state law applications centers on the New York Virtual Currency License and Wyoming and Delaware crypto initiatives. This chapter does not provide a comprehensive review of all legal issues related to cryptocurrency. Each legal issue about cryptocurrency is complex and requires separate analyses.

Keywords: Digital assets; tokenized assets; non-tokenized assets; federal securities law; tax law; blockchain

Introduction

Before discussing the law, understanding the "who, what, when, where, and why" of a digital asset is paramount. Investors should know what they are entitled to receive. Issuers need to understand their obligations to regulators and investors. Understanding the facts involves several lines of inquiry: (1) the parties (the "who" and "where"); (2) tokenomics (the "why"); (3) marketing and offering (the "how," "when," and "where"); (4) business structuring considerations (the "what"), and (5) whether the parties kept their promises.

The Emerald Handbook on Cryptoassets: Investment Opportunities and Challenges, 249–263

doi:10.1108/978-1-80455-320-620221017

The first section describes the various parties of a business transaction involving digital assets, followed by fundamental business questions about digital assets. The following sections discuss securities law considerations, specifically offering and marketing digital assets, business structuring and tax considerations, and New York and Wyoming digital asset regulations. The final section provides a summary and conclusions.

Who are the Players?

The first step in understanding digital assets, specifically tokenized and non-tokenized assets, is knowing the main parties. This task involves asking the following questions.

- Who or what is creating and issuing the digital asset?
- Does the issuer have a legal personality or is the token issuer a decentralized non-entity?
- In what jurisdictions are the token issuer and its sponsor incorporated or resident?
- Does a centralized or decentralized protocol govern the digital asset?
- Who are the potential regulators?
- Who receives the tokens? That is, who are the investors?

The Issuer

Entrepreneurs may create a project involving some element of crypto. Who are the entrepreneurs and innovators? Who is the business team? People often invest in a project based on the reputations of those behind it. High-quality people and business partners provide comfort to investors, regulators, and customers. Teams with business experience may be better suited to run a business than a group of wunderkinds who can solve technical problems but not adequately manage people or finances. A 20-year-old virtuoso with a vision and the ability to execute that vision may be better suited when paired with a 50-year-old chief executive officer with decades of experience.

Another issue involves the legal entity formed for this new business. Deciding on the type of entity requires tax planning and choosing where to incorporate it. States typically allow someone to establish a limited liability company (LLC) for less than $200. LLCs are attractive because they provide tax flexibility, economic flexibility, and the legal liability protection of a corporation but with fewer corporate formalities. Although many choose LLCs, some should weigh other business forms' benefits and considerations, such as limited partnerships and corporations.

Tax structuring is also incredibly important at this stage. Taxes affect the type of entity, as corporations have *double taxation*. A domestic corporation pays a corporate-level tax on its taxable income. Its shareholders pay tax on dividends paid by the corporation. Besides federal taxation, corporations also pay income and franchise taxes to states and certain cities where the corporation is incorporated and does business. Finally, taxes affect the decision to incorporate offshore or stay in the United States.

Deciding where to form entities is another critical decision. State laws differ. Some states are more business- or crypto-friendly than others. Suppose someone creates an entity outside the state where that person lives or maintains an office. In that case, the person should hire a company to function as a registered agent in the state of incorporation. This additional expense can be at least several hundred dollars. When forming new companies, many lawyers reflexively incorporate in Delaware.

However, a prudent approach is to look first to the state where the company's principals are located to avoid registered agent expenses or incorporate in Wyoming, a crypto-friendly state. Delaware and Nevada are popular states for incorporation because they do not impose a state-level tax on out-of-state activities, offer a well-developed body of corporate law, and may offer some degree of anonymity to shareholders. However, other states may provide a legal advantage unavailable elsewhere. For instance, Wyoming has engaged in several crypto-friendly laws. South Dakota is a popular jurisdiction to form trust companies for financial institutions' crypto custody. Regardless of where incorporation occurs, a company should generally qualify to do business in each state where it conducts business activities.

Investors

This section discusses two investor categories: early investors and token investors. A detailed discussion of venture capital (VC) investments into start-ups is beyond this section's scope. VC deals involve a high level of negotiation. Often the non-economic terms are as crucial to a start-up's success as is capital infusion. Non-monetary benefits include bringing in board members, creating synergies with other companies in which a VC firm invests, and providing mentorship, oversight, and management.

Early Investors. Start-ups need money to incorporate, pay outside advisors (e.g., legal, tax, accounting, and audit fees), acquire resources, and pay for outsourced items (e.g., developers and marketers). These costs can quickly get into hundreds of thousands of dollars and are necessary to get to an actual early round of funding from seed investors.

When the founders exhaust their capital, they look to friends and family. Investors at this stage invest in stock and usually other securities, such as warrants, preferred stock, or forward contracts. When an entity issues a digital asset, these early investors typically get a significant amount upon issuance. However, these are generally small investments, in the thousands or tens of thousands of dollars. But if a start-up attracts considerable attention, these early investments could be worth millions or billions.

These offerings should be exempt from registration under the Securities Act of 1933 under Rule 504 or Rule 506 of Regulation D. Under either type of exempt offering, 35 or fewer non-accredited investors can raise capital. Unlike Rule 504 offerings, offerings under Rule 506 allow for general solicitation and no limit to the funds obtained from accredited investors. However, Rule 506 offerings require additional disclosure. Therefore, raising funds from friends and family under Rule 504 may be more accessible, despite certain limitations.

A start-up may need to raise additional capital at a certain point. After the friends and family round, a company may attempt to raise a *series A round of funding*, a private offering to accredited investors, including angel investors and VC firms. These investors may also seek to be high in the capital stack, with common and preferred stock, and have access to the digital assets once the funding round launches. This round of funding is typically a private offering, exempt from registration under Rule 506 of Regulation D.

Token Investors. Determining who the token investors are can be a function of the digital asset and its *tokenomics*, which is the study of the economics of crypto tokens or cryptocurrencies. One potential investor category in a digital asset is a future customer, who may view the investment as buying a future product or service at a discount. Another investor category is a true investor, who sees value in a digital asset or promise in the start-up. A third investor category is a speculator. A speculator may invest in a token when it trades at pennies, hoping it catches on in the pages of Reddit or another online community and takes off "to the moon" in the parlance of such fora.

How or where a token trades may affect who invests. If an investor needs to convert dollars to ether (ETH) to Binance coin (BNB) and then BNB into an obscure digital asset, the investor may only be a crypto enthusiast and not an average investor. A final investor category is the average retail investor, who wants economic exposure without maintaining wallets and private keys. This investor may invest in an exchange-traded fund or a private fund that trades crypto. A retail investor may also own bitcoin through a traditional brokerage or Coinbase account.

Regulators

Regulators depend on where the company is formed and does business, the token issuer's business type, whether the digital asset is a security, and how the digital asset is issued. For instance, crypto companies in New York may need to apply for a BitLicense. New York's BitLicense applies to different crypto organizations, including those transmitting crypto, buying and selling cryptocurrency as a customer business, providing exchange services to customers, and issuing cryptocurrency. Crypto exchanges must also register and make filings with the Securities and Exchange Commission (SEC) and the Financial Industry Regulatory Authority (FINRA). Money transmitters must deal with each state having money transmission rules where they have customers. Selling tokens in a private offering (e.g., Reg D to accredited investors) or public offering (e.g., Reg A) requires the issuer to make certain filings to the SEC or state securities regulators (e.g., SEC Form D).

An essential item to consider is federal preemption. A start-up often must deal with a federal regulator, such as the SEC, instead of state regulators. However, suppose a start-up does not involve a federal regulator. In that case, that entity may have to deal with up to 50 state regulators and attorney generals. Although a start-up may not want to contend with the SEC, doing so may be strategic because it does not have to make individual filings in multiple states and comply with up to 50 state laws.

Service Providers

Crypto start-ups rely on outside advisers and service providers. For example, law firms incorporate businesses, draft operating agreements, employment agreements, investor documents, represent clients before regulators, prepare applications for business licenses and regulatory approvals, and structure businesses for tax efficiency. Accounting firms prepare tax returns, maintain financial books, prepare financial statements, and can help a start-up manage its business. Third-party services providers may include:

- external consultants to lobby the government;
- outside developers for coding;
- financial institutions to serve as custodians of digital assets or assist with "know your customer" (KYC) and anti-money laundering (AML) compliance;
- cybersecurity specialists;
- marketing; and
- investment bankers and other placement agents to help sell the digital asset.

A start-up must pay these service providers and establish a relationship governed under an appropriate contract. Here are a few guidelines between these two parties. First, a start-up company should usually own any work product developed by outside contractors. Third-party developers should not retain ownership of any code they wrote for hire.

Second, a start-up may be held liable for the actions of its service providers. If a social media influencer says, "Your investment will increase 10-fold," the SEC will have accessible evidence in its action against the start-up.

Finally, if a start-up pays a service provider in tokens, both the employer and service face tax, regulatory, and business issues. A discussion of these tax issues follows. From a business perspective, some service providers, such as law and accounting firms, want to receive fiat currency or highly liquid crypto for their services. Furthermore, in certain circumstances, insiders may be restricted in how they trade their employer's securities.

Tokenomics

As previously noted, *tokenomics* refers to the economics of a digital asset. At its most basic level, tokenomics means the business deal between the issuer and token holders. From a business perspective, the token offering must be worthwhile for investors. From a legal perspective, a clear understanding of the business terms of a digital asset sale may reduce legal costs. Therefore, tokenomics is important for crypto businesses when selling digital assets.

Without understanding tokenomics, lawyers may inadequately describe the digital asset in an offering prospectus, and ambiguities in offering documents may lead to investor confusion. Investors that feel wronged may sue the issuer or report the issuer to a regulator. Viewing a situation from an investor's viewpoint could help prevent future litigation. Crypto businesses and their lawyers that think about tokenomics should consider the following:

- What are the digital asset issuer's obligations and entitlements to the purchaser?
- Does a built-in economic benefit exist to owning the digital asset (i.e., the holder can redeem it for something of value), or is the potential return based only on the premise that the digital asset will appreciate given its speculative nature?
- Is the deal fair and balanced for all parties?
- Does the digital asset utility value? Can it redeem or use the tokens for goods or services with intrinsic value? How are the digital assets used or redeemed?

If an issuer can answer these questions, it may reduce the likelihood of a dispute with investors. It may also reduce the time lawyers need to understand the digital asset, adequately describe it in offering materials, and lead to corresponding savings in legal costs. As discussed in the next section, clearly defined tokenomics can also assist marketing efforts.

Marketing and Securities Law Considerations

A digital asset's marketing could have significant legal ramifications. Although a digital asset may not be a security, it could be a security offering. The SEC is active in policing these matters.

Since 2013, the SEC has brought over 75 cases against defendants relating to digital assets and initial coin offerings (ICOs), with only 11 cases brought before 2018 (Securities and Exchange Commission, 2021). In addition, at least 20 trading suspension cases involve digital assets.

The first case *SEC* v. *Shavers et al.* (2013), brought in 2013, alleged a Ponzi scheme involving bitcoin instead of dollars. Specifically, a federal judge ruled that the operator of Bitcoin Savings and Trust had operated a Ponzi scheme that defrauded investors. The judge awarded $40.7 million in damages following SEC charges of investment fraud. The crime alleged in the *Shavers* case was not a "crypto-crime." Instead, crypto was the medium used to commit the crime.

Since this first case, the SEC has brought enforcement actions that involved:

- the unregistered offering of securities, including ICOs, security token offerings (STOs), and the like, and including crypto lending and decentralized finance (DeFi) investment programs;
- operating online venues for trading securities using digital assets without registering the websites as broker-dealers or stock exchanges and other unregistered broker-dealers;
- defrauding investors in ICOs and the like;
- obtaining cease and desist orders where a company was selling digital tokens in an unregistered offering to investors and other violations of various US federal securities laws;
- additional digital asset denominated Ponzi schemes and other general fraud denominated in cryptocurrency, and disgorgement actions for selling restricted stock in a blockchain technology company at market price and not the fixed price under a registration statement;
- false marketing of a crypto-focused investment fund;

- misleading promotion of an ICO without proper disclosure;
- obtaining a cease-and-desist where a CEO misrepresented the use of proceeds of securities offer to invest in blockchain companies and digital assets; and
- market manipulation, including charging an iced tea company with stock manipulation by falsely stating it was pivoting into crypto.

Besides actions against issuers, promotors, and other bad actors, the SEC also released valuable guidance to the industry in the form of an investigative report – the DAO report (Securities and Exchange Commission, 2017) – and public speeches at industry events – notably a speech by SEC Director William Hinman (2018). Although this guidance is non-binding, issuers should understand how the SEC views cryptocurrency and how issuers and legal counsel can analyze whether a digital asset is a security and whether the offering is a securities offering.

Whether a digital asset is a security for federal securities law purposes depends partly on whether it is an investment contract. Under the Howey Test (*SEC* v. *Howey*, 1946), a transaction is an investment contract if:

- there is an investment of money;
- there is an expectation of profits from the investment;
- the investment of money is in a common enterprise; and
- any profit comes from the efforts of a promoter or third party.

The latter two elements generated considerable discussion among securities lawyers in the cryptocurrency context. Assume that bitcoin's price is market-driven and bitcoin transactions are verified through mining. However, does that satisfy the element requiring profits coming from the efforts of others? Most attorneys say no.

In the DAO report, the SEC analyzed whether tokens issued by a decentralized, autonomous organization might have been securities. For reference, a corporation or other business entity traditionally issues stock and other securities. The DAO is a "virtual" organization embodied in computer code and executed on a blockchain. The DAO sold tokens, intending to use the token sale proceeds to fund various projects and profit from them, thereby giving value to the DAO tokens. In applying the Howey Test, the SEC concluded that investors gave money to a common enterprise (i.e., the DAO) with a reasonable expectation of profit derived predominantly from the managerial efforts of others.

The DAO's facts are less important than the analysis applying the Howey Test to cryptocurrency. This analysis put the industry on notice of the SEC's litigating position. The conversation developed and distinguished between investment or security tokens, which authorities generally regarded as securities for federal securities law purposes, and utility tokens. Unlike security tokens, usually intended to offer only investment value, utility tokens offer holders non-investment value. Utility tokens might be redeemed for goods or services or used on a platform for the services provided. Could that non-investment-related value be enough to cause a digital asset not to be classified as a security?

SEC Director Hinman offered his view on this subject in a public speech. Hinman's view was that investors purchased digital assets with an expectation of profit derived from the efforts of others, regardless of any utility value of the digital asset. In Hinman's opinion, ether was not a security, but it might have been a security at its issuance. Hinman pointed to "sufficient decentralization" to indicate that something could be a security and lose its character as such as it develops. A digital asset only used on the platform where created could be viewed differently, even if its initial offering was a security offering.

Finally, Hinman identified several non-exhaustive factors to consider when determining whether a digital asset is a security. What are the roles of the sponsors and promotors? Did the sponsors retain a financial interest in the digital asset and remain incentivized to increase the digital asset's value? What are investors seeking when acquiring the digital asset? For example, are they seeking a return on their investment? Who controls the issuing entity? Does applying the Securities Act make sense?

Many in the industry latched onto Hinman's remarks. However, they were just one senior SEC official's view, not its official stance. If nothing else, Hinman's speech provided valuable insights to help determine whether a digital asset offering might be a security offering.

Digital Asset Offerings Under Regulation A of the Securities Act

On July 10, 2019, the SEC granted qualification to Blockstack Token LLC's sale of $28 million worth of digital tokens to the public under the SEC's Regulation A registration exemption (Blockstack Token LLC, 2019). This offering was the first-ever SEC-compliant public sale of securities tokens in the United States.

Congress amended Regulation A under the Securities Act of 1933 as part of the Jumpstart Our Business Startups Act of 2012. Many now call it "Regulation A+." Regulation A allows companies to raise up to $50 million in 12 months without the burden of the full range of disclosure obligations that come with a traditional initial public offering.

Until this approval, companies wanting to sell tokens that are securities could not do so, except in private sales under Regulation D of the Securities Act or a different exemption from the registration requirement of the Securities Act. Although this approach permits token sellers to raise funds, many token platforms are designed with tokenomics requiring freely tradeable tokens. Tokens sold according to Regulation D are not freely tradeable for the first year. By offering and selling tokens under Regulation A+, Blockstack can sell freely tradeable tokens to the public.

The day the SEC qualified Blockstack's Regulation A offer, it also qualified another Regulation A offering, YouNow, Inc.'s offering of up to 178 million Props Tokens. These tokens can reward users for in-app activities, administration, blockchain development, and subsequent sale to the public (YouNow, Inc., 2019). However, Regulation A offerings are limited to no more than $50 million annually (so-called "Tier 2" offerings). Any registrant wanting to register a larger amount of securities for sale must do so through a full-blown registration process. No one has successfully registered a token offering under that process.

Structuring Crypto Businesses: Tax, Legal, and Regulatory Considerations

At this point, entrepreneurs can communicate to their lawyers about what the business does or will do, where it operates, its owners and investors, customers to be served, and other pertinent information. This information is key to determining: (1) an efficient tax structure; (2) what licenses or registrations or exemptions from registrations need to be filed; (3) what key documents are needed; and (4) what else lawyers and other advisers need to do to help establish the business.

Tax Structuring

All crypto businesses are just businesses, and general tax planning considerations apply to crypto and traditional companies almost equally. This section discusses cryptocurrency taxation, specific token offerings, and tax considerations for structuring crypto start-ups.

Crypto Taxation. Image the following situation. A lawyer was on a conference call with a client who planned to launch a cryptocurrency-focused hedge fund. As the lawyer explained specific rules around in-kind contributions of bitcoin and ether, the client interjects, "But where in the tax code are cryptocurrencies mentioned? There are no rules right now!" The client learned that US federal income tax authorities and general tax principles apply to transactions in cryptocurrency.

The seminal piece of guidance is Internal Revenue Service (IRS) Notice 2014-21. The IRS released this notice before the Ethereum network's launch, but after the launch of Litecoin, Dogecoin, Ripple, and about a dozen others. In this notice, the IRS stated that cryptocurrencies readily convertible into fiat currency should be treated as property and not as currency. This ruling means that:

- special rules that apply to foreign currency transactions do not apply to crypto;
- if crypto is held as a capital asset, gains upon a sale would be capital gains;
- mining crypto by an individual was self-employment income;
- businesses that accept crypto as payment for goods or services must include crypto's fair market value in income as they received cash, and such amount was the business's tax basis in the crypto;
- employees and other service providers compensated in crypto must take the crypto into account for purposes of computing their income taxes and payroll or self-employment taxes; and
- general tax principles should be applied to crypto transactions without further guidance.

Although helpful, many unanswered questions remain. One issue involves valuation. Cryptos trade at different prices on different exchanges. Due to high volatility, an hour's difference could mean significant tax savings or tax costs.

Second, tax uncertainties exist when trading cryptos for other cryptos. For instance, a lack of clarity exists about whether crypto-for-crypto trades are eligible for tax deferral under section 1031 of the Internal Revenue Code of 1986, as amended. This section allowed for tax-deferred sales of real estate and property used in a trade or business. In 2017, section 1031 applied only to real estate. The IRS also came out in FAQs on its website that this section did not apply to crypto-for-crypto trades for tax years before 2018. This pronouncement was noteworthy at the time because few people reported their crypto gains. If the IRS had audited this issue, crypto traders might have had a large tax bill. Additionally, tracking is a complicated issue because investors may buy cryptos at different times and price points, trade cryptos for other cryptos, and trade one crypto at different prices on various exchanges. Additionally, some cryptos do not have a readily determinable US dollar equivalent. Some taxpayers may be unaware of these tax issues and trade crypto without keeping these records.

Third, the crypto space was rapidly evolving, and the IRS was largely silent on new developments. Hedge funds began trading crypto, which meant more investors and questions, including:

- Would a non-US domiciled hedge fund's crypto trading activities constitute a US trade or business for US federal income tax purposes?
- Could hedge funds or individual traders make a mark-to-market election on crypto?
- Firms tried to launch exchange-traded crypto funds to expand access to retail investors. Could these funds be structured as grantor trusts, publicly traded partnerships, or mutual funds?
- Investors could buy and trade bitcoin futures. Did wash sales and straddle rules apply to bitcoin specifically and crypto generally?
- New blockchain start-ups attempted to raise capital with token issuances in ICOs or STOs. What are the consequences to the issuing company?

Besides these questions, vast uncertainty prevailed as to how the tax authorities would treat smart contacts, airdrops, hard forks, DeFi, the tokenization of assets, and centralized bank decentralized currencies for tax purposes. Tax attorneys and certified public accountants had to determine reasonable tax positions without additional guidance when dealing with these and other issues.

Further guidance occurred in 2019 in Revenue Ruling 2019-24. In this ruling, the IRS provided advice on the federal income tax treatment of cryptocurrency received in an airdrop or a hard fork. A person receives tokens in an airdrop, usually because of existing ownership of another token. A hard fork occurs when a cryptocurrency on a blockchain undergoes a protocol change resulting in a permanent diversion from the legacy blockchain. The legacy cryptocurrency's owners receive units of the progeny cryptocurrency. The IRS stated that cryptocurrency received in an airdrop or a hard fork was a taxable event. Also, the value of the crypto received was ordinary income. A taxable event occurs when a taxpayer can sell the crypto received. Suppose a taxpayer's wallet does not support the crypto received in the airdrop or hard fork. In that case, the taxable event might occur days or weeks later, when the crypto might have significantly appreciated.

Given the scarcity of official IRS guidance, tax advisers must apply general tax principles to crypto. The tax positions related to acquiring, holding, or selling cryptocurrency depend on the transaction's specific facts. Some cryptocurrencies look and act more like gift cards that some can use to purchase services or goods from the crypto's issuer. Others look and act more like a transactional medium of exchange (currency). Still, other cryptos resemble financial products. How an issuer and taxpayer use crypto helps determine the tax consequences related to its ownership and sale.

- If a person buys cryptocurrency as an investment, the IRS taxes the gains from its sale as capital gains.
- If a person is a crypto dealer or otherwise uses it in a trade or business, gains from the sale of cryptocurrency are ordinary income.
- If someone uses crypto to pay for goods or services, the IRS taxes the person on the difference between that person's basis in the crypto and the value of the goods or services received.

Token Offerings

From a US federal income tax perspective, the economic rights and obligations of issuers and holders of digital assets are paramount in determining the proper tax treatment. According to Code sections 721(a) and 1032, a company's issuance of debt or equity does not generally recognize taxable income to the company. However, the sale of other property by a company does result in taxable income. Before 2018, the US federal corporate income tax rate was 35 percent. Authorities lowered the corporate tax rate beginning in 2018 to 21 percent. Consequently, an improperly structured ICO might have only been 65–79 percent effective after taxes.

Assuming the tokens were not characterized as debt or equity for US federal income tax purposes, the recognition of taxable income might not occur on day one. In early ICOs, issuers sold tokens before their creation and issuance under a "simple agreement for future tokens" ("SAFT"). For US federal income tax purposes, US issuers of tokens under a SAFT usually would not recognize income until token delivery. In addition, if the tokens were like gift cards, in the sense that the tokens entitled the holder to some future benefit from the issuer, the holder could elect to recognize income for US tax purposes during the subsequent tax year.

As mentioned previously, the issuance of debt and equity does not result in taxable income to the issuer. However, Delaware allows issuing equity on a blockchain. Tokenized equity issued by a Delaware corporation should typically be regarded as equity in a corporation for tax purposes. The analysis is unclear when a digital asset is not issued as tokenized equity or a tokenized debt instrument but may be treated as such.

Whether an instrument is a debt or equity for US federal income tax purposes depends on the facts and circumstances. A token can potentially be characterized as equity for US federal income tax purposes under certain circumstances: it is perpetual, has voting rights, has economic exposure to the issuer's growth or negative growth, and offers a right to distribute ongoing profits. The issuer typically makes this determination, which is binding on the investors, whether by statute or by contract.

Alternatively, characterizing a token as indebtedness for US federal income tax purposes may be possible if it has a limited term, offers little upside (i.e., interest payments that are not contingent on profits) and downside protection (i.e., principal protection), provides for a lump-sum or series of distributions and contains other signs of debt. The unconditional obligation to pay interest and repay the principal by a fixed maturity date is a hallmark of debt instruments. The right of token holders to enforce payment of principal and interest in the event of default indicates that the token is more likely to be characterized as debt for tax purposes. Understanding all economic terms regarding a digital asset is vital in determining how to describe a digital asset for tax purposes.

Crypto Business Structuring Considerations

New businesses must consider legal and tax factors from day one. The failure to consider liability protection, governance and capitalization flexibility, and taxes could be costly later in a business's life. Poor corporate structuring could result in costly litigation between founders or key employees, and inadequate tax planning could mean forgone tax savings.

Choice of Entity Considerations

A crypto start-up can be established as an LLC. LLCs offer incredibly flexible governance (member-management or an appointed manager). For example, they can allocate income and expenses similar to partnerships but limit their members' liability similar to a corporation. LLCs are also flexible from a tax perspective. Multi-member LLCs are partnerships for income tax purposes. However, they can elect to be a C or an S corporation for federal income tax purposes. By contrast, domestic corporations have corporate formalities, can only be taxed as a C or an S corporation, and offer less flexibility to get the right economics to their shareholders. For this reason, an LLC is a popular choice for a start-up business.

A US-based business can be taxed as a pass-through entity, such as a partnership or an S or C corporation, for tax purposes. Although a discussion of partnership-S and corporation-C corporations is beyond this section's scope, this section discusses one ownership benefit of qualified small business corporations (QSBCs).

Qualified Small Business Stock Considerations

If a company qualifies as a QSBC, each shareholder can exclude gain on the sale by meeting a five-year holding period. The amount of gain excluded from income is the greater of $10 million or 10 times the shareholder's tax basis in the QSBS stock. The requirements for this tax benefit generally are:

- The company was formed in the United States and classified as a C corporation for tax purposes.
- The taxpayer disposing of the QSBC stock must have acquired the stock at its original issuance for money, property other than stock in the issuer, or services provided to the company.

- The gross value of the company's assets is less than $50 million before and immediately after the stock issuance.
- At least 80 percent of the company's assets are used in the active conduct of one or more qualified trades or businesses, including research and development activities.
- Certain tax filings occur.

Structuring a business as a QSBC offers benefits to founders and investors. VC and private equity investors have realized most of the tax savings attributable to QSBS stock investment.

Equity-based or Token-based Compensation Considerations

Many start-up businesses want to attract and reward key employees by issuing tokens or equity. Issuing property for services is generally taxable. The issuing company must value the equity or tokens on their issuance date and determine and remit applicable withholding taxes, such as payroll taxes for employees. The service provider must take such value into account as income.

Suppose the issuance of tokens or equity is subject to a vesting schedule (i.e., if the vesting conditions are not satisfied, the tokens are forfeited). In that case, the taxable event occurs at the earliest of the following dates: (1) the date the service provider freely transfers the property to a third party, (2) the date the property is no longer subject to a substantial risk of forfeiture, or (3) the issue date if an election under Code section 83(b) occurs within 30 days of the property's issuance. The 83(b) election is usually advisable when the value at issuance is low but expected to appreciate by the time of vesting.

Regulatory Licenses and Registrations

Federal and state licensing and registration obligations may apply depending on what the business is doing and where the activities occur.

- Crypto exchanges may be required to register with the SEC as a broker-dealer or exchange. The business may also need to register with FINRA.
- A crypto-business that helps customers send money to people in other countries may be required to register as a money transmitter in the states where it operates.

NY BitLicense

New York enacted a requirement for certain crypto-businesses based or doing business in New York to apply for a virtual currency license, colloquially known as the BitLicense. The BitLicense applies to five types of incorporated companies or doing business in New York or with New York customers:

- receiving virtual currency for transmission or transmitting virtual currency;
- storing, holding, or maintaining custody or control of virtual currency on behalf of others;

- buying and selling virtual currency as a customer business; performing exchange services as a customer business; or
- controlling, administering, or issuing a virtual currency.

These conditions apply to many New York businesses where digital assets are integral to their business plan. Besides requiring filing an application, the New York Department of Financial Services imposes specific capitalization requirements and annual reporting obligations on licensees.

Wyoming

Wyoming has passed 24 crypto-friendly laws, making it a crypto-friendly state. One law allows a crypto business to apply for a watered-down bank charter, allowing it to become a special-purpose depository institution (SPDI) to offer banking services for crypto. Other states require a crypto business to undergo an expensive and time-consuming traditional bank charter process. Banks are subject to a strict regulatory and compliance regime relative to other financial institutions. Complying with all such regulatory requirements for banks in most cases does not make sense for crypto. The Wyoming SPDI is an example of state drafting laws specific to crypto.

Promises Kept: Ongoing Obligations

A company may have an annual reporting obligation to investors and regulators. These reports aim to provide transparency to investors and other interested parties. For instance, as part of the BitLicense requirements, licensees must report to the NY Department of Financial Services annually. Companies whose securities are registered under the Securities Act must report annually to the SEC. In addition, key investors typically ask to see audited financial statements each year. These reporting obligations require companies to collaborate with accountants, auditors, and attorneys.

Summary and Conclusions

US federal and state laws generally apply to cryptocurrency, even though they are not specific to cryptocurrency. This situation may create uncertainty and doubt about how a transaction fits within a particular legal or regulatory framework. However, it does not mean that cryptocurrency transactions are somehow outside the reach of existing US federal and state laws.

Notwithstanding the applicability of current law and regulation to cryptocurrency transactions, federal regulatory agencies, such as the SEC, CFTC, and the IRS, have already begun issuing guidance and writing rules specifically aimed at the cryptocurrency space. In addition, some states, such as Wyoming, Delaware, and New York, have enacted crypto-specific laws and regulatory regimes governing how a cryptocurrency business can operate. However, the legal aspects involving digital assets are still in their infancy. Federal and state legislative and regulatory bodies will continue to monitor the cryptocurrency space and ideally write thoughtful rules to help the industry grow and build public confidence.

Discussion Questions

1. Discuss how general securities laws might apply to a blockchain-based project or start-up company.
2. Discuss the treatment of digital assets for federal legal purposes.
3. Explain the factors founders and investors should consider when raising capital.
4. Explain whether profits on crypto investments are subject to taxation.
5. Describe the tax implications of paying for goods and services, including employees, in crypto.

References

Blockstack Token LLC. (2019). Prospectus. Retrieved from https://www.sec.gov/Archives/edgar/data/1725129/000162827919000230/younow1a.htm

Hinman, W. (2018, June 14). *Digital asset transactions: When Howey met Gary (plastic)*. Securities and Exchange Commission. Retrieved from https://www.sec.gov/news/speech/speech-hinman-061418

SEC v. *Howey*. (1946). 328 U.S. 293, 294. Retrieved from https://supreme.justia.com/cases/federal/us/328/293/

SEC v. *Shavers et al.* (2013). U.S. Dist. LEXIS 130781 (E.D. Tex., Sept. 18, 2014). Retrieved from chrome-extension://efaidnbmnnnibpcajpcglclefindmkaj/viewer.html?pdfurl=https%3A%2F%2Fwww.thompsonhine.com%2Fuploads%2F1137%2Fdoc%2FECLR_Volume_14_Issue_5_pg_22.pdf&clen=68362&chunk=true

Securities and Exchange Commission. (2017, July 25). SEC Release No. 81207, Report of investigation pursuant to Section 21(a) of the Securities Exchange Act of 1934: The DAO. Retrieved from https://www.sec.gov/litigation/investreport/34-81207.pdf

Securities and Exchange Commission. (2021). Cyber enforcement actions. Retrieved from https://www.sec.gov/spotlight/cybersecurity-enforcement-actions

YouNow, Inc. (2019). Prospectus. Retrieved from https://www.sec.gov/Archives/edgar/data/1725129/000162827919000230/younow1a.htm

Chapter 18

The Underlying Technology for Cryptoassets

Alevtina Dubovitskaya Ackerer and Damien Ackerer

Abstract

This chapter reviews the underlying technologies of cryptoassets, including fundamental cryptographic primitives used in distributed ledger technologies and permissionless blockchain technologies and their consensus protocols such as proof-of-work and proof-of-stake. It discusses the pros and cons of existing approaches to improve blockchain scalability and considers the requirements for security and decentralization. The chapter also examines the following techniques: layer 1 tuning, layer 1 sharding, and layer 2 solutions. It concludes with an overview of technologies to swap cryptoassets off-chain, technical requirements for cross-chain transactions, and reviews cross-chain atomic swap implementation using hashed time lock contracts.

Keywords: Cryptoassets; blockchain; distributed ledger technology; consensus protocols; scalability; layer 1 tuning; layer 1 sharding; layer 2 solutions.

Introduction

The use of cryptoassets in the financial services industry is increasing quickly (EY, 2021). Cryptoassets can be differentiated by their purpose and use, price volatility, and value type. However, all cryptoassets are private assets that depend primarily on cryptography and distributed ledger technology (DLT) as part of their perceived or inherent value (EBA, 2019).

This chapter reviews some technological aspects of cryptoassets and cryptographic primitives and principles of DLT on which cryptoassets rely. The CAP theorem (Gilbert & Lynch, 2002) inspired the blockchain trilemma (Scalability, 2021).

The Emerald Handbook on Cryptoassets: Investment Opportunities and Challenges, 265–282

doi:10.1108/978-1-80455-320-620221018

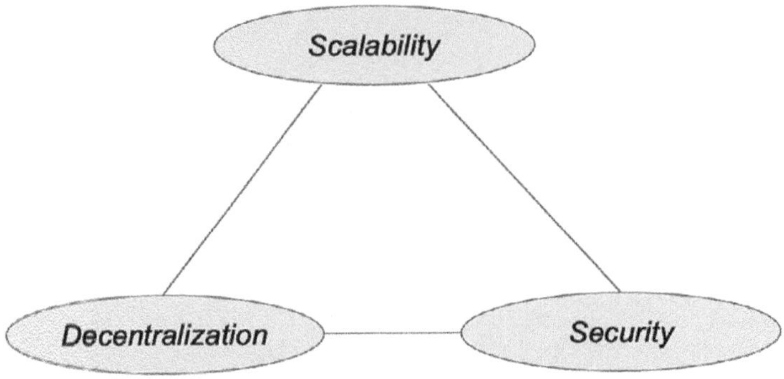

Figure 18.1. The Blockchain Trilemma. *Source:* The authors.
Note: The blockchain trilemma points out that three important properties of a blockchain system – decentralization, security, and scalability – cannot perfectly co-exist.

As Figure 18.1 points out, three critical properties of a blockchain system – decentralization, security, and scalability – cannot perfectly co-exist. This chapter reviews proposed solutions to improve blockchain scalability and balance these three properties. Next, the chapter discusses off- and on-chain cryptoasset trading, revises technical requirements for cross-chain transactions, and reviews cross-chain atomic swap implementation using hashed time lock contracts.

Foundations of Blockchains Technologies

The notion of distributed technology has existed for a long time. Blockchain technology relies on DLT, particularly consensus mechanisms to achieve data consistency. However, an important component of blockchain that differentiates it from a distributed ledger is cryptographic primitives and their use to ensure a ledger's immutability. This section first reviews cryptographic primitives employed by blockchain technology and then examines consensus protocols supporting various realizations of blockchain platforms (Dubovitskaya, 2018).

Cryptographic Primitives

Cryptographic primitives are mathematical techniques related to information security, such as confidentiality, data integrity, entity authentication, and data origin authentication (Menezes, Van Oorschot, & Vanstone, 2018). This section presents the concepts and primitives employed when issuing, storing, and managing cryptoassets: hash functions, Merkle tree, public-key infrastructure, digital signature, multi-party computations, threshold cryptography, and zero-knowledge proofs.

A *hash function* takes a message as input and produces an output called a hash code or hash. This function is deterministic and public, but the mapping should look random. In other words, a hash function $\boldsymbol{H}$ maps bit strings of arbitrary finite length to strings of fixed length $\boldsymbol{H}: \{0,1\}^* \rightarrow \{0,1\}^d$. A random oracle model is an ideal hash function model (Canetti, Goldreich, & Halevi, 2004).

This model assumes an oracle $\boldsymbol{H}$ exists such that on input $x \in \{0,1\}^*$, if $\boldsymbol{H}$ has not seen x before, it outputs a new random value $\boldsymbol{H}(\boldsymbol{x})$. Otherwise, it returns the previous output value. A random oracle gives a random value for all new inputs and deterministic answers to all inputs it has seen previously. It does not exist since it requires infinite storage. Therefore, practitioners use pseudo-random functions.

A hash value often serves as a compact representative image (message digest) of an input string. It can be used as if it were uniquely identifiable with that string. A hash function in an unrestricted sense is a function $\boldsymbol{h}$ that has at least the following two properties:

1. *Compression.* $\boldsymbol{H}$ maps an input x of an arbitrary finite length to an output $\boldsymbol{H}(\boldsymbol{x})$ of a fixed length.
2. *Ease of computation.* Given $\boldsymbol{H}$ and an input x, $\boldsymbol{H}(\boldsymbol{x})$ is easy to compute.

In addition, a secure cryptographic hash function has the following properties:

1. *Pre-image resistance.* Given $y \in \{0,1\}^d$, finding an x such that $\boldsymbol{H}(\boldsymbol{x}) = \boldsymbol{y}$ is difficult.
2. *Strong collision resistance.* Finding any pair of inputs x, x' such that $\boldsymbol{H}(\boldsymbol{x}) = \boldsymbol{H}(\boldsymbol{x}')$ is difficult.
3. *Weak collision resistance (target collision resistance, second pre-image resistance)*: Given x, finding x' such that $\boldsymbol{H}(\boldsymbol{x}) = \boldsymbol{H}(\boldsymbol{x}')$ is difficult.
4. *Pseudo-randomness.* The function behaves indistinguishably from a random oracle.
5. *Non-malleability.* Given $\boldsymbol{H}(\boldsymbol{x})$, generating $\boldsymbol{H}(\boldsymbol{f}(\boldsymbol{x}))$ for any function $\boldsymbol{f}$ is hard.

Modern secure cryptographic hash functions, such as the SHA-2 and SHA-3 families (NIST Special Publication 180-4, 2012), are usually used with a hash length that satisfies $\boldsymbol{h} \geq 256$ to provide strong security.

A *Merkle tree*, also called a *hash tree*, is a binary tree with nodes $\boldsymbol{a}_{i,j}$, where $\boldsymbol{i}$ denotes a node's level. A *node's level* is the distance from a node to a leaf: a leaf of the tree has level $\boldsymbol{i} = 0$, and is represented by a hash of a message $\boldsymbol{Y}_k$ and the root has level $\boldsymbol{i} = \boldsymbol{n}$. Figure 18.2 shows an example of a tree with four leaves.

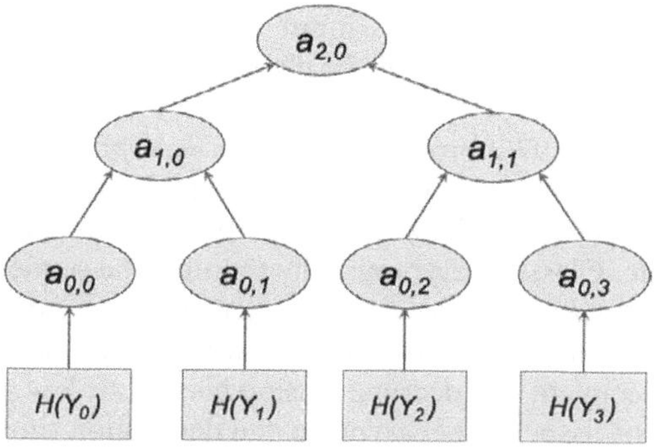

Figure 18.2. A Merkle Tree with Four Leaves. *Source:* The authors.
Note: The figure shows an example of a Merkle tree with four leaves.

The nodes on each level are numbered, starting from zero, so that $a_{i,0}$ is the leftmost node of level *i*. In the Merkle tree, the hash values h_i are a binary tree's leaves so that $H_k = a_{0,k}$. Each inner node of the tree is the hash value of the concatenation of its two children, so $a_{1,0} = H(a_{0,0} \| a_{0,1})$ and $a_{1,1} = H(a_{0,2} \| a_{0,3})$ (Merkle, 1980).

Such an organization of the hashes enables efficient verification of the data integrity by storing only the root of the tree ($a_{2,0}$ on Figure 18.2) and the list of the input messages, Y_k. Any modification of the input data results in a different hash stored at the leaf and, therefore, modification of the corresponding inner nodes and the tree's root. However, unlike naive hashing, changing one message does not require computing a hash over all the data. The required hash computations scale logarithmically in the number of data blocks. For instance, blockchain technology uses the Merkle tree's root for efficiently verifying the integrity of the transactions stored in a block (Okupski, 2014). A hash function and its use in a Merkle tree allow efficient data management and verification, despite whether data alteration happened.

What about data confidentiality and authenticity? Data confidentiality is a basic security property achieved through encryption. The standard approach for keeping sensitive data secret is to encrypt the data with a secret key only intended for the receivers. Classical cryptosystems, also called single-key or symmetric cryptosystems, use the same key for encryption and decryption. Assume that $\{E_e : e \in K\}$ is a set of encryption transformations, $\{D_d : d \in K\}$ is the set of corresponding decryption transformations, and K is the key space. Then, in symmetric encryption (*e*) and decryption (*d*) ciphers, the keys are the same ($e = d = k$, $k \in K$) meaning the encryption and decryption transformations are performed under the same secret key, *k*, or the encryption key can be calculated from the decryption key and vice versa.

A symmetric key encryption scheme consists of three algorithms.

1. Key generation takes as input a security parameter and outputs a secure key *k*.
2. An encryption algorithm takes as input a secure key *k*, and a message *m*, and outputs a ciphertext *c*.
3. A decryption algorithm takes as input a secret key *k* and a ciphertext *c*, outputs message *m*, or an error, if the ciphertext *c* is invalid.

Diffie and Hellman (1976) propose *public-key encryption*, a new type of cryptography that distinguishes between encryption and decryption keys. One key would be publicly known (public key, *pk*); the owner would keep the other (private key, *sk*) private. Classical cryptography requires the sender and recipient to share a common key (*k*), whereas public key cryptography does not. To send a secret message, a sender encrypts the message with the recipient's public key (*pk*) and sends it. The recipient can decrypt it using his private key (*sk*). In public-key encryption, a pair of associated encryption and decryption transformations (E_{pk}, D_{sk}) have the following property. Given a random ciphertext $c \in C$ and knowing E_{pk}, it is computationally infeasible to find the message $m \in M$ such that

$E_{pk}(m) = c$. Although two keys (*pk* and *sk*) are mathematically linked, given public key *pk*, determining the corresponding private key *sk* is infeasible.

Like symmetric encryption, a public key encryption scheme consists of three algorithms:

1. Key generation takes as input a security parameter and outputs a secret key *sk* and corresponding public key *pk*.
2. The encryption algorithm inputs a public key *pk*, and a message *m*, outputs a ciphertext *c*.
3. The decryption algorithm inputs a private key *sk* and a ciphertext *c*, outputs message *m*, or an error if ciphertext *c* is invalid.

Besides confidentiality, public-key cryptography can authenticate the data and their origin.

Signature schemes are another fundamental cryptographic primitive for authentication, authorization, and nonrepudiation (Goldreich, 2009), serving as an underlying technology of cryptoassets. *A digital signature* allows authenticating a message's source and contents in a mathematically provable manner. One party signs a message with a private key *sk,* and other parties can verify the signature's correctness using the corresponding public key (*pk*).

A digital signature scheme consists of the following probabilistic polynomial-time algorithms:

1. Key generation takes as input a security parameter and outputs a secret key *sk* and corresponding public (verification) key *pk*.
2. A signature generation algorithm inputs a private key *sk*, and a message *m*, outputs a signature *s*.
3. A signature verification algorithm inputs a message *m*, public (verification) key *pk,* and a signature *s*, outputs 1 for acceptance or 0 for rejection according to the input.

A digital signature scheme is correct if for any security parameters, generated pair of keys (*pk*, *sk*), and message *m*, the signature verification algorithm returns 1 for the corresponding signature of message *m*. Besides their use for signing digital documents and building classical cryptographic protocols such as key exchange, digital signature schemes are also critical components of more advanced cryptographic protocols, such as blind signatures (Chaum, 1984), group signatures (Bellare, Micciancio, & Warinschi, 2003), and anonymous credentials (Belenkiy, Chase, Kohlweiss, & Lysyanskaya, 2008).

Consensus Protocols

This section reviews various protocols used to maintain the up-to-date state of a distributed ledger, namely consensus protocols. According to Schneider (1990), the task of reaching and maintaining consensus among distributed nodes involves two elements: (1) a deterministic state machine that implements the logic of the service to be replicated; and (2) a consensus protocol to disseminate requests among the nodes, such that each node executes the same sequence of requests on its instance of the service.

Consensus means traditionally only the task of reaching an agreement on one single request (Cachin, 2017; Schneider, 1990). *Atomic broadcast* provides an agreement on a sequence of requests as needed for the state-machine replication (Anagnostou & Vassos Hadzilacos, 1993). The last section of this chapter discusses the atomicity property in the framework of the cross-chain asset exchange.

How a network defines a participant's identity and right to participate in the consensus enables distinguishing between permissionless and permissioned blockchain systems and public and private systems among the latter. *Hybrid consensus* relies on the Nakamoto consensus, as discussed below, to reelect committees over time, where each committee consists of recent online miners. A committee executes a classical, partially synchronous consensus instance (e.g., Practical Byzantine Fault Tolerance consensus algorithm) to confirm the transactions (Pass & Shi, 2017).

Participants use public and often permissionless blockchain technology implementations for cryptoassets. However, leveraging a permissioned-based approach is possible in finance, mainly to ensure regulatory compliance, such as privacy, regulations, know your customer, and anti-money laundering (AML) standards. For example, the implementation of permissionless blockchains has occurred for over-the-counter (OTC) financial derivatives transactions using Corda (Carare, Ciampoli, De Gasperis, & Facchini, 2021) and cross-chain security settlements using two permissioned blockchains – Hyperledger Fabric and Corda (Cross-chain, 2019). The form of consensus relevant to permissioned blockchain is technically known as an *atomic broadcast* (Cachin, 2017). Nakamoto consensus realizes a replicated state machine abstraction, where nodes in a permissionless network agree on a set and the order of committed transactions (Nakamoto, 2008). The protocol relies on chaining blocks of transactions: nodes express their acceptance of the block by creating the next block in the chain, using the hash of the accepted block as the previous hash. Nodes always consider the longest chain the correct one and work to extend it. If two nodes broadcast different versions of the next block simultaneously, some nodes may receive one or the other first. In this case, the nodes continue working on the first one they receive but save the other branch if it becomes longer; the nodes working on the other branch then switch to the longer one. New transaction broadcasts do not necessarily need to reach all nodes. If they reach many nodes, they eventually get into a block. Block broadcasts are also tolerant of dropped messages. If a node does not receive a block, it requests the missing block when it receives the next block and realizes it missed one.

In permissionless settings, the nodes' identities are unknown a priori. Therefore, defending against a so-called *Sybil attack*, where an attacker arbitrarily makes up many identities to outvote honest nodes, is imperative. Nakamoto consensus critically relies on proof-of-work to roughly enforce the idea of "one vote per hash power."

Proof-of-work (PoW), proposed as an underlying technology of bitcoin, is based on *mining, a* process of searching for a *nonce*, a random number stored in every block so that the resulting hash of a new valid block satisfies specific requirements. These requirements set the difficulty threshold for finding the nonce and determining the average number of hashes needed to mine one block. The difficulty threshold impacts the amount of energy spent to find such a nonce. In 2013, the amount of energy used by bitcoin mining was already comparable to the Irish national energy consumption (O'Dwyer & Malone, 2013). Existing PoW blockchains can achieve a throughput of not more than 60 transactions per second without significantly affecting the blockchain's security (Gervais et al., 2016).

Several proposals are available to modify PoW core operations, including the block generation rate and the basic primitives. Others have proposed several different PoW implementations using functions like script (Percival, 2009) and lyra2 (Simplicio, Almeida, Andrade, dos Santos, & Barreto, 2014). Two valid blocks can be found at approximately the same time, depending on network latency. This situation leads to a temporary fork during which two equal-length chains exist. Miners can choose either fork in this scenario. Due to the computational puzzle's random nature, one blockchain eventually extends further than the other. At this point, all miners should adopt it.

The greedy heaviest observed subtree (GHOST) protocol is a notable radical modification (Sompolinsky & Zohar, 2015). The basis of this protocol is the principle that all mined blocks should matter in the chain selection process, even those that did not end up in the main chain. To achieve this result, players store a tree of all mined blocks they received and then pick which chain to mine using the GHOST rule.

Proof-of-stake (PoS) proposes that the basis for selecting the participant who will create a new block is the amount of tokens owned by the participant. Instead of having participants mine by exchanging their wealth for computational resources, which are then exchanged for mining rewards in virtual mining, participants could exchange their wealth directly for the ability to append a new block to the ledger (Bonneau et al., 2015). Ouroboros is the first protocol based on PoS with rigorous security guarantees. However, Kiayias, Russell, David, and Oliynykov (2017) assume that the network is highly synchronous. Moreover, most randomly selected stakeholders are incorruptible in many epochs. An assumption is that these stakeholders form a committee responsible for executing the coin-flipping protocol to produce the randomness for the leader-election process.

Proof-of-burn bases the miner selection on the amount of tokens provably destroyed (i.e., sent to an unspendable address). However, providing a rigorous argument for or against the stability of virtual mining remains an open problem (Bonneau et al., 2015).

Smart Contracts

Blockchains may execute arbitrary, programmable transaction logic as smart contracts, as exemplified by Ethereum. The scripts in bitcoin were a predecessor of the concept. A smart contract functions as a trusted distributed application and gains its security from the blockchain and the underlying consensus among its peers. This method resembles the well-known approach of building resilient applications with state-machine replication (SMR) (Schneider, 1990). However, blockchains differ from traditional SMRs with Byzantine faults in the following ways: many distributed applications run concurrently; anyone may dynamically deploy applications, and the application code is untrusted, potentially even malicious (Androulaki et al., 2018).

Ethereum is an implementation of a permissionless programmable (i.e., supporting smart contract functionality) blockchain that enables any user to create and execute the code of arbitrary algorithmic complexity on the Ethereum platform: Ethereum Virtual Machine (EVM) (Buterin, 2014). One may view EVM as a large, decentralized computer. Creating two types of "accounts" is possible on EVM. A user's private key can control multiple *externally owned accounts* (EOA). The owner of the private key associated with the EOA can remain anonymous up to a certain degree and can send messages. A *contract account* is like an autonomous agent who lives in the Ethereum execution environment controlled by its smart contract code.

A smart contract encodes arbitrary state transition functions, allowing users to create systems with different functionalities by transforming the system's logic into code. In the case of a public blockchain such as Ethereum, smart contracts and all the transactions are public. In Ethereum, transaction processing is *Turing complete*. *Turing complete* refers to a machine that, with enough time, memory, and necessary instructions, can solve any computational problem, no matter how complex (Binance Academy, 2022). It can be used to implement any public functionality in a distributed way. Users must pay for the code execution. The transaction price limits the number of computational steps for the code execution to prevent infinite loops or other computational wastage. Users can participate in the consensus process to obtain the tokens to pay for the transaction's execution.

All programmable computations in Ethereum are subject to fees to avoid network abuse issues. Ethereum specifies the fee schedule in units of gas. Thus, any given fragment of programmable computation (i.e., creating contracts, making message calls, utilizing and accessing account storage, and executing operations on a virtual machine) has a universally agreed cost in terms of gas (Wood, 2014). Ethereum provides excellent scalability regarding the number of nodes and clients but has a limited transaction throughput.

Improving Blockchain Scalability

In both total transaction volume and the number of independent participants involved in processing them, the scalability of distributed ledgers is a significant challenge to their mainstream adoption (Kokoris-Kogias et al., 2018). Moreover, a blockchain system's three important properties – decentralization, security, and scalability – cannot perfectly co-exist. The following section examines existing approaches for improving a permissionless blockchain's scalability.

When referring to a blockchain, one typically references a layer 1 blockchain, which is where the formation of blocks occurs. Blockchain functioning relies on the rules set up on the communication or network layer over the internet. The hardware layer allows computing the received data and producing appropriate outputs. A faster network propagation mechanism can optimize the communication throughput on the network layer. Layer 1 blockchain also offers a few options for improving scalability, such as parameter tuning, sharding, and using different structures, such as directed acyclic graph (DAG) (Wang, Yu, Chen, & Xiang, 2020). Figure 18.3 shows two blockchain layers and outlines some of the most widespread approaches to improve scalability.

For example, block time interval and block size affect the PoW blockchain's scalability. Reducing the time interval and increasing the block size improve performance by allowing more transactions. However, it might increase the risk of blockchain forks, leading to slower network propagation and reducing security (Qin & Gervais, 2018). Using alternative digital signatures schemes, such as the BLS scheme (Boneh, Gentry, Lynn, & Shacham, 2003) that generate an aggregated multisignature, can decrease a transaction's size and allow packing more transactions in a block without changing the block size. However, it may also introduce security risks as the current design of BLS signature schemes is yet to be perfected. Additionally, verifying such cryptographic tools requires more time and computational power than other signature schemes (Unitychain, 2021).

Sharding schemes seem to be the most effective candidate because they can overcome performance and scalability problems. A sharding scheme splits the processing of transactions among smaller groups of nodes, called *shards*. As a result, shards can work in parallel to maximize performance and improve throughput while requiring significantly less communication, computation, and storage overhead, allowing the scheme to work in large systems (Zamani, Movahedi, & Raykova, 2018). Increasing the transaction throughput can occur when more participants join the network. More committees can be formed to process transactions in parallel (Wang, Shi, Nixon, & Han, 2019).

Using different blockchain structures, such as a DAG, is another scaling solution on layer 1. To avoid consuming competitive transactions caused by linear sequenced blocks, DAG-based blockchain systems, like the one proposed by Sompolinsky and Zohar (2013), structure the transactions in the form of graph topology. Such systems can improve performance by requiring less communication, computation, and storage overhead. However, the sources of existing open-sourced projects and solutions are scarce. Wang et al. (2020) provide a recent review of scalability solutions based on DAG.

Layer 2 blockchain is a layer built to "off-load" some work performed on layer 1 (main chain). Layer 2 solutions improve scalability by handling transactions off the main chain, do not require any changes on the main chain, and often rely on the main chain security. Figure 18.3 also shows scaling layer 2 solutions. A description of layer 2 solutions follows.

- *Payment channel* is a decentralized network that allows off-chain transactions with privacy among participants, enabling instantaneous contract processing at negligible costs. The payment channel's basic idea is to let two parties, say Alice and Bob, "lock" some coins in a smart contract on the blockchain so that dynamically changing each party's amounts in the contract can occur without interacting with the blockchain. The parties can then

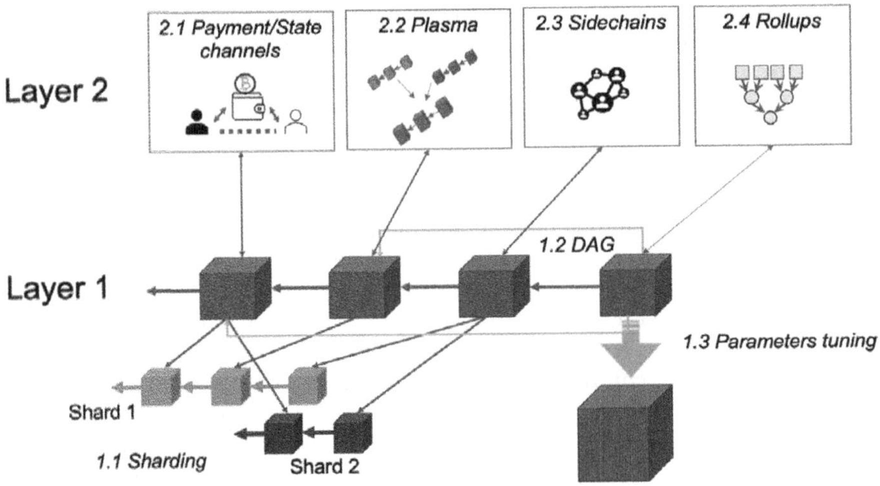

Figure 18.3. Scalability Solutions on Layer 1 and Layer 2 Blockchains.
Source: The authors.
Note: This figure shows two blockchain layers and outlines some general approaches to improve scalability.

update the distribution of these coins "off-chain" by exchanging signatures of the new balance that each party owns in the channel. When the parties decide to close the channel, the blockchain will realize the latest signed off-chain distribution of coins. Another use of the main chain is to resolve a dispute between the parties about the current off-chain balance of the channel (Dziembowski, Eckey, Faust, Hesse, & Hostáková, 2019). One extension of a payment channel is the lightning network on bitcoin (Poon & Dryja, 2016), allowing users to "route" transactions securely over a longer path of channels. A state channel is another extension supporting off-chain execution of general state updates.

- *Plasma* is a series of smart contracts that coordinates many blockchains with a root blockchain. Plasma blockchain is a framework enabling the creation of child chains composed of a tree hierarchy. Achieving this construction involves composing smart contracts on the main blockchain using fraud proofs, whereby enforcing state transitions occur on a parent blockchain. Like in the lightning network, the withdrawal requires time to exit (Poon & Buterin, 2017).
- A *sidechain* is a separate blockchain network connected to the main blockchain (layer 1) with a *two-way peg*, a mechanism allowing bidirectional transfer of assets at a fixed exchange rate and mediated by a group of servers (federation) determining when used tokens are locked up and released. Sidechains may have consensus protocols that could completely differ from the main chain's protocol. Sidechains are isolated from the main chain and do not rely on the security of the layer 1 blockchain. Therefore, the damage is entirely confined to the sidechain in case of attack or a maliciously designed sidechain (Singh et al., 2020).

- *Rollups* are a concept that keeps the whole transaction data on-chain while moving the transaction computation off-chain enables efficiency gains. Rollups are somewhat related to plasma but claim to be trustless. By publishing just enough data on-chain, rollups resolve the data availability problem that all the previously discussed layer 2 scaling solutions suffer from. The transactions are bundled into a Merkle tree root to decrease the data size stored on-chain and increase security guarantees. Ethereum's consensus protocol does not validate the transactions but relies on zero-knowledge proofs or fraud proofs (Schaffner, 2021).

Technologies Used to Swap Cryptoassets

Blockchain participants may eventually want to swap their cryptoassets for other cryptoassets or fiat currencies for investment or trading purposes. The fundamental property that a solution for swapping assets must ensure is atomicity: either transferring all assets in the agreed quantities occurs, or no transfer occurs. Without atomicity, a trader could send an asset without ever receiving anything in exchange, and most individuals are likely to avoid such a trading environment. Most modern commercial and financial platforms rely on a trusted intermediary guaranteeing atomicity. In a trustless distributed environment with one or multiple blockchains, special logic is necessary to ensure the atomicity of transactions. An *atomic swap* is a coordination task where two parties agree to exchange assets. Either both parties receive each other's original assets upon successful execution or nothing in the event of failure (Garcia-Molina, 1983). Atomic swaps are easily achievable on a single ledger by implementing smart contracts such as automated market-making protocols (Xu, Vavryk, Paruch, & Cousaert, 2021). The conventional approach uses a centralized exchange (CEX) for cross-chain asset swaps, characterized by high efficiency and transaction speed, such as Coinbase, Binance, FTX, and Kraken. However, this approach requires intermediary fees and trust in the exchange regarding the privacy and transparency of its matching mechanisms. In addition, CEXs are vulnerable to different kinds of attacks, from wallet hacking to a distributed denial-of-service (DDoS) attack (Moore & Christin, 2013). A *DDoS attack* is a malicious attempt to disrupt the regular traffic of a targeted server, service, or network by overwhelming the target or its surrounding infrastructure with a flood of internet traffic (Cloudflare, 2022).

To address some issues with CEXs with an intermediary, decentralized exchanges (DEXs) have recently become a popular tool for cross-chain asset swaps, such as Uniswap, Sushiswap, and 0x. In such a peer-to-peer environment, the transacting agents typically do not know each other. Thus, they have exposure to potential malicious behaviors from their counterparty. Therefore, a major challenge in such settings is achieving the atomicity of the cross-ledger transaction. Either the execution of the entire transaction occurs, or nothing happens in case of failure.

Perhaps surprisingly, most transactions for cryptoassets happen off-chain in systems like those used by financial institutions for traditional assets such as equity shares and commodities. However, 2021 highlighted the viability of on-chain cryptoasset trading, rising from almost zero to between 5 and 10 percent of total monthly volumes (CMC, 2022).

Off-Chain Swap on CEXs

Market participants commonly use CEXs to acquire and trade cryptoassets. A *CEX* is a financial intermediary allowing buyers and sellers to trade anonymously from each other, but not an intermediary, on a platform built by an intermediary. However, a CEX uses official identification documents to verify a trader's identity. The platform controls the cryptoassets or fiat currencies transferred by traders. Hence, it is custodial because an intermediary must approve transfers in and out of the platform. CEXs use a central limit order book (CLOB) to record available buy and sell orders. Transactions are typically fast and cheap as they happen on dedicated and isolated high-performance servers running highly optimized order matching engines. Therefore, trading on a CEX requires considerable trust in the intermediary.

Some exchanges have experienced increased transparency and regulatory compliance in recent years. This situation also allows some platforms to connect with the traditional financial system, thus enabling transfers in fiat currencies using standard banking protocols such as credit cards and bank transfers. Hence, these platforms function as a ramp for individuals who want to buy cryptoassets using fiat currencies. Most technologies used by CEXs are not blockchain specific except for the wallet components needed to transfer cryptoassets in and out of the platform. Chapter 22 provides a further discussion on CEXs.

OTC operations are also frequent for large financial transactions. These transactions typically involve professional investors and actors who provide liquidity for large transactions. An important difference with CEXs is that OTC transactions are typically *post-trade settled*, meaning the transfer of coins and tokens can happen hours or even days after the agreement on the swap's terms.

On-chain Swaps with DEXs

The Ethereum blockchain has thousands of tokens. The number of protocols enabling the swapping of these assets without an intermediary continues to increase. However, implementing a CLOB exchange directly on a blockchain is challenging due to the volume of transactions. Each pair sends millions of orders per day, such as BTC/USDT on a CEX. Therefore, following the same CLOB design could be costly and slow due to the time-consuming mining process and gas fees paid to miners, with further limitations caused by the blockchain's storage capacity.

For these reasons, DEXs have developed so-called automated market maker (AMM) algorithms embedded in smart contracts. An AMM smart contract controls *liquidity pools*, which are cryptoassets contributed by market participants. This contract allows market participants to swap assets from and to these pools. When using an AMM to exchange a token for another token, a trader sends a token swap request and the tokens to be sold to the AMM smart contract. The AMM automatically determines the transaction prices based on the available liquidity pools, typically by using a conservation function to determine the number of tokens the pool wants to swap. If the AMM swap rate is within an acceptable range specified in the trader request, the AMM's liquidity pool receives the traders' tokens. It automatically sends the requested tokens to the trader. If the swap rate is unacceptable, the AMM smart contract automatically returns the trader's tokens to the trader's wallet and no transaction occurs. The liquidity pools receive compensation for providing liquidity by receiving a fee on each transaction. Xu, Vavryk, et al. (2021) provide further discussion on DEXs.

Cross-chain Swap with Hashed Time Lock Contracts

Some protocols have adopted hash time lock contracts (HTLCs). As first proposed on a bitcoin forum by TierNolan (BW, 2022), these contracts aim to achieve atomicity of cross-chain transactions without direct communications between the ledgers. Studying and improving HTLCs are of great interest (Kirsten & Davarpanah, 2018; Liu, 2018; Xu, Ackerer, & Dubovitskaya, 2021; Zyskind, Kisagun, & Fromknecht, 2018). The rest of this section presents an overview of HTLCs.

Assume that two agents want to swap their respective assets stored on two different blockchains. An HTLC requires the two agents separately lock their holdings on their separate blockchains, using the hash of a secret generated by one of the users. Users can unlock the assets upon revealing the hash's preimage. The users have accounts (wallets) on two disconnected ledgers ($Chain_a$ and $Chain_b$) executing smart contracts.

Suppose Alice wants to send assets on $Chain_a$ to Bob in exchange for assets on $Chain_b$ from Bob. In step 1, Alice initiates the transaction by generating a secret (a key) used to unlock the asset, which transfers later. She then deploys a smart contract on $Chain_a$ that locks her assets until time t_a. This contract would transfer the assets to Bob only if the secret generated by Alice is revealed and entered into the smart contract. To verify the secret, Alice reveals its hash as part of the smart contract (Figure 18.4, Step 1). A critical feature of this contract is that after time t_a, if the secret has not been revealed, the smart contract expires, unlocking and returning Alice's assets to her wallet.

In Step 2, Bob can verify the contract deployed by Alice on $Chain_a$ and use the hash submitted by Alice to deploy a similar contract on $Chain_b$ (Figure 18.4, Step 2), specifying the amount he will transfer to Alice and the expiry time t_b. Until then, Bob's assets are locked on $Chain_b$.

In Step 3, Alice can verify the contract deployed on $Chain_b$, unlock the assets, and initiate their transfer to her wallet by revealing the secret on $Chain_b$. Upon the secret's revelation in the mempool of $Chain_b$ (even before confirmation of Alice's transfer), Bob can use the revealed secret to unlock the assets on $Chain_a$ and complete the cross-ledger transaction. In the best-case scenario, this mechanism enables the exchange of atomic cross-ledger assets without relying on a trusted party and connection between ledgers. If Alice does not unlock the assets on $Chain_b$ before t_b, the assets are transferred back to Bob. Thus, she has no incentive to reveal the secret (after t_a and before t_b) as that would allow Bob to execute the smart contract on $Chain_a$ and transfer the assets to his wallet while keeping his assets on $Chain_b$. Once the secret is revealed, Bob's assets are transferred to Alice. He should execute the smart contract on $Chain_a$ immediately to complete the

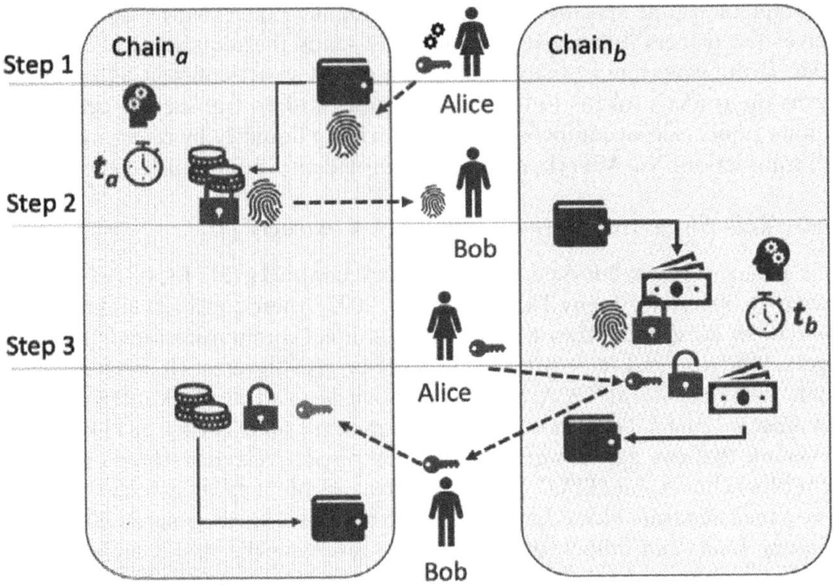

Figure 18.4. Hash Time Lock Contract.
Notes: This figure highlights an HTLC's steps, showing the cross-chain transfer of the tokens owned by Alice on *Chain*$_a$ to Bob. In exchange, Alice receives the corresponding amount of tokens from Bob, on *Chain*$_b$.

transaction. Otherwise, he transferred his assets without receiving Alice's assets. In practice, extending the above HTLCs logic can include additional incentive mechanisms such as capital collateral and reputation.

Summary and Conclusions

This chapter discusses the underlying technologies of cryptoassets, including fundamental cryptographic primitives and DLTs and recently developed permissionless blockchain technologies. The blockchain community has recently proposed various approaches to improve scalability and attain VISA-like transaction throughput. The chapter reviews techniques applicable to layer 1 and layer 2 blockchains. It also considers the blockchain trilemma, pointing out that decentralization, security, and scalability cannot co-exist perfectly. The chapter concludes by offering an overview of technologies to swap cryptoassets, a dynamic research and development space due to the growing popularity and number of cryptoassets.

Discussion Questions

1. List security properties public-key cryptography (asymmetric encryption and digital signature) can provide.

2. Identify an important barrier to adopting blockchain technology and discuss the challenges of overcoming this barrier.
3. Discuss a fundamental property that a solution for swapping assets must ensure.
4. Define layer 1 blockchain and discuss the possibilities to improve its scalability.
5. Identify a main use of an HTLC.

References

Anagnostou, E., & Hadzilacos, V. (1993). Tolerating transient and permanent failures. In *International workshop on distributed algorithms* (pp. 174–188). Berlin: Springer. Retrieved from https://link.springer.com/chapter/10.1007/3-540-57271-6_35#editor-information

Androulaki, E., Barger, A., Bortnikov, V., Cachin, C., Christidis, K., De Caro, A., … Yellick, J. (2018). Hyperledger fabric: A distributed operating system for permissioned blockchains. In *Proceedings of the thirteenth EuroSys conference* (pp. 1–15). Association for Computing Machinery. Retrieved from https://dl.acm.org/doi/proceedings/10.1145/3190508

Belenkiy, M., Chase, M., Kohlweiss, M., & Lysyanskaya, A. (2008). P-signatures and noninteractive anonymous credentials. In R. Canetti (Ed.), *Theory of cryptography conference* (pp. 356–374). Berlin: Springer.

Bellare, M., Micciancio, D., & Warinschi, B. (2003). Foundations of group signatures: Formal definitions, simplified requirements, and a construction based on general assumptions. In E. Bihamfor (Ed.), *International conference on the theory and applications of cryptographic techniques* (pp. 614–629). Berlin: Springer.

Binance Academy. (2022). Turing complete. Retrieved from https://academy.binance.com/en/glossary/turing-complete

Boneh, D., Gentry, C., Lynn, B., & Shacham, H. (2003). A survey of two signature aggregation techniques. *RSA CryptoBytes*, *6*(2), 1–9.

Bonneau, J., Miller, A., Clark, J., Narayanan, A., Kroll, J. A., & Felten, E. W. (2015). Sok: research perspectives and challenges for bitcoin and cryptocurrencies. In *2015 IEEE symposium on security and privacy* (pp. 104–121). Piscataway, NJ: IEEE.

BW. (2022). Bitcoin Wiki: Atomic cross-chain trading. Retrieved from https://en.bitcoin.it/wiki/

Buterin, V. (2014). Ethereum: A next-generation smart contract and decentralized application platform. Retrieved from https://github.com/ethereum/wiki/wiki/%5BEnglish%5D-White-Paper

Cachin, C. (2017). *Blockchains and consensus protocols: Snake oil warning*. In *2017 13th European dependable computing conference (EDCC)* (pp. 1–2). Piscataway, NJ: IEEE.

Canetti, R., Goldreich, O., & Halevi, S. (2004). The random Oracle methodology, revisited. *Journal of the ACM*, *51*(4), 557–594.

Carare, A., Ciampoli, M., De Gasperis, G., & Facchini, S. D. (2021). Case study: The automation of an over the counter financial derivatives transaction using the CORDA blockchain. In *International congress on blockchain and applications* (pp. 128–137). Cham: Springer.

Chaum, D. (1984). Blind signature system. In *Advances in cryptology* (p. 153). Boston, MA: Springer.

CMC (2022). ConMarketCap. Retrieved from https://coinmarketcap.com

Cloudflare (2022). What is a DDoS attack? Retrieved from https://www.cloudflare.com/learning/ddos/what-is-a-ddos-attack/

Cross-chain (2019, November). Deutsche Börse, Swisscom and partners successfully settle securities transactions via tokens in Switzerland. Retrieved from https://www.swisscom.ch/en/about/news/2019/11/19-wertpapiertransaktionen-mi.t-tokens.html

Diffie, W., & Hellman, M. (1976). New directions in cryptography. *IEEE Transactions on Information Theory*, *22*(6), 644–654.

Dziembowski, S., Eckey, L., Faust, S., Hesse, J., & Hostáková, K. (2019). Multi-party virtual state channels. In *Annual international conference on the theory and applications of cryptographic techniques* (pp. 625–656). Cham: Springer.

Dubovitskaya, A. (2018). *Privacy-preserving data exchange and aggregation in healthcare*. Ph.D. thesis, EPFL.

EBA. (2019). Report with advice for the European Commission on crypto-assets. Retrieved from https://www.eba.europa.eu/sites/default/documents/files/documents/10180/2545547/67493daa-85a8-4429-aa91-e9a5ed880684/EBA%20Report%20on%20crypto%20assets.pdf?retry=1

EY. (2021). Crypto-assets—The global regulatory perspective. Retrieved from https://assets.ey.com/banking-and-capital-markets/ey-crypto-assets-the-global-regulatory-perspective.pdf

Garcia-Molina, H. (1983). Using semantic knowledge for transaction processing in a distributed database. *ACM Transactions on Database Systems*, *8*(2), 186–213.

Gervais, A., Karame, G. O., Wüst, K., Glykantzis, V., Ritzdorf, H., & Capkun, S. (2016). On the security and performance of proof of work blockchains. In *Proceedings of the 2016 ACM SIGSAC conference on computer and communications security* (pp. 3–16).

Gilbert, S., & Lynch, N. (2009). Brewer's conjecture and the feasibility of consistent, available, partition-tolerant web services. *ACM SIGACT News*, *33*(2), 51–59.

Goldreich, O. (2009). *Foundations of cryptography: Volume* 2, Basic *applications*. Cambridge: Cambridge University Press.

Kiayias, A., Russell, A., David, B., & Oliynykov, R. (2017). Ouroboros: A provably secure proof-of-stake blockchain protocol. In *Annual international cryptology conference* (pp. 357–388). Cham: Springer.

Kokoris-Kogias, E., Jovanovic, P., Gasser, L., Gailly, N., Syta, E., & Ford, B. (2018). Omniledger: A secure, scale-out, decentralized ledger via sharding. In *2018 IEEE symposium on security and privacy (SP)* (pp. 583–598). Piscataway, NJ: IEEE.

Kirsten, J., & Davarpanah, H. (2018, August 20). Anonymous atomic swaps using homomorphic hashing. Retrieved from https://ssrn.com/abstract=3235955

Liu, J. A. (2018). *Atomic swaptions: Cryptocurrency derivatives*. Ithaca, NY: Cornell University. arXiv preprint arXiv:1807.08644.

Menezes, A. J., Van Oorschot, P. C., & Vanstone, S. A. (2018). *Handbook of applied cryptography*. Boca Raton, FL: CRC Press.

Merkle, R. C. (1980). Protocols for public key cryptosystems. In *1980 IEEE symposium on security and privacy*. Piscataway, NJ: IEEE.

Moore, T., & Christin, N. (2013). Beware the Middleman: Empirical analysis of bitcoin-exchange risk. In *International Conference on financial cryptography and data security* (pp. 25–33). Berlin: Springer.

Nakamoto, S. (2008). Bitcoin: A peer-to-peer electronic cash system. *Decentralized Business Review*, October 31, pp. 1–9. Retrieved from https://www.debr.io/article/21260-bitcoin-a-peer-to-peer-electronic-cash-system

NIST Special Publication 180-4. (2012). *Secure hash standard (SHS)*. Gaithersburg, MD: National Institute of Standards and Technology.

O'Dwyer, K. J., & Malone, D. (2014). Bitcoin mining and its energy footprint. Irish signals and systems conference 2014 and 2014. In *25th IET China–Ireland international conference on information and communications technologies (ISSC2014/CIICT 2014)* (pp. 280–285).

Okupski, K. (2014). *Bitcoin developer reference*. Working Paper, Eindhoven University of Technology.

Pass, R., & Shi, E. (2017). Hybrid consensus: Efficient consensus in the permissionless model. In *LIPIcs-Leibniz international proceedings in informatics, 1. Schloss Dagstuhl-Leibniz-Zentrumfuer Informatik*.

Percival, C. (2009). Stronger key derivation via sequential memory-hard functions. Retrieved from https://sites.cs.ucsb.edu/~rich/class/old.cs290/papers/scrypt.pdf

Poon, J., & Buterin, V. (2017). Plasma: Scalable autonomous smart contracts. Retrieved from https://www.plasma.io/plasma-deprecated.pdf

Poon, J., & Dryja, T. (2016). The Bitcoin lightning network: Scalable off-chain instant payments. Retrieved from https://www.bitcoinlightning.com/wp-content/uploads/2018/03/lightning-network-paper.pdf

Qin, K., & Gervais, A. (2018). An overview of blockchain scalability, interoperability and sustainability. Retrieved from https://www.eublockchainforum.eu/sites/default/files/research-paper/an_overview_of_blockchain_scalability_interoperability_and_sustainability.pdf

Scalability. (2021). The scalability trilemma in blockchain. Retrieved from https://medium.com/@aakash_13214/the-scalability-trilemma-in-blockchain-75fb57f646df

Schaffner, T. (2021). Scaling public blockchains. Retrieved from https://wwz.unibas.ch/fileadmin/user_upload/wwz/00_Professuren/Schaer_DLTFintech/Lehre/Tobias_Schaffner_Masterthesis.pdf

Schneider, F. B. (1990). Implementing fault-tolerant services using the state machine approach: A tutorial. *ACM Computing Surveys*, *22*(4), 299–319.

Simplicio, M. A., Jr, Almeida, L. C., Andrade, E. R., dos Santos, P. C. F., & Barreto, P. S. L. M. (2014). *The Lyra2 reference guide*. Technical Report v2. 3.2.

Singh, A., Click, K., Parizi, R. M., Zhang, Q., Dehghantanha, A., & Choo, K.-K. R. (2020). Sidechain technologies in blockchain networks: An examination and state-of-the-art review. *Journal of Network and Computer Applications*, *149*(7), 102471.

Sompolinsky, Y., & Zohar, A. (2013). Accelerating bitcoin's transaction processing. Fast money grows on trees, not chains. In IACR Cryptology ePrint Archive, 2013 (881). Retrieved from https://eprint.iacr.org/2013/881.pdf

Sompolinsky, Y., & Zohar, A. (2015). Secure high-rate transaction processing in bitcoin. In *International conference on financial cryptography and data security* (pp. 507–527). Berlin: Springer.

Unitychain. (2021). *Scalability magic: BLS signatures*. Retrieved from https://www.unitychain.io/blog/scalability-magic-bls-signatures/

Wang, G., Shi, Z. J., Nixon, M., & Han, S. (2019). Sok: sharding on blockchain. In Proceedings of the 1st ACM *conference on advances in financial technologies*, (pp. 41–61). Association for Computing Machinery.

Wang, Q., Yu, J., Chen, S., & Xiang, Y. (2020). *SoK: Diving into DAG-based blockchain systems*. Ithaca, NY: Cornell University. arXiv preprint arXiv:2012.06128.

Wood, G. (2014). Ethereum: A secure decentralised generalised transaction ledger. *Ethereum Project Yellow Paper*, *151*, 1–32.

Xu, J., Ackerer, D., & Dubovitskaya, A. (2021). A game-theoretic analysis of cross-chain atomic swaps with HTLCs. In *2021 IEEE 41st international conference on distributed computing systems (ICDCS)* (pp. 584–594). Piscataway, NJ: IEEE. Retrieved from https://ieeexplore.ieee.org/xpl/conhome/9546301/proceeding

Xu, J., Vavryk, N., Paruch, K., & Cousaert, S. (2021). *SoK: Decentralized exchanges (DEX) with automated market maker (AMM) protocols*. Ithaca, NY: Cornell University. arXiv preprint arXiv:2103.12732.

Zamani, M., Movahedi, M., & Raykova, M. (2018). Rapidchain: scaling blockchain via full sharding. In *Proceedings of the 2018 ACM SIGSAC conference on computer and communications security* (pp. 931–948). Retrieved from https://ieeexplore.ieee.org/xpl/conhome/9546301/proceeding

Zyskind, G., Kisagun, C., & Fromknecht, C. (2018). Enigma catalyst: A machine-based investing platform and infrastructure for crypto-assets. Retrieved from http://www.bixiaobai.com/uploads/white_paper/pdfs/269.pdf

Chapter 19

Central Bank Digital Currencies: Opening Pandora's Box or Paving the Future of Money?

Dimitrios Salampasis, Patrick Schueffel, Russell Dominic and Duncan Cameron

Abstract

This chapter reviews developments concerning central bank digital currencies (CBDCs). It introduces, analyzes, and discusses the potential implications of CBDCs on the existing cryptoassets landscape. The chapter also provides an overview of the different approaches to adopting and implementing this new form of money. Additionally, it compares traditional cryptocurrencies, privately issued stablecoins, fiat currencies, and CBDCs. Although vastly divergent opinions exist on digital money's purpose, benefits, and use cases, CBDCs can provide opportunities for innovation and experimentation at a central bank and systemic level. CBDCs may pave the way for democratizing access to unbundled financial services while rethinking the overall purpose of money, monetary systems, and global business.

Keywords: Central bank digital currencies; cryptoassets; cryptocurrencies; stablecoins; fiat currencies; digital money

Introduction

Decentralized finance (DeFi) has emerged as an alternative, disintermediated, and mainly unregulated value proposition within financial services. Cryptocurrencies and the digital assets landscape are undergoing meteoric developments offering alternative units of account and novel payment systems, primarily due to the advancements in cryptographic and distributed ledger technologies (DLTs). Facebook's failed plans to launch Diem, a private, fiat-backed digital currency,

The Emerald Handbook on Cryptoassets: Investment Opportunities and Challenges, 283–306

doi:10.1108/978-1-80455-320-620221019

increasing fears of potential intense financial speculation and endangered financial stability. Incumbents, FinTechs, BigTechs, and central banks are actively exploring and experimenting with the concept of programmable money. Stronger financial inclusion remains a top agenda item on global calls, especially in the advent of a dematerialized cashless economy. This complex reality has redefined the concept and the purpose of fiat, private, and public money and may shape entire monetary and financial landscapes. In a broader context, although technological innovations contribute toward a global shift in the architectural designs of extant financial systems, the rapid adoption of digital assets begins to question the role governments and central banks play as monopolized custodians of monetary and financial institutions.

The Era of Central Bank Digital Currencies

In response to the declining global usage of physical cash and the continuous demand for disruptive financial innovation, central banks worldwide are accelerating research and development (R&D) by exploring and experimenting with alternative policy options. According to the Atlantic Council (2022) CBDC tracker, there are 11 projects launched, 14 in the pilot phase, 26 in the development phase, 47 in the research phase, 10 inactive and 2 cancelled. Central banks are looking into a new pilot scheme of publicly issued digital money, aptly called a CBDC, moving beyond their traditional passive and inertial approaches. The COVID-19 pandemic has challenged peoples' trust and confidence toward fiat currencies, urgently seeking viable alternatives within contactless environments (Lee, Yan, & Wang, 2021). Some could consider CBDCs a historic and radical innovation in the evolutionary journey of money (Peneder, 2021). They can potentially lead to fundamental and profound structural changes in monetary policy with macroeconomic, monetary regulation, system-changing, and business competition implications (Keister & Sanches, 2019; Shen & Hou, 2021).

The dichotomy between stability or heavy financial regulation and innovation has always been inherent to the DNA of financial services. Moreover, central banks are generally conservative, staid, cautious, and inertial (Bordo & Levin, 2017). Several foundational forces of change may lead to the introduction and potential adoption of this new form of publicly issued digital money as an alternative form (Cunha, Melo, & Sebastião, 2021; Lee et al., 2021). These forces include the digitization of universally accessible retail payments, the substitution effect stemming from the emergence of other forms of money, and the increased competition within the international monetary system due to the meteoric rise of cryptocurrencies (Echarte Fernández, Náñez Alonso, Jorge-Vázquez, & Reier Forradellas, 2021).

Definition of a CBDC and Value Proposition

Coeuré and Loh (2018, p. 3) state, "CBDC is not a well-defined term." CBDCs have certain common denominators. For instance, CBDCs are a central bank liability denominated in an existing unit of account, serving as a medium of exchange and a store of value. Furthermore, as the name suggests, CBDCs exist only in digital form and are "digital money" (Nolting, Heinz, & Köhling, 2020). Today, a fair share of central bank currency exists digitally, namely the sight deposits held by commercial banks at the central bank. This trend will remain with "physical" cash (coins and notes) continuing to convert into a digital form. Hence, some refer to CBDCs as digital base money (Mersch, 2017).

According to the International Monetary Fund, a CBDC is a "digital representation of sovereign currency that is issued by a jurisdiction's monetary authority and appears on the liability side of the monetary authority's balance sheet" (Kiff et al., 2020, p. 5). Lee et al. (2021, p. 54) more narrowly define a CBDC as

> a new type of electronic liabilities of the central bank, which can be used as a means of payment and value storage, and yet retain most of the desirable characteristics of M0 and M1.

M0 is the total of all physical currency, including coinage (i.e., M0 = Federal Reserve notes + US notes + coins. M1 is M0 (cash/coin) outside the private banking system plus demand deposits, travelers' checks, and other checkable deposits + most savings accounts. Agur, Ari, and Dell'Ariccia (2022) view a CBDC as a new type of fiat money that expands access to central bank reserves to the public instead of restricting it to commercial banks. Keister and Sanches (2019) contend that the introduction of a CBDC consists of a set of use cases compared to physical cash bearing both positive and negative returns. Bordo and Levin (2017, p. 19) summarize the value proposition of a CBDC as a "costless medium of exchange, secure store of value, and stable unit of account."

Extant research suggests that a CBDC, as a digitized legal tender, is a centralized digital version of fiat money designed to serve as a monetary tool and a payment instrument (Shen & Hou, 2021). This perspective may pave the way toward an era of an improved international monetary system (Xu & Zou, 2021), large-scale financial intermediation, financial inclusion, and transformative innovation in the history of banking and money (Fernández-Villaverde, Sanches, Schilling, & Uhlig, 2021). Tong and Jiayou (2021) place CBDCs among the three categories of digital currencies together with private, encrypted, decentralized digital currencies (e.g., Bitcoin and Ether) and global stablecoins (e.g., USDT and Diem). Bindseil (2019, p. 303) considers a CBDC as "a third form of base money" together with overnight deposits with a central bank and banknotes.

As a CBDC is central bank money, but in a digital form, it has a unique value proposition. It has the risk-free aspects of central bank money but is highly fungible in digital settings. Hence, unlike notes and coins, it is suitable for transactions on the internet.

Why Central Banks Establish CBDCs

Several reasons explain central banks' interest in exploring and potentially launching a CBDC. The primary drivers are financial inclusion and financial digitization, especially considering unbanked populations. The issuance, storage, and circulation of materialized fiat money are costly. Hence, a CBDC may reduce issuance, storage, and transaction costs while increasing efficiency in payments, financial markets, and the real economy. Data recording and tracking can bring better accuracy in transaction authentication (higher auditability), preventing illegal transactions, money laundering, tax evasion, anonymous cash (preserving the privacy of exchanges), and usage of unregulated virtual currencies.

The introduction of a CBDC could also allow central banks to overcome the "zero lower bound" (ZLB) problem since they can optimally adjust interest rates to align with inflation, contrary to a deposit-driven economy (Shen & Hou, 2021). The *ZLB* is a macroeconomic problem occurring when the short-term nominal interest rate is at or near zero, causing a liquidity trap and limiting the central bank's capacity to stimulate economic growth. The digital nature of a CBDC can bring ecosystemic and universal lens within financial and economic activities, opening the competitive landscape of payments while reducing the number of intermediaries. CBDCs' interoperability can optimize cross-border payments, remittances, e-commerce transactions (i.e., clearing and settlement systems and reduction/elimination of brokerage costs), and leverage a sovereign digital currency as a competitive and more attractive vehicle for global business.

Additionally, sovereign CBDCs may increase international exchange and global influence while leading a more harmonized, controlled, and integrated monetary and fiscal policy. The digital and potentially blockchain-enabled infrastructure behind a CBDC can bring safety, transparency, efficiency, speed, and enhanced user experience. Such an infrastructure can also reduce the environmental footprint of maintaining a cash-led economy (payment system). A CBDC may or may not have blockchain or DLT technology as an underlying infrastructure, at least in its purest forms. However, different architectural variations could exist.

Finally, a CBDC could be the centralized response to the increasing competition stemming from using unregulated, decentralized cryptocurrencies and non-government backed stablecoins for domestic and international transactions. Central banks may want to preserve public sovereignty by ensuring that public money will still be in demand and remain the preferred unit of account, medium of exchange, and store of value compared to other private/open-source digital currencies (Peneder, 2021; Viñuela, Sapena, & Wandosell, 2020). Table 19.1 summarizes the main reasons for central banks to establish a CBDC.

Why Central Banks Do Not Establish CBDCs

A CBDC's potential adoption has challenges and potential risks. A key concern is related to the disintermediation of commercial banks. A CBDC's disintermediation effect could potentially lead to transformative dynamics within financial markets, disrupting the relationship between central and commercial banks. Some expect challenges to commercial banks' intermediary role of attracting deposits and offering financial services to consumers. Such challenges are likely within an account-based scheme where financial consumers can open and hold accounts directly, with the central bank shifting completely the extant banking relationship practices. This scenario could pose an existential threat to commercial banks due

Table 19.1. Advantages of CBDCs.

Efficiency	• Reduces friction within extant payment systems
	• Lowers the cost of a transaction
	• Increases the speed and safety of transactions
	• Ensures the finality of transactions
	• Decreases the reliance on clearinghouses
Taxation	• Provides an effective tax base
	• Reduces or limits tax evasion
	• Increases tax revenues
Flexible monetary policy	• Offers flexibility
	• Provides optimal interest rates
	• Minimizes expansionary fiscal or monetary policies due to increased money supply
	• Pays interest to the token itself
Payments	• Offers a backdrop to privately managed payments
	• Avoids a breakdown during a crisis
Financial inclusion	• Enables underbanked and unbanked societies to access financial products/services

Source: Developed by the authors based on Allen et al. (2020).

Note: This table summarizes the main advantages of central banks adopting a CBDC.

to reduced deposits and decreased money supply, resulting in a collapse in bank liquidity. Similarly, a CBDC's centralized character might result in competition distortion with central banks replacing commercial banks as the primary vehicles of retail and business payments, along with credit issuance, further undermining market neutrality.

In addition, some central banks do not see any advantage or benefit of adopting a CBDC over existing payment systems. Other potential reasons for central banks not establishing a CBDC are a lack of demand preference toward private digital/virtual currencies and failed pilot projects. Table 19.2 summarizes the major reasons for central banks not wanting to establish a CBDC.

Public–Private Partnership of Money

No single accepted theory is available on how money came into existence (Davies, 2010). This situation is probably because money has various purposes. Money reduces transaction costs compared to barter trading because it provides a gauge for value and makes traditional bartering no longer a prerequisite for a deal (Menger, 1892). Hence, money likely emerged in the private sector. Soon afterward, sovereigns would have understood its practicability and adopted it for tax collection and borrowing purposes (Graeber, 2011).

Table 19.2. Disadvantages of CBDCs.

Disintermediation	• Results in potential systemic destabilization
Government involvement	• Creates a potential difficulty in balancing central-bank oversight and innovation
Regulatory compliance	• Creates additional complexity in developing regulatory and compliance tools and mechanisms
	• Requires a need to upskill to rapidly address financial innovations and structural changes
Loss of privacy	• Creates potential ethical issues with managing private and sensitive information
Technological immaturity	• Involves a potential lack of expertise in developing complex technical solutions

Note: This table summarizes the main disadvantages of central banks adopting a CBDC.

Over time, rulers started issuing coins, generating seigniorage by charging a markup on the physical costs of money. *Seigniorage* is a government's profit by issuing currency, especially the difference between the face value of coins and their production costs. Today, central banks still create legal tender and collect seigniorage, but the more significant part of money creation involves commercial banks (McLeay, Radia, & Thomas, 2014). Under the fractional reserve system, commercial banks can create loans for borrowers of the balance held at the central bank. In the Eurozone, for instance, the current reserve requirement is a maximum of 1 percent, which means that commercial banks can loan out at least EUR 100 on every Euro they deposit with the European Central Bank (2021).

In this private–public partnership, the coins and notes in circulation, which constitute a country's legal tender, along with the deposits commercial banks hold at the central bank, represent central bank currency, also known as base or sovereign money. By comparison, the money issued by commercial banks constitutes bank money, also known as credit, book, or deposit money. A saver's balance on a bank account as sight, time or savings deposits is a payment promise or "IOU" issued by a commercial bank (Swiss National Bank, 2007). Figure 19.1 depicts the distinct types of monetary aggregates.

Stakeholders

From the origins of money when payments in standardized goods such as metals began to replace barter trade, to today's financial services industry, an entire ecosystem has emerged around money. Similarly, a CBDC will not emerge in a vacuum. It will also affect various stakeholders. Those stakeholders consist of two groups: (1) the provider side ensuring issuance and distribution of CBDCs, and (2) the consumer side using a CBDC. The former group includes central banks, commercial banks, credit card firms, payment companies, and infrastructure providers. The latter group comprises all entities and individuals who adopt a CBDC as money. Big tech firms that primarily rely on the internet as a

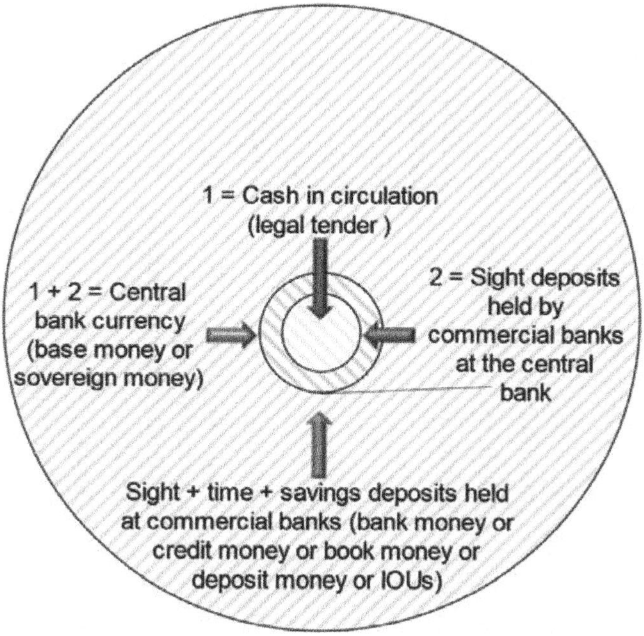

Figure 19.1. Depicting Money Aggregates. *Source:* Developed by the authors. *Note*: This figure displays a schematic depicting money aggregates.

distribution channel are clearly among the prime candidates to swiftly adopt a CBDC for their business models.

Attributes of Central Bank Money

Central bank money is fiat money, meaning it is a currency and is not representative of another asset. Instead, governmental decree or parties engaging in trade who agree on its value assign value.

Central bank money consists of cash in circulation (i.e., a nation's legal tender) and sight deposits held by commercial banks at the central bank. As a central bank liability, it is money that has "no liquidity risk, no credit risk, no market risk" (Panetta, 2021). Central bank money does not bear any liquidity risk because a central bank can meet its short-term debt obligations. It remains liquid, given that it is indebted in its domestic currency. Being unable to convert assets into cash is not a problem for central banks because they can potentially create more money to meet obligations. Similarly, credit risks rarely threaten central banks. They can meet their obligations under the agreed terms if such obligations involve only debts denominated in their domestic currency. From a domestic point of view, no market risks can occur because losses in positions arising from market variables do not affect the domestic central bank money.

Table 19.3. A Comparison of Six Types of Money.

Feature	Physical Cash	Electronic Cash	CBDC	Crypto	Stablecoin	Bitcoin
Legal tender	Yes	No	Yes	No	No	No [Except for El Salvador]
Infinite	Yes	Yes	Yes	Depends	Yes [In most existing cases]	No
Stable (pegged)	Yes	Yes	Yes	Depends	Yes [In most existing cases]	No
Anonymity	Yes	No	Depends	Depends	Pseudo anonymity	Pseudo anonymity
Programmable	No	No	Yes	Depends	Yes	No
Centralized	Yes	Yes	Yes	No	No	No
Regulated	Yes	Yes	Yes	No	No	No
Transaction speed	High	High	High	Depends	Medium	Low
Counterparty risk	No	Yes	No	No	Yes [counterparty must warrant backing]/ No [DLT securing trustless operations]	No
Fungible	Yes	Yes	Yes	Depends	Depends	Yes
Issued by	Central banks	Commercial banks	Central banks	Private entities	Private entities	Private entities
Physical Point of Sale (POS) usability	Yes	Yes	Yes	Yes	Yes	Yes
Online usability	No	Yes	Yes	Yes	Yes	Yes

Note: This table provides a comparison of six types of money against certain features.

Comparing and Contrasting

Table 19.3 compares six distinct types of money. Physical cash is the starting point. Electronic cash is the second category created by commercial banks under the fractional reserve regime. The third class is a CBDC, which can emerge in various forms so that its characteristics are not currently well defined. Next is crypto, comprising a broad range of cryptocurrencies like stablecoins and bitcoin. Due to their significance, the latter two categories represent separate types.

Possible Representations

CBDCs are possible in different representations. Three possibilities are conceivable involving the organization level. A CBDC could be issued: (1) solely on a wholesale level (e.g., interbank payments and securities settlements), (2) on an individual level (general purpose/retail), and (3) to end-users via intermediaries as an intermediate CBDC. Two other realizations are feasible regarding ledger design. Entries could represent a CBDC on ledgers as account-based or token-based. Figure 19.2 and Table 19.4 show these combinations.

Account Versus Token-based system The basis of the discussion around adopting an account versus token-based system concerns a conflict between divergent views of representing value through tokenization of financial instruments or improvements within account-based systems (McLaughlin, 2021). An account-based system requires payer verification. A token-based system requires an asset's verification of the validity of a payment transaction (Garratt, Lee, Malone, & Martin, 2020). It serves on an anonymous basis akin to cash today. Another name for a token based CBDC is a "digital banknote" (Auer & Böhme,

Figure 19.2. CBDC Representations. *Source:* Developed by the authors extending the work by Lee et al. (2021).
Note: This figure shows the main CBDC representations combining ledger design and organizational level.

Table 19.4. CBDC Representations, Attributes, and Design Considerations.

Representation	Attributes	Design Considerations
Retail (general purpose)	• Digital version of cash	• Role of central banks and the private sector regarding accessibility and usage
	• Universally accessible medium of exchange and store of value	• One-tier or two-tier system
	• Unit of account – sovereign currency	• Account-based, token-based, or hybrid system
	• Convertible one-for-one in other forms of money	• In-person, online, and offline usability
	• Legal tender	• National or international interlinkages
	• Involves corporations, small businesses, and individuals	• Interest rate
	• Could lead to a complete replacement of cash	• Degree of privacy (account-based no privacy; token-based privacy by default)
		• Blockchain/DLT technology and consensus algorithm harmonization (R3 Corda or Quorum) or not (conventional-centralized ledger; potentially distributed storage but centralized control of information)
		• Centralized, partially decentralized, or fully decentralized
		• Questionable future role of cash

Representation	Attributes	Design Considerations
Wholesale	• Restricted-access digital token	• Limited to commercial banks, clearing institutions, or other entities traditionally having access to central bank reserves
	• New infrastructure for securities settlements	• Centralized, partially decentralized, or fully decentralized
	• Accessible only by a limited range of participants	• Blockchain/DLT technology and consensus algorithm harmonization (R3 Corda or Quorum) or not (conventional-centralized ledger; potentially distributed storage but centralized control of information)
	• Bank-to-bank (interbank) payments	
	• Real-time settlement of cross-border financial transactions	
	• Possible threat to the banking system	

Note: This table summarizes the two CBDC representations and their associated attributes and design considerations.

2020a, p. 90). The two models have different economic implications. The following section presents the two systems.

Account-based Model: Retail, Wholesale, and Intermediated. A CBDC is a transferable deposit account with a central bank, requiring the identity verification of the "would-be-payer." If issued as an account based CBDC, the end-user is credited/debited with the corresponding amounts of a CBDC. The corresponding additions/subtractions involve individual user or business accounts. For this purpose, a commercial bank or a central bank should directly identify the end-user. Commercial banks or a central bank record all transactions on a ledger. These institutions could keep records at both levels. A party could outsource account servicing and technical maintenance to third-party providers. A CBDC is not a circulating currency but includes transferable account balances held within a central bank. This situation could lead to an exponential growth of public central bank accounts, raising questions about governance and account management capacity. Consequently, central banks would be more prone to cyber-attacks when receiving instructions to pay unauthorized parties by transferring money from accounts belonging to the central bank. Table 19.5 summarizes the key advantages and disadvantages of an account based CBDC.

Token-based Model: Retail, Wholesale, and Intermediated. Contrary to an account-based system, a token-based system is entirely new. A token's treatment legally depends on the purpose and the ad hoc granted rights questioning the legality of a token based CBDC scheme (Wagner, Bruggink, & Benevelli, 2021). A token based CBDC comes closest to a digital version of physical cash. A central bank issues a liability in the form of a digital token. The CBDC, created as a token, has a specific denomination. In this case, the central bank circulates digitally issued tokens in a centralized manner, and the central ledger would only

Table 19.5. Account-based System: Advantages and Disadvantages.

Advantages	**Disadvantages**
Public access to central bank accounts	Technical and infrastructure issues related to governance and management
Enhancement of financial inclusion	Capacity to oversee and engage with payments (retail scenario)
Promotion of fiscal and monetary policy	Infrastructure and system cost
Speed and security of cross-border transaction settlements	Potential bank runs (retail scenario)
Tracking transactions to avoid illicit activities	Customer privacy issues

Note: This table summarizes the main advantages and disadvantages of an account-based CBDC system.

register issuance and redemption. This process involves storing individual liabilities on digital wallets and not on accounts.

Like cash, a user can pass on a token in a financial transaction to another holder. This "immediate" transfer of ownership would not require database reconciliation. The issuer keeps a record of the issued token but does not record who holds specific tokens because users can pass on these tokens by simply using private/public keys. In that way, a central bank only knows the total amount of CBDC tokens withdrawn and the total amount spent.

Similarly, commercial banks are only aware of how many tokens their clients withdrew. They do not know the amount spent by an individual or the purpose of the expenditure (Grothof & Moser, 2021). Other members of the blockchain network must confirm the transaction. The expectation is that the network would be permissioned to adopt a centrally distributed private model consistent with the ad hoc central bank's objectives and monetary policy goals. A single entity would control the digital ledger.

A token-based CBDC could facilitate cross-border transactions if both parties have digital wallets. Moreover, a token-based CBDC would be more secure due to encryption, especially within cross-border transactions. Table 19.6 summarizes the key advantages and disadvantages of a token based CBDC.

Architectural Design

Given the different possible representations of a CBDC, various architectural designs are also conceivable. We can refine the three categories discussed a bit further into *direct, indirect,* and *intermediated* (including a *hybrid* special case) CBDCs explained below:

Table 19.6. Token-based System: Advantages and Disadvantages.

Advantages	Disadvantages
Easy cross-border transactions	Transaction speed (consensus algorithm)
Promotion of financial inclusion	Cost of implementation (infrastructure consistent with broader monetary policy objectives)
Higher degree of anonymity	Cybersecurity issues (decentralized network)
Higher security due to encryption	Nature of tokens (interest and fees)
Implementation of monetary policy	Blurry differences compared to existing privately issued digital currencies (stablecoins)
Less central bank bureaucracy	

Note: This table summarizes the main advantages and disadvantages of a token-based CBDC system.

- an *indirect* CBDC deployed on the wholesale level,
- a *direct* CBDC directly provided to the retail level, and
- an *intermediated* CBDC, including a hybrid design as a special case of the intermediated design.

Developers can roll out each design category in conjunction with an account or a token based CBDC (Lee et al., 2021), rendering six distinctive design models. Figure 19.3 shows these design variants.

Indirect (Two-tiered) or Synthetic. A central bank issues an indirect or synthetic CBDC to commercial banks on a wholesale level. It is an account based CBDC with a central bank operating a ledger that records all transactions between it and the commercial banks and potentially among the commercial banks.

The client holds a claim against the commercial bank in this setup, not a central bank. However, the commercial bank must back its clients' claims by actual CBDC holdings at the central bank. As the client holds no CBDC, this architectural design model is an "indirect or synthetic" CBDC. The intermediary (i.e., the commercial bank) manages the client's onboarding and know your customer (KYC). The central bank restricts itself to payments on a wholesale level.

Direct. In contrast to an indirect or synthetic CBDC, a direct CBDC is issued to end clients, including businesses, individuals, and other non-banking organizations. In this architectural design model, the central bank operates a ledger that records all CBDCs that it issues either as an account- or token-based CBDC. The CBDC with the end-user represents a direct claim on the central bank.

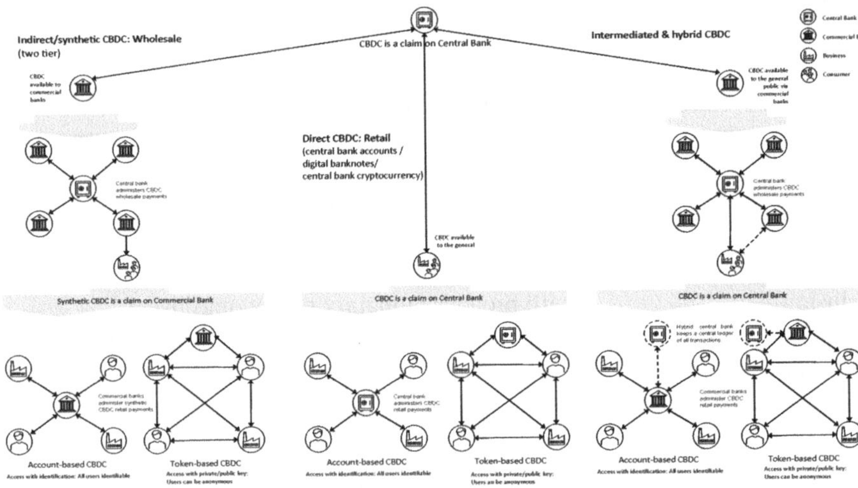

Figure 19.3. Architectural Design Variants. *Source:* Developed by the authors synthesizing information and extending the work by the Bank for International Settlements (2021), Nolting, Heinz, and Köhling (2020), and Auer & Böhme (2020a). *Note*: This figure shows the key variants of the three CBDC architectural designs.

Intermediated. An intermediated architectural model foresees intermediation between the central bank and an end-user by commercial banks. However, it differs from an indirect or synthetic CBDC in that the issued CBDC is a claim against the central bank, whether in possession of commercial banks or end-users. From the central bank's perspective, a disadvantage of the intermediated model is that it must honor claims for which it has no record (Auer & Böhme, 2020b).

Intermediated (Hybrid). A special case of the intermediated architectural model is a hybrid one, where there is a direct claim on a central bank, but intermediaries are responsible for managing the payments. It mitigates the risks for central banks because they keep a ledger of all transactions (Fatás, 2021). Moreover, accomplishing a high degree of technological resilience occurs through a "hybrid design via the central bank operating a back-up infrastructure (hence the name hybrid – [...])" (Auer & Böhme, 2020a, p. 12). Table 19.7 summarizes the key attributes of the three possible representations of a CBDC.

Infrastructure

A CBDC's introduction is likely to pose infrastructure requirements by the issuing central bank to execute payments digitally as a database to register the CBDC and an application to execute CBDC payments. Central banks traditionally are not known for building payment infrastructure or payment services and are likely to push these requirements onto commercial and retail banks. Regardless of the service provider, a CBDC's infrastructure must support various functional requirements and security features (Han, Yuan, & Wang, 2019). The following discussion is indicative only as there is no standardization around CBDC infrastructure.

Functional Requirements

The underlying infrastructure must allow for centralized issuance and central banks because the sovereign state's representatives must issue or manage the currency's issuance. Moreover, such an infrastructural architecture must allow for transferability (i.e., the money in circulation is a means of payment among parties) and accessibility (i.e., a user can securely access the CBDC in the form of data at the user's electronic device). Furthermore, another consideration is the provision of offline functionality. A CBDC user may be unable to directly communicate with the main ledger when performing transactions through the electronic device. Finally, such infrastructure must support the provisions brought forward by Anti-Money Laundering/Financial Action Task Force (AML/FAFT) regulations.

Security Properties

The underpinning infrastructure must support the no double-spend requirement as a minimum security feature. No CBDC used by one user can be used again to pay for other transactions. Next, it must be counterfeit-proof, implying that

Table 19.7. Architectural Designs Attributes.

Architecture	Attributes
Direct	• The CBDC represents a direct claim on a central bank • A central bank maintains the central ledger • A central bank executes all retail payments • A central bank or intermediaries manage onboarding, including KYC processes
Indirect or synthetic	• The CBDC does not represent a direct claim on a central bank but represents a claim on the financial intermediaries • Financial intermediaries operate all retail payments • A central bank operates all wholesale payments • Consumers cannot directly access central bank money • Financial intermediaries perform onboarding, including KYC processes
Intermediated	• The CBDC represents a direct claim on a central bank • A central bank maintains the wholesale ledger • Financial intermediaries operate all retail payments • Consumers cannot directly access central bank money • Financial intermediaries perform onboarding, including KYC processes
Intermediated (Hybrid)	• The CBDC represents a direct claim on the central bank • A central bank maintains the wholesale ledger • Financial intermediaries operate all retail payments • Consumers cannot directly access central bank money • Financial intermediaries perform onboarding, including KYC processes • A central bank operates a backup technical infrastructure, providing the ability to restart payment systems in case of failure by financial intermediaries

Note: This table summarizes the three CBDC architectural designs and their main associated attributes.

no one can forge an officially issued CBDC. A CBDC also requires non-repudiation, meaning that a payer cannot successfully dispute a transaction's validity. This security property requires recording all parties' actions from the transaction's initiation to the end, including the payer, recipient, and transaction verifier. In addition, the infrastructure must allow for verifiability, requiring validation of all transaction records created in the system. Some experts demand anonymity as a critical feature to support a CBDC infrastructure. Considering the abovementioned discussion of account- and token-based models, whether anonymity will be an inherent feature remains uncertain.

Compatibility

CBDC compatibility remains a central challenge within international financial systems, especially concerning the ability to host multiple CBDCs on the same infrastructure and platform. The sharing of such a CBDC infrastructure can pose significant governance challenges. The Bank for International Settlements has conceptualized three multiple CBDC (m-CBDC) models to reduce friction and barriers to enable seamless cross-border monetary services. The three models are (1) m-CBDC arrangements based on compatible CBDC systems, (2) m-CBDC arrangements based on linking multiple CBDC systems, and (3) m-CBDC arrangements based on single multi-currency systems. In a recent research report, Oliver Wyman and JP Morgan estimate that adopting a full-scale m-CBDC network could result in about a $120 billion savings in transaction costs by global corporates on an annual basis (Ekberg et al., 2021).

CBDC Implications for the Blockchain and Cryptoassets Landscape

This section examines selected implications related to blockchain technology, interoperability, and cryptoassets. It also compares CBDCs with other forms of money, particularly stablecoins.

Implications of Blockchain Technology

Blockchain technology can potentially benefit various sectors, including the public sector, by improving complex processes cost-effectively (Blakstad & Allen, 2018). Although Bitcoin and Ethereum are mainstream decentralized large-scale payment systems, blockchain's role as an underlying infrastructure of a centrally governed payment system is still relatively unexplored. Cited concerns include decentralization, scalability, security, limited oversight, and insufficient know your customer, anti-money laundering/counter financing of terrorism (AML/CFT), and pseudo-anonymity of transactions. The experimentation on CBDCs and the emergence of private blockchain and CBDCs as service/infrastructure providers have propelled technological developments and innovations through discipline and application intersectionality, bringing enhanced and novel use cases to market.

Different schools of thought exist on blockchain serving as an infrastructure for CBDCs. Jung and Jeong (2021) believe that blockchain is vital to developing a CBDC ecosystem. The main attributes include shared value and transfers of ownership via the integrated platform, smart contracts, and programmable and transparent audit records. Impetus exists for blockchain to evolve because it calls for the evolution of the blockchain landscape required to serve stakeholders with public sector oversight. Incompatibility issues may push stakeholders to create and adopt harmonized blockchain to avoid fragmentation. This relationship strongly depends on the appetite of each central bank and a CBDC's role within a jurisdiction. Some expect more innovation in enterprise-level permissioned or hybrid networks consistent with required CBDC attributes and functionalities.

Some also contend that a CBDC-managed payment system may allow central banks to detect illegal activities (Lee et al., 2021) but at the cost of personal security and privacy. Although a blockchain-enabled CDBC limits the risk of information tampering, the whole blockchain ecosystem is not risk-free. A blockchain-enabled CDBC may encounter personal information security issues (Lee et al., 2021). For instance, malevolent parties may target the centralized trusted network for geopolitical purposes, resulting in lost stakeholders' private keys and asset theft.

A blockchain-enabled CDBC requires several actions to support the benefit of transparency and trust. For example, all participants in the ecosystem should observe all transactions in the ledgers and duplicate them into their ledger. Although viable solutions to this issue include encryption and obfuscation methods (Priem, 2020), dilemmas arise for this type of solution. On the one hand, the obfuscation technique makes detecting malevolent activities difficult. At the same time, without the applicability of further encryption in a blockchain-enabled CDBC, bad actors could exploit shared or public information.

CBDC Interoperability

Blockchains are hermetic systems, meaning that swapping assets from one chain to another is difficult (Finlow-Bates, 2020). An example is swapping native bitcoin on the Bitcoin blockchain into Ethereum (ether) on the Ethereum blockchain. This situation creates significant issues for *interoperability*, meaning the ability of disparate chains to talk to each other, share data, or execute transactions.

Some techniques, namely "atomic cross-chain swaps" and "bridges," are maturing that allow users to execute separate transactions to simultaneously transact on both chains (Lys, Micoulet, & Potop-Butucaru, 2019). Recently, significant developments have gone into building cross-chain compatibility via centralized services or multi-chain decentralized exchanges.

CBDC technical architectures are unlikely to be "blockchains" in the sense of being open, permissionless ledgers. They are more likely to align to a private distributed-ledger system with limited exposure to underlying code and tightly controlled transaction permissions (Coeuré & Shin, 2021). They also are likely to face demanding design decisions around enabling interoperable products and services.

China's recent CBDC development paper highlights a need to support existing infrastructure and enable interoperability between CBDC systems of different jurisdictions and incumbent payment systems (People's Bank of China, 2021). Although the promise of interoperability is desirable, significant technical and political limitations may result in market fragmentation. Jurisdictions will develop CBDCs in different forms due to cultural factors and policy demands, resulting in diverging architectures.

The Relationship Between CBDCs and Stablecoins

Stablecoins play a critical role in the crypto ecosystem, with roughly $125 billion worth of these assets available on-chain, with a substantial percentage of that centralized on Ethereum. A few key tokens, including Tether ($68.64 billion) and USD Coin ($30.28 billion), seem to dominate the ecosystem (Cryptoslate, 2021).

Stablecoins, as a new cryptocurrency asset class, mostly operate on the principle of pegging. The on-chain token is linked or pegged to an asset off-chain considered stable, most often fiat currencies (Finlow-Bates, 2020) or a set of exchange-traded commodities like precious metals. Stablecoins serve as an optimal hedging instrument for cryptocurrency traders since their definition is relative to the risk profile of the assets in their reserves (Catalini & de Gortari, 2021). For example, Tether and USDC are pegged to reserves of US dollars, held in bank accounts by the institutions that issued the tokens. The main categories of stablecoins are: (1) fiat-collateralized, (2) asset/commodity-collateralized, (3) crypto-collateralized, (4) non-collateralized, and (5) consortium. Catalini and de Gortari (2021) propose a slightly different categorization: (1) fully backed in a protocol's investment token, (2) partially backed in a protocol's token, (3) backed in crypto with low collateralization, (4) backed in risky off-chain assets, (5) backed in crypto with high collateralization, (6) 1:1 fiat-backed in high-quality liquid assets (HQLAs) + capital requirements/buffers, and (7) CBDC digital token convertible 1:1 with reference asset.

Interoperability between different CBDCs will differ from interoperability between CBDCs and permissionless blockchain networks. The former is a priority to enable cross-border settlements.

Notable critics suggest that the advent of CBDCs could remove the need for stablecoins, as a CBDC may be a less risky alternative to users (Powell, 2021), given the ongoing concern around stablecoins. The guarantee of stablecoin "stability" is often based on the ability to redeem the token for the underlying asset. For example, can someone redeem $100 for $100 in cash from the issuer? The basis of this guarantee is an agreement, albeit with no underlying contract or promise between the holder and issuer. Tether has come under scrutiny for failing to disclose adequate evidence to redeem all issued Tether on-chain (Schoenberg, Robison, & Faux, 2021). Absolving these risks relies on a centrally backed digital currency.

Additionally, developing countries continue to recognize the threat of global stablecoins to international monetary policy and consistently highlight the risk of illicit activity happening in the crypto ecosystem (Foley, Karlsen, & Putniņš, 2019). Assuaging many of these concerns relies on a centrally backed, transparent, and highly auditable CBDC-type stablecoin.

However, interoperability between CBDCs and the wider crypto ecosystem will not be a priority for CBDC protocols for two key reasons:

- The architectural design of permissioned CBDCs is likely to prevent this level of interoperability. As mentioned earlier, blockchains or permissioned-CBDC ledgers are hermetic systems. Middleware or integration layers between sovereign state-owned ledgers and public, permissionless ledgers are unlikely to exist anytime soon. Until there is a standardized regulatory acceptance of cryptoassets, many will view interoperability as an unnecessary implementation risk to any sovereign digital currency.

- For central banks to retain sovereignty and monetary control is likely against their interests to enable interoperability with the broader crypto ecosystem. Interoperability would also hinder the regulator's ability to manage tax evasion, control policy and rates, ensure the finality of transactions, and even limit the safety and protection of users.

A likely conclusion is that stablecoins will persist as a critical element of the crypto ecosystem. Additionally, there has been significant growth in the popularity of stablecoins that do not rely on 1-to-1 pegging to existing off-chain assets like the US dollar, including:

- crypto-reserve stablecoins that rely on other crypto-assets as collateral to maintain stability, like MakerDAO and Synthetix; and
- algorithmic stablecoins that rely on the open market and complex user incentives to constantly rebalance their token against a stable target, like Celo and Terra.

Users consider CBDCs or fiat currencies stable as they represent a claim or are "redeemable" against the central bank. One principle that supports these alternative stablecoins is that a credible commitment to market-making is economically identical to allowing redemptions or claims against a central bank (Qureshi, 2021). Therefore, even with the maturing of CBDCs globally, stablecoins are likely to continue within the crypto ecosystem that, by design, decouples them from central bank money, paving the way toward a co-existence scenario.

The Relationship between CBDCs and Other Cryptoassets

The relationship between CBDCs and other types of privately issued cryptoassets depends on the appetite for innovation, co-existence, and the plurality of options. By nature, a CBDC backed by an institution has the public policy objective and accountability. A CBDC's central attribute and its scope and usage will determine the trust quotient and attractiveness compared to other forms of crypto-led assets. Central banks may push to issue a CDBC as a policy response if use of cryptoassets is heavy and erodes the public benefit (Bank of Canada, 2020). A philosophical consideration is also important on the preference of public/permissionless/open source versus central/permissioned and pegging. Crypto holders may not want to switch to a CDBC as it lacks price volatility, which many use to gain value. Additionally, they may want to avoid changing to a CDBC if it lacks anonymity or is subject to excessive control. CBDCs will also come together with a solid regulatory portfolio, which will create more or fewer barriers to entry or eliminate certain cryptocurrencies. CBDCs may not replace cryptoassets unless the jurisdiction imposes a complete ban, as in the recent example of China. All will come down to consumer and user trust and an acceptable risk level.

Summary and Conclusions

This chapter explores different CBDC definitions and provides reasons for and against creating a CBDC. Moreover, it considers the broader DLT-ecosystem in which CBDCs operate and highlights its stakeholders. The chapter also examines the attributes constituting a CBDC and highlights the various representations CBDC can take, including the architectural designs and minimum requirements that they would need to fulfill. Lastly, as CBDCs are likely to have massive external effects, the chapter compares CBDCs to other cryptoassets and assesses potential CBDC implications on the blockchain and cryptoasset landscape.

This detailed analysis of CBDCs reveals the topic's multifaceted nature. The symbiotic cooperation between public and private stakeholders provides the grounding for the digital evolution, effectiveness, and value proposition of CBDCs. Virtually no aspect of CBDCs is unchangeable. CBDC deployment is at the intersection of integration (extant conventional and emerging/alternative payment systems), current and anticipated consumer needs, regulatory clarity, and policy-level innovation, among others. Some perceive CBDCs as a utopian vehicle for accessibility, inclusion, and democratization and a dystopian way as a vehicle for control, data exploitation, and money multiplication. Therefore, all shareholders need a constructive dialogue from a feasibility and desirability standpoint to create this new type of money to benefit its stakeholders.

Discussion Questions

1. Describe a CBDC and its two variants.
2. Describe the types of CBDCs.
3. List several potential reasons for central banks establishing a CDBC.
4. Explain the main differences between CDBCs and cryptocurrencies.
5. Identify the main differences between an account-based and a token-based system.
6. Identify the advantages and disadvantages of CBDCs.

References

Agur, I., Ari, A., & Dell'Ariccia, G. (2022). Designing central bank digital currencies. *Journal of Monetary Economics*, *125*(January), 62–79.

Allen, S., Čapkun, S., Eyal, I., Fanti, G., Ford, B., Grimmelmann, J., … Zhang, F. (2020). *Design choices for central bank digital currency: Policy and technical considerations*, No. w27634. National Bureau of Economic Research. Retrieved from http://www.nber.org/papers/w27634

Atlantic Council. (2022). Central bank digital currency tracker. Retrieved from https://www.atlanticcouncil.org/cbdctracker/

Auer, R., & Böhme, R. (2020a). The technology of retail central bank digital currency. *BIS Quarterly Review*, March, pp. 85–100. Retrieved from https://www.bis.org/publ/qtrpdf/r_qt2003j.htm

Auer, R., & Böhme, R. (2020b). *CBDC architectures, the financial system, and the central bank of the future*. VoxEU.org – CEPR's Policy Portal. Retrieved from https://voxeu.org/article/cbdc-architectures-financial-system-and-central-bank-future

Bank for International Settlements. (2021, June 28). *BIS annual economic report 2021*. Basel: BIS. Retrieved from https://www.bis.org/publ/arpdf/ar2021e.htm

Bank of Canada. (2020, February 25). Contingency planning for a central bank digital currency.. Retrieved from https://www.bankofcanada.ca/2020/02/contingency-planning-central-bank-digital-currency

Bindseil, U. (2019). Central bank digital currency: Financial system implications and control. *International Journal of Political Economy*, *48*(4), 303–335.

Blakstad, S., & Allen, R. (2018). Central bank digital currencies and cryptocurrencies. In *FinTech revolution: Universal inclusion in the new financial ecosystem*. Cham: Palgrave Macmillan.

Bordo, M. D., & Levin, A. T. (2017). *Central bank digital currency and the future of monetary policy*, No. w23711. National Bureau of Economic Research. Retrieved from https://www.nber.org/papers/w23711

Catalini, C., & de Gortari, A. (2021). On the economic design of stablecoins. Retrieved from https://ssrn.com/abstract=3899499

Coeuré, B., & Loh, J. (2018, March 12). *Central bank digital currencies*. Committee on Payments and Market Infrastructures and Markets Committee. Bank for International Settlements. Retrieved from https://www.bis.org/cpmi/publ/d174.htm

Coeuré, B., & Shin, H. S. (2021, June 23). III. CBDCs: An opportunity for the monetary system. Retrieved from https://www.bis.org/publ/arpdf/ar2021e3.htm

Cryptoslate. (2021, October). Stablecoin coins. Retrieved from https://cryptoslate.com/cryptos/stablecoin/

Cunha, P. R., Melo, P., & Sebastião, H. (2021). From bitcoin to central bank digital currencies: Making sense of the digital money revolution. Future Internet, *13*(7), 1–19.

Davies, G. (2010). *History of money*. Cardiff: University of Wales Press.

Echarte Fernández, M. Á., Náñez Alonso, S. L., Jorge-Vázquez, J., & Reier Forradellas, R. F. (2021). Central banks' monetary policy in the face of the COVID-19 economic crisis: Monetary stimulus and the emergence of CBDCs. *Sustainability*, *13*(8), 2–18.

Ekberg, J., Ho, M., Chia, T. Y., Liu, L., Mallela, N., Patel, H., & Khatri, S. (2021). *Unblocking $120 billion value in cross-border payments: How banks can leverage central bank digital currencies for corporates*. Oliver Wyman and JPMorgan Chase & Co. Retrieved from https://www.oliverwyman.com/our-expertise/insights/2021/nov/unlocking-120-billion-value-in-cross-border-payments.html

European Central Bank. (2021). *How to calculate the minimum reserve requirements*. Frankfurt: European Central Bank. Retrieved from https://www.ecb.europa.eu/mopo/implement/mr/html/calc.en.html

Fatás, A. (2021). *The conflict between CBDC Goals and design choices*. VoxEU.org – CEPR's Policy Portal. Retrieved from https://voxeu.org/article/conflict-between-cbdc-goals-and-design-choices

Fernández-Villaverde, J., Sanches, D., Schilling, L., & Uhlig, H. (2021). Central bank digital currency: Central banking for all? *Review of Economic Dynamics*, *41*, 225–242.

Finlow-Bates, K. (2020). Defining finance. In *Move over brokers here comes the blockchain*. Satakunta: Thinklair TMI.

Foley, S., Karlsen, J. R., & Putniņš, T. J. (2019). Sex, drugs, and bitcoin: How much illegal activity is financed through cryptocurrencies? *Review of Financial Studies*, *32*(5), 1798–1853.

Garratt, R., Lee, M., Malone, B., & Martin, A. (2020). *Token-or account-based? A digital currency can be both* (No. 20200812). Federal Reserve Bank of New York Liberty Street Economics. Retrieved from https://libertystreeteconomics.newyorkfed.org/2020/08/token-or-account-based-a-digital-currency-can-be-both.html

Graeber, D. (2011). *Debt: The first five thousand years*. New York, NY: Melville House.

Grothoff, C., & Moser, T. (2021). *How to issue a privacy-preserving central bank digital currency*. SUERF Policy Brief 2021, No. 114. Retrieved from https://www.suerf.org/suer-policy-brief/27227/how-to-issue-a-privacy-preserving-central-bank-digital-currency

Han, X., Yuan, Y., & Wang, F.-Y. (2019). A blockchain-based framework for central bank digital currency. In *2019 IEEE International conference on service operations and logistics, and informatics (SOLI)* (pp. 263–268). Piscataway, NJ: IEEE.

Jung, H., & Jeong, D. (2021). Blockchain implementation method for interoperability between CBDCs. *Future Internet*, *13*(5), 1–14.

Keister, T., & Sanches, D. R. (2019). *Should central banks issue digital currency?* Working Paper No. 19–26, Federal Reserve Bank of Philadelphia. Retrieved from https://ssrn.com/abstract=3399069

Kiff, J., Alwazir, J., Davidovic, S., Farias, A., Khan, A., Khiaonarong, T., … Zhou, P. (2020). *A survey of research on retail central bank digital currency*. IMF Working Paper WP/20/104.

Lee, D. K. C., Yan, L., & Wang, Y. (2021). A global perspective on central bank digital currency. *China Economic Journal*, *14*(1), 52–66.

Lys, L., Micoulet, A., & Potop-Butucaru, M. (2019). Atomic swapping bitcoins and ethers. In *38th symposium on reliable distributed systems (SRDS)* (pp. 372–374). Piscataway, NJ: IEEE.

McLaughlin, T. (2021). Two paths to tomorrow's money. *Journal of Payments Strategy & Systems*, *15*(1), 23–36.

McLeay, M., Radia, A., & Thomas, R. (2014). *Money creation in the modern economy*. Monetary Analysis Directorate. Bank of England Quarterly Bulletin Q1. Retrieved from https://www.bankofengland.co.uk/quarterly-bulletin/2014/q1/money-creation-in-the-modern-economy

Menger, K. (1892). On the origin of money. *The Economic Journal*, *2*(6), 239–255.

Mersch, Y. (2017). *Digital base money: An assessment from the ECB's perspective*. Speech at the Farewell Ceremony for Pentti Hakkarainen, Deputy Governor of Suomen Pankki–Finlands Bank, Helsinki. Retrieved from https://www.ecb.europa.eu/press/key/date/2017/html/sp170116.en.html

Nolting, C., Heinz, G., & Köhling, S. (2020). *Central bank digital currencies – Money reinvented*. CIO Special. Frankfurt: Deutsche Bank Wealth Management. Retrieved from https://www.db.com/news/detail/20200914-central-bank-digital-currencies-money-reinvented?language_id=1

Panetta, F. (2021, July 14). *Preparing for the Euro's digital future*. The ECB Blog. Frankfurt: European Central Bank. Retrieved from https://www.ecb.europa.eu/press/blog/date/2021/html/ecb.blog210714~6bfc156386.en.html

Peneder, M. (2021). Digitization and the evolution of money as a social technology of account. *Journal of Evolutionary Economics*, *25*(May), 1–29.

People's Bank of China. (2021, June). Progress of research and development of E-CNY in China. Retrieved from http://www.pbc.gov.cn/en/3688110/3688172/4157443/4293696/2021071614584691871.pdf

Powell, J. (2021, July). Federal chair Jerome Powell, semi-annual monetary report before the Senate Banking Committee. Retrieved from https://www.youtube.com/watch?v=Qqi58Xzp78I&t=1715s

Priem, R. (2020). Distributed ledger technology for securities clearing and settlement: Benefits, risks, and regulatory implications. Financial Innovation, *6*(1), 1–25.

Qureshi, H. (2021, April 27). *A visual explanation of algorithmic stablecoins*. Dragonfly Research. Retrieved from https://medium.com/dragonfly-research/a-visual-explanation-of-algorithmic-stablecoins-9a0c1f0f51a0

Shen, W., & Hou, L. (2021). China's central bank digital currency and its impacts on monetary policy and payment competition: Game changer or regulatory toolkit? *Computer Law & Security Review*, *41*(July), 105577.

Schoenberg, T., Robinson, M., & Faux, Z. (2021). Tether executives reportedly to face bank fraud probe. Australian Financial Review, July 17. Retrieved from https://www.afr.com/markets/currencies/tether-executives-reportedly-to-face-bank-fraud-probe-20210727-p58d8l

Swiss National Bank. (2007, February). *The monetary base and the M1, M2 and M3 monetary aggregates.* Retrieved from https://www.snb.ch/en/mmr/reference/histz_geldmengen_book/source/histz_geldmengen_book.en.pdf

Tong, W., & Jiayou, C. (2021). A study of the economic impact of central bank digital currency under global competition. *China Economic Journal*, *14*(1), 78–101.

Viñuela, C., Sapena, J., & Wandosell, G. (2020). The future of money and the central bank digital currency dilemma. *Sustainability*, *12*(22), 9697.

Wagner, E., Bruggink, D., & Benevelli, A. (2021). Preparing Euro payments for the future: A blueprint for a digital Euro. *Journal of Payments Strategy & Systems*, *15*(2), 165–187.

Xu, Z., & Zou, C. (2021). What can blockchain do and cannot do? *China Economic Journal*, *14*(1), 4–25.

Part V

Other Cryptoasset Issues

Chapter 20

Trade Settlements

Hugo Benedetti, Ehsan Nikbakht and Giga Zukhubaia

Abstract

The current security trade settlement life cycle presents several inefficiencies derived from intermediaries involved in the transaction between buyers and sellers. This chapter examines distributed ledger technology (DLT), the underlying technology of all blockchain applications, including trade settlements. It also reviews the implications of using blockchain in trade settlements for cryptoassets. Emerging blockchain technology provides investors, exchanges, regulators, and countless potential intermediaries with the most up-to-date technology with the highest efficiency, transparency, credibility, and automation enabled by smart contracts. Smart contracts allow an ecosystem to manage the process of trade settlements starting from execution to clearing and then settlement. These contracts reduce reconciliation and recordkeeping costs and streamline repetitive processes present in today's trade settlement system. The chapter highlights the benefits of implementing DLT in financial markets globally in all trading aspects, including cryptoassets.

Keywords: Cryptoassets; trade settlements; distributed ledger technology; smart contracts; blockchain; ecosystem

Introduction

The history of trade settlements in the United States began in the nineteenth century. Investors had to prefund transactions in full unless they secured a "call" loan from an independent party. The increase in demand for such services led to creating the Clearing House, a banking association and payments company owned by the largest commercial banks in the United States. The New York Stock Exchange Clearing House emerged in 1892 to improve the system further. In the 1920s, the stock market's popularity and an increase in volume caused

The Emerald Handbook on Cryptoassets: Investment Opportunities and Challenges, 309–325

doi:10.1108/978-1-80455-320-620221020

the creation of the Stock Clearing Corporation. The Depository Trust Company (DTC) launched in the 1960s, becoming the Central Securities Depository (CSD).

To catch up with the innovation and various technologies required conducting stock market trade settlements electronically to cope with further increased volume and complexity. Later, however, after the consolidation of different markets around the United States, the Depository Trust and Clearing Corporation (DTCC) emerged to unite the equity markets (Monahan, 2019). In 2021, the United States had around 20 stock exchanges, including the New York Stock Exchange, Nasdaq, IEX, Chicago Stock Exchange, Miami International Securities Exchange, CBOE Stock Exchange, Boston Options Exchange, and others (Securities and Exchange Commission (SEC), 2021).

Several intermediaries participate in today's trade settlement process. Many intermediaries connect to settle the trades facilitated between security buyers and sellers, with varying settlement times depending on the type of security and transaction. The current system for trade settlements is *delivery versus payment* (DvP), which is a smart contract. A *smart contract* is a program stored on a blockchain that executes when predetermined conditions are satisfied. Their primary use is to automate an execution agreement so that participants are confident of an outcome with no intermediaries involved and without losing time. A smart contract's implementation on blockchain infrastructure could develop an alternate ecosystem that provides trade execution without needing a central authority. Smart contracts could directly connect all market participants and allow disintermediated and near-instantaneous transactions. This tool is even more appealing to the growing sector of cryptoassets since those assets use blockchain infrastructure, allowing a direct implementation of smart contract trade and settlement.

Current Trade Settlement Process

Markets currently use the DvP. This method of trade settlements reduces principal and liquidity risk. *Principal risk* involves losing the entire value involved in a transaction due to a counterparty's default or insolvency. *Liquidity risk* derives from parties' inability to sell or buy securities within a reasonable time and price. The current system does not eliminate principal risk because the risk transfers to the CSD (Chiu & Koeppl, 2018).

Fig. 20.1 shows the three steps in trade settlements in the United States financial markets and other countries (Spaulding, 2021).

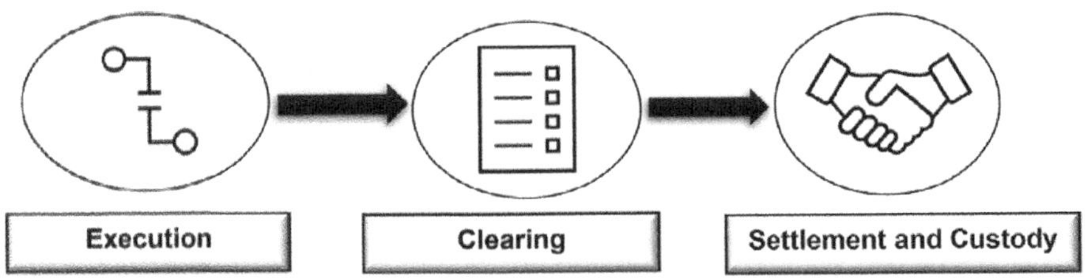

Fig. 20.1. Trade Settlement Life Cycle.
Note: This figure shows the three main steps in the trade settlement life cycle.

1. *Execution*. The buyer and seller agree on a security's specified amount and price needing settlement. Thus, execution is when the potential buyer bids a price and the potential seller asks the same price, lifting the offer.
2. *Clearing*. This step ensures the buyer has available funds and the seller has available securities to sell. A *central counterparty* (CCP) acts as an intermediary between buyers and sellers. Thus, it serves as a counterparty for both parties. Transaction failure risk remains because it transfers to the CCP (Arissen, 2019). In this stage, the information is recorded and transferred for settlement. Before moving information for settling, it needs to be verified to reconcile the data.
3. *Settlement and custody*. This step involves officially changing records and moving assets from one account to another or moving funds from one party to another. It finalizes the transfer and makes changes to the ledger's record. Two intermediaries are involved: the CSD and the custodian. The custodian's purpose is to hold funds and release them when necessary. The CSD delivers and ensures the transaction's settlement between the buyer and seller (Arissen, 2019). *Clearing* is the final record of moving information on the ledger using a DvP. Clearing consists of two types.
   - *Bilateral clearing* is when the parties go through the steps necessary to settle the transaction (Spaulding, 2021).
   - *Central clearing* uses a clearinghouse to settle the transaction. Clearinghouse members involve broker-dealers. Investors and all other parties involved in transactions must have an account with clearing members. Notably, clearinghouse members are responsible for clearing the trades to the clearinghouse and other parties involved. If discrepancies exist in the transaction, member firms take financial responsibility. If a member firm becomes insolvent, the clearinghouse bears the financial burden.

Netting Transactions During Trade Settlements, Margin Trading, and Pre-funding

In the United States, the current system takes two business days (T+2) to settle an equity trade transaction between two parties. The clearinghouse nets the transactions on the first day and officially settles the transactions between the two parties on the second day. It sums up all daily transactions from the member firms and nets them the following day. This action results in members making transactions on net payments and securities and not for all transactions occurring daily within the member firms. For options, a clearinghouse is a counterparty ensuring the delivery of the securities and payments.

Despite netting down the transactions, a clearinghouse still records all transactions. Multilateral netting is in place to further reduce the number of transactions. Instead of the member firms sending all the transactions to DTCC, they only send the aggregate transactions netted throughout the day. The member broker firms aggregate trades and payments throughout the day and send them to DTCC (Spaulding, 2021).

To illustrate, consider a member firm registered with DTCC. On the same day, the member firm's customers bought 1,000 shares of Apple, and two other customers sold 500 shares each. If these customers bought and sold at the same prices, the transfer would involve only the difference in the quantity bought and sold. When millions of transactions occur daily, this process eliminates many transactions for the brokers, reducing transaction-based risks and costs. A logical economic reason exists for netting between the clearinghouse and member firms. However, the clearinghouse only records specific buyers and sellers of securities in the trade settlement process and netting. This process also affects the collateral required by clearinghouses from the member firms. Member firms must post collateral depending on the number of transactions, volatility, and risk of the securities involved, imbalance of buying and selling, and other factors. These characteristics change continuously throughout the day (Spaulding, 2021).

The origins of the current interconnected infrastructure of trade settlement find their roots in the early twentieth century. Investment banks and hedge funds use prime brokerage agreements with brokers to facilitate their activities with the markets and clearinghouses. Prime brokerages function as intermediaries between large investment banks for custody of assets, credit lending depending on the transaction volume, the amount borrowed for margin trading, and short-sell trading (Daly, 2022).

Margin trading and short selling are a big part of the financial market's infrastructure. Margin trading requires extending credit, resulting in high net exposure for the investors involved. Short selling is like a net exposure because the securities are short (borrowed). The current infrastructure does not require pre-funding. Today, investors can execute a trade and have no funds/securities available now but have the funds or securities available the next trading day for clearing and settlement. Large institutional investors rely on this system. Real-time settlement requires prefunding by the investors to purchase the securities or have securities immediately available when they sell them. Designers set up the system so that prefunding would cause significant issues and conflicts of interest with numerous parties because many of them rely on margin and day trading netting activities.

Intermediaries

Intermediaries include brokers, issuer CSD, investor CSD, two global custodians, two local custodians, registrar, CCP, two clearing members, and the Society for Worldwide Interbank Financial Telecommunication (Arissen, 2019). These organizations, agencies, and companies enable trading to be settled with little risk that usually accompanies trade settlements.

Fig. 20.2 shows the connections between the intermediaries involved in trade settlements. The graph also illustrates the chronological order in which trade settlements occur in the current system, starting from order routing for execution, clearing, and settlement.

Settlement Time and Risks in the Current System

Various securities have different ways and time frames for the trade settlement. For most stock trades, settlement occurs two business days after the order

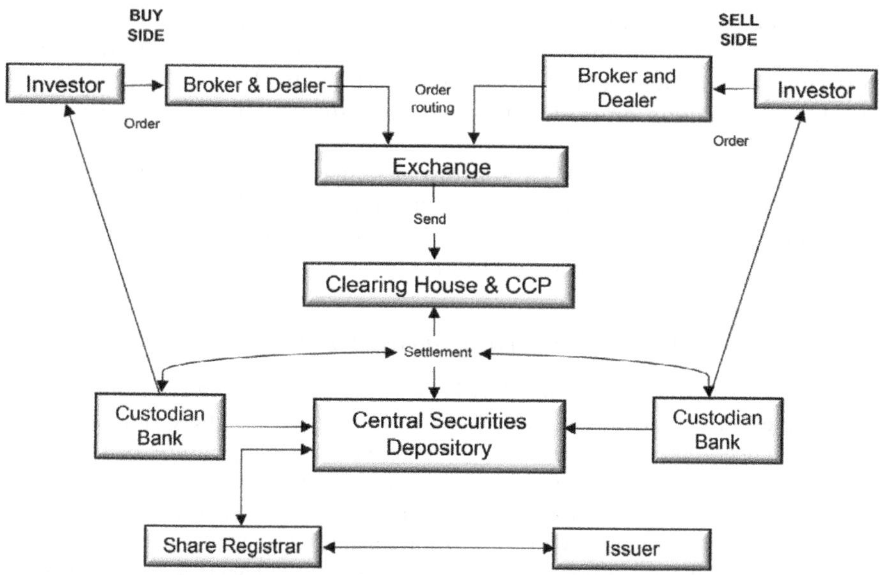

Fig. 20.2. Trade Settlement Infrastructure and Participants.
Note: This figure shows the major participants from the buy and sell sides.

executes, or T+2 (trade date plus two days). For example, if an investor executes an order on Monday, the settlement typically occurs on Wednesday. For some products, such as mutual funds, settlement occurs on a different timeline. For example, some equity and bond funds settle on the next business day, while other funds may take up to three business days to settle. To illustrate, if an investor exchanges shares of one fund for another within the same fund family, the trade usually settles on the next business day. Stock options settle on the next business day following the trade (T+1). Options of futures contracts, government securities, and foreign exchange (FX) spot market take two business days to settle (T+2). However, USD, CAD, EUR, RUB, and TRY trades settle in one business day (T+1) (Caytas, 2016).

As mentioned earlier, the current system of trade settlements involves some risks. The most important are principal risk when settlement instructions do not match (i.e., a buyer and seller have different trade objectives) and missing cash and securities. According to Arissen (2019), three CCPs have already gone bankrupt. The reason is that the risk remains is because it transfers to the CCP, who bears the risk in return for a trade settlement fee. In 2020 settlement failures intensified, further hinting that the system is prone to volatility risk (Burne, 2020).

Current System's Cost

The price tag investors pay to ensure the systems run properly defines the current system's cost. Today's system has a hidden cost associated with trade settlements. For example, Oliver Wyman's 2015 study reports that the revenue to major trade settlement entities was around $5 billion for clearing-related services and $43 billion for settlement and custody-related services (Arissen, 2019). According to Bech, Hancock, Rice, and Wadsworth (2020), the banking industry annually spends $17–24 billion on trade settlements and $65–80 billion on clearing and settlements.

Examining the extent of DTCC's involvement in trade settlement in the United States is also essential. According to its annual report, DTCC processed securities valued at $2.33 quadrillion in 2020 compared to $2.15 quadrillion in 2019 and $1.85 quadrillion in 2018 (DTCC, 2020a).

A Proposition by DTCC and Further Implementation

According to the statistics gathered by DTCC, there is more than $13 billion held in margin every day to mitigate risk. The clearing corporation holds and manages the margin account, as in the case of other assets. The clearinghouse believes that moving to T+1 could help to reduce the margin amount held daily by 41 percent (DTCC, 2021). Vladimir Tenev, Robinhood's CEO, called for simultaneous real-time trade settlements. Murray Pozmanter, DTCC's head, commented that reducing trade settlement times would take phases to achieve this goal. However, DTCC does not have the authority to change the time needed to settle trades. Real-time trade settlements require refunding the trades, potentially reducing market liquidity (Fitzgerald, 2021).

DTCC already provides same-day settlements for more than a million transactions daily. The DTC and National Securities Clearing Corporation (NSCC) have built an infrastructure to facilitate same-day clearing and settlement. The NSCC, collaborating with the DTC, can clear and settle transactions settled before 11.30 a.m. Eastern Standard Time the same day. Netting also happens for same-day transactions, which reduces the cost and risk. Netting may make the US financial market highly efficient. It reduces the number of transactions and the value of transactions by around 98 percent for settlement cycles. For example, DTCC, on an average day, netted down $1.77 trillion to just $38 billion in 2020 (Hillery, 2021).

DTCC also settles trades without involving the NSCC for settling with big brokers and institutional investors. Some contend that no need exists for distributed ledger technology (DLT) to make these trades settle in seconds. The importance of netting and excluding prefunding, not a lack of technological improvement, makes instantaneous real-time trade settlements possible (Hillery, 2021).

DTCC reports several reasons traders do not need settlement on a real-time basis. Real-time trade settlements would jeopardize the netting process, thus losing netting's benefit. Without netting, risk increases, and markets could become illiquid. Also, having real-time settlements would increase the difficulty for brokers to have a margin available for trades and increase the time to set up the financing process (Hillery, 2021).

DTCC supports the move to T+1 trade settlement soon. It contends that netting and margin financing would continue to remain smooth. DTCC has a roadmap to transition to T+1 trade settlement and plans to continue offering same-day settlement if the demand allows. Further, in May 2020, DTCC introduced Project Ion. This project explores DLT's benefits for accelerating settlement and reducing risk and transaction costs (Hillery, 2021).

Blockchain Technology's Value Proposition for Trade Settlements

Significant benefits may accrue from adopting blockchain technology in the trade settlements process in the United States and elsewhere. These benefits include reduced settlement latency, lower operation and custodial risk, higher transparency for the parties involved (e.g., issuers, investors, and regulators), and the certainty of settlement, operations, and correctability. Blockchain registries would also eliminate the need for reconciliation, eliminating database redundancies related to reconciliation. Finally, blockchain would increase data security with its immutability characteristic and cryptographic protection (Symons et al., 2016).

Theoretically, settling trades between investors instantaneously is possible. However, not all investors or investment and trading companies may prefer that approach. They usually use a margin on which trades settle at a later date. Blockchain can enable settling trades upon an investor's request. A faster trade settlement would add additional expenses for investors, as they would need to fulfill payments faster.

Blockchains for implementing trade settlements could be permissioned or permissionless. A permissionless system would have no central authority. Adopting this mechanism would be uncertain to the public and other regulatory parties. Having hierarchical permissioned DLT would enable relevant parties to access the necessary data for their operations. For example, regulators like the SEC would have a private key to access additional data and for specific purposes.

For example, the *proof-of-stake* (PoS) protocol must be implemented to verify transactions in trade settlements (Arissen, 2019; Chiu & Koeppl, 2018). *PoS* is a consensus algorithm to confirm transactions and produce newly released blocks on the blockchain (Tar, 2018). PoS also ensures that no party can take advantage of this core mechanism on a blockchain. Parties needing the most access and control over the infrastructure exchanges and other intermediaries would hierarchically have the highest stake. Alternatively, proof-of-work (PoW) could be a more viable option for a permissionless system for trade settlements. In this model, miners validate trades on the blockchain and earn a commission (reward). Potentially, the CSD and DTCC would be the main miners to enhance trust in the system. Trade settlements could be free with enough miners and participants in the system (Chiu & Koeppl, 2018).

Blockchain's Risks in Trade Settlements

Permissionless blockchain systems involve several risks at the microstructure level since the DLT could be prone to forking attacks. If a buyer or seller alters the ledger, the original transaction is inconsistent with the public ledger, causing a settlement failure. Suppose a buyer enters a position, but the price decreases before executing the trade. This situation gives the buyer an incentive to alter its position by requesting the blockchain miners modify the original trade order. If a set of miners changes the original trade order, the blockchain will present a "fork." In that case, there are two different blockchain versions of the transaction log, one with the original trade order and another with the modified order. To reduce the probability of "forking," blockchains should include appropriate incentives and penalties to encourage proper miner behavior (Chiu & Koeppl, 2018).

Another risk comes from specific user groups in permissionless systems. A group can engage in double-spending, for which it needs to win the competition for some number of blocks. Double-spending occurs after a set of transactions has settled. The transaction's originator rewrites the blocks that contain them, effectively removing the set of transactions from the log. Unlike a *fork attack*, which leaves two distinct versions of a blockchain transaction, a double-spending attack eliminates the transaction with the caveat that many examples of double-spending attacks exist in PoW blockchains. They are enabled through hash renting to overpower regular blockchain farmers.

Another way that dishonest users can pose some risk to a DLT is by breaking the cryptographic protections and stealing users' holdings. Yet, this event is improbable since breaking the cryptographic protections is almost impossible (Chiu & Koeppl, 2018). Other risks involved in implementing permissioned blockchain for trade settlements include operational, security, and legal risks, and settlement and connectivity issues (Löber, 2017).

Typically, blockchain technology duplicates the information between all parties to increase transparency. All parties have a copy of a ledger (Priem, 2020). This situation could result in privacy and competition issues and thus violate some laws, such as the General Data Protection Regulation. All participants would have information about the transaction. However, encryption methods should eliminate deviation from accepted standards and regulations (Priem, 2020).

Blockchain trade settlement infrastructure could affect ownership identification. Currently, DTCC holds all the securities on behalf of custodians and brokers, and custodians and brokers keep a registry of the identities of the securities end-owner. Under blockchain, each transaction is linked to the end-owner's address, potentially resulting in information leakage. Also, a blockchain system would affect securities lending and require modifying the infrastructure (Irrera, 2016).

Smart Contracts – A Must in Trade Settlement

Smart contracts are a necessity of DLT regarding trade settlements. Smart contracts allow automation and high integration with the blockchain protocol. A significant advantage of using DLT is its ability to implement smart contracts and build other frameworks on top of it.

The blockchain ecosystem built by smart contracts can enable the entire life cycle of trade settlements, from executing to clearing and settling the transactions. Several hypotheses are available on how the ecosystem should work. Bech et al. (2020) developed one variant called an *atomic settlement smart contract* that entails instantly transferring securities using smart contracts on a DLT platform. Below are an ecosystem's specifications concerning smart contracts for trade settlements.

1. An investor converts cash into cash tokens on the chain.
2. The project owner converts securities into tokenized securities. In general, tokenization is a blockchain representation of an underlying asset. A tokenized security is a derivative in the form of a blockchain token in which the underlying asset is the security itself (Stoner, 2021).
3. The buyer receives the tokenized security in exchange for the cash token.
4. The seller receives cash tokens in exchange for tokenized security.
5. The seller has the option to convert cash tokens into cash.
6. The buyer has the option to convert the tokenized security into the underlying security.

Implications of Blockchain Trade Settlements

Major investors and institutional investors are not keen on instantaneous trade settlements. They fear that they would need to prefund all trades, changing the whole landscape of financial markets and affecting multiple, if not most, participants. DTCC can make real-time clearing and settlements occur without using DLT. As it explores DLT, DTCC could launch the network if the advantages outweigh the disadvantages (DTCC, 2021).

DTCC can offer real-time trades soon without using blockchain technology. The entity already settles around a million transactions daily with the same-day settlement. The reason DTCC does not move to real-time settlements is not a technological hurdle. Instead, financial institutions have expressed no demand. The entire infrastructure revolves around the current system. Investors are accustomed to the current system, where they do not need to prefund when executing the transaction. Investors must be sure they have funds or securities the next day when clearing happens (DTCC, 2021).

DTCC proposes shortening the period needed to settle trades from T+2 to T+1. It maintains that this change would significantly improve the system without sacrificing any netting benefits or requiring prefunding. The clearinghouse also wants to offer real-time settlements to the investors who want to do so with prefunding and without the benefit of netting, incurring higher costs for this type of transaction (DTCC, 2021).

Implications for Cryptoassets

A link exists between cryptoassets and blockchain trade settlements since both have similar fundamentals. *Cryptoassets* are digitized assets that use cryptographic techniques to generate a medium of exchange of transactions. Examples of cryptoassets include cryptocurrencies, utility coins, stablecoins, tokenized securities, and security tokens. Unlike traditional central banking systems and fiat currencies, a blockchain infrastructure forms the basis for cryptoassets.

A *utility token* is a crypto token that serves some use case within a specific ecosystem, such as funding its development. Users can employ utility tokens to purchase services and products built on that ecosystem. A *stablecoin* is any cryptocurrency designed to have a relatively stable price, typically through being pegged to a commodity or currency or having its supply regulated by an algorithm. A *tokenized security* is a blockchain representation of a security that exists off-chain. A *security token* is a blockchain native instrument subject to existing securities law (Lambert, Liebau, & Rosenbloom, 2021).

Four major cryptoassets participants are exchanges, banks, miners, and custodians. Exchanges are online matching platforms. Most of the more than 210 exchanges are centralized (Daye, Guan, Swift, & Pugachevsky, 2019). A centralized exchange (CEX) consists of order placement, order cancelation, and order matching functionalities. Most CEXs rely on third-party providers, possibly leading to a single-point failure. They are also vulnerable to system failures and cybersecurity risks. A decentralized exchange (DEX) does not need a third-party provider. DEXs reduce single-point failure and the risk of server inaccessibility. Some exchanges are hybrids composed of centralized and decentralized functionalities (Daye et al., 2019).

Cryptoasset exchanges face regulatory uncertainty, which likely decreases over time (Daye et al., 2019). According to the European Central Bank, cryptoasset risks mainly result from the lack of an underlying claim (fundamental value), unregulated nature, and absence of a formal governance structure. Depending on their interconnectedness, the current financial system and economy could also face exposure to cryptoasset risks. According to Chimienti, Kochanska, and Pinna (2019), cryptoassets are prone to cyberattacks, frauds, and hacking. In addition, the G20 Ministers of Finance and Central Bank Governors (G20 Communique, 2018, par. 9) recognize that cryptoassets "raise issues with respect to consumer and investor protection, market integrity, tax evasion, money laundering, and terrorist financing."

Different Alternatives

Introducing blockchain technology should offer varying time settlements. Some investors want to settle their trades in real-time; others may be more leveraged using margin trading and prefer a T+2 settlement. With technological improvements, a system could have varying settlement times according to an investor's preferences.

Another alternative is to change the entire system. However, financial market stakeholders are unlikely to continue making such extensive changes. The system would require prefunding trades, freeing up some collateral but posing a burden on large investors. Having prefunded transactions would enable the blockchain ecosystem to settle trades in real time. Real-time settlements do not require netting. Netting's purpose in today's system is to batch the trades resulting in fewer transaction lines and reducing transaction costs. If blockchain can reduce transaction costs without netting, it would be a viable option. However, suppose the blockchain system of trade settlement turns out to be more expensive without netting. In that case, the system could have varying settlement times depending on investor needs.

Further research should analyze networking costs, start-up costs, and the economics of the technology. The following section examines ongoing projects implementing blockchain technology in financial market trade settlements worldwide.

Blockchain Technology Projects

This section examines blockchain projects in different countries.

Australia – Australian Securities Exchange (ASX) Chess Project

Australian financial markets currently use the Clearing House Electronic Subregister System (CHESS) for trade settlements, managed by the Australian Securities Exchange Settlement Pty Limited (ASX Settlement). In January 2016, ASX with Digital Asset decided to develop a prototype of trade settlement using DLT. In December 2017, ASX announced that the blockchain ecosystem designed by Digital Asset would replace CHESS in Australia (ASX, 2011).

Although the initial starting date was April 2021, ASX delayed the date to April 2023 due to increased trading volume and required additional testing. This project aims to use DLT for trade settlements in Australian markets and replace the legacy system of CHESS (Barbaschow, 2020).

Estonia – Tallin Stock Exchange

In January of 2017, Nasdaq, the operator of the Tallinn Stock Exchange, successfully experimented with proxy voting, company registration, and public pension registration using blockchain technology. Blockchain allowed investors to vote online securely. Nasdaq introduced this initiative because of blockchain's key characteristics of distributed ledger and immutable record without a central authority. Nasdaq considered selling this technology to CSD. In addition, DTCC plans to use blockchain for credit default swaps (Irrera, 2017). This global electronic marketplace is likely to develop further use cases of blockchain implementation.

India – Securities and Exchange Board of India (SEBI)

Ajay Tyagi, SEBI's Chief Executive, announced in mid-2020 the move toward real-time trade settlements in Indian financial markets gradually using blockchain technology. He encouraged developers to create a pilot program and assess it in real time. Such a program would improve the Indian financial markets' trade settlement process, which takes two business days (The Hindu Business Line, 2021).

Japan – Japan Exchange Group "B-POST"

The Japan Exchange Group announced in mid-2020 several pilots to evaluate DLT in Japanese financial markets, with one using a post-trade settlement.

Programs also include using lending and collateral management for margin trading. The expected completion was initially late 2021 (Ledger Insights, 2020).

The United States – Nasdaq Linq

On December 30, 2015, authorities confirmed the success of the Nasdaq Linq project to complete and record private security transactions using DLT. Using blockchain reduced settlement time and risk and eliminated the need for paper stock certificates. The initiative also announced the possibility of exploring trade settlements for transactions in US secondary markets. Some contend that this technology would allow a trade to settle in less than 10 minutes (Briganti, 2015).

According to Nasdaq, DLT can reduce costs by decreasing duplicate processes, settlement time, collateral requirements, and operational overhead (Bajpai, 2017). Van de Velde et al. (2016, p. 20) suggest:

> I.T. and operations expenditure in capital markets is currently close to \$100–150 billion per year among banks. On top of that, post-trade and securities servicing fees are in the region of \$100 billion. Significant capital and liquidity costs are also incurred because of current delays and inefficiencies within market operations.

Germany – Deutsche Börse and Deutsche Bundesbank

In 2016, Deutsche Börse and Deutsche Bundesbank introduced a prototype for blockchain-based trade settlements for securities (Bajpai, 2017). The Korean Exchange Group, Moscow Exchange, London Stock Exchange, and Santiago Exchange have similar initiatives promoting blockchain technology and testing pilot systems in their financial markets' infrastructure (Bajpai, 2017).

Projection – DTCC Case Study

To further increase the efficiency and cost savings with trade settlements, DTCC is exploring new ways to implement up-to-date technology to trade settlements. It is currently working on the Digital Accelerated Settlement Service. This project aims to control netting and risk management and offer broader access to T+0 and possibly real-time trade settlements. In 2019, DTCC with NSCC settled transactions valued at more than \$1.85 quadrillion (DTCC, 2020a).

DTCC switched to T+2 instead of T+3 daily capital requirements for clearing trades through NSCC decreased by 25 percent, freeing up the \$1.36 billion requirements. It aims to reduce risk, decrease capital requirements, release "trapped liquidity," and lessen insolvency risk. DTCC's interest in exploring new technology like DLT is to facilitate better service to US financial markets in post-trade settlements. However, DTCC is not keen on forcing operational and technical changes to clearance and settlement (DTCC, 2020a).

Nevertheless, DTCC is engaged in continuous research and a vision of integrating DLT into the capital markets. Importantly, it plans to evaluate blockchain technology thoroughly before adjusting the financial market accordingly. For this reason, DTCC initiated Project ION (DTCC, 2020b).

Project ION aims to identify if DLT reduces cost and risk in the industry. Its primary mission is to develop a system around DLT that retains the significant benefits of the current netting and risk management system. The project intends to digitize the assets to ensure netting in real-time, at day's end or the end of sliced time intervals during an intraday trading session. Project ION will have a compatible API interface for easier adjustments to the current system. Most importantly, Project ION will encompass the pre-funding settlement model.

Paxos

Paxos is a DLT platform that works on building sustainable ecosystems for financial systems worldwide. It offers various products and services like crypto brokerage, settlement, post-trade, and stablecoins like PAX Gold, itBit, and others (Paxos Settlement Service, 2021).

Paxos offers settlement services for US equity markets, commodities, and FX markets. The company uses DvP with a permission-based distributed ledger for settlement services for equities facilitating trade settlements on a blockchain platform. It provides a pilot for US equities, integrated with DTC and internal broker-dealer infrastructures. Paxos promises cost and capital savings by freeing up clearing capital. The platform also promises blockchain benefits, reducing structural costs (Paxos Settlement Service, 2021).

Fig. 20.3 shows the proposed steps in the PAXOS settlement system, starting from trade execution, clearance, and settlement, and ending with fund proceeds.

Another service offered by Paxos is FX market settlements. The services encompass: (1) reduced settlement risk via simultaneous settlement, (2) decreased information leakage by using a blockchain interface, (3) lower costs than manual processing, and (4) increased efficiency and visibility via multilateral payment netting which works for any counterparty. This blockchain ecosystem is compliant with multiple guidelines and regulations worldwide. Fig. 20.4 shows PAXOS settlement solutions for FX and commodities markets and market participants.

Regulation

Regulators have been among the most important parties involved in trade settlements and blockchain implementation regulations. They are aware of DLT

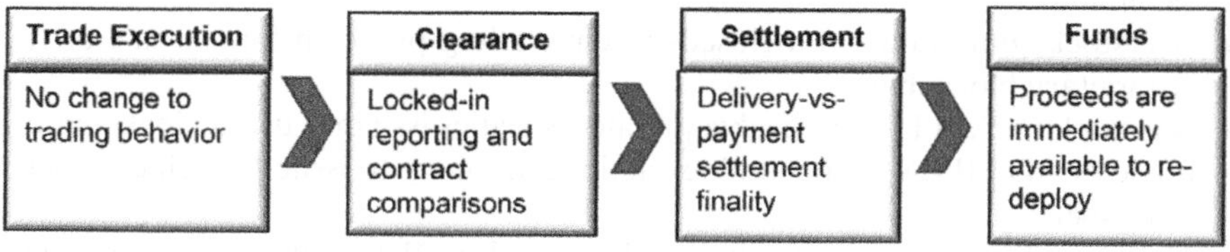

Fig. 20.3. Paxos Settlement Service.
Note: This figure presents the proposed steps in Paxos Settlement Service.

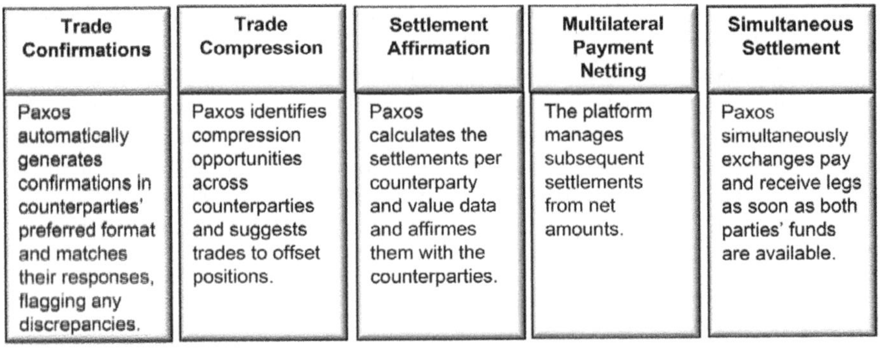

Fig. 20.4. Paxos Settlement Solution for FX and Commodity Markets.
Note: This figure presents the steps proposed in the Paxos settlement solution for FX and commodity markets.

and its potential. Regulators have introduced some rules and guidelines on this technology. Below are several developments in blockchain regulations and their implementation in financial markets (Priem, 2020).

- European securities markets authority published a report outlining DTL's potential risks and benefits when applied to financial markets.
- The Financial Stability Board developed in July 2018 a framework and identified metrics to monitor the financial stability implication of cryptoassets.

Regulators need guidance on implementing DLT in financial markets. Some anticipate that Gary Gensler, SEC chairperson, will introduce regulations and guidance on blockchain and various blockchain-based cryptoassets, including securitized tokens.

Recent Developments

Below is the list of recent developments for DLT on trade settlements as outlined by Peters and Vishnia (2016), McDowell (2018), Bech et al. (2020), and Priem (2020):

- The Australian Stock Exchange cooperated with Digital Assets to use DLT to clear and settle equity transactions.
- Nasdaq and SEBI created a mutual fund trading platform based on blockchain technology.
- Overstock.com launched a closed-system trading platform for the sale of its proprietary blockchain.
- Nasdaq launched Linq to enable private securities issuance using blockchain.
- French CSD "ID2S" applied blockchain technology to issue French commercial paper.
- The Canadian Securities Exchange developed a DLT securities clearing and settlement platform to allow companies to issue equity and fixed income securities via security token offerings.

- The World Bank and the Commonwealth Bank of Australia issued security tokens called Bond-I, maintained and issued by DLT.
- The Bank of England intends to support transfers of account-based securities in exchange for cash tokens (AvT transfer) and tokenized securities in exchange for cash in accounts (TvA).
- ID2S and DLT-based CSD for European commercial paper interoperate with TARGET-2 Securities to settle the payment leg achieving TvA arrangements.

Summary and Conclusions

This chapter discusses the current financial trade settlement infrastructure, the usability of blockchain DLT for trade settlements and the risks involved with blockchain-based systems, regulations, and recent developments. The blockchain DLT provides an enhanced and more efficient alternative infrastructure (ecosystem) for trade settlements of different financial assets, including cryptoassets. However, a prerequisite for implementing this idea is making significant infrastructural changes in the current ecosystem. Many initiatives to use blockchain for trade settlements are under implementation. Despite many challenges, the prospect of implementing blockchain DLT in the trade settlement process is promising, including varied expectations of major stakeholders in the current system.

Discussion Questions

1. Describe the process that defines the current trade settlement infrastructure.
2. Explain the importance of transaction netting, margin trading, and pre-funding.
3. Identify several benefits provided by blockchain implementation in trade settlement.
4. List some ongoing projects/initiatives that bring blockchain to trade settlement infrastructure.

References

Arissen, S. (2019, July). *Blockchain for post-trade settlement, clearing and custody of financial instruments*. Nijmegen: Radboud University. Retrieved from https://www.ru.nl/publish/pages/769526/master_thesis_report.pdf

ASX. (2011). CHESS Clearing House Electronic Subregister System. Retrieved from https://www.asx.com.au/documents/research/chess_brochure.pdf

Bajpai, P. (2017, June 12). *How stock exchanges are experimenting with blockchain technology*. New York, NY: Nasdaq. Retrieved from https://www.nasdaq.com/articles/how-stock-exchanges-are-experimenting-blockchain-technology-2017-06-12

Barbaschow, A. (2020, October 27). *ASX's blockchain-based CHESS replacement pushed to April 2023*. ZDNet. Retrieved from https://www.zdnet.com/article/asxs-blockchain-based-chess-replacement-pushed-to-april-2023/#:~:text=The%20Australian%20Securities%20Exchange%20(ASX,running%20for%20around%2025%20years

Bech, M., Hancock, J., Rice, T., & Wadsworth, A. (2020). On the future of securities settlement. BIS Quarterly Review (March), 67–83. Retrieved from https://www.bis.org/publ/qtrpdf/r_qt2003i.pdf

Briganti, W. (2015, December 30). *Nasdaq Linq enables first-ever private securities issuance documented with blockchain technology*. New York, NY: Nasdaq. Retrieved from https://ir.nasdaq.com/news-releases/news-release-details/nasdaq-linq-enables-first-ever-private-securities-issuance

Burne, K. (2020, October). *How to succeed in fixing settlement fails*. New York, NY: BNY Mellon. Retrieved from https://www.bnymellon.com/us/en/insights/aerial-view-magazine/how-to-succeed-in-fixing-settlement-fails.html

Caytas, J. D. (2016, June 22). Developing blockchain real-time clearing and settlement in the E.U., U.S., and globally. Columbia Journal of European Law. Retrieved from http://blogs2.law.columbia.edu/cjel/preliminary-reference/2016/developing-blockchain-real-time-clearing-and-settlement-in-the-eu-u-s-and-globally-2/

Chimienti, M. T., Kochanska, U., & Pinna, A. (2019). Understanding the crypto-asset phenomenon, its risks and measurement issues. ECB Economic Bulletin, 5(May). Retrieved from https://www.ecb.europa.eu/pub/economic-bulletin/articles/2019/html/ecb.ebart201905_03~c83aeaa44c.en.html

Chiu, J., & Koeppl, T. V. (2018, September). *Blockchain-based settlement for asset trading*. Bank of Canada Staff Working Paper, No. 2018-45. Bank of Canada, Ottawa. Retrieved from https://www.bankofcanada.ca/wp-content/uploads/2018/09/swp2018-45.pdf

Daly, L. (2022, February 17). *What is a prime brokerage agreement?* The Ascent. Retrieved from https://www.fool.com/the-ascent/buying-stocks/prime-brokerage-agreement/

Daye, W., Guan, C., Swift, L., & Pugachevsky, D. (2021). *Understanding the cryptoasset market*. OKCOIN & Quantifi. Retrieved from https://www.quantifisolutions.com/wp-content/uploads/2021/06/Quantifi-OKCoin-Understanding-the-Cryptoasset-Market.pdf

DTCC. (2020a). *2020 annual report*. DTCC. Retrieved from https://www.dtcc.com/annuals/2020/pdf/DTCC_2020_AR_Print.pdf

DTCC. (2020b, May). *Project ION case study*. DTCC. Retrieved from https://www.dtcc.com/~/media/Files/Downloads/settlement-asset-services/user-documentation/Project-ION-Paper-2020.pdf

DTCC. (2021, May). *Daily total U.S. treasury trade fails*. DTCC. Retrieved from https://www.dtcc.com/charts/daily-total-us-treasury-trade-fails#qna

Fitzgerald, M. (2021). Wall Street clearing firm proposes 1-day trade settlement after Robinhood controversy. CNBC, February 24. Retrieved from https://www.cnbc.com/2021/02/24/wall-street-clearing-firm-proposes-1-day-trade-settlement-after-robinhood-controversy.html

G20 Communique. (2018, March 19–20). Communique. G20 Argentina 2018. Retrieved from https://back-g20.argentina.gob.ar/sites/default/files/communique_-_finance_and_central_banks_-_march_2018.pdf

Hillery, M. (2021, April 19). *Ask the expert: Same day, every day – How same-day settlement works at DTCC*. DTCC. Retrieved from https://www.dtcc.com/dtcc-connection/articles/2021/april/19/ask-the-expert-same-day-every-day-how-same-day-settlement-works-at-dtcc

Irrera, A. (2017). Nasdaq successfully completes blockchain test in Estonia. *Reuters*, January 23. Retrieved from https://www.reuters.com/article/nasdaq-blockchain/nasdaq-successfully-completes-blockchain-test-in-estonia-idUSL1N1FA1XK

Lambert, T., Liebau, D., & Roosenboom, P. (2021). Security token offerings. *Small Business Economics*, 1–27. Retrieved from https://link.springer.com/content/pdf/10.1007/s11187-021-00539-9.pdf

Ledger Insights. (2020, July 2). *Tokyo stock exchange owner JPX progresses blockchain post trade pilots*. Leader Insights. Retrieved from https://www.ledgerinsights.com/tokyo-stock-exchange-jpx-blockchain-post-trade-pilots/

Löber, K. (2017, February). *Distributed ledger technology in payment, clearing, and settlement. Bank for international payments, committee on payments and market infrastructures*. Bank for International Settlements. Retrieved from https://www.bis.org/cpmi/publ/d157.pdf

McDowell, H. (2018). Canadian securities exchange releases blockchain clearing platform. Global Custodian, February 15. Retrieved from https://www.globalcustodian.com/canadian-securities-exchange-releases-blockchain-clearing-platform/

Monahan, K. (2019, June 7). *Steampunk settlement, deploying futuristic technology to achieve an anachronistic result*. DTCC. Retrieved from https://www.dtcc.com/dtcc-connection/articles/2019/june/07/steampunk-settlement-deploying-futuristic-technology-to-achieve-an-anachronistic-result

Paxos Settlement Service. (2021). Retrieved from https://www.paxos.com/securities

Peters, G., & Vishnia, G. (2016, August 31). *Overview of emerging blockchain architectures and platforms for electronic trading*. Heriot Watt University. Retrieved from https://researchportal.hw.ac.uk/en/publications/overview-of-emerging-blockchain-architectures-and-platforms-for-e

Priem, R. (2020). Distributed ledger technology for securities clearing and settlement: Benefits, risks, and regulatory implications. Priem Financial Innovation, *6*(11), 1–25. Retrieved from https://jfin-swufe.springeropen.com/articles/10.1186/s40854-019-0169-6

Securities and Exchange Commission. (2021). *National securities exchanges*. SEC. Retrieved from https://www.sec.gov/fast-answers/divisionsmarketregmrexchangesshtml.html

Spaulding, W. C. (2021). *Execution, clearing, and settlement*. This Matter. Retrieved from https://thismatter.com/money/stocks/settlement-and-clearing.htm

Stoner J. (2021, June 14). Tokenized stocks from Apple, Tesla, and Amazon now available through Bittrex Global. Retrieved from https://www.securities.io/tokenized-stocks-from-apple-tesla-and-amazon-now-available-through-bittrex-global/

Symons, P., Peeters, I., Yli-Jaakkola, J., Delhez, A.-M., Scott, A., Mead, J., & Kingsley, B. (2016, May). *Blockchain settlement, regulation, innovation, and application*. Euroclear. Retrieved from https://www.swift.com/file/34341/download?token=qqx60Nus

Tar, A. (2018). Proof-of-work, explained. Cointelegraph, January 17. Retrieved from https://cointelegraph.com/explained/proof-of-work-explained#:~:text=1.-,What%20is%20Proof%2Dof%2DWork%3F,the%20network%20and%20get%20rewarded

The Hindu Business Line. (2020). SEBI chief moots real-time settlement of trades in stock market. *BusinessLine*, July 22. Retrieved from https://www.thehindubusinessline.com/markets/ajay-tyagi-moots-real-time-settlement-of-trades-in-stock-market/article32158127.ece

Van de Velde, A. S., Sartorius, K., Dalton, I., Allchin, C., Dougherty, M., Ryan, P., & Rennick, E. (2016, February). *Blockchain in capital markets—The prize and the journey*. Euroclear and Oliver Wyman. Retrieved from https://www.oliverwyman.com/content/dam/oliver-wyman/global/en/2016/feb/BlockChain-In-Capital-Markets.pdf

Chapter 21

A Closer Look Into Decentralized Finance

Hugo Benedetti and Sebastián Labbé

Abstract

Decentralized finance is a technological infrastructure built on a blockchain networking environment that supplies transparent, uncensorable, and decentralized financial services and products. This infrastructure offers the opportunity to replicate traditional financial instruments on a decentralized platform and incorporate added features provided by blockchain technology. It also allows the creation of new instruments native to blockchain technology unavailable through traditional financial institutions. This chapter presents an in-depth analysis of the inner workings of stablecoins, decentralized exchanges, automated market makers, liquidity pools, decentralized lending, synthetic instruments, and asset management. It also provides specific examples for each application and presents some current challenges the sector faces.

Keywords: Decentralized finance; stablecoins; decentralized exchanges; automated market makers; liquidity pools; decentralized lending; synthetic instruments

Introduction

Decentralized finance (DeFi) has evolved rapidly in recent years with the promise of using the internet, cryptography, and code to optimize the efficiency and transparency of people's finances using decentralized blockchain networks. This area consists of different blockchains in the form of applications that together enable functions that until a few years ago were only possible through the traditional finance system, with barriers to entry difficult to overcome depending on an individual's economic or geographic situation.

The Emerald Handbook on Cryptoassets: Investment Opportunities and Challenges, 327–340

doi:10.1108/978-1-80455-320-620221021

Free access to this new form of finance has also propelled its growth. Economists and others often ignore concerns about inflation for developed countries with strong currencies because it is low, or alternative financial instruments that protect against it are readily available. On the contrary, if one explores the context of developing countries with domestic currencies with high inflation due to negligent economic measures, a sustained pressure exists to sell domestic currencies for foreign currency, resulting in governments restricting access to these currencies. Access to these new instruments that only require an internet connection allows people to access free markets of stable currencies and digital assets safely, without needing intermediaries to restrict the free circulation of money. This new form of digital finance has a bright future in an increasingly connected world, given the rapid spread of the internet and smart devices capable of storing the cryptographic keys needed to make transactions.

DeFi is a technological infrastructure based on a blockchain networking environment built to provide financial services and products without a central authority (Deshmukh, Geest, Gogel, Resas, & Sillaber, 2021; Gogel, 2021; Schär, 2020). This infrastructure has different foundational pieces, including decentralized applications (DApps) using smart contracts to replicate the services of traditional finance.

First appearing in the 1990s, a *smart contract* is "a set of promises, specified in digital form, which includes the same protocols where actors execute these promises" (Szabo, 1996, p. 1). Additionally, a smart contract is a program or protocol devised to execute, control, or automatically document events or actions if certain conditions are met (Fries & Paal, 2019). Blockchain's emergence as a solution for peer-to-peer (P2P) transfers of value and a method of decentralized execution of contracts allowed this idea to come to life in 2015, with Ethereum as the first blockchain network compatible with executing smart contracts (Buterin, 2014).

Among the fundamental building blocks of DeFi's exponential growth are overcollateralized stablecoin projects, such as MakerDAO (DAI), Synthetix (sUSD), and Liquity (LUSD). These stablecoins are debt instruments backed by volatile cryptoassets held in an over-collateralized reserve, with a dynamic interest rate adjusted algorithmically by predetermined formulas or according to decisions made by decentralized autonomous organizations (DAOs). Stablecoin's creation allows for a decentralized, digital, and self-custodial alternative to traditional fiat currencies or fiat-backed stablecoins.

A second relevant DeFi application is decentralized exchanges (DEXs). These markets differ from their centralized counterparts. Users do not delegate the custody of their assets to a third party, enabling them to trade on a P2P in a secure and trustless format through a smart contract-based order book. These markets function 24/7 and are accessible ubiquitously to any user with a compatible wallet interface. Moreover, some web-based crypto wallets have embedded DEXs functionalities into their user interface, allowing users to trade directly from their wallet application, bypassing the need to connect to a DEX protocol. As DEXs rely on blockchain infrastructure, they can only trade blockchain-compatible assets. Therefore, using fiat currencies is limited to fiat-backed cryptocurrencies or fiat-based stablecoins.

Besides P2P trading, some DEXs have also implemented the concept of an *automated market maker* (AMM), a smart contract that groups sellers and buyers of cryptocurrencies without needing preset market orders. People participate in these markets through so-called *liquidity pools* (LP), consisting of dynamically adjusted portfolios of tradable tokens. Users who contribute liquidity to the pools usually receive returns from trading fees and additional rewards as newly issued tokens. Examples of DEX are Uniswap, Sushiswap, Balancer, Kyber, and Bancor.

Another fundamental building block is P2P lending, such as Compound and Aave. These protocols allow for overcollateralized lending through dynamic interest rates based on the demand for the protocol's liquidity pool. These overcollateralized loans theoretically have no risk of bad debt because they have sufficient backing or collateral to be repaid in the event of liquidation. Settlement mechanisms are open and rely on information provided by "oracles." An *oracle* is an interface providing information from a blockchain network to smart contracts. Oracles can deliver different types of information depending on the smart contract's requirements (Beniiche, 2020). Some P2P protocols allow a *flash loan instrument*, a loan issued, settled, and repaid in the same blockchain block, allowing for instantaneous arbitrage and debt swaps from one blockchain protocol to another.

Decentralized insurers acting as mutuals mitigate the risks of blockchain-related events such as hacking, smart contract malfunctions, and events external to blockchain networks. Armor, Nexus Mutual, and Unslashed are examples of decentralized insurance projects that provide insurance to DeFi protocols. Other projects have gone beyond ensuring blockchain-based applications to offer insurance on more traditional events like flight delays or catastrophic weather, such as floods, hurricanes, and tornados.

Another DeFi product is a derivative instrument. Some protocols allow exposure to traditional asset types external to blockchain technologies, such as market indexes, stocks, and commodities. Applications, including Synthethix, Mirror, and Uma, use market information from oracles and algorithms from betting markets to generate synthetic tokens. A *synthetic token* tracks an external asset's price without possessing the underlying asset or any related traditional instrument (Brooks, Jurisevic, Spain, & Warwick, 2020). Markets, where buyers take a long or short position depending on market conditions, make this situation possible. Users can also exchange these synthetic tokens in decentralized markets.

Lastly, decentralized asset managers allow users to manage their cryptoassets automatically according to specific investment and portfolio optimization algorithms. The core premise is searching for the best investment strategies through decentralized governance. Some examples are Yearn Finance and Beefy Finance, which focus on the growth of digital assets, regardless of their volatility. Within this category, investors can buy index portfolios in a decentralized market. These portfolios can be pure indexes or actively managed by the community and developers. Set Protocol, Index Coop, Basket Dao, and Indexed Finance are examples of decentralized asset managers.

Composability is a crucial property of these applications. It allows creating higher complexity services or applications by assembling and combining a different set of smart contracts and decentralized applications, potentially from different blockchain networks. A smart contract creates a volume-weighted price on each collateral asset using prices obtained from several DEXs to algorithmically determine the collateralization ratios of stablecoins. In turn, each DEX can use the stablecoin as a price denominator in the exchange. If price differences exist between different DEXs, an AMM contract can arbitrage the price differences, creating a more efficient price and greater liquidity across markets. Several blockchains with smart contract capabilities are available. Thus, each can host its stablecoins, DEXs, and AMM projects. Smart contracts can interconnect (bridge) different blockchains and allow interaction across stablecoins, DEXs, and AMMs. Lastly, as the interconnection between smart contracts and blockchains increases, dependency and reliance also increase. Therefore, if a hack, an exploit, or a bug occurs in a smart contract, its impact is likely to spread through the network and affect other ecosystem components.

The chapter proceeds as follows. The following section presents the economic dynamics of the three main stablecoin issuance mechanisms: asset-backed, cryptoasset-backed, and algorithmic/seigniorage-based. The next section describes DEXs, AMMs, and their interrelation. The subsequent section presents decentralized lending, derivatives, and asset managers, followed by a section on the current DeFi challenges. The final section contains a summary and conclusions.

Stablecoins

Most agree that money should be a store of value, a medium of exchange, accountable, and recognizable (Mankiw, 2019; Moin, Sekniqi, & Sirer, 2020). Smart contracts allow physical and digital assets to have these characteristics by representing them in tokens. However, native cryptoassets are known for their price volatility, reducing their capacity as a store of value. Stablecoins reduce price volatility by formulating smart contracts to follow a reference price or peg. Different types of stablecoins are available. However, the most common mechanism design involves asset-backed reserves, mainly fiat currencies such as the US dollar, Euro, or Yen, overcollateralized cryptoasset-backed, such as bitcoin, ethereum, or another broadly used cryptoasset, and dual seignorage algorithmic tokens. These mechanism designs attempt to maintain the stablecoin price equal to its peg or redemption price. The following subsections present and compare these stablecoin economic mechanisms.

Asset-backed Stablecoins

In this system, a traditional asset fully backs each stablecoin. The creating and destructing ("burning") stablecoins result from an increase or reduction in the asset reserve. Most commonly, the reserve is US dollars, held in custody by an intermediary, which may or may not be a regulated custodian. Some companies have caused controversy by using fixed income securities considered "cash and cash equivalent" instead of US dollars (Grant Thornton LLP, 2021).

The asset-backed reserve mechanism was the first stablecoin design, having its origins in 2012, when the Mastercoin project described the possibility of issuing digital assets on the Bitcoin network, operating on a second layer (Willet, 2013). Subsequently, part of the Mastercoin team founded Realcoin in 2014 (Casey, 2014). This project, later renamed "Tether," managed different digital assets operating on the Mastercoin Project's Omni network. Other cryptocurrency exchanges and blockchain networks later used the stablecoin "USDT," issued by Tether. It was a primary instrument to store and safeguard liquidity in the different cryptocurrency markets (Griffin & Shams, 2020). Despite this stablecoin's success, doubts arose about the integrity of Tether reserves. In March 2021, after a ruling by the New York courts, authorities forced Tether to disclose publicly its detailed reserve instruments.

Newer projects sought greater transparency with regular audits, institutional-grade custody, and fully insured reserves. In 2018, the US-based companies Circle and Coinbase created USDC, a stablecoin fully backed by US dollar reserves. In 2018, Stasis launched EURS, a stablecoin fully backed by Euro reserves. Also, in 2018, Paxos launched a white-label stablecoin, providing stablecoin issuance to third parties. Its most relevant stablecoin is BUSD, used by the leading crypto exchange Binance as its proprietary stablecoin. At the end of 2021, Tether represented 45.99 percent ($78.12 billion) of the dollar-denominated stablecoin market, followed by USDC with 29.32 percent ($49.66 billion) and BUSD with 8.82 percent ($15.02 billion) (Gecko Labs Pte. Ltd, 2022).

Overcollateralized Crypto-backed Stablecoins

MakerDAO was one of the first projects to propose creating decentralized stablecoins pegged to the dollar by generating debt-collateralized positions. Users deposit cryptoassets, such as bitcoin, ether, and liquidity pool tokens, into a smart contract "vault" and use them as collateral to generate a debt instrument. This instrument equals a certain number of tokens, "DAI," each with a value pegged to $1. Users can issue any amount between 25 and 75 percent of the collateral value with a dynamically agreed interest rate ("stability rate"). Adjustment of a DAI's price occurs through the market, with the stability rate being the mechanism to incentivize the token's price to tend to the peg. The collateral can be unlocked if the full borrowed value of DAI plus the stability rate is paid (Moin et al., 2020). Control of a protocol's stability rate occurs through constituents voting on a DAO. The DAO's constituents must deposit their governance tokens in a smart contract to vote on protocol decisions. These decisions can be executed, such as adding or removing collateral types and vaults, adjusting global protocol parameters, replacing smart contracts, or polls designed to assess the DAO's sentiment regarding possible changes in the protocol (MakerDAO, 2021).

As opposed to asset-backed stablecoins, decentralized cryptoasset-backed stablecoins do not require a central controlling and issuing authority, a custodian to hold reserves, or an auditor to verify the integrity and value of reserves. The smart contract performs all these processes. Holders of the protocol's token determine changes to the smart contract.

A criticism of this decentralized stablecoin model is that it still suffers from the problem of tracking the peg's value. This value is usually a traditional currency subject to inflation, despite working well as a store of value, unit of account, and medium of exchange. Additionally, some newly accepted collaterals are centralized asset-backed stablecoins, like USDC, PAX, TUSD, GUSD, and USDT), increasing regulatory risk if those assets become regulated. On the other hand, the governance model has barriers to entry due to the fluctuating cost of blockchain transactions. During specific periods of high demand for blockchain transactions, the dynamically adjusted transaction cost has made participating in governance voting economically unfeasible for retail token holders. This situation is detrimental to the protocol's decentralization.

Liquidity is a decentralized cryptoasset-backed stablecoin project, holding overcollateralized ether reserves to issue its stablecoin LUSD. The project minimizes potential regulatory risks by not having a front-end interface and only interacting with smart contracts. Any website or app-based interface can connect to the smart contract and function as an intermediary between users and the liquidity protocol. Besides this back-end-only infrastructure, the protocol offers a 0 percent interest rate on loans, a collateral requirement of only 110 percent, and a one-time issuance rate of 0.5 percent, charged at debt repayment.

Fig. 21.1 presents the price evolution of LUSD and ether. The figure shows that while the price of ether in US dollars fluctuated wildly, a 25 percent decrease followed a 100 percent increase, closely maintaining the peg of LUSD ($1r).

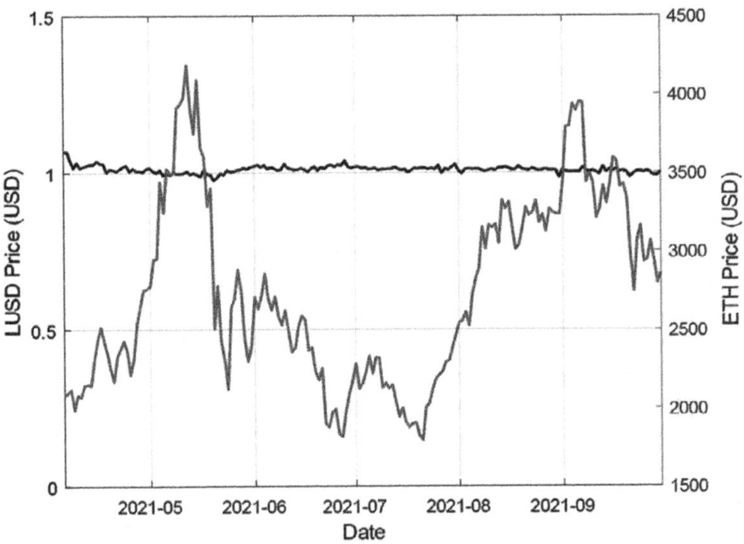

Fig. 21.1. Price Evolution of LUSD and Ether: from April 1, 2021 to September 30, 2021. *Source:* Coinmarketcap.com.

Note: This figure shows LUSD and ether prices in US dollars between April 1, 2021 and September 30, 2021, using price data from coinmarketcap.com.

Algorithmic Seignorage Stablecoins

The third stablecoin mechanism relies on the issuance and destruction of monetary units or reserves to maintain the stablecoin's peg value. The most common framework depends on using two tokens simultaneously. One token acts as a stablecoin and backs its value on reserves of the other token, usually a utility and governance token. The most representative example of this type of token is UST, a stablecoin backed by Luna, the native token of the Terra blockchain. In this case, the protocol controls the issuance and burning of UST tokens (Kereiakes, Kwon, Di Maggio, & Platias, 2019). When UST's value exceeds the dollar value in markets monitored by an oracle, the protocol creates more UST. It simultaneously burns part of Luna token reserves, balancing the total issued value of UST and LUNA. When UST's value drops below $1, the system sells LUNA and buys UST tokens in the open market.

Fig. 21.2 presents the price evolution of UST and LUNA. UST's price remains close to the peg, while the reserve token's price varies widely, from around $0.40 in the last quarter of 2020 to $25.00 in the last quarter of 2021, after reaching highs near $45.

A less traditional project, Ampleforth, developed a single token algorithmic stablecoin. The AMPL tokens follow a continuous rebasing, meaning that the number of tokens in circulation can increase or decrease automatically according to the token's price evolution in the monitored markets. The number of tokens

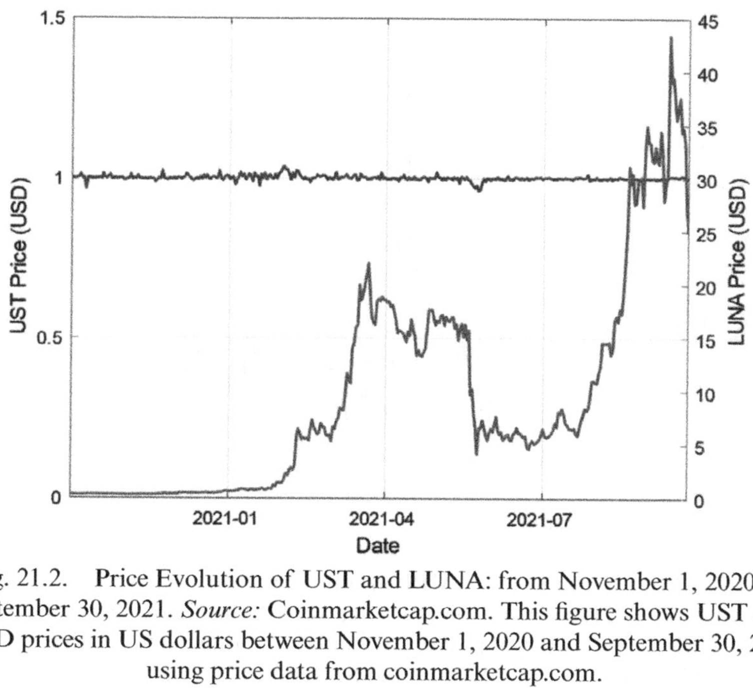

Fig. 21.2. Price Evolution of UST and LUNA: from November 1, 2020 to September 30, 2021. *Source:* Coinmarketcap.com. This figure shows UST and LUSD prices in US dollars between November 1, 2020 and September 30, 2021, using price data from coinmarketcap.com.

in any crypto wallet containing AMPL increases when AMPL's price increases, aiming to return to the peg price equal to the 2019 inflation-adjusted $1 benchmark. The increase in the total circulating supply of AMPL delivered directly to all current holders of the token should decrease the market price by increasing the selling pressure due to the inflation of tokens in circulation. At the same time, when AMPL's value drops, the number of tokens in the wallet also decreases, removing market liquidity and potentially bringing the token's price back to the inflation-adjusted $1. This mechanism, called "rebasing," occurs every 24 hours. A smart contract oracle calculates AMPL's time-weighted average price from the main marketplaces. It then gradually increases or decreases the total amount of tokens in circulation. The rebasing mechanism has not been as effective as initially intended, leading to a large price disparity relative to the target peg. As Fig. 21.3 shows, AMPL's price reached lows below $0.50 and highs of over $3.50.

Lastly, the FRAX project proposed a hybrid solution to stablecoin design (Frax, 2020). It combines collateralized issuance with algorithmic rebasing. A potential problem with collateralized stablecoins is that the collateral base does not increase by the same magnitude during positive demand shocks. FRAX proposes a dual reserve, with a fraction of reserves held in a stablecoin and the rest in a proprietary token (FXS). The share of collateral held on each adjusts algorithmically. If FRAX's price exceeds its $1 peg, FXS held in reserve is burned, reducing the share of collateral backed by FXS and increasing the share backed

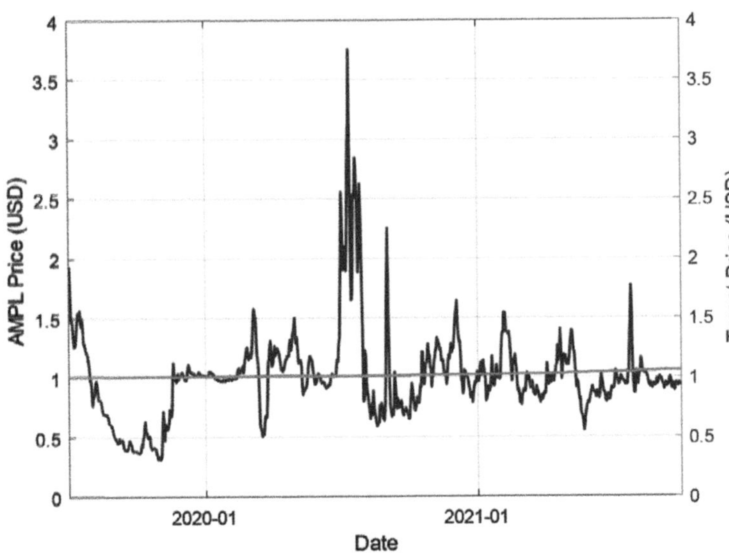

Fig. 21.3. Price Evolution of AMPL and Its Target Price: from July 1, 2019 to September 30, 2021. *Source:* Coinmarketcap.com. This figure shows the evolution of AMPL and its target prices, 2019 inflation-adjusted $1, both expressed in US dollars, between July 1, 2019 and September 30, 2021, using price data from coinmarketcap.com.

by stablecoins. If FRAX's price is below the peg, additional FXS are minted and held in reserves, increasing the share of reserves backed by FXS and reducing the share backed by stablecoins.

Decentralized Exchanges

Before 2014, users mostly exchanged cryptocurrencies on centralized exchanges (CEXs). This approach went against Bitcoin's original ethos regarding exchanging fiat currencies for cryptocurrencies. Thus, a need existed to relinquish direct control of the cryptocurrency and transfer ownership to a centralized intermediary, the CEX. Hackers targeted many CEXs between 2014 and 2020 (Crystal Analytics Team, 2021). For example, Mt. Gox's hack in February 2014 accounted for about 6 percent of bitcoin's total supply.

To bring bitcoin's ethos to the cryptocurrency markets, different developers created DEXs that operated on top of Bitcoin as a second layer, such as Bitshares, NXT, Mastercoin, and Counterparty. Developers designed these platforms to abstract the marketplace's complexity while using the security of the Bitcoin blockchain when settling transactions. However, the Bitcoin programming system's limitations and the limitations on the size and type of information stored in the Bitcoin blockchain made these solutions complex to program, use, and isolated from each other.

In 2016, Vitalik Buterin proposed a DEX based on an automated market maker (AMM) (Buterin, 2016). With this approach, any user could participate in an AMM smart contract by depositing two equal-valued amounts of tokens in a liquidity pool. When a counterparty trades against the AMM, it removes a certain amount of one token and increases the amount of the other. The relative value of each token held in the LP changes and reflects the new relative price of each token. In addition, users pay a liquidity fee, which goes to the liquidity providers.

In 2018 Hayden Adams implemented this idea in a project called Uniswap (Adams, Zinsmeister, & Robinson, 2020). During the so-called DeFi summer in 2020, it became the first DEX to hold over $1 billion in assets and outperform Coinbase Pro's (a US-based CEX) daily volume. Uniswap's success shows that a DEX can provide liquidity levels similar to world-class CEXs. Additionally, any token can be "listed" using an AMM smart contract without regard for its potential market cap or liquidity levels. The latter led to creating initial decentralized offerings instead of initial exchange offerings by funding liquidity pools on an AMM. This feature enables token issuers to distribute primary issuance tokens to users and provide liquidity to current token holders.

During the Uniswap boom in late August 2020, an anonymous developer, known by the pseudonym Chef Nomi, copied the code, named the copy Sushiswap and executed what came to be known as a *vampire attack*, draining liquidity from the victim and transferring it to the attacker. Sushiswap distributed its token (Sushi) to users who deposited Uniswap liquidity pool tokens into a smart contract. The value of newly issued Sushi tokens offered liquidity providers an annual percentage yield equivalent to over 1,000 percent. During the attack, over $800 million was moved from Uniswap to Sushiswap.

The project Balancer aspires to be an AMM based on a market value-weighted portfolio index. Liquidity providers deposit multiple tokens into a liquidity pool, creating a portfolio of tokens available for trading. As users trade against the portfolio, the weights of each asset and their relative prices change, effectively rebalancing the portfolio. With each trade, the portfolio receives trading fees. Therefore, liquidity providers who deposit into Balancer's liquidity pool participate in a self-rebalancing market portfolio and get a share of all fees received from trader interactions.

A drawback of AMM is *impermanent loss*, which refers to the temporary losses occurring in liquidity pools due to large and sudden price changes that generate an imbalance in the value of the token reserves. Most smart contract AMMs are passive traders, not initiating transactions on behalf of the liquidity pool. The smart contract waits for external traders to interact and trade against the liquidity pool. This feature creates a dependency on external traders to arbitrage price differences between the relative prices within the liquidity pool and the relative prices in other markets (DEXs, CEXs, or other AMMs).

Suppose an initial price of 2,000 UST per ETH. A liquidity pool should have in reserve 2,000 UST per ETH. Therefore, if the contract initially had 20,000 UST and 10 ETH, it would have a total value locked of 40,000 UST. If the price of ETH doubles to 4,000 UST in external markets, traders could still buy 1 ETH by depositing 2,000 UST into the contract. After one transaction of 1 ETH, the contract would have 22,000 UST and 9 ETH. ETH's internal relative price would now be 2,444 UST (22,000 UST divided by 9 ETH). This process would continue until the internal relative price equals the external relative price. A smart contract predetermines the price impact of each trade to prevent users from withdrawing (purchasing) large amounts of tokens and taking unfair advantage of the protocol. However, it is vulnerable to large price changes. The *impermanent loss* is the difference in the portfolio's value to the value of a buy-and-hold strategy on the same assets. To compensate for this potential loss, liquidity providers receive compensation in trading fees charged on each transaction.

Decentralized Lending, Derivatives, and Asset Management

The idea of a P2P credit market is not new. Since 2005 companies have operated solutions using the internet to enable direct lending between retail customers (Lee & Lee, 2012). The emergence of smart contracts permitted creating protocols that allow this kind of P2P transaction in a decentralized manner.

In 2018, a protocol called ETHLend and later renamed Aave, created a lending marketplace on Ethereum. Due to the pseudo-anonymous nature of blockchain networks, which limits reputation building and legally enforces delinquent debt, lending markets have only been collateral-based. Collateralized loans reduce or eliminate debt repayment risk and allow using the collateral for low-risk investments such as staking, offsetting part of a debtor's interest cost. Interest rates adjust dynamically and depend on the usability of the deposited assets. These markets also enable leveraged long and short investing. In a leveraged long position, a debtor uses the newly acquired debt, usually a stablecoin, to purchase additional amounts of the collateral asset token. In leveraged shorts, users deposit stablecoins as collateral and borrow the volatile cryptocurrency they expect to decrease in price. If the price decreases, their collateralization ratio increases, allowing additional debt issuance and increasing the short position.

Another application that emerged with a similar idea is Compound. This application uses collateral deposits to provide liquidity to AMMs. Hence collateral receives additional revenue from trading fees, further reducing the cost of borrowing. The yield received from trading fees surpassed the interest charge during specific periods, leading to a negative borrowing cost in some cryptoassets.

Smart contracts can also create derivative instruments by holding collateral reserves and distributing future flows derived from them according to a predetermined set of rules. As presented in the previous sections, users can deposit volatile cryptoassets and create a new asset of stable value. The same mechanism allows protocols to transform volatile assets into new tokens, which could track the price of volatile non-blockchain-related assets such as commodities, stocks, bonds, and exchange rates.

In the case of the Synthethix protocol, individuals can deposit the protocol token (SNX) to generate synthetic dollars, which serve as collateral in the synthetic stock and derivatives market. Any synthetic derivative's value in the platform derives from markets where people favoring an outcome take a long position on the token, while those against it take a short position. The platforms support contracts on synthetic stocks, fiat currencies, indices, options, and perpetual futures, among others.

An implementation that best demonstrates DeFi's composability is asset management Dapps. The segment started with Yearn Finance, a dApp launched in 2020 in response to the difficulties observed by users in choosing the most profitable investment option among different protocols. As investment returns fluctuate based on the supply and demand of liquidity on a particular token in each market. Yearn Finance automatically tracks returns on each market and deploys funds to the highest paying market. As token transactions have fixed fees, pooling funds reduces the average transaction cost per user, increasing returns compared to individual strategies. Yearn Finance currently employs multiple strategies per token. In the case of Ethereum, the protocol uses seven different strategies to generate returns. A team of developers actively updates and monitors these strategies.

Challenges

Although DeFi has many advantages over traditional finance, it still has several unresolved issues. Exponential project growth occurred during 2021, reflecting developer and user interest in this new form of finance. However, developers do not yet have enough experience to create robust and secure code in such immature fields, leading to security flaws overlooked by developers, auditors, and users.

A leading area of uncertainty concerns an applicable legal and tax framework. Different jurisdictions have not adapted regulations for digital assets. This legal limbo generates distrust in investors. Consequently, some refrain from investing due to unclear legal and tax implications. By contrast, other jurisdictions take advantage of this situation. They strategically adopt a less restrictive attitude to attract investors from other countries. For example, El Salvador legalized using bitcoin as legal tender. For El Salvador, a dollarized country without a domestic fiat currency and an economy dependent on remittances in foreign currency (Anzoategui, Demirgüç-Kunt, & Martínez Pería, 2014), DeFi expands access to international capital markets without the limitations of traditional intermediaries, remittances, and payment systems. Some European countries adopted much lower taxes on profits from cryptoasset investments.

The transparency in code execution in most blockchain protocols allows for front running by competing agents and transaction reordering by miners. Daian et al. (2019) and Obadia (2021) discuss and measure the total value extracted through the reordering, inclusion, or censorship of transactions within the blocks when included in the blockchain. This problem is like that observed in traditional finance with free trading applications. In this instance, some market participants sell information about the volume of orders from retail investors to generate profits from arbitrage, a phenomenon called *payment for order flow*. Proposals are available to solve this problem, such as *fair sequencing order*, which attempts to order transactions fairly across blocks.

Another problem is the safekeeping of digital assets. Although sufficient education about computer security is available, the risk of losing digital assets due to phishing techniques or lack of risk prevention is still common. Fraud frequently occurs in this space. According to Chainanalysis (Chainanalysis Team, 2021), scams represent the most prominent form of cryptocurrency-based crime by transaction volume, with over $7.7 billion worth of cryptocurrency taken from victims worldwide in 2021. Also, the basis of the programming language for most of these apps is still novel. Therefore, developers who lack sufficient experience may be unaware of all possible issues.

In 2021, DeFi-related hacks accounted for about 75 percent of the major hacks related to cryptocurrencies, totaling almost $1.3 billion (CertiK, 2022; CipherTrace, 2021). This situation further strengthens the position that DeFi is still a novel ecosystem with potential but faces many challenges to overcome before mainstream adoption.

Summary and Conclusions

This chapter presents some DeFi building blocks, namely stablecoins, DEXs, AMMs, decentralized lending, smart contract-based synthetic instruments, and automated asset managers. The chapter briefly explains the mechanics behind code execution and discusses some currently available protocols and projects for each element. It ends by reviewing some challenges faced by the DeFi industry.

Discussion Questions

1. Identify and explain three stablecoin implementation designs.
2. Explain the arbitrage process that allows liquidity pools to reach market prices without relying on oracles or market price feeds.
3. Describe the term impermanent loss.
4. Discuss the mechanisms that allow negative interest rates on crypto asset collateralized loans.

References

Adams, H., Zinsmeister, N., & Robinson, D. (2020, March). *Uniswap v2 Core*. Uniswap.org. Retrieved from https://uniswap.org/whitepaper.pdf

Anzoategui, D., Demirgüç-Kunt, A., & Martínez Pería, M. S. (2014). Remittances and financial inclusion: Evidence from El Salvador. *World Development*, *54*(C), 338–349.

Beniiche, A. (2020, March 19). *A study of blockchain oracles*. Ithaca, NY: Cornell University. https://arxiv.org/abs/2004.07140v2

Brooks, S., Jurisevic, A., Spain, M., & Warwick, K. (2020). Synthetix Litepaper. Retrieved from https://synthetix.io/

Buterin, V. (2014). *A next-generation smart contract and decentralized application platform*. Ethereum White Paper. Retrieved from http://buyxpr.com/build/pdfs/EthereumWhitePaper.pdf

Buterin, V. (2016, October 3). *Let's run on-chain decentralized exchanges the way we run prediction markets*. Reddit.com. https://www.reddit.com/r/ethereum/comments/55m04x/lets_run_onchain_decentralized_exchanges_the_way/

Casey, M. J. (2014). Dollar-backed digital currency aims to fix bitcoin's volatility dilemma. The Wall Street Journal, July 8. Retrieved from https://www.wsj.com/articles/BL-MBB-23780

CertiK. (2022). State of DeFi security 2021. Retrieved from https://certik-2.hubspotpagebuilder.com/the-state-of-defi-security-2021

Chainanalysis Team. (2021, December 16). *The biggest threat to trust in cryptocurrency: Rug pulls put 2021 scam revenue close to all-time high*. Chainanalysis.com. Retrieved from https://blog.chainalysis.com/reports/2021-crypto-scam-revenues/

CipherTrace. (2021, August). *Cryptocurrency crime and anti-money laundering report, August 2021*. Ciphertrace.com. Retrieved from https://ciphertrace.com/cryptocurrency-crime-and-anti-money-laundering-report-august-2021/

Crystal Analytics Team. (2021, June 25). *The 10 biggest crypto exchange hacks in history*. Crystalblockchain.com. Retrieved from https://crystalblockchain.com/articles/the-10-biggest-crypto-exchange-hacks-in-history/

Daian, P., Goldfeder, S., Kell, T., Li, Y., Zhao, X., Bentov, I., … Juels, A. (2019, April 10). *Flash boys 2.0: Frontrunning, transaction reordering, and consensus instability in decentralized exchanges*. Ithaca, NY: Cornell University. https://arxiv.org/abs/1904.05234v1

Deshmukh, S., Geest, A., Gogel, D., Resas, D., & Sillaber, C. (2021, June 8). *Decentralized finance (DeFi) policy-maker toolkit*. Weforum.org. Retrieved from https://www.weforum.org/whitepapers/decentralized-finance-defi-policy-maker-toolkit

Frax. (2020). Frax: Fractional-algorithmic stablecoin protocol. Retrieved from https://docs.frax.finance/overview

Fries, M., & Paal, B. P. (Eds.). (2019). *Smart contracts*. Tübingen: Mohr Siebeck. Retrieved from https://library.oapen.org/handle/20.500.12657/24858

Gecko Labs Pte. Ltd. (2022). Stablecoins by market capitalization. Retrieved from https://www.coingecko.com/en/categories/stablecoins

Gogel, D. (2021, June). *DeFi beyond the hype – The emerging world of decentralized finance*. Wharton: University of Pennsylvania. Retrieved from https://wifpr.wharton.upenn.edu/wp-content/uploads/2021/05/DeFi-Beyond-the-Hype.pdf

Grant Thornton LLP. (2021, September 1). Circle reserve account report. Retrieved from https://www.centre.io/hubfs/pdfs/attestation/2021 Circle Examination Report July 2021 Final.pdf?hsLang=en

Griffin, J. M., & Shams, A. (2020). Is bitcoin really untethered? *Journal of Finance*, *75*(4), 1913–1964.

Kereiakes, E., Kwon, D., Di Maggio, M., & Platias, N. (2019). Terra money: Stability and adoption. Retrieved from https://www.terra.money/Terra_White_paper.pdf

Lee, E., & Lee, B. (2012). Herding behavior in online P2P lending: An empirical investigation. *Electronic Commerce Research and Applications*, *11*(5), 495–503.

MakerDAO. (2021). Learn about MakerDAO. Retrieved from https://makerdao.world/en/learn/MakerDAO

Mankiw, N. G. (2019). *Macroeconomics* (10th ed.). New York, NY: Worth Publishers.

Moin, A., Sekniqi, K., & Sirer, E. G. (2020). SoK: A classification framework for stablecoin designs. In J. Bonneau & N. Heninger (Eds.), *Financial cryptography and data security. FC 2020*. Lecture Notes in Computer Science (vol. 12059, pp. 174–200). Cham: Springer.

Obadia, A. (2021, February 22). *Quantifying MEV: Introducing MEV-explore V0*. Medium.com. Retrieved from https://medium.com/flashbots/quantifying-mev-introducing-mev-explore-v0-5ccbee0f6d02

Schär, F. (2020). Decentralized finance: On blockchain- and smart contract-based financial markets. *Review, Federal Reserve of Saint Louis*, *103*(2), 153–174.

Szabo, N. (1996). Smart contracts: Building blocks for digital markets. *Extropy* 16. Retrieved from https://www.fon.hum.uva.nl/rob/Courses/InformationInSpeech/CDROM/Literature/LOTwinterschool2006/szabo.best.vwh.net/smart_contracts_2.html

Willet, Jr. (2013). MasterCoin complete specification vs. 1.1 (Smart property edition). Retrieved from https://sites.google.com/site/2ndbtcwpaper/

Chapter 22

Cryptocurrency Exchanges and the Future of Cryptoassets

Antonio Brasse and Samuel Hyun

Abstract

This chapter differentiates between centralized and decentralized exchanges (DEXs), emphasizing the importance of regulations and compliance related to the market's development and expansion for cryptoasset trading and investment. It also explains the pros and cons of using different methods to trade cryptocurrencies or virtual currencies and their tradeoffs. The chapter discusses how centralized and DEXs emerged, their history and potential future, and the possible role of future regulations and regulatory clarity around how they may operate. Additionally, it compares cryptoasset markets to other more traditional markets such as equities, real estate, and foreign exchange.

Keywords: Cryptocurrencies; cryptoassets; centralized exchanges; decentralized exchanges; regulations; compliance

Introduction

From a macro perspective, cryptocurrency exchanges have offered a gateway for investors and traders to invest in a new emerging asset class. Comparing the cryptocurrency market since about 2017 shows a significant increase in demand for cryptocurrencies and crypto-related products. Although mainstream adoption of cryptocurrencies is occurring, all cryptocurrency exchanges need to scale up in response to the demand for new functionality and features.

The Emerald Handbook on Cryptoassets: Investment Opportunities and Challenges, 341–353

doi:10.1108/978-1-80455-320-620221022

Centralized Versus Decentralized Exchanges

Centralized exchanges (CEXs) are trading platforms that function as an intermediary between traders to buy or sell cryptocurrencies, whether between each other or fiat currencies such as the US dollar. These exchanges also maintain custody of the cryptoassets and fiat funds if the exchange also serves as a fiat gateway. CEXs are responsible for safeguarding customer assets.

Not all CEXs facilitate trading into and out of fiat currencies. Most centralized crypto exchanges only support the trading between cryptocurrencies or cryptoassets. Most exchanges cannot support fiat gateways directly, regardless of whether they are centralized or decentralized. They lack a basic regulatory framework, such as know your customer (KYC) protocols that are required to secure banking partnerships to offer various fiat options.

Decentralized exchanges (DEXs) facilitate the exchange of cryptoassets by matching and executing trades through smart contracts, allowing traders to reach each other, and set an agreed-upon price. DEXs do not hold customer funds in custody. The trader is responsible for private keys and wallets.

DEXs allow users to buy and sell digital assets without any intermediary organization responsible for processing transactions and instead allow for self-executing smart contracts to facilitate the transaction. Since users are transacting trades without an intermediary, these DEXs do not have a requirement of KYC or anti-money laundering (AML) regulatory standards typically required when using a CEX. As a result, users process trades within a non-custodial framework, meaning DEX users are responsible for their assets. The user must manage all wallets, private keys, and seed phrases. A *wallet* is a device or piece of software code or program that allows someone to transfer or store cryptoassets. A *private key* is a secret number used in cryptography, like a password. In cryptocurrency, holders also use private keys to sign transactions and prove ownership of a blockchain address. A private key is necessary to move or transfer cryptoassets. Having appropriate levels of security over it can protect a user from theft of cryptoassets. A *seed phrase* is a list of words that needs to be secured as it would be necessary to recover cryptoassets.

Although many users perceive that being responsible for their assets is a great feature, others prefer to have a central point of authority/intermediary, like a bank or exchange, be responsible for the custody of cryptoassets. For example, if one loses a private key or a password, that person may be unable to access the wallet containing all the cryptoassets. DEXs offer various liquidity options to ensure trade order and execution optimization, which conventional order book models, other decentralized liquidity protocols, and liquidity aggregation tools reinforce.

Currently, all DEXs lack regulatory compliance due to how they operate. Because DEXs facilitate peer-to-peer (P2P) trading between cryptoassets, there is no KYC layer or distinction between what might be considered a security, commodity, or other regulated asset class. Consequently, no DEX can directly facilitate fiat deposits, withdrawals, and trading. Additionally, DEXs are not truly decentralized because they still facilitate P2P trading via a centralized domain or website. They still function as intermediaries between traders despite not taking custody of investor assets or funds. A truly decentralized crypto transaction would be one person transferring bitcoin (BTC) to another person's wallet address with no intermediaries.

CEXs and DEXs can differ. However, CEXs have far more variations, particularly involving regulations/compliance, security, and liquidity.

Consider telephone connections to visualize the general differences between a CEX and DEX. In the past, the telephone company would route calls for a particular region through a switchboard location. This approach allows for a more efficient connection of callers, reducing the potential distance between some callers. For example, callers in different cities would connect to a central hub in their location, and those central hubs would be connected. This way, a caller in New York can be routed to someone in Chicago more efficiently through appropriate hubs shortening the distance or latency. This situation is comparable to a CEX. Of course, if the switchboard fails, no callers can connect, but this is the tradeoff. The alternative would be to connect people directly with cables or wires to facilitate calls. This approach is comparable to a DEX.

Sticking with the phone example where everyone is connected can create significant inefficiencies. However, if one connection goes down, it does not take down an entire network the way it would happen if a switchboard went down. Continuing the decentralized example of telephone connections, building a network of everything being connected directly to each other requires time. An example of how a decentralized phone connection may work is a caller in New York trying to call someone in Chicago, but Chicago and New York are not connected. Thus, a caller would get routed through Los Angeles to Chicago because direct connections exist from New York to Los Angeles and from Los Angeles to Chicago. This situation creates inefficiencies, lags, and latency issues because individuals must travel further to make the call to Chicago.

A CEX is not more or less secure than a DEX. The issue is more about which counterparty is responsible for securing the cryptoassets. CEXs have this responsibility, whereas the responsibility with DEXs lies with the individual or entity placing a trade since cryptoassets move in and out of personal wallets.

Although most cryptocurrency trading volume and activity exist within CEXs, the demand for DEXs continues to grow. Ultimately, determining which type of exchange is better depends on a person's needs, concerns, and priorities. Thus, both exchange types can co-exist based on their purposes and audiences.

The Benefits of CEXs

Compared to DEXs, CEXs have deeper liquidity, better pricing, and faster execution times for placing trades on cryptoassets. CEXs oversee all trading aspects, from matching to settling trades, providing custody of the cryptoassets or fiat, and aggregating liquidity from multiple sources. CEXs offer better efficiency and scalability due to trader experience in equity and foreign exchange (forex) markets.

Yet not all CEXs are created equal. Most exchanges are CEXs lacking these benefits. However, many CEXs offer these benefits. Hence, global access is available.

The Disadvantages of CEXs

CEX disadvantages are subjective and depend on a person's needs, concerns, and CEX type. CEXs are generally unregulated, non-compliant, and "offshore," meaning they are not subject to regulatory oversight from the most developed countries, like the United States and the United Kingdom.

A CEX's main disadvantage concerns security. News often appears around hacking a CEX, resulting in losses to crypto customers. For example, the Crypto.com hack resulted in investors losing $35 million (Brewster, 2022).

The hacked CEXs are often "offshore" types. Because they circumvent basic compliance protocols, these CEXs frequently do not have cybersecurity measures and other technology and operational controls representing best practices or a minimum baseline. Hackers use phishing scams to steal funds (Merrill, 2021). These exchanges generally only require their users to enter their email and password to access the exchange's services, such as trading, depositing, and withdrawing crypto. They often do not require two-factor authentication (2FA). Even when CEXs mandate 2FA, it is sometimes insufficient because the basis of such authentication may be short message service (SMS), better known as text messaging or email addresses. Since most people have their email address recovery option tied to their mobile number, SMS, and email address, 2FA is vulnerable to subscriber identification module (SIM) hacks (Moon, 2021).

Hackers have stolen billions of dollars because of phishing attacks and SIM hacks. Yet, CEXs such as BlockQuake have reduced this risk by mandating app-based 2FA, such as Google Authenticator. Thus, even if hackers phish or SIM hack accounts, they generally lack access to the authentication app because hackers physically need access to a smartphone. This situation limits their ability to steal customer funds. Besides customer-level account hacks, exchange companies have been subject to phishing scams where backend systems with the ability to move funds lack 2FA and other security protocols.

Another main disadvantage of using some CEXs is that a person is subject to that company's unfairly restrictive policies. A company often has the discretion to deem what activities it views as acceptable, regardless of legality. In turn, a company punishes its users by closing their accounts. Many proponents of decentralized finance (DeFi) and democratized economies often say, "not your keys, not your crypto." Although users may have legal rights to their crypto sitting on a CEX via the "for the benefit of" relationship, the exchange controls everything. However, a CEX may not always act on behalf of its customers' wishes. Investors should research a CEX to ensure it is compliant, security-driven, and customer-focused.

A Deeper Look into DEXs

When investors think of DEXs, DeFi often comes to mind. *DeFi* is a system by which financial products become available on a public decentralized blockchain network. Thus, DEXs fall under the world of DeFi as a financial product for users to execute buy and sell orders for cryptocurrencies through a decentralized blockchain network protocol (Napoletano & Schmidt, 2021). Many different types of DEXs (decentralized applications – dApps) specialize in a specific financial instrument, including automated market makers (AMM), order books, and atomic swaps.

AMMs have significantly increased activity within DEXs as protocols, including Uniswap and Sushiswap. The protocols permit tackling the ever-existing issue of inadequate liquidity within DEXs. From a technology standpoint, AMMs utilize liquidity pools in the form of smart contracts with complex algorithms to determine trading pair liquidity and resulting market prices (Sergeenkov, 2021). This approach differs from an order book since market pricing from AMMs results from the protocol employing liquidity pool protocols to determine an asset's price instead of an existing order book.

Order books provide a simple supply and demand for a specific asset, including a record of all open buy and sell orders for all users to see. Users can see the order book's depth, as this information is often held on-chain during trades while funds remain off-chain in the wallet.

Atomic swaps act as a P2P process to swap cryptocurrencies across different blockchain networks without a CEX or intermediary. Users maintain control of their assets throughout the process and can do so autonomously by utilizing specific smart contracts, including a HashLock and TimeLock key (Fitzpatrick, 2019). A HashLock key distributes traded cryptocurrency only when all parties have signed off on their respective transactions. In contrast, a TimeLock key provides a safety mechanism that returns traded cryptocurrency to traders if they do not complete the trade within a specified time (Fitzpatrick, 2019). Both are security controls designed to ensure a P2P transaction is efficiently confirmed and executed.

The development of DeFi and DEXs has enhanced the trading experience. A prime example includes introducing DEX aggregators such as 1inch exchange, Paraswap, and Matcha, enabling users or traders to buy and sell large volumes of cryptoassets. These aggregator protocols aggregate liquidity across many existing platforms to execute trades safely and autonomously. Users can accomplish this task by clicking a button across different blockchains by linking an associated wallet address to the DeFi protocol (Sephton, 2022).

DeFi originated from specific borrowing and lending platforms offered to users, like traditional finance. Today, many people cannot access specific financial tools that would otherwise allow for better financial security and optimizing their finances. With DeFi, any user with internet access and a crypto wallet can borrow, lend, and earn interest on cryptocurrencies in yield farming, liquidity mining, and staking (Geroni, 2021).

Specific DeFi protocols such as AAVE, Compound, or Spell allow users to deposit digital assets into liquidity pools while earning interest in real time. Users also can borrow these assets through over-collateralized loans to optimize capital efficiency. These DeFi protocols have offered worldwide exposure to many common financial instruments that often are inaccessible.

Decentralized autonomous organizations (DAOs) have played a crucial role in the world of decentralization. A *DAO* is an organizational model structure that allows communities (an individual or entity) to make decisions for a specific protocol. This task involves having the organization run entirely on a blockchain-specific protocol that is fully autonomous, with encoded smart contract rules. This "trustless" decision-making framework advocates for proper governance for everyone involved in the protocol. An example includes an Ethereum DeFi lending and borrowing protocol accessible to anyone who has Ethereum or an ERC-20 Token in their non-custodial wallet address. The DeFi protocol functions on algorithmic smart contracts that allow users to borrow and lend their digital assets. However, as usage of the protocol increases, a need exists to create a DAO to make suggestions and changes. By creating a DAO within a specific DeFi lending and borrowing protocol, all participants (i.e., usually those holding the protocol's governance token) can propose any changes they want. A majority vote results in a proposal's passage. The underlying team that created the DeFi protocol makes the appropriate changes in the smart contract. This approach facilitates DEXs and DeFi applications to scale up rapidly.

Although DAOs are structured to distribute decision-making power and involvement to the users, an underlying firm is still responsible for managing the protocol(s). Many are likely to refute that creating a completely decentralized ecosystem is possible because some point of centralized authority is needed to operate the business (Harsimran, 2021). However, DeFi enables many companies to function in a more decentralized manner. Investors are beginning to appreciate that they can be involved in the potential success of a business/coin/token, which usually results in a stronger community and sustainability. To put this situation in perspective, the total amount locked up into DeFi protocols (TVL) was approximately $10 billion in June 2020. In October 2021, that number rose 10-fold to $100 billion. Current statistics on DeFi's value are available at https://defipulse.com/.

Although the previous example involves the DeFI sector, DAOs apply to existing blockchains, including BTC. It was one of the first DAOs with an open participation consensus protocol connecting a network of participants autonomously. Although BTC currently lacks complex governance mechanisms used by DeFi protocols, DAOs are beginning to provide a decentralized form of corporate governance as transparent and self-governing organizations are on the rise.

CEXs and Cryptoassets: Regulated Versus Unregulated

A CEX's advantages and disadvantages depend on the level of exchange regulation from the perspective of general laws and best practices applying to exchanges (whether CEX or DEX) and how an exchange handles laws around the cryptoassets offered.

Practically all DEXs and most CEXs currently do not perform KYC or sufficient KYC and AML checks to comply with domestic and international laws. All exchanges require these checks to facilitate the exchange and movement of money or money equivalents. For the exchanges not performing these checks or performing them insufficiently, all investors need to provide an email address and possibly some personal information that is not verified. People interested in avoiding these identity checks can use the information and an email address not generally associated with their real identity to trade on these platforms.

People have different reasons for using an exchange that does not perform these KYC and AML checks. Some are only concerned with maintaining privacy. However, laws across multiple jurisdictions mandate KYC and AML checks involving any third-party service that facilitates trading, exchanging, and moving any asset considered a money equivalent like cryptoassets. Although some users may want to maintain their privacy, their ability to do so may be short-lived. However, platforms performing full KYC are responsible for complying with privacy laws such as Europe's general data protection regulation. Thus, they protect their customers' personal information from being breached by hackers or viewed/accessed by unauthorized individuals.

Those who want to avoid KYC and AML checks are likely to intentionally circumvent laws that have transactions falling under money laundering activity. These exchanges have insufficient controls to check the presence of illegal activity such as money laundering.

Examples of illicit activities facilitated by the exchanges that fail to perform sufficient KYC and AML checks include tax evasion, movement of funds related to drug activity and sex trafficking of minors, and financing terrorism. These financial activities link to serious crimes that have a devastating impact on people. Therefore, laws involving KYC and AML are necessary for crypto exchanges to protect the public.

As shown by the growth of equity, real estate markets, and forex exchange, regulatory clarity is likely to have a similar effect on the crypto markets. After establishing the passage of rules and regulations across these other markets, consumers experienced better transparency, accountability, clarity, uniformity, and compliance. With greater regulatory clarity and compliance comes more trust in those markets. With trust comes more participants and growth. Crypto markets are likely to realize similar results. Despite crackdowns related to KYC guidelines (Kaaru, 2022), the market capitalization of cryptoassets has grown (Ledesma, 2021).

Different laws may apply, depending on the attributes of a particular cryptoasset, cryptocurrency, or token. Additionally, each country or jurisdiction may have different definitions for various asset classes. Each country defines the meaning of money, currency, or legal tender, an investment contract, security, commodity, and derivative. For example, most countries see BTC as a commodity. Therefore, few restrictions exist around offering it for trading beyond KYC and AML requirements. However, the government in El Salvador considers BTC as legal tender and as good as its local currency (Tidy, 2021).

The United States has a legal precedent called the "Howey test." The Howey Test refers to the US Supreme Court case for determining whether a transaction qualifies as an "investment contract." Authorities use it to determine whether an investment contract exists. This investment qualifies as a security if it involves (1) an investment of money, (2) in a common enterprise, (3) with the expectation of profit, and (4) derived from the efforts of others (Reiff, 2021). A security is subject to disclosure and registration requirements under the Securities Act of 1933 and the Securities Exchange Act of 1934. This test considers a cryptocurrency under securities laws. Most other countries do not have this concept. US authorities view any cryptocurrency meeting the Howey Test as a security under current laws. However, other countries may consider the same cryptoasset a spot market commodity and subject to different regulations.

Exchanges must manage the intricacies of the various cryptoassets. For example, they need to have proper KYC requirements to identify a user's country of residence. Exchanges also need to work with their legal team to determine a particular cryptoasset class based on each country's regulations. The exchange can then list and offer cryptoassets to citizens or residents of various countries to comply with applicable laws.

In the United States, the two main regulators are the securities and exchange commission (SEC) and the commodity futures trading commission (CFTC). Another popular asset class in the crypto markets is derivatives. The CFTC is the agency with jurisdiction over derivatives, but other agencies may be involved depending upon the underlying asset and the derivative instrument's structure. For example, since US regulators view BTC as a commodity, BTC futures are generally under the CFTC, which approved their trading in December 2017 (Cheng, 2017).

If a crypto exchange wants to trade tokens in the United States as securities, it must have a broker-dealer license. Additional registrations and licenses would be required to offer crypto derivatives in the United States. Most exchanges, including regulated ones, generally do not have these licenses or registrations. They cannot provide these types of tokens to US persons. In many cases, they cannot offer these tokens to Canadian persons because Canada has similar registration and licensing requirements.

The SEC recently approved a BTC futures exchange-traded fund (ETF) (De & Nelson, 2021). Authorities consider BTC a commodity, and its associated futures contract falls under the CFTC. However, once wrapped into an ETF and available for trading on stock exchanges, the ETF product also comes under SEC rules. Hence, authorities view this specific ETF product as a security in the United States and many other jurisdictions.

Crypto exchanges need to consider a tradeable asset's various attributes to determine an appropriate audience. Taking such action is necessary to avoid unnecessary regulatory scrutiny, potential fines, criminal charges, and the risk of closure. Exchanges also need to ensure certain assets are only legally offered to the right people by following proper KYC guidelines.

Exchanges that do not perform KYC or determine a cryptoasset's legal asset class often fail to comply with the laws of most countries and are most at risk of disappearing with customer funds without any available consumer recourse. In the case of CEXs, these exchanges frequently lack proper technology controls to protect customer funds from being stolen.

Potential users need to factor in a CEX's advantages and disadvantages in their analysis. They should choose a regulated platform if they seek deep liquidity, competitive, consistent pricing, and a secure place to trade devoid of market manipulation.

Traders or investors who want a more obscure cryptoasset available on an "offshore" face increased cybersecurity and market manipulation risks. Consequently, they should double-check the cryptoasset's pricing and hold the asset in a personal wallet for security purposes.

Regulations Around DEXs

Governments and other entities increasingly demand regulation and compliance, affecting CEXs and DEXs. Regulations toward the cryptocurrency/blockchain space are ever-changing, emphasizing CEXs that are entirely responsible for the custody of customer assets. Nonetheless, much discussion surrounds how to apply regulations to DEXs.

Although various federal and state government agencies are involved in providing crypto-related regulations, a lack of clarity still exists. This lack of clarity is also not limited to the United States, further exacerbating the problem. Questions on how to regulate a smart contract or treat a transaction on a DEX and off-chain/off-platform order books require much tailoring and time. As cryptocurrency and blockchain have a worldwide presence, regulators must be mindful to avoid confusion as people and businesses look to transact internationally across borders. If differences are too great, this situation could bring commerce in this sector to a standstill or fragment it enough to make its uses inefficient. Without KYC and AML requirements, regulators are beginning to pay attention and act, as seen in the example with Uniswap (Michaels & Osipovich, 2021). Uniswap has not taken any corrective actions to date. Although securities must follow strict trading and reporting rules, regulators treat most cryptocurrencies as commodities, which are not subject to the same level of scrutiny as securities. However, with the ever-growing space and current investigations by the SEC on Uniswap, regulations are likely to come into the DeFi space at an increasing rate (Michaels & Osipovich, 2021).

DEX's use by blockchain users has exploded in recent years. According to real-time analytics sources such as CoinMarketCap, as of March 20, 2022, many of the largest DEXs process over $1 billion worth of transactions. For example, Uniswap V3 has over $1 billion in daily transactional volume. *The Wall Street Journal* announced that the SEC is investigating one of Uniswap's leading developers (Michaels & Osipovich, 2021). This investigation concerns many DEX users and DEX dApps developers about the legal status and the regulatory enforcement future of DEX. Specifically, the concerns involve a lack of KYC checks and their impact on illegally offering securities to US residents.

When CEXs started to operate, regulators quickly asserted their right to supervise these exchanges. In particular, the SEC determined that if the cryptoasset exchanged was a token that the SEC views as a security, the SEC requires a CEX to register just like any other national securities exchange, such as the New

York stock exchange and NASDAQ. Similarly, the financial crimes enforcement network (FinCEN) ruled that if the cryptoasset exchanged is a blockchain token transmitted from one location to another, it can supervise the exchange because the transaction is a money transmission. Thus, CEXs must create an AML policy and adopt AML and KYC procedures. Regulators could contact these CEXs and insist they adopt these policies to remain in business in the United States.

However, this situation left open a few questions. For example, what must DEXs do to comply with these regulations? Would regulators insist that DEXs abide by the same regulations as CEXs?

In 2018, the SEC first confronted a DEX called EtherDelta (Fries, 2021). EtherDelta operated a DEX that brought together buyers and sellers of tokens using a website, smart contract, and an order book. The SEC brought an action against EtherDelta's founder for operating an unregistered national securities exchange. In the action, the SEC suggested that it did not believe the exchange was decentralized because EtherDelta operated the website, controlled the order book, and could upgrade the smart contract. The action resulted in a $400,000 settlement. This case left open what the SEC would do if it had to face a true DEX and evaluate whether it was subject to SEC regulation. What kind of action can authorities implement if an entity operates an unregistered securities exchange when a DEX has no operator?

Currently, much uncertainty exists on how the SEC and FinCEN will regulate DEXs. *The Wall Street Journal*) reports that the SEC's investigation of Uniswap does not clarify matters (Michaels & Osipovich, 2021). The SEC has taken no formal action. Gary Gensler, SEC Chairperson, has made statements about DeFi platforms suggesting that they are not immune from regulatory oversight. Stating that DeFi platforms may not be immune also does not clarify the situation. Identifying which DeFi platforms, including DEXs, are subject to this oversight creates a complicated situation for regulators.

Although the EtherDelta action provides some guidance, a lack of direction still exists about how the SEC will interpret its regulations when applying them to a DEX. Regulators have good reason to pause before deciding to supervise DEXs. Investors wanting to exchange one form of blockchain token for another do not just use DEXs. These exchanges are now a fundamental part of the blockchain infrastructure, including gaming platforms focusing on creating and exchanging non-fungible tokens and various dApps.

Some applications are based in the United States, but many are not. Thus, if US regulators shut down a DEX, this action could have a global impact. By contrast, a US regulator can go to a CEX operator and require them to exclude US users. This option is unavailable with a DEX because no person or entity is often available to make that request. Regulators also lack information about DEX users, such as their jurisdiction. This situation enables a DEX to wall off those users. US regulators may be in a position where their only options are to let the DEX operate or shut it down. Suppose the SEC can shut down a DEX. Taking this action could cause more harm than good for potential US participants because the DEX could move outside of the United States, where other jurisdictions view its operations as legal. This situation could put the United States at a competitive disadvantage.

Without explicit regulatory guidance about DEXs, DEXs can identify and mitigate potential regulatory risks through discussions with their appropriate counsel. Developers trying to build applications that use these DEXs should also discuss with their counsel the possibility of secondary liability that may arise if the SEC were to treat that DEX as an unregistered national securities exchange. Additionally, app developers should discuss the possibility of money transmission issues due to the transfers to and from the DEX. DEX users, or even dApps users using the DEX, should analyze and compare the regulatory risk between different DEXs because not all DEXs have the same closure risk.

The Future of Crypto Exchanges and Cryptoassets

What does the future hold for crypto exchanges and cryptoassets? Examining the overall landscape of cryptocurrencies, virtual currencies, and digital blockchain-based assets shows that much potential growth remains. Currently, the cryptocurrency markets represent just over 1 percent of the global economy. These markets are barely scratching the surface. This situation is comparable to when internet and web-based stocks entered the mid-to-late 1990s.

The crypto markets are still in the early adoption phase. Just as internet-based businesses have morphed, transformed, and grown, a similar scenario is likely to happen for cryptoassets and their underlying blockchains, given the movement from crypto 1.0 to the next generations and iterations of blockchain-based assets. Security and commodity-based tokens will show further development. Better safeguards will emerge to prevent or reverse the loss or theft of these next-generation tokens and cryptoassets. Blockchain technology will transform industries such as cross-border payments involving using stablecoins, data storage, identity management and verification, and supply chain management. Such actions will create new economies of scale that are more democratized and decentralized, allowing more people to participate. As this landscape grows, larger swaths of the population will participate as their understanding develops. Most people still do not understand blockchain or cryptocurrencies, their purposes, or utility. This situation will eventually change just as it did for internet-based services.

The future of crypto exchanges looks bright, at least for those choosing to be compliant and regulatory-minded and work alongside traditional financial institutions. The current phase of crypto exchanges is like how the retail forex brokerage space was the "Wild West" about two decades ago. Just as regulatory clarity came to the forex space, that same regulatory clarity will arrive in the crypto exchange space. As that happens, a consolidation of crypto exchanges is likely to occur similarly for forex brokers. The only ones likely to survive and grow are those that obey financial regulations.

A rise of next-generation, regulatory-compliant crypto exchanges is likely to occur, including best practices involving cybersecurity and internal controls. Many types of crypto exchanges can thrive in the future. Just as dozens of stock exchanges exist globally, each making billions of dollars annually, many next-generation exchanges will do the same as more retail and institutional market participants enter the space.

DEXs will also have a place. Although most people have no interest in having custody of their cryptoassets, some in the crypto audience feel more comfortable doing so. For this reason, a need exists for DEXs to service this segment. Thus, DEXs will morph and transform from their current state. Today, almost all DEXs are unregulated. That situation will likely change. DEXs interested in continuing to operate and grow their businesses will need to address regulations around KYC and AML. DEXs and CEXs failing to address basic regulations will inevitably result in blacklisting. As a result, they will have difficulty operating at scale and making significant profits legally.

Summary and Conclusions

This chapter explored CEXs and DEXs and their current and future roles involving cryptoassets. It concludes that both types of exchanges and cryptoassets will continue to grow and support their specific niches. New regulations will clarify the space and set baseline requirements and standards that add consistency and uniformity. These changes should create more trust from people and increase cryptoasset usage and trading. This situation is like what occurred when the internet became accessible to the masses, resulting in the growth of internet-based companies. This space is here to stay and will continue to transform and be transformative.

Discussion Questions

1. Identify and discuss the primary differences between CEXs and DEXs.
2. Discuss whether CEXs and DEXs can be regulated.
3. Explain whether the future of cryptocurrency and trading lies with CEXs or DEXs.
4. Identify lessons learned from past markets and industries as DEXs enter the mainstream.

References

Brewster, T. (2022). Crypto.com admits $35 million hack. *Forbes*, January 20. Retrieved from https://www.forbes.com/sites/thomasbrewster/2022/01/20/cryptocom-admits-35-million-hack/?sh=7e55ad575133

Cheng, E. (2017). CME to launch bitcoin futures in three weeks after green light from regulator; Bitcoin jumps. *CNBC*, December 1. Retrieved from https://www.cnbc.com/2017/12/01/cme-says-its-launching-bitcoin-futures-on-dec-18.html

De, N., & Nelson, D. (2021, October 16). SEC approves bitcoin futures ETF, opening crypto to wider investor base. Coinbase. Retrieved from https://www.coindesk.com/policy/2021/10/15/sec-approves-bitcoin-etf-opening-crypto-to-wider-investor-base/

Fitzpatrick, L. (2019). A complete beginner's guide to atomic swaps. *Forbes*, September 2. Retrieved from https://www.forbes.com/sites/lukefitzpatrick/2019/09/02/a-complete-beginners-guide-to-atomic-swaps/?sh=30cbf6886178

Fries, T. (2021). SEC charges EtherData founder with operating an unregistered securities exchange. *Tokenist*, May 13. Retrieved from https://tokenist.com/sec-charges-etherdelta-founder-with-operating-an-unregistered-securities-exchange/

Geroni, D. (2021). *Staking vs. yield farming vs. liquidity mining – key differences. 101blockchains*, November 18. Retrieved from https://101blockchains.com/staking-vs-yield-farming-vs-liquidity-mining/

Harsimran, K. (2021). Are DEX's truly decentralized? *Bezinga*, September 11. Retrieved from https://www.benzinga.com/markets/cryptocurrency/21/09/22898396/are-dexs-truly-decentralized

Kaaru, S. (2022). Binance knowingly ignored AML, KYC checks and Changpeng Zhao knows it: Report. *Coingeek*, January 28. Retrieved from https://coingeek.com/binance-knowingly-ignored-aml-kyc-checks-and-changpeng-zhao-knows-it-report/

Ledesma, L. (2021). Crypto market cap surges to record $2.7T. Coindesk, October 21. Retrieved from https://www.coindesk.com/markets/2021/10/21/crypto-market-cap-surges-to-new-record-27-trillion/

Merrill, J. (2021). Scammers scoop UP misspelled cryptocurrency URLs to rob your wallet. The Washington Post, October 8. Retrieved from https://www.washingtonpost.com/technology/2021/10/08/cryptocurrency-scam-websites/

Michaels, D., & Osipovich, A. (2021). Regulators investigate crypto-exchange developer uniswap labs. The Wall Street Journal, September 3. Retrieved from https://www.wsj.com/articles/regulators-investigate-crypto-exchange-developer-uniswap-labs-11630666800

Moon, M. (2021). Coinbase hackers exploit multi-factor flaw to steal from 6,000 customers. Engadget, October 10. Retrieved from https://www.engadget.com/coinbase-hack-mfa-exploit-102924471.html

Napoletano, E., & Schmidt, J. (2021). Decentralized finance is building a new financial system. *Forbes*, April 2. Retrieved from https://www.forbes.com/advisor/investing/defi-decentralized-finance/

Reiff, N. (2021). *What is the Howey test?* Investopedia, July 5. Retrieved from https://www.investopedia.com/terms/h/howey-test.asp

Sephton, C. (2022, January 15). *What is a DEX aggregator?* Coinmarketcap. Retrieved from https://coinmarketcap.com/alexandria/glossary/dex-aggregator

Sergeenkov, A. (2021). *What is an automated market maker?* Coindesk, August 20. Retrieved from https://www.coindesk.com/learn/2021/08/20/what-is-an-automated-market-maker/

Tidy, J. (2021). Fear and erxcitement in El Salvador as bitcoin becomes legal tender. *BBC*, September 7. Retrieved from https://www.bbc.com/news/technology-58473260

Discussion Questions and Answers: Chapters 2–22

Chapter 2. The Cryptoasset Auditing and Accounting Landscape

1. Explain the current accounting consensus for how organizations should account for cryptoassets.
   The current consensus is to account for all cryptoassets as indefinite-lived intangible assets. Another instrument similarly classified is goodwill, which an organization can only write down via an impairment loss and never mark up in value. The current accounting for cryptoassets does not reflect the economic realities of the crypto market or the use case of crypto at many organizations.

2. Describe two differences between stablecoins and central bank digital currencies (CBDCs).
   Stablecoins and CBDCs differ in two main ways. First, private sector organizations generally issue and manage stablecoins, but a central government or central bank issues CBDCs. Second, stablecoins compete with fiat currency, but CBDCs serve to replace, digitize, or augment existing fiat currencies.

3. Define a non-fungible token (NFT) and discuss how it differs from other cryptoassets
   An NFT is a digital, virtual, or cryptoasset that can be tracked, monitored, and accounted for in a traceable and transparent manner. It differs from other cryptoassets since an NFT is a unique digital asset (non-fungible), cannot be exchanged for one another as equivalents, and cannot be subdivided. Unlike other cryptoassets like decentralized crypto, stablecoins, and CBDCs that can be used for transactions, NFTs cannot be used for transactional purposes.

4. List three changes needed to the audit processes as cryptoassets become more mainstream.
   Three changes needed for the audit processes are:

   - account for how blockchain and cryptoassets affect current workflows and audit processes,
   - consider the role of specialized or continuous audits in the face of more readily available and verifiable information, and
   - account for being able to audit, confirm, and review how smart contracts interact and drive transactions centered around blockchain and cryptoassets.

5. Identify two financial reporting and disclosure considerations organizations should use related to cryptoassets.
   Two financial reporting and disclose considerations needed in a blockchain and cryptoasset-based environment are:

   - What information needs to be reported related to the specific blockchain and cryptoassets used in an organization? and
   - How much detail should be reported surrounding how an organization categorizes and values various cryptoassets, especially if the organization holds and trades a variety of these assets?

Chapter 3. The Crypto Investing Landscape

1. Discuss the main US rules and regulations for fund managers investing in digital assets and how they differ from traditional fund managers.
   Private and public fund managers who invest in digital assets must adhere to the same rules and regulations as non-digital asset fund managers for registration, advertising, fraud, and market manipulation. These regulations are the '33 Act, '34 Act, and '40 Act.

2. Identify the three main categories of digital assets determined by the Financial Conduct Authority (FCA) and those under its regulation.
   These three main groups of digital assets are:

   - *Exchange tokens* are digital assets not issued or backed by any central authority and intended and designed for use as a means of exchange. These are outside the FCA's perimeter.
   - *Security tokens* are digital assets contracted for fractions of an existing asset like real estate, corporate stock, artwork, collectibles, or other valuable assets. They are within the FCA's perimeter.
   - *Utility tokens* are digital assets that allow the holder to access a service or a current or prospective product. Utility tokens acting as fiat cash may be e-money within the FCA's perimeter. Utility tokens where the exact fiat value is unknown and, therefore, would not function as a type of e-money would be outside the FCA's perimeter.

3. Explain the operational risks unique to digital assets funds: asset custody, portfolio management, counterparties, and service providers.
   Digital asset funds have several specific operational risks.

   - *Asset custody.* Digital assets are essentially bearer assets. Hence, digital custody is essential. Institutional custody providers generally limit asset custody to bitcoin, ether, and other highly liquid cryptocurrencies. For investors who are not allowed to self-custody their investments, this restriction limits the number of cryptoassets they can hold.
   - *Portfolio management.* Although several thousand crypto assets are available, only a few cryptocurrencies constitute most of this asset class's market

value and liquidity. Investors wanting to diversify broadly need to consider investing in lower market value and less liquid assets.
- *Counterparties and service providers*. Traditional counterparties have not yet developed substantial expertise in the cryptoasset class. Therefore, investors must perform additional due diligence and vet new and less well-known service providers.

4. Explain three challenges in determining the net asset values (NAVs) of a fund's investment in digital assets traded on crypto exchanges.
   Investors face several challenges in determining a fund's NAVs involving digital assets.

   - Digital asset exchanges trade continuously and have no closing time. These factors create a challenge in determining an official cutoff time for coin pricing.
   - Most digital assets trade on multiple exchanges with no primary exchange. When there is no primary exchange, determining the sets of exchanges a fund manager should use to extract coin prices is challenging.
   - Digital asset exchanges express coin prices in different currencies. The challenge is determining the different exchange rates when obtaining coin prices.

Chapter 4. Cryptocurrencies

1. Explain the double-spending problem.
   The double-spending problem is the risk that some can spend a digital currency can be spent twice. If someone sends a digital currency via an e-mail-like system, no one can verify how much of that currency exists and whether a given digital "coin" is a copy or an original.

2. Define bitcoin and discuss if it represents cash, currency, a financial asset, a medium of exchange, a commodity, or something else.
   Bitcoin is a decentralized digital currency without a central bank or single administrator. It can be sent from user to user on the peer-to-peer bitcoin network without intermediaries. Although bitcoin may have been conceived as digital cash, this cryptocurrency and its uses have evolved. Bitcoin can be described more as a financial asset. A cryptocurrency's utility is more like an investment/store of value and not purely a medium of exchange.

3. Explain how so-called privacy coins differ from bitcoin.
   Privacy coins are a class of cryptocurrencies powering private and anonymous blockchain transactions by obscuring their origin and destination. Thus, privacy coins strive to enable anonymous blockchain transactions to provide users with the highest possible degree of privacy. By contrast, bitcoin is pseudo-anonymous. That is, all transactions can be transparently assessed and monitored.

4. Discuss whether cryptocurrency prices are correlated and why this situation might occur.
   The prices of most cryptocurrencies are positively correlated. This situation might occur because bitcoin holds more than 40 percent of cryptocurrencies' total market capitalization value.

Chapter 5. Security Tokens

1. Explain the difference between utility and security tokens.
   Utility tokens are typically payment instruments for an issuer's products or services that may be developed in the future. In contrast, security tokens are "investment contracts" according to the Howey Test. For a token issuer to pass the Howey Test, the issuer or the security token offering (STO) needs to involve an investment of money, be a common enterprise, have a profit expectation, and involve the effort of others. If a token is determined to be an investment contract and hence a security token, then securities law applies with several partly far-reaching ramifications for the issuer.

2. List several advantages of security tokens over traditional securities.
   Security tokens offer several advantages over traditional securities. For example, security tokens include automated and more rapid settlements due to blockchain technology and smart contracts. Due to interoperability standards, they also offer potential integration with different entities, systems, and products. Finally, security tokens can provide more efficient securities markets because of greater market participation due to fractional ownership and potentially more liquid markets. They also offer higher market completeness due to the expected financial innovations enabled by interoperability standards and other aspects of the new technology.

3. Explain some regulatory challenges to the broader adoption of security tokens.
   Key regulatory challenges to more widespread adoption of security tokens include:

   - *Cross-border transactions*. There is a lack of clarity about who has jurisdiction and how competencies and potential conflicts of interest among enforcing agencies will be regulated.
   - *Teams, firms, and issuers without physical offices*. A lack of clarity exists about who has jurisdiction.
   - *Legal standardization*. Although technical standardization is relatively advanced, legal standardization across jurisdictions is not. This situation poses impediments to the usage and value of interoperability.
   - *Use as collateral*. When and under what conditions are security tokens accepted as collateral? Collateralization is a key prerequisite for broader industry adoption because of its importance for refinancing.

4. Explain the typical STO process.
   The STO process has seven stages.

   - Stage 1 involves the company's foundation.
   - Stage 2 deals with the STO's design. It includes developing the token distribution structure and governance rights, selecting the jurisdiction, appointing financial and legal advisors to help with the regulatory process, and preparing required documents, such as a prospectus.
   - Stage 3 involves setting up the technology, including a decision about the underlying blockchain platform and the coding of the security tokens.
   - Stage 4 concerns reaching out and negotiating with outside stakeholders to help with the STO, such as financial advisors, brokers, and custodians.
   - Stage 5 is fundraising. The STO fundraising process takes longer than utility token initial coin offerings (ICOs) because it is more likely that the institutional investors who participate in the offering require traditional roadshows and one-to-one meetings.
   - Stage 6 is the token exchange listing, which establishes a liquid market for a security.
   - Stage 7 is trading the security token and complying with regulatory standards, such as ensuring sufficient liquidity and complying with regulatory disclosure obligations.

Chapter 6. Utility Tokens

1. Discuss the difference between utility tokens and cryptocurrencies.
   Utility tokens provide consumptive rights on services and products through a blockchain-based platform. They serve as the exclusive means of payment in the ecosystem developed by the issuer. Cryptocurrencies are digital assets issued on blockchain to serve as a currency by functioning as a medium of exchange, a unit of account, and a store of value. A utility token can be used as a cryptocurrency outside of an issuer's platform, but its primary function is to enhance and allow value creation within its ecosystem.

2. Explain the concept of tokenomic design.
   A tokenomic design involves the rules and regulations that control token issuance, distribution, allocation, and potential destruction. It also describes the different token uses and how it enables the transactions and interactions within a network. Tokenomic design can enhance value creation and determine the allocation of value to network participants.

3. Describe three mechanisms token issuers use to raise funds using utility tokens.
   The three mechanisms are initial coin offerings (ICOs), initial exchange offerings (IEOs), and initial DEX (decentralized exchange) offerings (IDOs). During an ICO, the issuer sells tokens to the public using blockchain infrastructure,

commonly without intermediaries. The mechanics can be as simple as requesting funds to be transferred to the issuer's account. Once a target amount has been collected, the issuer creates the tokens and distributes them to each contributor. The ICO process relies on the issuer's correct behavior. A cryptoasset exchange acts as an intermediary in an IEO and orchestrates the token sale process. Therefore, the IEO process depends on the exchange's correct behavior. A decentralized cryptoasset exchange fulfills the intermediary's role in an IDO, providing a verifiable allocation process. The IDO process relies on the proper coding of the allocation parameters.

4. Discuss the potential benefits of reward programs such as farming.
Farming consists of distributing newly issued or allocating treasury tokens to users as a reward for locking up their tokens for a certain period. This lock-up directly reduces the token's total circulating token supply and indirectly signals users' expectations of future token valuation. Suppose the return in additional tokens compensates for a token's alternative cost, either as consumable for an issuer's services or revenues from selling in the secondary market. In that case, users should be willing to farm tokens. Providing farming rewards allows issuers to engage early adopters and investors in network development, gain access to additional investors, promote and showcase a project, and manage supply and demand shocks to secondary markets.

Chapter 7. Stablecoins

1. Explain the purpose of stablecoins.
Their creators introduced stablecoins to mitigate the price volatility risk of cryptocurrencies. Stablecoins provide the benefits of digital currencies, such as low cost and immutable transactions, without exposing users to the risk of possible strong price fluctuations.

2. Identify an application of stablecoins in traditional finance or banking.
The low cost, immutable transactions, and 24/7 availability make stablecoins a beneficial application area for cross-border transfers and remittances.

3. Distinguish between the different forms of stablecoins.
Different methods are available to back stablecoins, including traditional assets such as fiat or gold, digital assets such as cryptocurrencies, or algorithms to maintain the price peg dynamically.

4. Discuss the benefits and risks of central bank digital currencies (CBDCs).
CBDCs can provide citizens with cheap and easily accessible digital cash. However, based on the design, a CBDC could also be used to surveil citizen behavior and control, such as by excluding specific individuals from the monetary system. Accordingly, carefully planning a CBDC's design and governance is critical.

Chapter 8. Tokenized Assets and Securities

1. Explain the difference between tokenized securities and security tokens.
   Although asset-backed tokens or tokenized securities represent a pre-existing asset or security, security tokens constitute newly created securities. Therefore, tokenized securities can exist outside the blockchain, where the underlying asset does not disappear. By contrast, security tokens are blockchain native and do not exist outside the blockchain.

2. Describe some tokenization benefits of traditional assets.
   Tokenization benefits of traditional assets include:

   - Increased efficiency and reduced cost, driven by automated processes and fewer intermediaries.
   - Increased transparency and security, provided by blockchain infrastructure and cryptographic record-keeping.
   - Improved compliance and traceability delivered by programming from smart contracts that allow embedding rules directly on the tokenized asset.
   - Facilitated innovation, supported by the primarily open-source nature of blockchains, third-party developers' multiple layers and applications, and their interconnection with traditional financial and operational infrastructure.

3. Explain the steps of the tokenization process.

   - *Ecosystem assembly*. Analyze and plan an ecosystem of industry specialists and partners to ensure the tokenized instrument's successful issuance and the existence of the supporting infrastructure and services required for its use case.
   - *Token creation*. Code and program the token based on identifying the adjacent asset, the token identifier, the divisibility options, and the ecosystem partners with which the token can interact.
   - *Compliance setup*. Automate compliance requirements for any jurisdiction, such as know your customer (KYC) or anti-money laundering (AML) obligations and ownership and transfer restrictions.
   - *Token distribution*. Set the norms to transfer tokens to their intended recipients directly or through broker-dealer agents and custody services.
   - *Corporate actions execution and management*. State clear and transparent rules on when and how corporate actions would occur.

4. Discuss the importance of oracles in the asset tokenization process.
   Oracles are essential for asset-backed tokens since they provide and transform the off-chain information into on-chain information that smart contracts need to process when off-chain events occur automatically. Tokenization's benefits regarding automatization, security, speed, compliance, efficiency, and costs would be impossible without the necessary oracles linked with a token's smart contract.

Chapter 9. A Comparative Review of Cryptoasset Products

1. Identify and describe four cryptoasset characteristics.
   Cryptoassets exhibit four main characteristics that enable their core functionalities. They are cryptographically secure, use distributed ledger technology (DLT), permit excluding third-party intermediaries, and enable the tokenization of assets and data, both intangible and tangible.

   - *Are cryptographically secure.* Using cryptography provides the fundamentally secure nature of cryptoassets. They typically use a standard cryptographic algorithm of the National Institute of Standards Technology, such as SHA-3 or KECCAK-256.
   - *Use DLT.* DLT stores data and conducts transactions on a distributed, peer-to-peer (P2P) basis. DLT enables removing intermediaries and a trustless system void of any central authority, allowing users to verify a transaction's validity within the network rather than relying on the trust placed in a central authority.
   - *Exclude third-party intermediaries.* Excluding third-party intermediaries using P2P networks allows participants to transact directly with one another rather than relying on the traditional custodial practices of the conventional banking and payments infrastructure.
   - *Enable tokenization.* Tokenization allows for the digital representation of an asset, utility, or any form of data enabling secure storage, ease of transfer, and verification of digital asset ownership. Intangible and tangible assets can be represented digitally through tokenization.

2. Explain the similarities and differences between the four main methods to tokenize assets.
   The four main types of tokenized assets used in crypto and distributed systems are currency, platform, utility, and transactional tokens. They are not necessarily mutually exclusive and have different use cases. Cryptosystems may use a combination of token types depending on their use cases:

   - *Currency tokens.* Currency tokens are the most common type of digital token. Their main use is for transactional purposes, similar to how fiat currency behaves, with the added benefits of DLT and cryptographic security.
   - *Platform tokens.* These tokens enable users to interact with decentralized applications and are the basis for their respective mechanisms. Typically, the uses of these tokens involve smart contracts. However, decentralized platforms can pay them out to provide rewards to users for using their services and refunding transaction fees.
   - *Utility tokens.* Utility tokens represent tokenized rights or access granted to users of a decentralized platform, such as voting rights or other forms of on-chain governance.
   - *Transactional tokens.* Transactional tokens serve as units of account and resemble the properties of traditional currencies and even currency tokens.

However, transactional tokens' primary purpose is to facilitate transactions that would otherwise experience friction with traditional currency, such as cross-currency exchanges.

3. List and describe the risks and criticisms of using cryptocurrency as an open-source project.
   Regulatory concerns stem from regulators regarding the open-source nature of cryptocurrency projects. Many regard the decentralized nature of these projects as potentially insecure because any individual with engineering skills can contribute to projects and their audit source code.
   The open-source nature of crypto-related projects is a key security feature of a cryptocurrency, allowing for incremental improvement of protocols by a decentralized group of developers. Such projects also enable the participating community to help direct the development of crypto ecosystems in which they choose to participate. Open-source projects typically require using remote version control technology such as Git. They allow developers to submit their code changes for review. If these changes pass specific tests, the result is usually auditing the proposed code and merging the changes into the main source code repository.
   Crypto-related projects usually require a form of improvement proposal process involving a governance mechanism to decide whether to implement the changes to the underlying protocols. Centralizing the development of protocols undermines the decentralized, P2P, and trustless characteristics of cryptoassets.

4. Summarize the benefits of cryptoassets on a decentralized exchange (DEX) compared to a centralized infrastructure.
   DEXs have overcome some criticisms of centralized exchanges (CEXs) that have become widely popularized in the cryptoasset trading community. DEXs leverage decentralized blockchain technology to allow P2P trading of cryptoassets. They also aid in increasing the efficiency of price discovery mechanisms for cryptoassets using automated market makers, enabling users to stake their tokens in liquidity pools that serve as the primary source of liquidity of specified trading pairs in a specified price range. Limit order book protocols allow users to trade cryptoassets without intermediaries or custodial accounts at CEXs. Conversely, CEXs rely on custodial wallets to hold a user's position. Users never own the cryptoassets in their account until they transfer those cryptoassets to an external crypto wallet owned by them.

5. Describe the current limitations of cryptoassets as a digital asset class in financial markets and potential solutions to these issues.
   Cryptoassets have drawbacks. First, financial market participants have not widely accepted or adopted cryptoassets as mediums of exchange due to current technical and political restrictions. Second, the lack of scalability limits decentralized blockchain networks, leading to slow speeds and high transaction fees. Third, politicians and environmental regulators scrutinize cryptoassets

due to their association with criminal activities and ecological risks from parallelized graphics processing unit (GPU) clusters.

In terms of solutions, user-friendly crypto wallet services and cryptocurrency credit cards may increase cryptoasset adoption rates and reduce technical limitations. Likewise, improvements in Arbitrum and ZK-rollup have increased the scalability of specific cryptoassets, such as Ethereum. Additionally, increased demand for proof-of stake (PoS) is likely to reduce the popularity of GPUs and proof-of-work (PoW)-based methods, eventually offsetting the environmental harm of cryptoassets.

Chapter 10. Decentralized Finance

1. Identify and explain the five stages of the decentralized finance (DeFi) stack.
   The DeFi stack involves units of value, transaction layers, oracles, markets, and wallets.

   - *Units of value* typically involve stablecoins, which hold their value against the US dollar. Transaction layers are layer 1 solutions that allow building applications with smart contracts on top of them.
   - An *oracle* is a third party that provides on-chain smart contracts with the external off-chain information (real-world data) needed to execute those contracts. An example is bitcoin's price in a derivatives contract. A smart contract's effectiveness rests heavily on its access to accurate information. Most oracles seek out data from many different sources to ensure accuracy.
   - *Markets* include DeFi borrowing, asset management, staking, lending, yield farming, derivatives, and insurance. Markets are the various avenues where DeFi could apply.
   - *Wallets* keep digital assets safe by storing private keys. A hardware wallet allows cold storage. Such a wallet is not connected to the internet, so remote hackers cannot gain access. Online wallets involve storing private keys in an app or via software.

2. Explain the main challenge to DeFi scalability.
   DeFi is currently not as interoperable as it could be. It must address inherent issues that hinder siloed blockchains from establishing inter-blockchain communication. DeFi becomes challenging to transfer value, data, and assets across different blockchain networks without a third-party intermediary. Interoperability is necessary to enable clients to scale their business on a large scale. Each blockchain is analogous to an individual economy. If each economy or the blockchain cannot cross-communicate and exchange value, DeFi cannot grow and supersede traditional finance, which is highly interoperable. Although third-party custodial services facilitate transferring value among blockchains of different networks, such services make the ecosystem centralized like traditional finance, defeating the basic purpose of blockchain – decentralization.

3. List several DeFi business models.
   Several DeFi business models are available.

   - *Decentralized currency.* A *decentralized currency* refers to the method/currency not tied to or backed by any central entity and acts as a means of storage, transfer of wealth, and utility.
   - *Decentralized fundraising.* Some methods of decentralized fundraising are an initial coin offering (ICO), initial exchange offering (IEO), security token offering (STOs), and decentralized autonomous organization (DAO). An ICO is the most popular method and involves raising money by issuing new tokens and coins to the crowdfunder. It enables money to be raised worldwide without border restrictions enabling even retail investors to participate, unlike traditional initial public offerings (IPOs).
   - *Decentralized payment service.* A decentralized payment service is a payment network that facilitates the cross-border transfer of currencies and wealth without trusting a third-party intermediary agent.
   - Decentralized contracting. A *smart contract* is a popular decentralized contract that automatically executes different contract stages between two intermediaries without a third-party intervention at any stage after meeting each preprogrammed condition in an agreement.

4. Explain whether stablecoins backed by the government and Federal Deposit Insurance Corporation are a form of currency and payment.
   No government agency backs stablecoins. Instead, they are decentralized and carry the same inherent risks as other cryptocurrencies. Although recent uses of stablecoins include many banking services, the government fears the consequences of stablecoins if they completely replace traditional banking institutions. Since the government does not control stablecoins or cryptocurrencies, it cannot step in if anything goes wrong.

5. Discuss the government regulations on stablecoins.
   Discussions are currently underway in the US Congress to pass legislation to regulate the stablecoin market and usage. No guidelines are available on managing stablecoins. Thus, the market remains largely decentralized and uncontrolled. However, ongoing suggestions for regulation include requiring the registration of stablecoin issuers as banking institutions. They would be subject to the same regulations as traditional banks and avoid fraud and money laundering in organizations offering stablecoins.

6. Discuss whether equity option pricing models work on cryptocurrency options and the possibility of accurately pricing crypto options and developing a crypto hedging strategy.
   Equity option pricing models do not necessarily work on cryptocurrency options. Crypto price movement is highly volatile and even more unpredictable than stock movement. The assumptions about stock price movements and equity markets are inappropriate for the crypto market. Thus, new pricing

models must be developed with appropriate assumptions about crypto prices. Some have implemented Monte Carlo simulations and artificial intelligence (AI) methods to approximate crypto option prices. Based on those simulations, they can form a trading strategy.

Chapter 11. Blockchain and Crypto Exchange-traded Funds

1. Explain the concept of pooled fund investing and its advantages and disadvantages.
   Pooled fund investing involves collecting money from investors and combining it into a single investment fund. Since the fund has more purchasing power, it reduces costs through economies of scale. Pooled fund investing provides a low-risk opportunity for investors to grow their money. A disadvantage is that individual investors have less control over the group's investment decisions, which may benefit only specific individuals in the group. Diversification can limit an investment's upside since less risk can lead to fewer rewards.

2. List several different regulators involved in the exchange-traded fund (ETF) approval process.
   The Securities Act of 1933 and the Securities Exchange Act of 1934 created the Securities and Exchange Commission (SEC), charged with maintaining a fair securities market and protecting investors from fraud and manipulation. The Investment Company Act of 1940 led to the creation of the Commodity Futures Trading Commission (CFTC), which is responsible for the regulatory oversight of derivatives traded on the exchanges. The main goal of these acts is to protect investors.

3. Identify two major benefits of investing in an ETF rather than individual stocks.
   An ETF enables investors to diversify their portfolios by investing in a basket of assets instead of individual stocks. Diversification assumes that if one investment underperforms, the others may offset this underperformance. Since ETFs use the concept of pool fund investing, the costs associated with purchasing ETFs are lower than buying individual stocks. The entry point for investment can be as low as a couple of hundred dollars.

4. Explain the difference between a hot and cold wallet.
   Investors use hot and cold wallets to store cryptocurrencies. A hot wallet is connected to the internet and vulnerable to online attacks. Cold wallets are offline, and external storage devices are effective when private keys or passwords are secure. Cold storage is a way to hold coins offline, making them unhackable unless having physical possession and the private keys to access within. Flaws with cold wallets means investors need a safe place to hide them and must have a high level of trust in the organization.

5. Explain why Proshares received approval to list its bitcoin ETF on a national exchange.
   Proshares Bitcoin ETF enables investing in bitcoin futures contracts, not bitcoin. Futures contracts are derivative securities regulated by the CFTC. The CFTC provided oversight to Proshares Bitcoin ETF for four years, giving the SEC enough comfort that investors have protection through the Investment Company Act of 1940.

Chapter 12. Approaches to Cryptocurrency Valuation

1. Discuss whether cryptocurrencies and other cryptoassets have intrinsic value.
   A polarized debate exists on whether cryptoassets have intrinsic value. Intrinsic value refers to what is valuable for its own sake. By contrast, extrinsic value refers to something valuable for something else's sake. Most scholars believe that exchange tokens or cryptocurrencies are devoid of intrinsic value. However, others believe that a cryptocurrency's intrinsic value involves the total of all properties, making it suitable as a medium of exchange. For example, the total cost of mining hardware and energy investments can serve as a proxy to estimate their intrinsic value.

2. Explain the common approaches to valuing the main types of cryptoassets.
   Common approaches to valuing cryptoassets depend on the type of asset. In theory, security tokens are the least challenging to value. The market approach incorporates market prices while considering the liquidity level and development stage. Cash flows to the security token's holder form the basis for the income approach. Analysts can use the market approaches and cost approach for mineable tokens for utility tokens. The quantitative theory of money (QTM) is another option in the valuation process.

   Analysts can value cryptocurrencies using (1) the income approach, (2) the market approach, and (3) the cost approach. The income approach considers the cryptoasset features of medium of exchange and storage of value and applies QTM and network effects such as Metcalfe's law. The market approach uses an approach inspired by the price/earnings (*P*/*E*) ratio, a widely used metric in conventional equity market valuations. This approach emphasizes the transaction value and token utilities, with metrics such as the network value-to-transaction ratio and the price-to-utility ratio. Finally, the cost approach calculates mining costs as a lower bound for valuations.

3. Discuss the primary challenges in valuing cryptocurrencies.
   Valuing cryptocurrencies involves several challenges.

   - Cryptocurrencies lack fundamental value because they have no underlying claim, such as the right to a future cash flow or to discharge any payment obligation. This situation makes their valuation difficult and subject to speculation. Cryptocurrencies may experience extreme price movements (volatility risk), exposing their holders to potentially significant losses.

- Adopting a valuation multiple is also challenging because financial metrics like revenues or earnings often lack comparability between assets.
- Valuation methods based on discounting future cash flows require assumptions about the discount rate. Discount rates are critical assumptions under the income approach. However, their estimation for investments in early-stage ventures is highly subjective. Adopting the traditionally accepted models, such as the capital asset pricing model (CAPM), is similarly challenging in determining an appropriate discount rate because market data such as betas are unobservable, comparable quoted companies do not exist, and subjective risk premia assumptions are required.
- Many cryptocurrencies are illiquid, resulting in different valuation challenges.

4. Discuss the leading network effects in cryptocurrency valuation.
   A network's value is proportional to the square of the number of its users. This relationship is because the number of unique connections in a network of n nodes can be expressed mathematically as $n(n-1)/2$, which is asymptotically proportional to n^2. This logic similarly applies to cryptocurrencies. Suppose that bitcoin's number of unique addresses proxies the number of bitcoin users. Metcalfe's law captures a token's long-term value by measuring the number of its users. Nevertheless, the validity of this law for cryptocurrencies is questionable in the short run. Besides the difficulty of quantifying a network's value, the mathematical justification for Metcalfe's law measures only the potential number of contacts. However, a network's social utility depends upon the number of nodes in contact. In addition, the law simplistically assumes that all nodes are of equal value or benefit.

   The transaction volume per unique address is another critical factor to consider. This modification would make Metcalfe's law-based models more suitable for token valuation analysis. An explanation for this situation is that the number of users reflects a token's long-run value, while the transaction volume per unique address mirrors a token's daily usage. Therefore, analysts should factor in the transaction volume per unique address when estimating short-run price variation.

Chapter 13. Cryptoassets in a Portfolio Context

1. Explain an initial coin offering's (ICO) attributes.
   In an (ICO), a token holder values a token based on supply and demand for the underlying tokenized product using a coding algorithm based on cryptography writing and solving codes on a blockchain network. This process is like a stock initial public offering (IPO) for raising capital, enabling investors to buy coins for their portfolios. An ICO derives its value from an underlying process, such as a transaction or sale in a company. These transactions recorded on a blockchain allow new coins to be minted and added to the supply.

2. Identify and discuss the factors to consider in a portfolio containing cryptoassets. Several factors are relevant to consider in a portfolio with cryptoassets.

   - *Total money supply related to crypto*. A proxy for this factor the total market capitalization, measured by is the total number of an asset multiplied by the market price.
   - *A cryptoasset's speed or velocity*. Speed refers to how fast a cryptoasset is used or spent in the flow of the currency. This concept is analogous to the Federal Reserve (Fed) velocity of the money supply. A regulatory regime does not control the usage. This issue is currently a policy debate at domestic and international levels.
   - *The average volume of each transaction using cryptoassets*. A cryptoasset's popularity increases with its average volume, the more popular that cryptoasset, which may lead to a more pronounced network effect. The network effect is the impact of growing usage by different parties. More cryptoassets use leads to an overall acceptance in the market and higher prices due to rising demand.
   - *The number of cryptoasset transactions*. The number of transactions affects volume and liquidity in the market.

3. Describe the stock-to-flow method and its use in valuing crypto.
   Investors may use the stock-to-flow approach to value crypto in a portfolio. Pricing is a significant factor in investment decision-making before adding crypto to a portfolio. In the stock-to-flow approach, a commodity's value appreciates over the long run due to its scarcity. Supply and demand are the main determinants of valuation without cash flow. Thus, the limited supply and rising demand may increase crypto's value. Based on the stock-to-flow approach, some investors may value cryptos following the bitcoin model in terms of supply and demand. This perspective values crypto in a portfolio based on its "store of value" expectation. Using this concept, a cryptocurrency's value may increase despite the absence of cash flows, as expected in the case of traditional assets such as stocks or bonds.

4. Discuss how crypto hedge funds operate and their usage in blockchain networks.
   After bitcoin's success, entrepreneurs created many cryptocurrency funds catering to growing market demand. Regulators are slowly establishing a framework to manage cryptocurrency activities. Hedge fund trading in this market is not subject to the same regulations as traditional funds. A particular segment of hedge funds strongly advocates cryptocurrencies. It maintains that using crypto is a secure payment method using blockchain networks and more reliable than the process in fee-charging credit institutions. Portfolio managers consider different types of crypto rather than specific cryptos because they believe that not all cryptos are perfectly correlated. Additionally, financial institutions may use cryptocurrencies in search of higher yields.

Chapter 14. Protection of Portfolios and Financial Consumers from Cryptoasset Frauds

1. Identify the primary differences between traditional financial assets and cryptoassets in terms of portfolio and consumer protection.
   Fundamentally, cryptoassets have different characteristics than traditional assets, such as stocks and bonds. Cryptoassets are part of a novel asset class emanating from their underpinning technology. They do not necessarily have any underlying assets, making them volatile and risky instruments. Moreover, they might not be regulated or supervised. Furthermore, their decentralized nature enables fraudsters to reach out to portfolio managers and financial consumers worldwide while allowing them to stay anonymous. These characteristics of cryptoassets almost unarm traditional portfolio and consumer protection mechanisms, requiring new investment and risk management strategies for portfolio managers and consumers in the cryptoasset space.

2. Define asymmetric technology and explain how it changes the effectiveness of financial supervision.
   Asymmetric technology refers to the increased technological gaps between supervisors and their responsibility areas. Under asymmetric technology risks, financial supervisors face increased investor protection challenges, and financial consumers face exposure to higher cryptoasset risks.

3. Define the innovation abuse hypothesis and explain why it is relevant to the cryptoasset market.
   The innovation abuse hypothesis refers to intentional abuses of innovations, particularly taking advantage of regulatory and supervisory gaps, delicate market conditions, and consumer greed. Potential white-collar fraudsters tend to go where the money is and abuse innovations as brand-new deception materials and transformation periods as perfect time frames to realize their plans. Cryptoassets are financial innovations that rely on revolutionary technologies, such as distributed ledger technology or blockchain.

4. Discuss how regulators and supervisors view consumer protection in the cryptoasset domains.
   Financial regulators and supervisors include the Securities and Exchange Commission, Commodity Futures Trading Commission, and Financial Industry Regulatory Authority in the United States, the European Securities and Markets Authority, European Banking Authority, and European Insurance and Occupational Pensions Authority in the European Union, and the Financial Conduct Authority in the United Kingdom. They have frequently warned financial consumers of the extraordinary risks of cryptoassets. The prevailing warning theme revolves around "protect yourself" since regulators and supervisors have limited protection powers in the cryptoasset space.

5. Explain who can protect portfolios and financial consumers most effectively.
   Although economies have various consumer protection responsibilities and mechanisms, portfolio managers and consumers can protect themselves much better and more effectively by making sound decisions and avoiding suspicious financial products and services. This view is a typical investment rule. However, it has much more value in the cryptoasset space. Therefore, the mainstream reactions of regulatory and supervisory agencies worldwide in the cryptoasset domain have been strongly signaling a let the buyer beware policy for portfolio managers and consumers. These signals mainly apply to individual financial consumers, leaving all responsibilities on buyers or consumers and stressing the need for a stronger financial literacy requirement.

Chapter 15. General Institutional Considerations of Blockchain and Emerging Applications

1. Identify the test the Securities and Exchange Commission (SEC) uses to determine if something is a security and the components making up the test.
   The SEC uses the Howey Test to determine whether something is an investment contract and a security. This test four primary parts: (1) whether an investment of money has occurred, (2) whether an expectation of profits exists from the investment, (3) if the money is invested in a common enterprise, and (4) how the profit of this common enterprise is distributed. This test applies to all financial instruments that come under SEC's scrutiny. It determines whether something falls under the regulatory oversight of the SEC.

2. Define a smart contract and explain its main use cases.
   Smart contracts contend that different kinds of contractual clauses, such as collateral, bonding, and delineation of property rights, can be embedded into the hardware and software of an underlying blockchain. Within this definition, the potential use cases for smart contracts are extensive but have a crucial role in decentralized finance (DeFi) and decentralized applications. Other use cases are in the payments, confirmation, real estate, and supply chain sectors. Once programmed, smart contacts can automate or streamline processes in a transaction or series of transactions.

3. Discuss the advantages and disadvantages of internal versus outsourced compliance resources.
   Specifics involve the internal development or outsourcing of compliance resources, but the decision consists of several categories. Cost, legal compliance, and the sophistication of the proposed products and services drive this decision-making process. Organizations seeking to acquire customers and handle customer funds require more regular and higher caliber compliance planning and implementation. This situation is especially important for crypto

organizations seeking to enter the DeFi space since many proposed products and services involve customer/investor assets.

4. Identify the four general guidelines for reporting cryptocurrency and blockchain transactions accurately and adequately.
   As specified by Deloitte, the four general guidelines for reporting cryptocurrency are (1) applicability, (2) compliance requirements, (3) understanding the disruption and modifications caused by crypto, and (4) how internal operations need to evolve. These guidelines are generalized best practices and reflect the still-developing nature of the cryptoasset sector. No standard-setting body has yet issued crypto-specific accounting standards.

5. Explain the main risks inherent to DeFi in contrast to traditional finance.
   As DeFi continues to expand and evolve, investors and policymakers should be aware of the risks involved with this space. Examples include smart contract risks (hacking), the possibility of a 51 percent attack (brute force hacking of the platform), and oracle risk (where off-chain data are corrupted and subsequently added to the blockchain itself). Besides these risks, an investor should know that insurance typically does not cover DeFi activities.

Chapter 16. Custody, Provenance, and Reporting of Blockchain and Cryptoassets

1. Summarize the issues around institutions using cryptoassets in custody, provenance, and reporting.
   Institutions using cryptoassets as a financial intermediary or medium of exchange face custody, provenance, and reporting issues. In terms of custody, they face losing their cryptoassets or having them stolen if they do not choose their cryptoasset custodian carefully. The lack of proper custody could result in losing cryptoassets forever, resulting in severe repercussions for institutions, especially those handling retirement and hedge funds. Regarding provenance, institutions cannot do business with other institutions, companies, and individuals who cannot prove they own certain cryptoassets. Since limited resources for provenance, like know your customer (KYC) data and the underlying blockchain technology, are available, proving cryptoasset ownership is still challenging. Lastly, reporting cryptoasset income and ownership is particularly challenging because of limited tax and regulatory guidelines. Institutions face confusing reporting requirements and could incur severe penalties, including significant fines and jail time for non-compliance.

2. Identify the key takeaways from the Infrastructure Act coming into effect in 2024.
   The Infrastructure Act has three pages related explicitly to cryptoasset regulatory changes that may significantly affect those embracing cryptocurrencies and blockchain technology. According to the Infrastructure Act, the main takeaways include the controversial designation of brokers in the digital asset

market and the expansive definition of virtual assets subject to tax reporting. For example, reporting non-fungible tokens (NFTs) may be necessary. Additionally, traditional reporting requirements have changed to include certain digital asset transactions involving more than $10,000. Holders of cryptoassets are not responsible for reporting wholly new information. Despite the confusion surrounding the information requiring reporting, owners can incur severe criminal penalties if they do not report select information.

3. Explain the best custody option for institutions holding cryptoassets.
   The best custody option for institutions holding cryptoassets is third-party custody. This option is best for those institutions that do not understand blockchain technology entirely or want the sole responsibility of managing their accounts. The preferred choice for institutions in terms of custody is custodial banks. A few reputable US custodial banks have the legal right to offer custody of cryptoassets. These banks are worth considering if institutions want the best security for their assets. However, drawbacks associated with keeping crypto-asset keys in a custody bank include limiting the transaction amounts and freezing assets.

4. Identify three issues institutions wanting to use cryptoassets face and explain why they are important.
   Three issues faced by institutions wanting to use cryptoassets are (1) tax accounting, (2) money laundering, and (3) financial fraud and data theft. If institutions disregard these issues, they could experience severe consequences.

5. Identify several financial reporting issues institutions face to account for cryptoassets.
   No authoritative guidance exists for cryptoassets, such as cryptocurrencies, NFTs, stablecoins, and central bank digital currencies. Institutions must process and consistently report identical or similar cryptoassets. This situation can be challenging as new cryptoasset variants enter the market regularly and existing constructions change.

Chapter 17. Tokenized and Non-tokenized Assets: Legal Considerations

1. Discuss how general securities laws might apply to a blockchain-based project or start-up company.
   Authorities often write laws with general applicability. Thus, laws not explicitly relating to cryptocurrency can still apply. A digital token offering may also be an offering of an investment contract and, therefore, a security for federal securities law purposes. These laws include but are not limited to Regulation A of the Securities Act, the NY BitLicense, and the Securities Act of 1933 and 1934. The legal framework surrounding cryptocurrency and blockchain applications is still evolving and subject to case-by-case interpretation.

2. Discuss the treatment of digital assets for federal legal purposes.
   Given existing opinion letters and public comments, a widely regarded view is that bitcoin and ether are commodities and not securities, but that might not be the case. Examples of digital assets reveal that they most likely should not be viewed as securities. The legal proceedings and discussions about what legal or financial classification specific cryptocurrencies should belong are ongoing and are evaluated on a facts-and-circumstances basis. The lack of regulatory clarity and treatment in the United States, combined with regulators' partial oversight of crypto, creates a complicated compliance landscape. Yet, authorities classify crypto as property for federal tax purposes, with other legal classifications still relatively ambiguous.

3. Explain the factors founders and investors should consider when raising capital.
   Founders and investors should consider several factors when raising capital. For example, the intended offering's structure plays a vital role in how the government taxes the proceeds raised from an offering. An improper structure could trigger legal action related to an unregistered security offering. It could also result in an effective tax rate between 20 and 40 percent. Another factor concerns how the fundraisers plan to deploy the proceeds. For instance, are the offering and proceeds raised connected to the business's core operations? Regulators often look at this factor, leading to increased scrutiny if not correctly structured and disclosed. Another factor to consider when raising capital is an entity's legal structure. Although a C or S corporate structure can offer benefits, an LLC's flexibility and limited liability make it popular.

4. Explain whether profits on crypto investments are subject to taxation.
   Profits on crypto investments are generally subject to taxation. Trading between cryptos is a taxable event, requiring investors and traders to take the gain or loss into account for tax purposes. Merely buying and holding crypto does not result in any taxable income, gain, or loss until it is sold, becomes worthless or abandoned, or is hard-forked resulting in distributing new crypto to an investor. Generally, any transaction, transfer, or exchange involving crypto incurs a tax filing and a potential tax liability due to the IRS's classification and treatment of crypto as property.

5. Describe the tax implications of paying for goods and services, including employees, in crypto.
   Assuming no restrictions on the crypto, the government taxes an employee upon the initial payment and at a later sale. The payment's value is ordinary income at the payment date, subject to applicable wage withholding or self-employment taxes. That amount also becomes the employee's initial tax basis in the crypto. Any difference between that tax basis and a later sales price is the employee's capital gain or loss. Suppose the crypto involves a restriction at the initial payment. In that case, the taxable event usually does not occur

until the crypto becomes no longer subject to a substantial risk of forfeiture. This double taxation treatment continues to present an obstacle to firms seeking to pay external vendors or employees in crypto.

Chapter 18. The Underlying Technology for Cryptoassets

1. List security properties public-key cryptography (asymmetric encryption and digital signature) can provide.
   Public-key cryptography provides confidentiality and authenticity of the data and its origin. Asymmetric encryption ensures confidentiality and data authenticity. *A digital signature* allows authentication of the source and data.

2. Identify an important barrier to adopting blockchain technology and discuss the challenges of overcoming this barrier.
   The scalability of distributed ledgers in total transaction volume and the number of independent participants in processing them create a challenge to their mainstream adoption. According to the blockchain trilemma, decentralization, security, and scalability cannot perfectly co-exist. Therefore, improving scalability without compromising decentralization, security, or both is challenging.

3. Discuss a fundamental property that a solution for swapping assets must ensure.
   A fundamental property that a solution for swapping assets must ensure is atomicity. Either the transfer of all assets in the agreed quantities occurs, or no transfer occurs. Without atomicity, a risk occurs of transferring an asset without receiving anything in exchange.

4. Define layer 1 blockchain and discuss the possibilities to improve its scalability.
   Layer 1 blockchain is where the chain of blocks (transactions) formation occurs. Options for improving scalability include parameter tuning (increasing the block size, reducing the block time interval, and using an aggregate signature), sharding, and using different blockchain structures, such as a directed acyclic graph (DAG).

5. Identify a main use of a hash time lock contract (HTLC).
   A An HTLC is a way to achieve atomicity of cross-chain transactions without direct communications between the ledgers.

Chapter 19. Central Bank Digital Currencies: Opening Pandora's Box or Paving the Future of Money?

1. Describe a central bank digital currency (CBDC) and its two variants.
   A CBDC is a conceptual digital currency backed by a sovereign currency. It is a new form of central bank money created to serve the purpose of a medium of exchange, a store of value, and a stable unit of account. A CBDC is either an electronic record or a digital token of a country's official currency. Central

banks are exploring assorted designs, representations, and infrastructure peculiarities to align CBDCs to their monetary and systemic strategies. CDBCs represent an account-based or a token-based system, each with different economic implications.

2. Describe the types of CBDCs.
The two types of CBDCs are wholesale and retail. Wholesale CBDCs use the existing tier of banking and financial institutions for conducting and settling transactions. Retail CBDCs involve transferring a digital currency backed by a central government directly to consumers. Such CBDCs are not mutually exclusive. Hybrid or combinatory models can co-exist in the same economy depending on the objective, usability, and underlying infrastructure.

3. List several potential reasons for central banks establishing a CDBC.
The following are potential reasons for central banks establishing a CDBC:

    - providing financial inclusion by giving unbanked stakeholders easier access to money and financial digitization,
    - modernizing a fiat currency,
    - offering cost efficiency in multi-areas, such as lower transaction cost,
    - providing higher auditability through data recording and tracking,
    - preventing illicit activity,
    - preserving the privacy of exchange,
    - increasing management efficiency, and
    - preserving the relevancy and demand for public money.

4. Explain the main differences between CDBCs and cryptocurrencies.
A CDCB is not a cryptocurrency in its purest form. It is a centrally controlled monetary vehicle represented in an account-based or a token-based system. A country's monetary authority or central bank control, regulate, and govern. A CDCB's issuance, supply, and monetary attributes are controlled, regulated, and governed. Because of their centralized nature, CDBCs may erode citizens' privacy. By contrast, cryptocurrencies are decentralized, open-source, private digital assets transacted via a permissionless blockchain network. They are not pegged to any fiat currency or basket of assets, and their value depends on supply and demand dynamics and algorithmic trading. Cryptocurrencies can have an unlimited supply and be traded, speculated, or capped. Nodes are incentivized to contribute by receiving monetary rewards in the native coin.

5. Identify the main differences between an account-based and a token-based system.
In an account-based system, the identity is linked to CBDC ownership, a transaction is an update in the balance of the payee and the payer, and identification is required to authorize transactions. In a token-based system, CBDC

ownership is linked to a particular proof. Transactions are executed and verified using cryptography and digital signatures. The transaction is a change of a token's ownership.

6. Identify the advantages and disadvantages of CBDCs.
   The main advantages of CBDCs include:

   - providing a simplified implementation of monetary policy,
   - eliminating third-party risk,
   - establishing a direct connection between central banks and consumers, empowering financial inclusion, and
   - preventing illicit activities, illegal transactions, and tax evasion.

   The significant disadvantages of CBDCs include:

   - creating the risk of monopoly and abuse of control data and transactions between banks and consumers,
   - producing the risk of privacy and data breaches, depending on the infrastructure,
   - creating uncertainty around the regulatory and legal issues involving CBDCs, especially concerning cross-border transactions and transfers, and
   - opening a geopolitical puzzle with strong economies substituting weaker economies.

Chapter 20 Trade Settlements

1. Describe the process that defines the current trade settlement infrastructure.
   The process defining the current trade settlement infrastructure consists of three stages: (1) execution, (2) clearing, and (3) settlement and custody. Execution is when a buyer and a seller agree upon a specified amount and price of securities. Clearing involves verifying that the buyer has available funds to purchase the securities and that the seller has the selected security. The central counterparty acts as an intermediary to bear the counterparty risk for the investors. Settlement and custody make the final delivery of funds and securities to the seller and the buyer. This last step alters the ledger to sync with the transaction.

2. Explain the importance of transaction netting, margin trading, and prefunding.
   Netting transactions, margin trading, and the lack of prefunding are essential parts that make up the current infrastructure of trade settlements.

   - Netting transactions occur during the settlement by consolidating the transactions between sellers and buyers. The clearinghouse determines the net amount the member firms must commit. There is no need to perform all transactions. Thus, the number of transactions after netting decreases, lessening transaction costs and risks.

- Margin trading and short selling extend credit to investors and give them higher net exposure to their long/short positions.
- The current trade settlement infrastructure does not require prefunding. An investor can execute a trade and have funds available the next day, enabling firms and individual investors to day trade and trade on margin.

3. Identify several benefits provided by blockchain implementation in trade settlement.
   Some benefits that blockchain implementation in trade settlement infrastructure can bring are:

   - reducing settlement latency,
   - lowering operational and custodial risk,
   - bringing higher transparency for issuers, investors, and regulators,
   - providing the certainty of settlement,
   - allowing correctability,
   - eliminating reconciliation,
   - reducing database redundancies,
   - increasing data security, and
   - cryptographic protection.

4. List some ongoing projects/initiatives that bring blockchain to trade settlement infrastructure.
   Multiple projects showcase the effectiveness of incorporating blockchain technology into financial systems and openness to new technology breakthroughs. Some significant initiatives occur in different parts of the world. For example, in 2017, the Australian Stock Exchange announced moving from the Clearing House Electronic Subregister System (CHESS) to a new prototype incorporating distributed ledger technology (DLT) in trade settlements. Similarly, Deutsche Börse and Deutsche Bundesbank followed suit by developing a prototype of trade settlements based on the blockchain ecosystem. India and Japan also integrate blockchain technology in their trade settlement ecosystems. In addition, other projects such as Nasdaq Linq, Project ION, and PAXOS try to bring DLT to trade settlement infrastructure.

   - In 2015, the Nasdaq Linq project successfully implemented and tested blockchain in private security transactions and announced further studies exploring the possibility of bringing this to US secondary markets.
   - In 2016, Deutsche Börse and Deutsche Bundesbank developed a prototype for blockchain-based trade settlements.
   - In 2017, the Australian Stock Exchange (ASX) announced the planned replacement of CHESS with a prototype developed by Digital Asset. Digital Asset implemented DLT technology for trade settlements.
   - In 2020, India's Securities and Exchange Board announced the move toward real-time trade settlements using blockchain technology.

- In 2020, the Japan Exchange Group announced pilot programs to evaluate blockchain technology for post-trade settlement.
- Project ION, initiated by DTCC, explores the benefits of blockchain implementation in trade settlements without withdrawing benefits in the current system.
- PAXOS uses delivery versus payment with a permission-based distributed ledger for settlement services. PAXOS claims significant cost savings and capital reductions that are needed as collateral.

Chapter 21. A Closer Look into Decentralized Finance

1. Identify and explain three stablecoin implementation designs.
   Below are three stablecoin implementation designs.

   - *Asset-backed stablecoins.* This system is based on a traditional asset fully backing each stablecoin. A stablecoin's creation and destruction ("burning") depend on the increase or decrease in the asset reserve. The reserve is mainly US dollars held in custody by an intermediary, which may or may not be a regulated custodian.
   - *Overcollateralized crypto-backed stablecoins.* In this model, collateral locked into a smart contract backs each stablecoin. Users deposit cryptoassets, like bitcoin, ether, and liquidity pool tokens, into a smart contract "vault" and use them as collateral to generate a debt instrument up to a certain amount, typically between 25 and 75 percent of the collateral value. Suppose the price of the collateral falls below a certain threshold. In that case, the liquidation of collateral occurs to guarantee the face value of the issued debt. As opposed to asset-backed stablecoins, decentralized cryptoasset-backed stablecoins do not require a central controlling and issuing authority, a custodian to hold reserves, or an auditor to verify the integrity and value of reserves.
   - *Algorithmic seignorage stablecoins.* This mechanism relies on issuing and destroying monetary units or reserves to maintain the stablecoin's peg value. Most applications use two tokens simultaneously. One token acts as a stablecoin and backs its value on the other token's reserves, usually a utility and governance token. If the value of the stablecoin increases, the protocol issues new stablecoins and distributes them proportionally to the reserve token holders. If the value of the stablecoin decreases, the protocol sells governance tokens, buys back stablecoins, and potentially burns stablecoins to restore price parity.

2. Explain the arbitrage process that allows liquidity pools to reach market prices without relying on oracles or market price feeds.
   Liquidity pools are passive smart contracts that rely on arbitragers' actions to reach market prices. When the pool's internal relative price differs from the market price, arbitrageurs trade against the protocol to restore price parity.

3. Describe the term impermanent loss.
   Impermanent loss refers to the difference in the portfolio value observed by a liquidity pool investor after a large price shock compared to a buy-and-hold strategy of the assets initially held in the liquidity pool.

4. Discuss the mechanisms that allow negative interest rates on cryptoasset collateralized loans.
   Cryptoassets held as collateral typically occur in liquidity pools, earning trading fees distributed to debtors. If the trading fees are higher than the interest charged on crypto-backed loans, the effective interest rate can be negative.

Chapter 22. Cryptocurrency Exchanges and the Future of Cryptoassets

1. Identify and discuss the primary differences between centralized exchanges (CEXs) and decentralized exchanges (DEXs).
   A DEX allows smart contracts for transactions. A CEX is an intermediary of sorts in the process. Some CEXs have fiat onramps, where users can deposit fiat such as US dollars to begin trading. DEXs only manage crypto and crypto trading because they lack the regulatory compliance to accept fiat currency. The custody of assets also differs between DEXs and CEXs. DEX users are responsible for the custody of their cryptoassets. By contrast, CEX users rely on the CEX to provide custody for cryptoassets and fiat deposits, where applicable.

2. Discuss whether CEXs and DEXs can be regulated.
   CEXs can be regulated. Signals worldwide indicate authorities intend to regulate these crypto exchanges. Regulating a DEX is more complicated. Some form of "facilitation" occurs with a DEX. Those responsible for the DEX may not be identifiable. Thus, a regulator's ability to impose fines or other penalties for a DEX's failure to comply is problematic.

3. Explain whether the future of cryptocurrency and trading rests with CEXs or DEXs.
   The answer depends on what investors and traders want to accomplish. Centralized options may have better-established policies to remain compliant. Yet, CEXs often do not have the variety of crypto-to-crypto trading provided by DEXs. DEXs often involve regulatory ambiguity regarding risk management, insurance, and money transmitter laws. They may also lack the ability to offer custodial services. Although some individuals may want complete self-custody, this situation comes at the cost of liquidity and the best pricing often offered by CEXs. Therefore, the preference for DEX or CEX options depends on an investor's interests, the risk appetite of the retail or institutional partner, and the desired crypto-related outcome.

4. Identify lessons learned from past markets and industries as DEXs enter the mainstream.
   Clear and appropriate regulation can lead to market growth rather than an adverse impact. However, care is needed to avoid regulatory overreach. There is a need for objective and flexible regulation to protect investors and users, especially given the hacks and breaches that occur as DEXs continue to attract capital and attention.

Index

Printed and bound by CPI Group (UK) Ltd, Croydon, CR0 4YY
16/09/2026
14963021-0001